BATMAN
LEGENDS OF THE
DARK KNIGHT

VOLUME 2

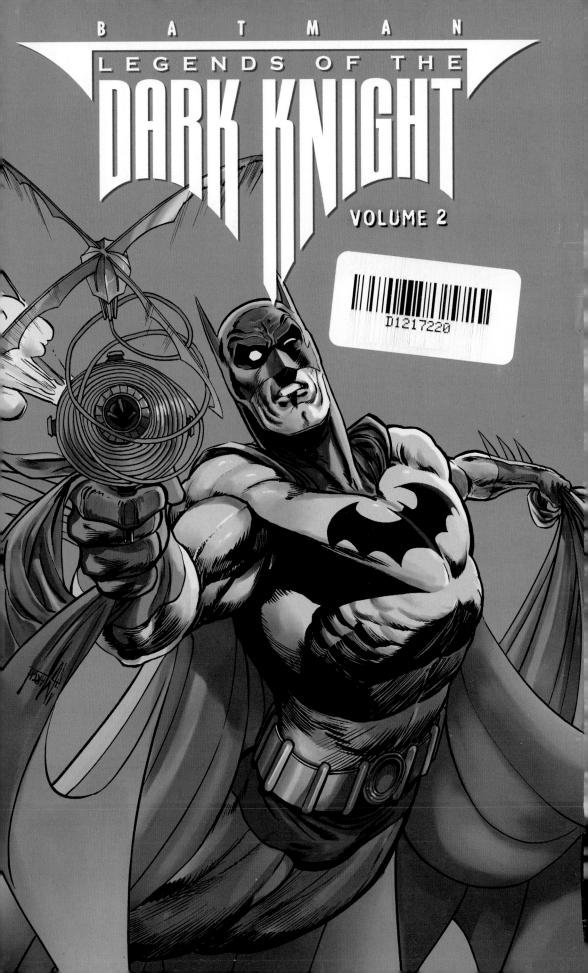

D1217220

BATMAN
LEGENDS OF THE
DARK KNIGHT

VOLUME 2

Jeff PARKER · Michael AVON OEMING · Rob WILLIAMS
JOE HARRIS · Paul TOBIN · RICARDO SANCHEZ
CHRISTOS GAGE · RAY FAWKES · DAVID TISCHMAN
WRITERS

GABRIEL HARDMAN · MICHAEL AVON OEMING · JUAN JOSE RYP
JASON MASTERS · Tradd MOORE · SERGIO SANDOVAL
JHEREMY RAAPACK · STEPHANE ROUX · CHRIS SPROUSE · KARL STORY
ARTISTS

Elizabeth BREITWEISER · Nick FILARDI · IKARI STUDIO
JIM CHARALAMPIDIS · REX LOKUS · CARRIE STRACHAN
COLORISTS

Saida TEMOFONTE
LETTERER

Jheremy RAAPACK & Wendy BROOME
COLLECTION COVER ARTISTS

BATMAN created by BOB KANE

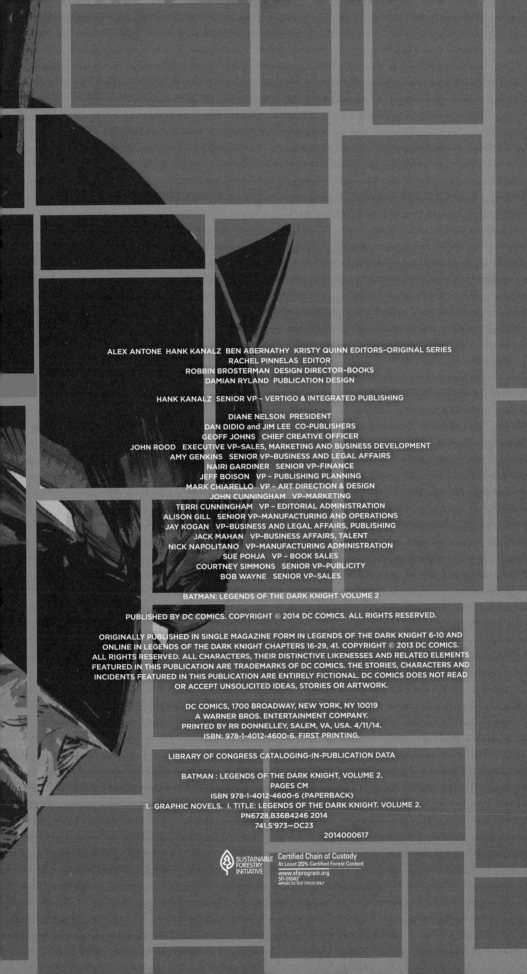

ALEX ANTONE HANK KANALZ BEN ABERNATHY KRISTY QUINN EDITORS–ORIGINAL SERIES
RACHEL PINNELAS EDITOR
ROBBIN BROSTERMAN DESIGN DIRECTOR–BOOKS
DAMIAN RYLAND PUBLICATION DESIGN

HANK KANALZ SENIOR VP – VERTIGO & INTEGRATED PUBLISHING

DIANE NELSON PRESIDENT
DAN DIDIO and JIM LEE CO-PUBLISHERS
GEOFF JOHNS CHIEF CREATIVE OFFICER
JOHN ROOD EXECUTIVE VP–SALES, MARKETING AND BUSINESS DEVELOPMENT
AMY GENKINS SENIOR VP–BUSINESS AND LEGAL AFFAIRS
NAIRI GARDINER SENIOR VP–FINANCE
JEFF BOISON VP – PUBLISHING PLANNING
MARK CHIARELLO VP – ART DIRECTION & DESIGN
JOHN CUNNINGHAM VP–MARKETING
TERRI CUNNINGHAM VP – EDITORIAL ADMINISTRATION
ALISON GILL SENIOR VP–MANUFACTURING AND OPERATIONS
JAY KOGAN VP–BUSINESS AND LEGAL AFFAIRS, PUBLISHING
JACK MAHAN VP–BUSINESS AFFAIRS, TALENT
NICK NAPOLITANO VP–MANUFACTURING ADMINISTRATION
SUE POHJA VP – BOOK SALES
COURTNEY SIMMONS SENIOR VP–PUBLICITY
BOB WAYNE SENIOR VP–SALES

BATMAN: LEGENDS OF THE DARK KNIGHT VOLUME 2

PUBLISHED BY DC COMICS. COPYRIGHT © 2014 DC COMICS. ALL RIGHTS RESERVED.

ORIGINALLY PUBLISHED IN SINGLE MAGAZINE FORM IN LEGENDS OF THE DARK KNIGHT 6-10 AND
ONLINE IN LEGENDS OF THE DARK KNIGHT CHAPTERS 16-29, 41. COPYRIGHT © 2013 DC COMICS.
ALL RIGHTS RESERVED. ALL CHARACTERS, THEIR DISTINCTIVE LIKENESSES AND RELATED ELEMENTS
FEATURED IN THIS PUBLICATION ARE TRADEMARKS OF DC COMICS. THE STORIES, CHARACTERS AND
INCIDENTS FEATURED IN THIS PUBLICATION ARE ENTIRELY FICTIONAL. DC COMICS DOES NOT READ
OR ACCEPT UNSOLICITED IDEAS, STORIES OR ARTWORK.

DC COMICS, 1700 BROADWAY, NEW YORK, NY 10019
A WARNER BROS. ENTERTAINMENT COMPANY.
PRINTED BY RR DONNELLEY, SALEM, VA, USA. 4/11/14.
ISBN: 978-1-4012-4600-6. FIRST PRINTING.

LIBRARY OF CONGRESS CATALOGING-IN-PUBLICATION DATA

BATMAN : LEGENDS OF THE DARK KNIGHT, VOLUME 2.
PAGES CM
ISBN 978-1-4012-4600-6 (PAPERBACK)
1. GRAPHIC NOVELS. I. TITLE: LEGENDS OF THE DARK KNIGHT. VOLUME 2.
PN6728.B36B4246 2014
741.5'973—DC23

2014000617

SUSTAINABLE
FORESTRY
INITIATIVE

Certified Chain of Custody
At Least 20% Certified Forest Content
www.sfiprogram.org
SFI-01042
APPLIES TO TEXT STOCK ONLY

GOTHAM SPIRIT

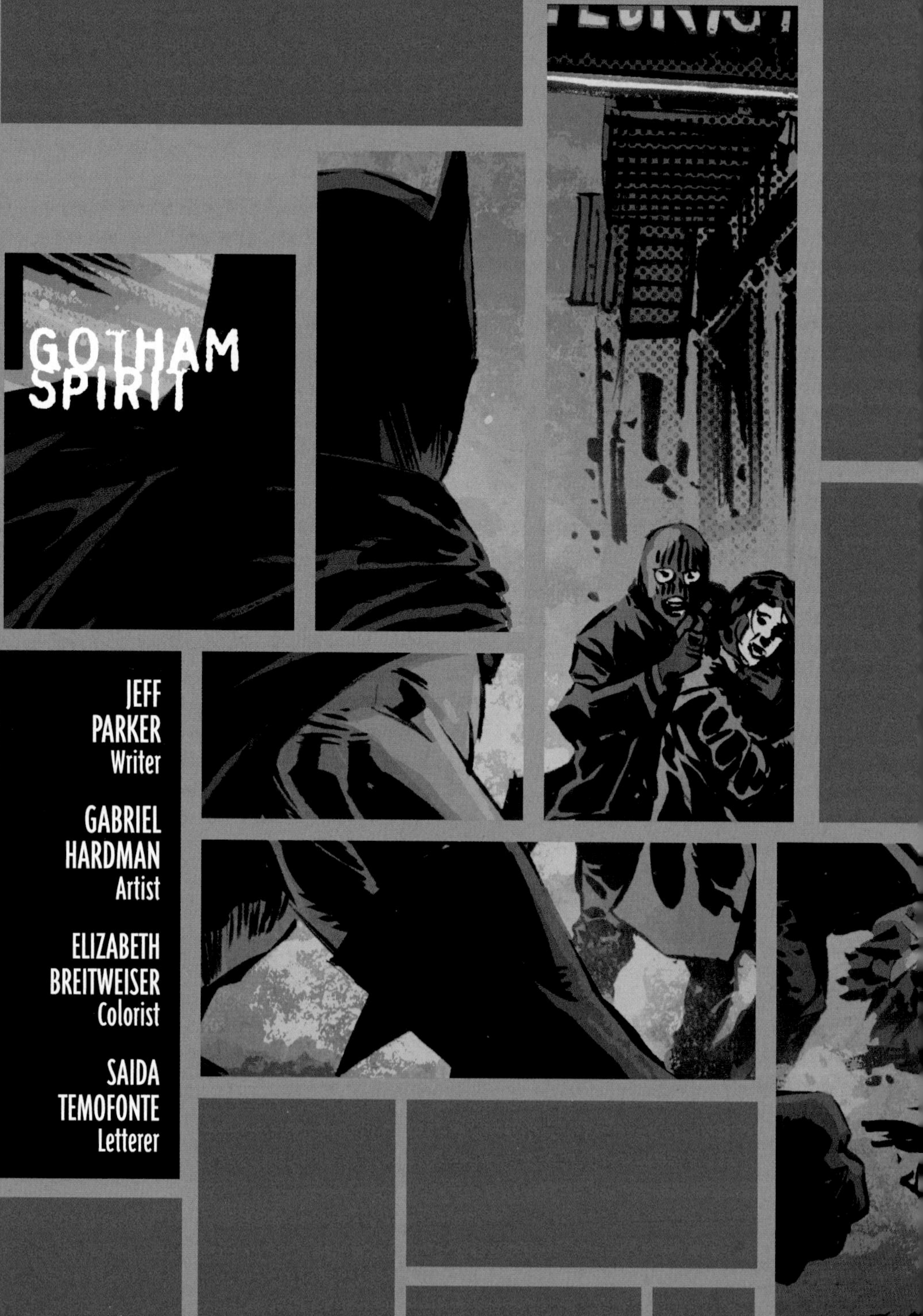

JEFF PARKER
Writer

GABRIEL HARDMAN
Artist

ELIZABETH BREITWEISER
Colorist

SAIDA TEMOFONTE
Letterer

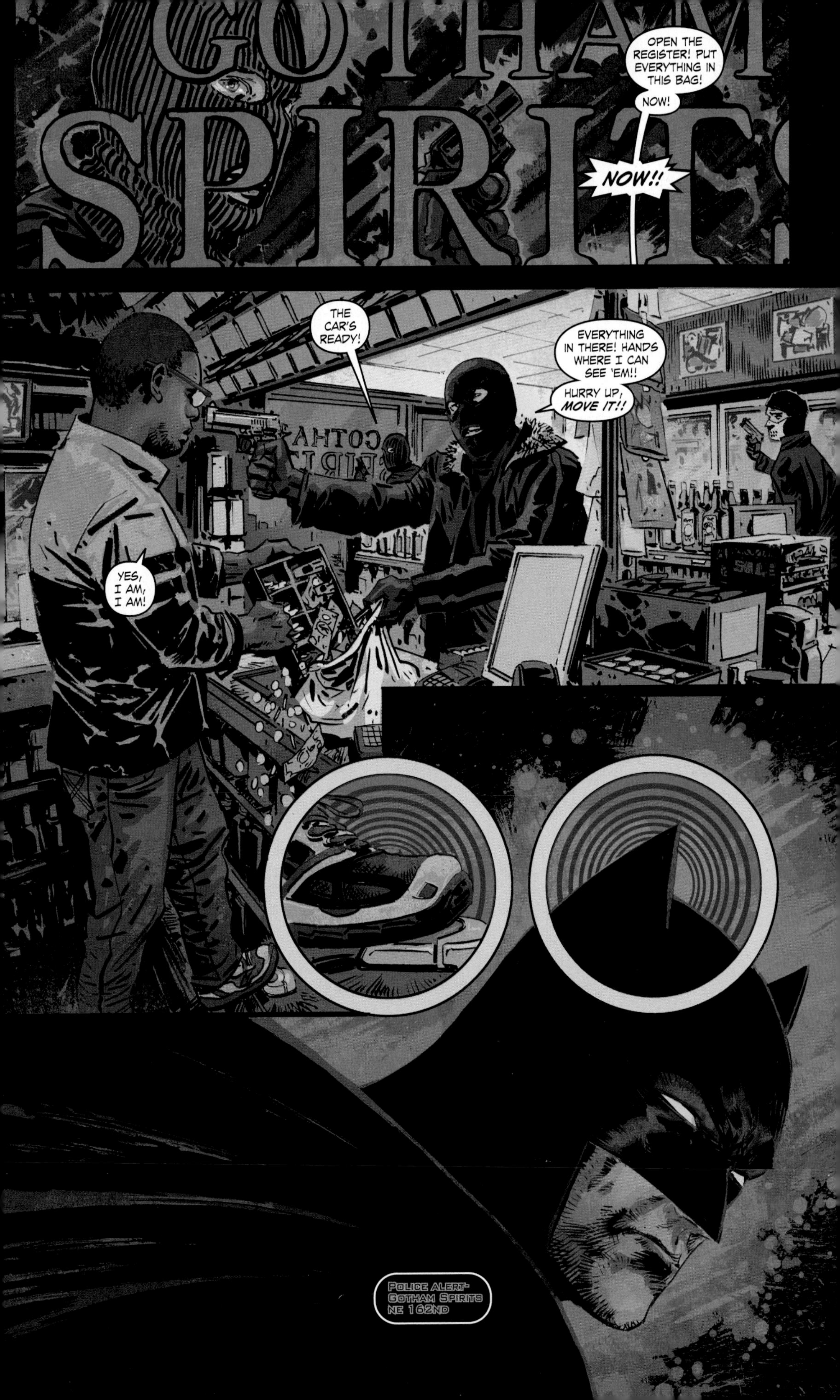
GOTHAM SPIRITS
OPEN THE REGISTER! PUT EVERYTHING IN THIS BAG!
NOW!
NOW!!
THE CAR'S READY!
EVERYTHING IN THERE! HANDS WHERE I CAN SEE 'EM!!
HURRY UP, MOVE IT!!
YES, I AM, I AM!
POLICE ALERT-
GOTHAM SPIRITS
NE 162ND

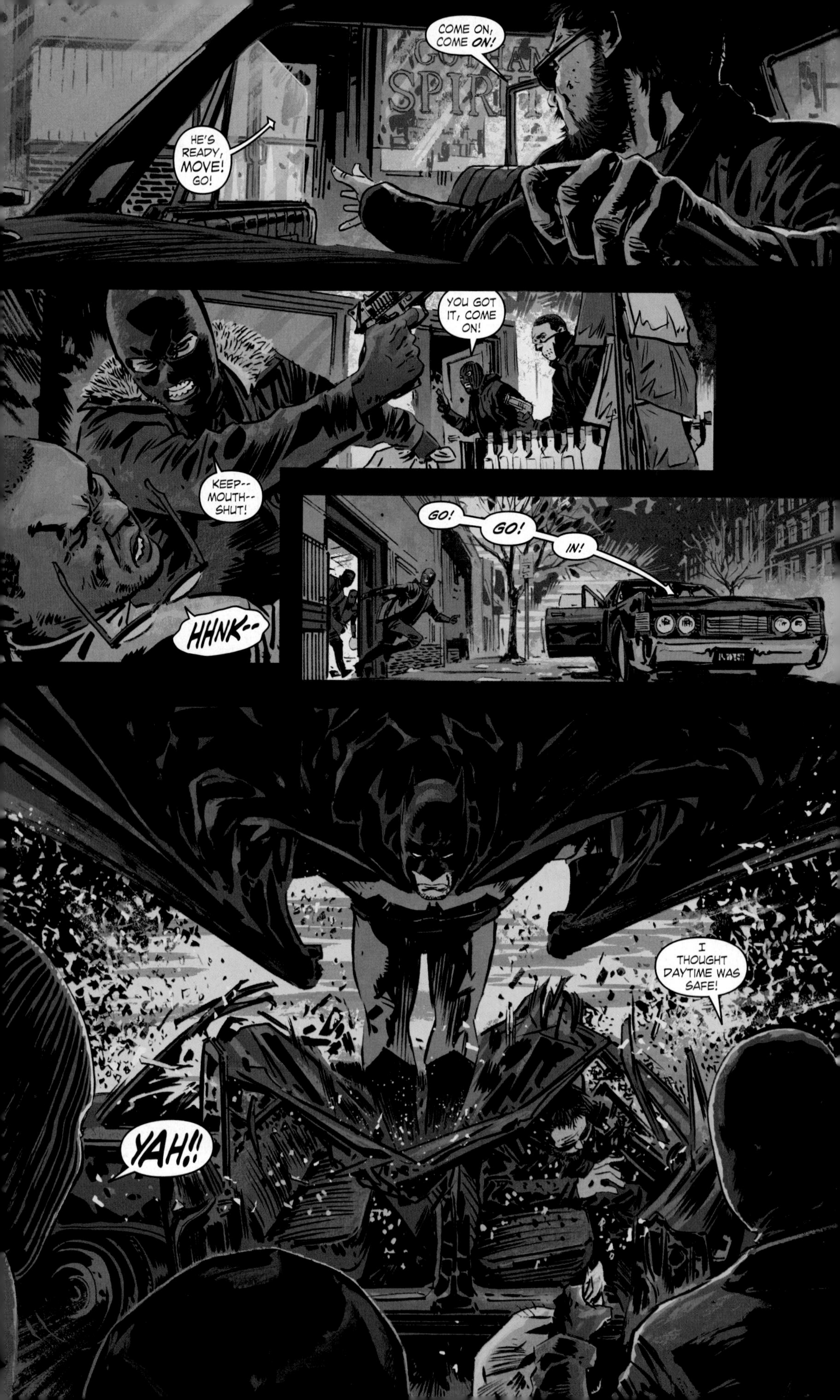

COME ON, COME ON!
HE'S READY, MOVE! GO!
YOU GOT IT, COME ON!
KEEP-- MOUTH-- SHUT!
HHNK--
GO!
GO!
IN!
I THOUGHT DAYTIME WAS SAFE!
YAH!!

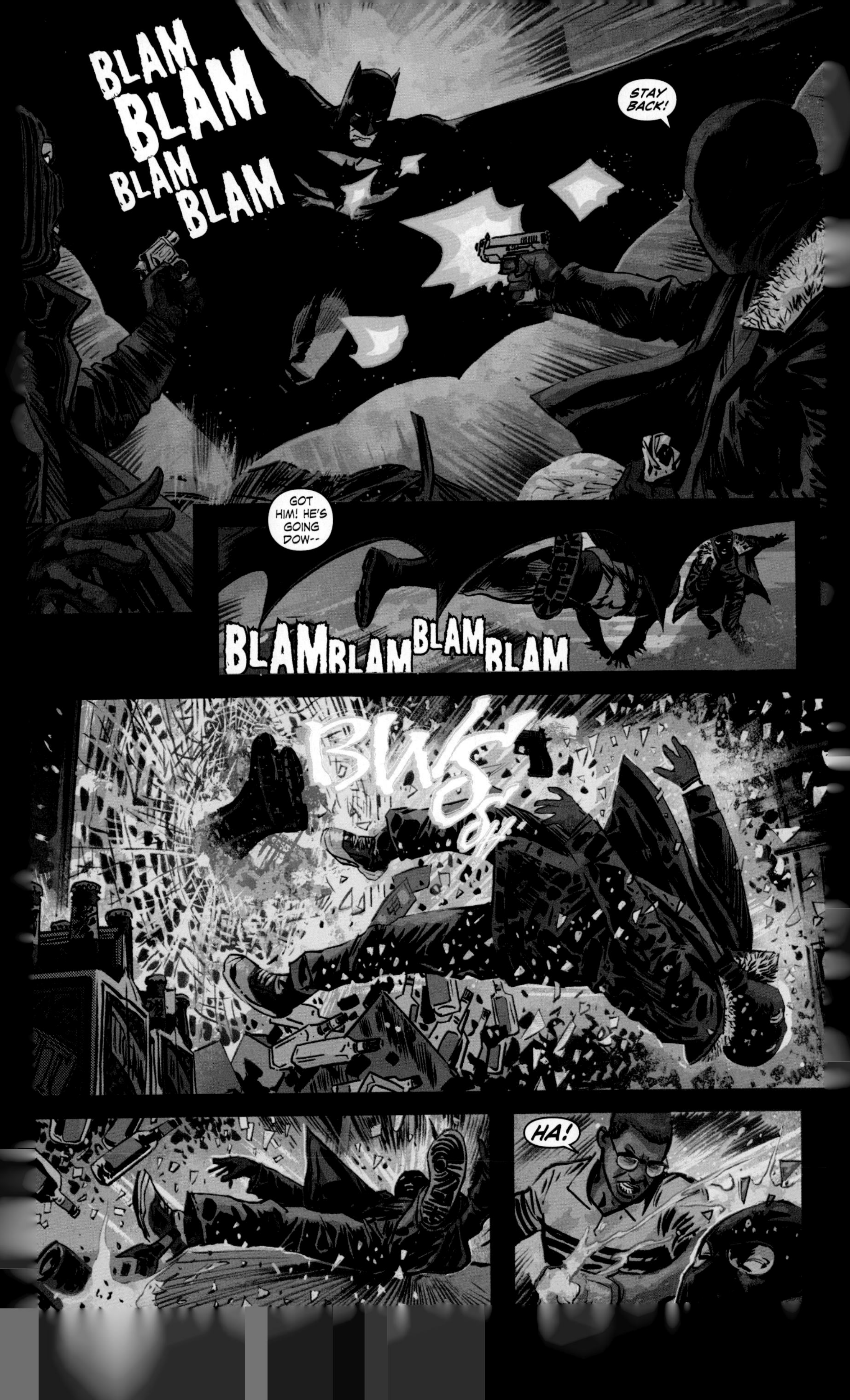
BLAM BLAM BLAM BLAM
STAY BACK!
GOT HIM! HE'S GOING DOW--
BLAMBLAMBLAMBLAM
BWOOSH
HA!

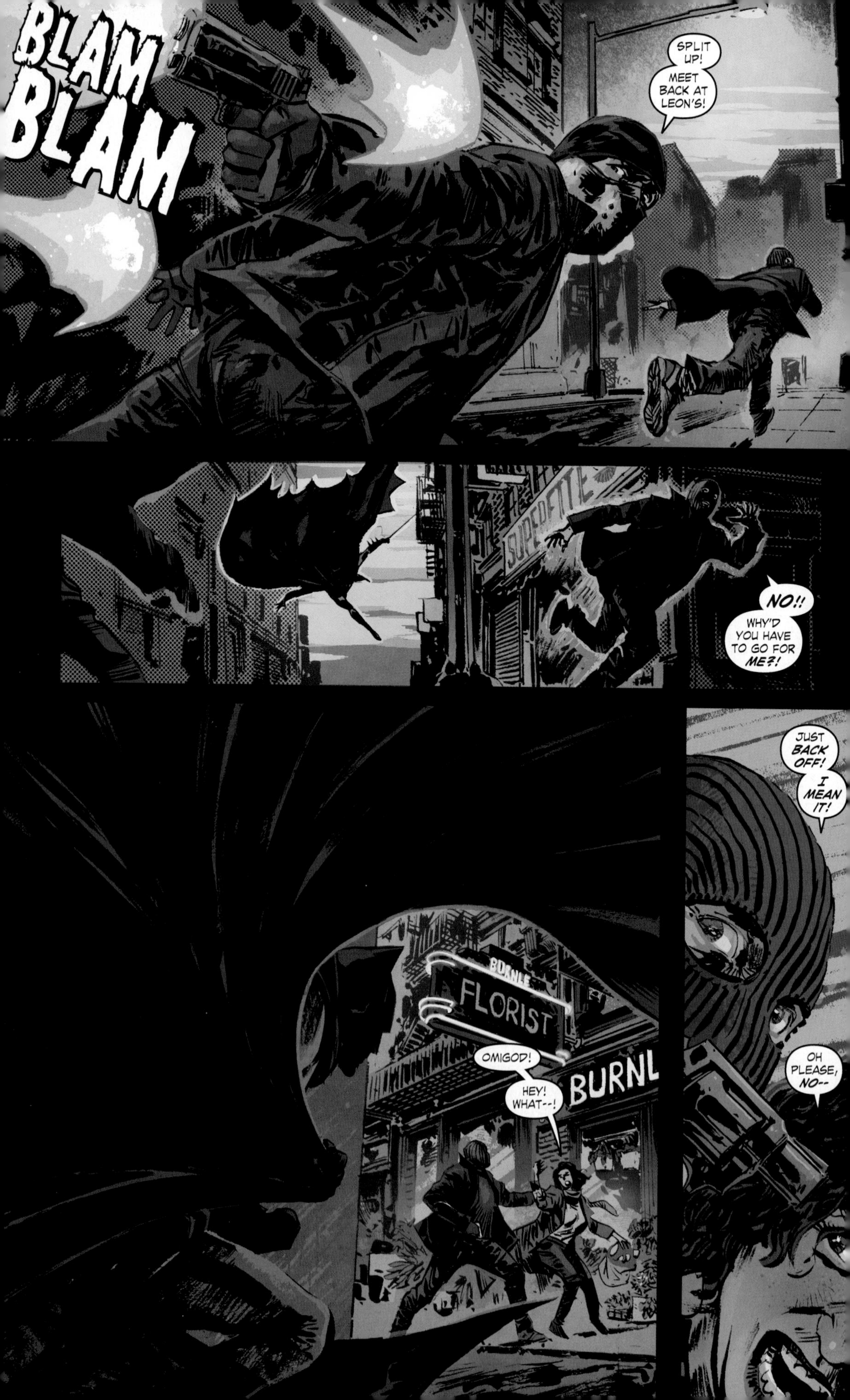
BLAM BLAM
SPLIT UP! MEET BACK AT LEON'S!
SUPERETTE
NO!! WHY'D YOU HAVE TO GO FOR ME?!
JUST BACK OFF! I MEAN IT!
FLORIST
OMIGOD!
HEY! WHAT--!
BURNL
OH PLEASE, NO--

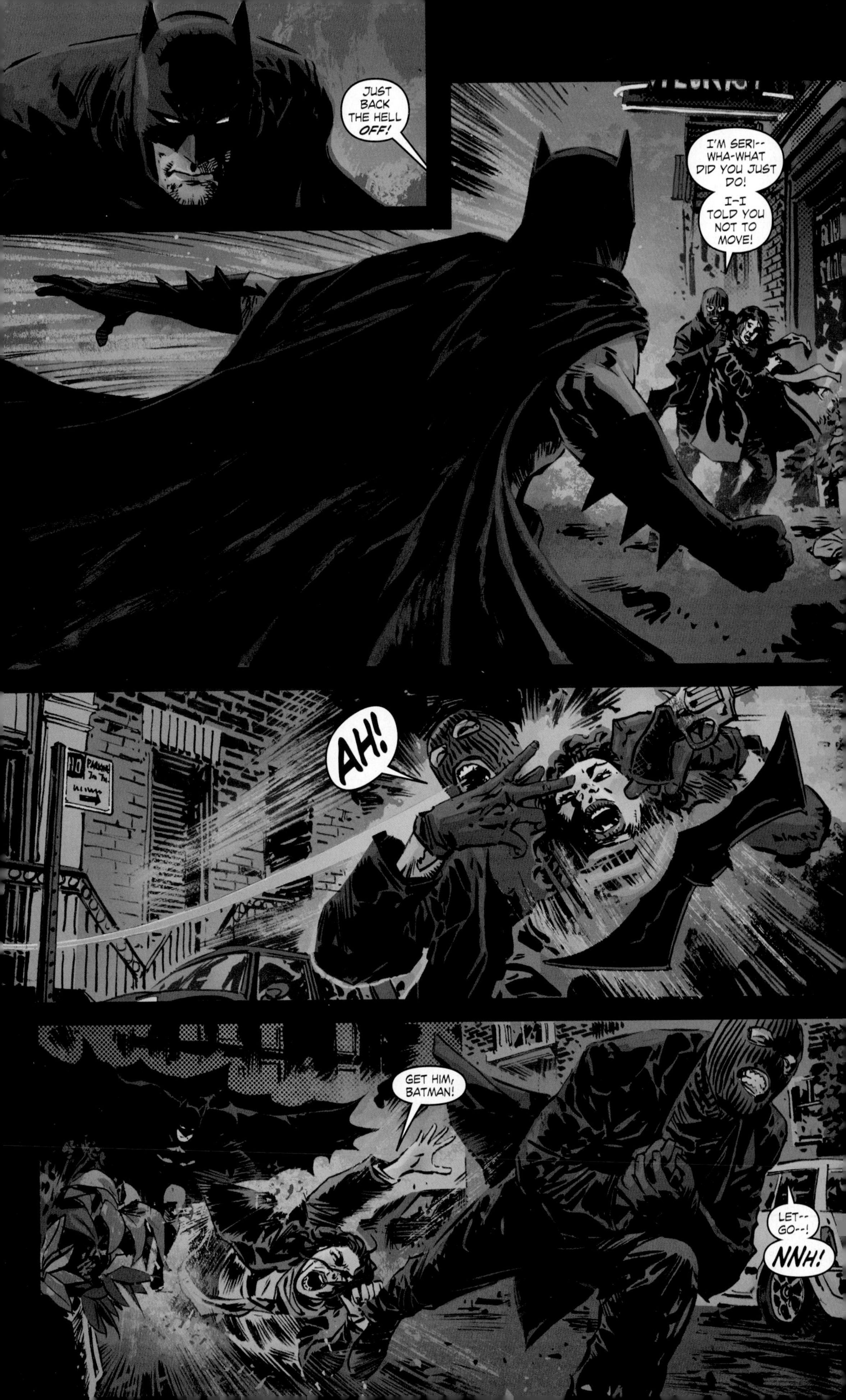
JUST BACK THE HELL OFF!
I'M SERI-- WHA-WHAT DID YOU JUST DO!
I-I TOLD YOU NOT TO MOVE!
AH!
GET HIM, BATMAN!
LET-- GO--!
NNH!

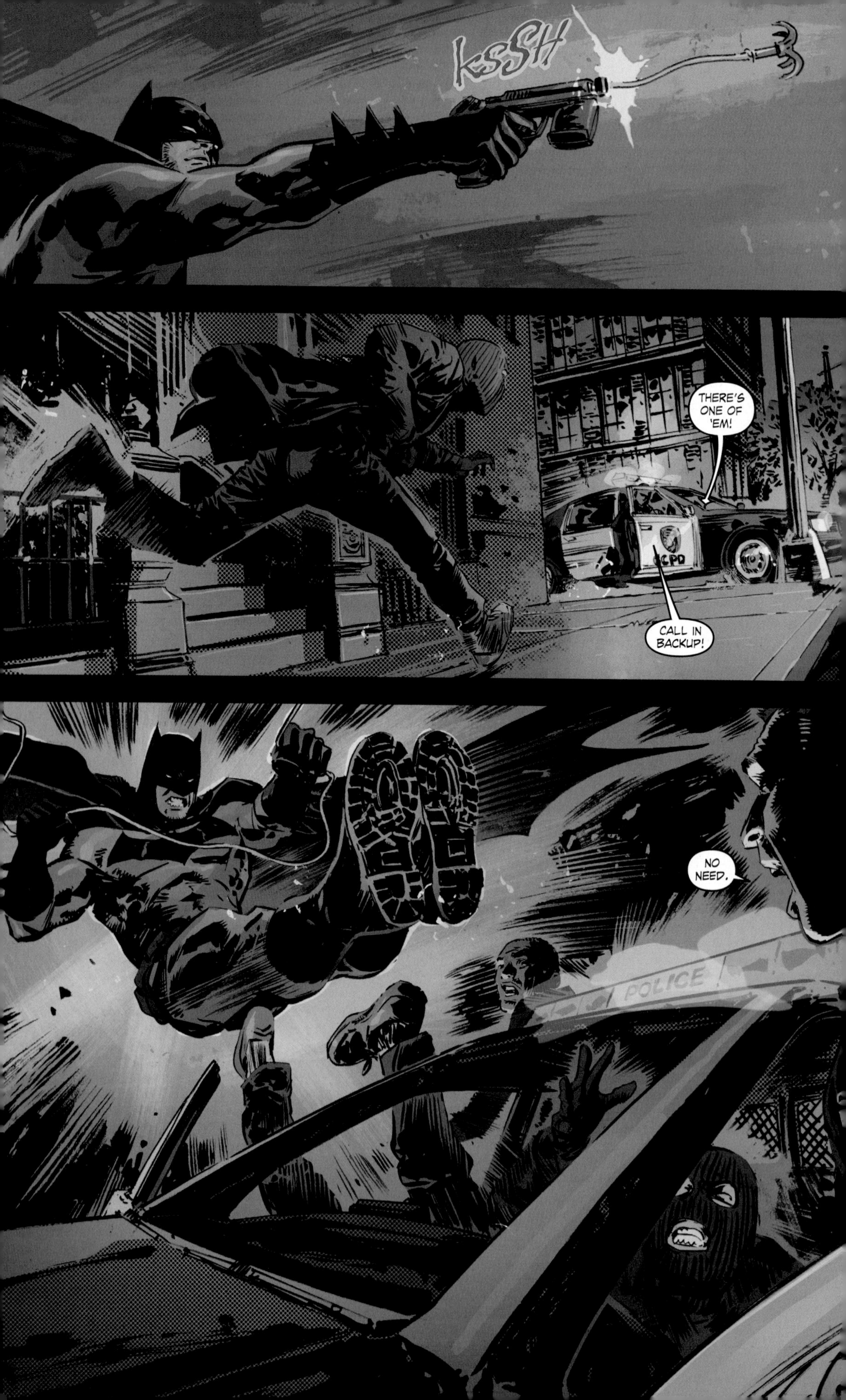

KSSH
THERE'S ONE OF 'EM!
CALL IN BACKUP!
NO NEED.
GCPD
POLICE

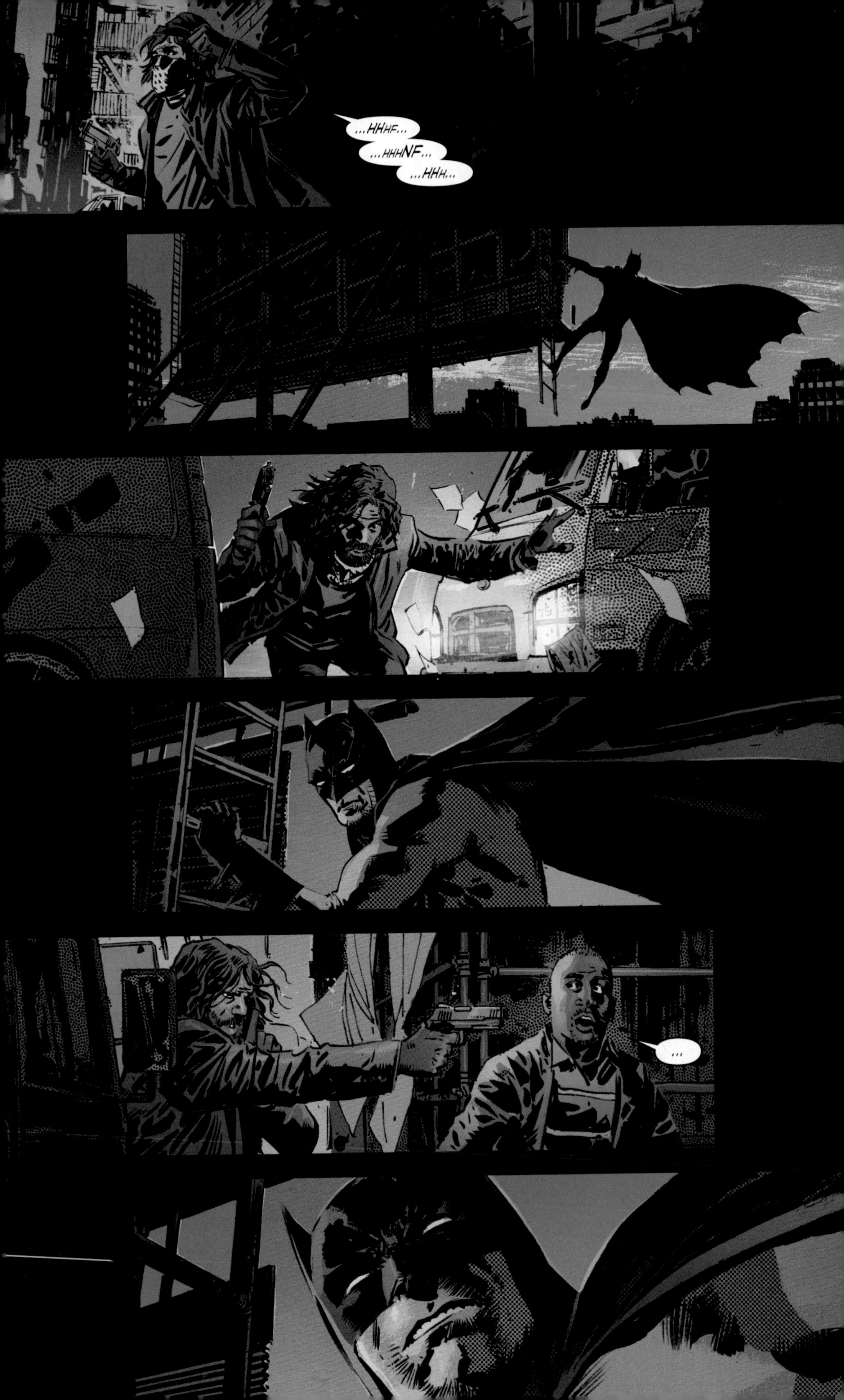
...HHHF...
...HHHNF...
...HHH...
...

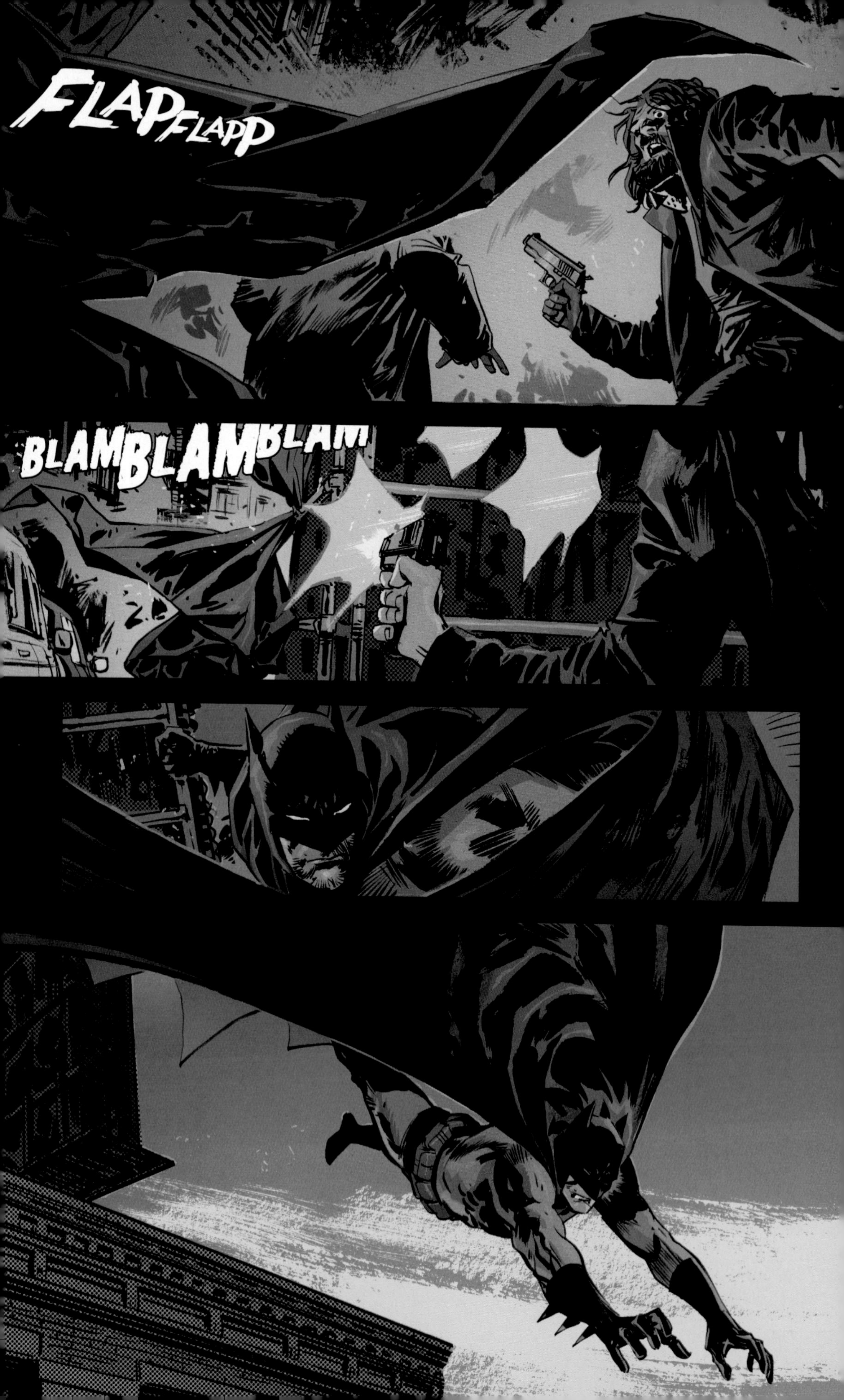
FLAPFLAPP
BLAMBLAMBLAM

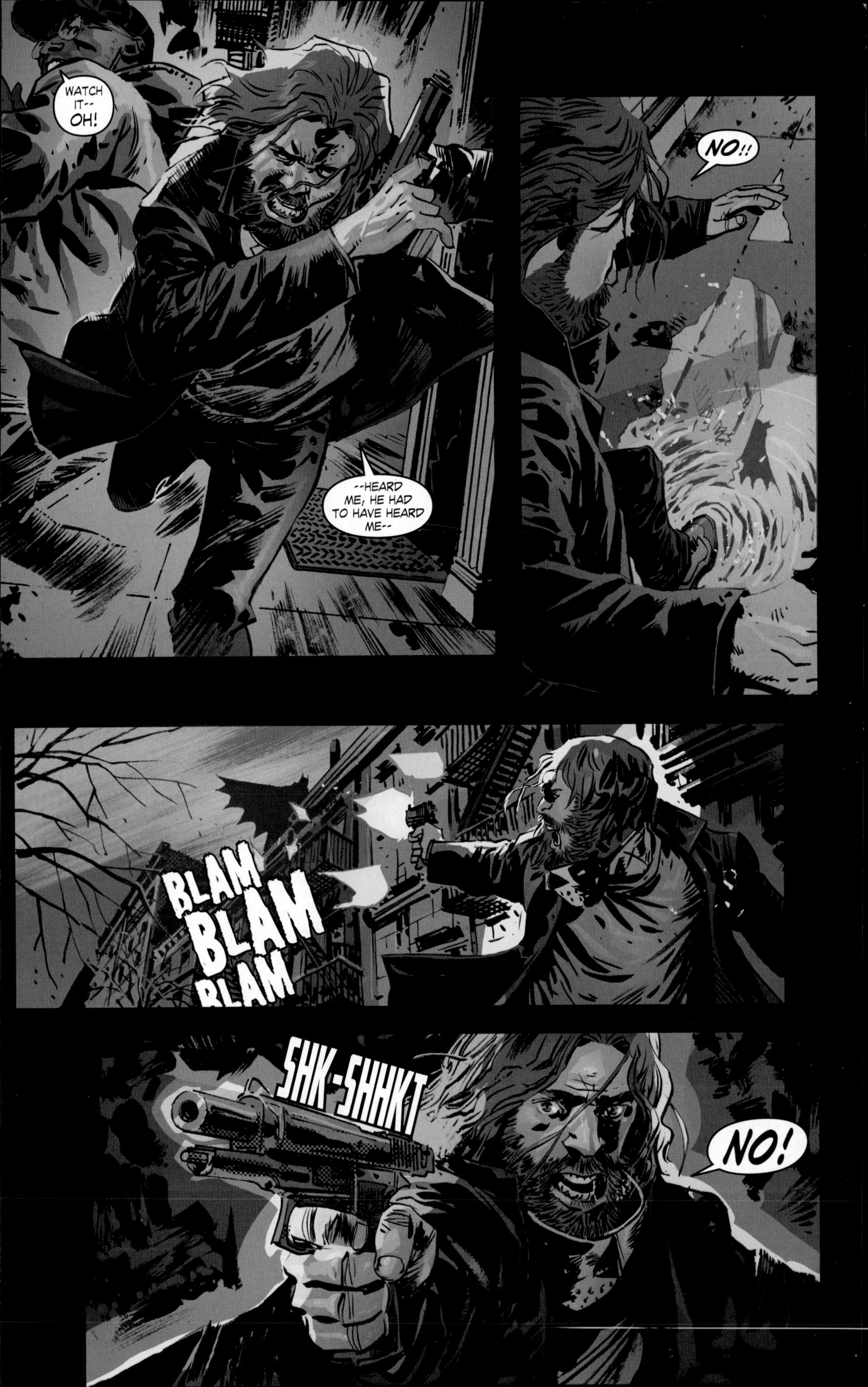
WATCH IT-- OH!
--HEARD ME, HE HAD TO HAVE HEARD ME--
NO!!
BLAM
BLAM
BLAM
BLAM
SHK-SHHKT
NO!

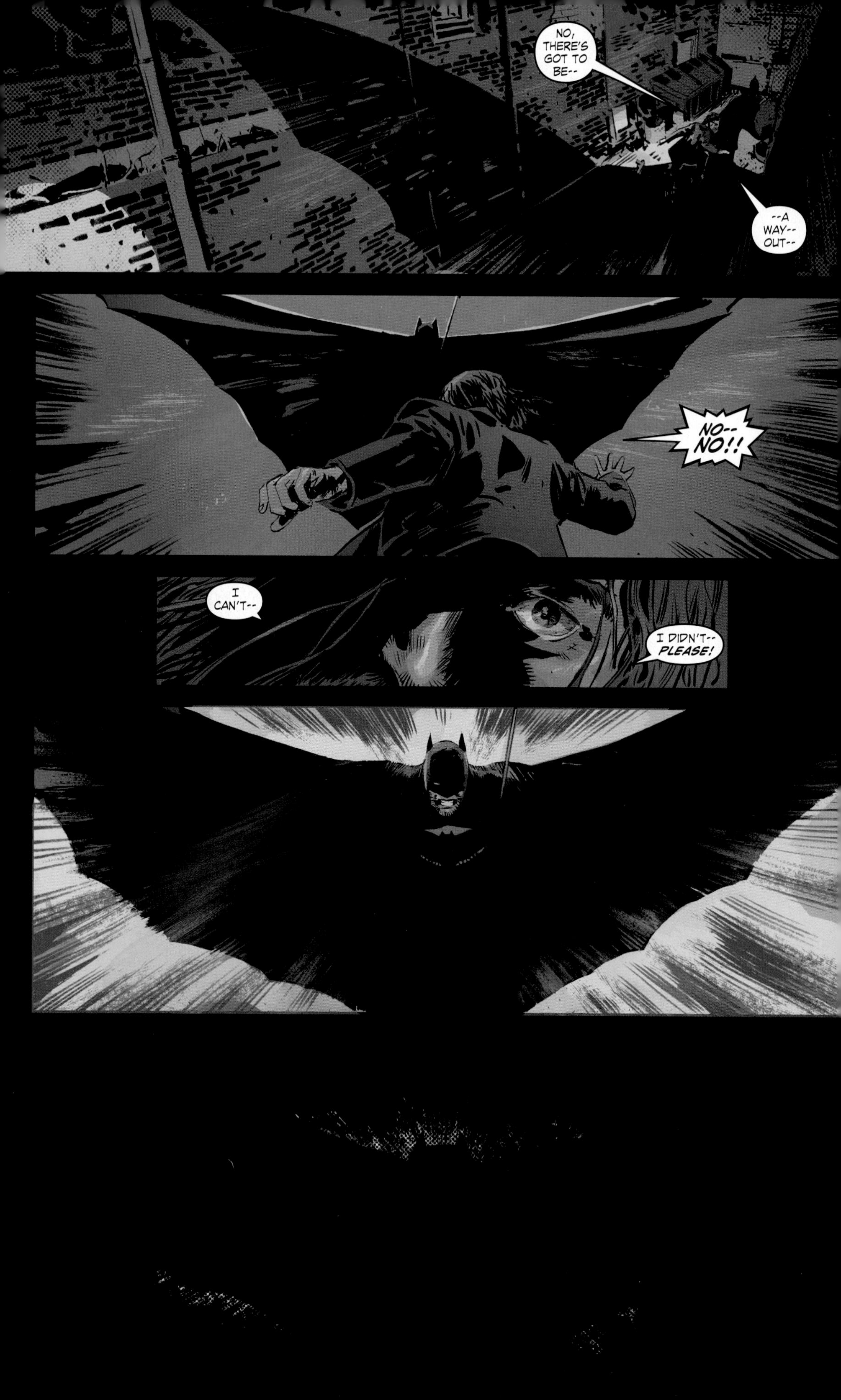
NO, THERE'S GOT TO BE--
--A WAY-- OUT--
NO-- NO!!
I CAN'T--
I DIDN'T-- PLEASE!

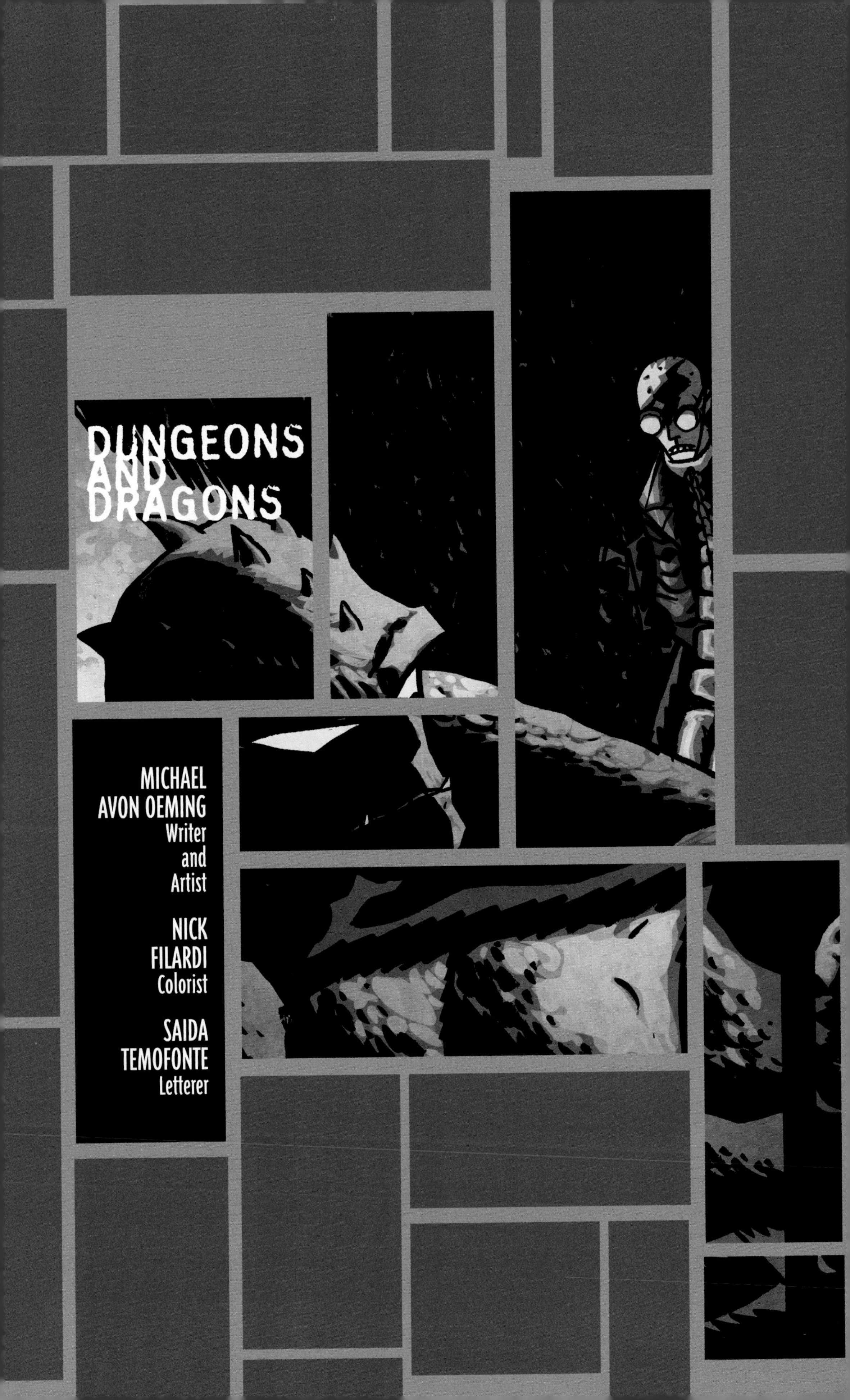
DUNGEONS AND DRAGONS
MICHAEL AVON OEMING Writer and Artist
NICK FILARDI Colorist
SAIDA TEMOFONTE Letterer

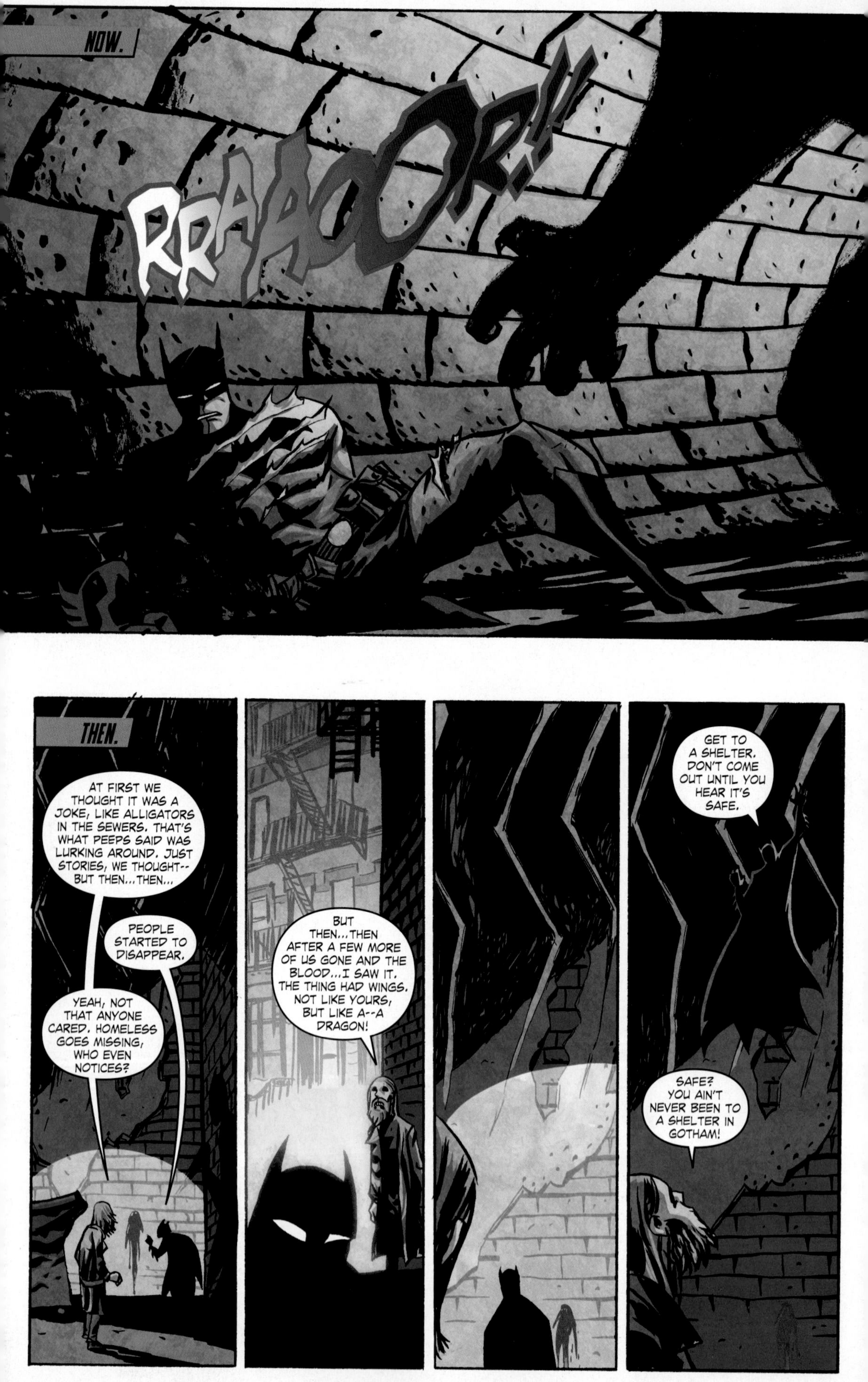
NOW.
RRAAOOR!!
THEN.
AT FIRST WE THOUGHT IT WAS A JOKE, LIKE ALLIGATORS IN THE SEWERS. THAT'S WHAT PEEPS SAID WAS LURKING AROUND. JUST STORIES, WE THOUGHT-- BUT THEN...THEN...
PEOPLE STARTED TO DISAPPEAR.
YEAH, NOT THAT ANYONE CARED. HOMELESS GOES MISSING, WHO EVEN NOTICES?
BUT THEN...THEN AFTER A FEW MORE OF US GONE AND THE BLOOD...I SAW IT. THE THING HAD WINGS. NOT LIKE YOURS, BUT LIKE A--A DRAGON!
GET TO A SHELTER. DON'T COME OUT UNTIL YOU HEAR IT'S SAFE.
SAFE? YOU AIN'T NEVER BEEN TO A SHELTER IN GOTHAM!

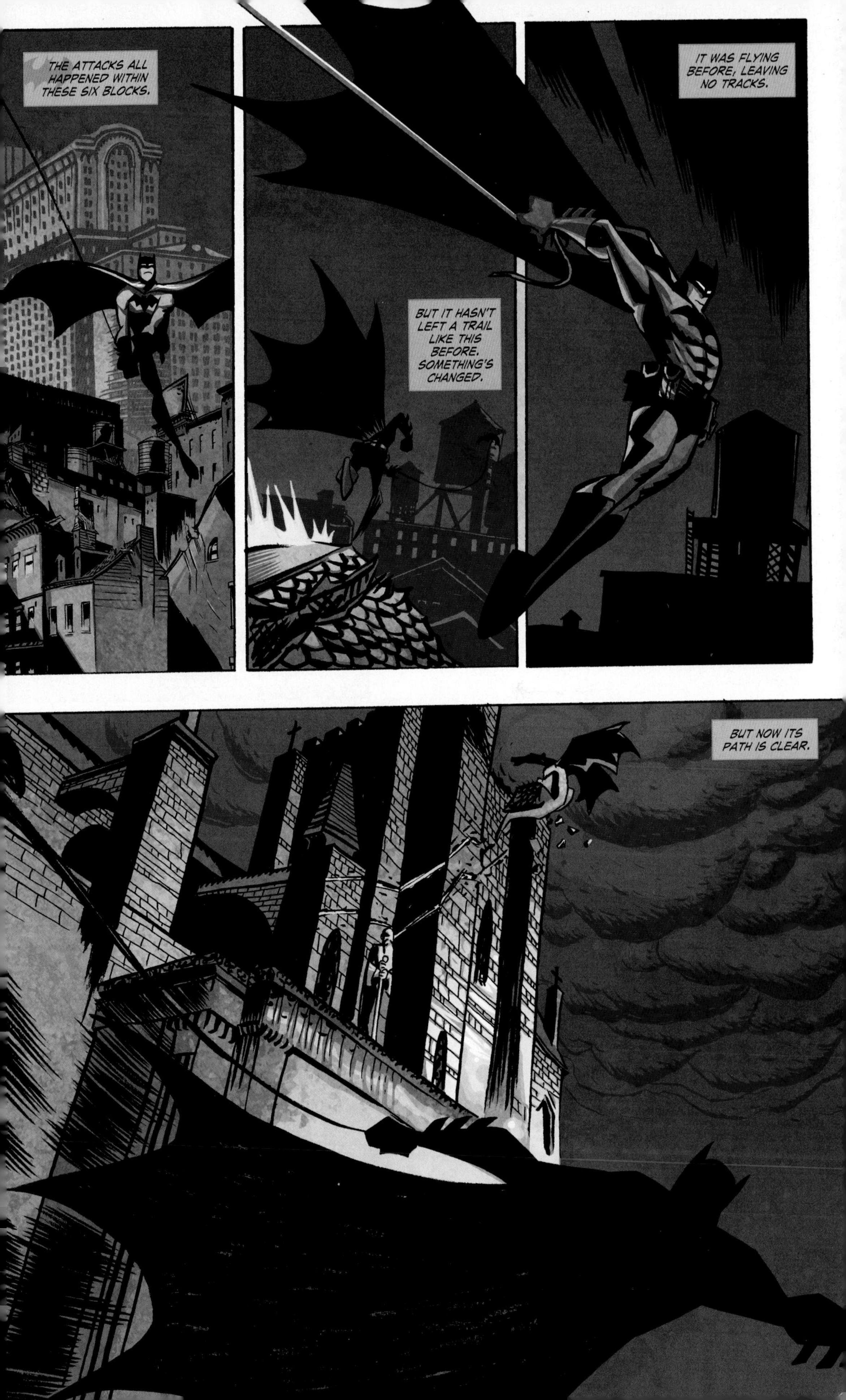
THE ATTACKS ALL HAPPENED WITHIN THESE SIX BLOCKS.
BUT IT HASN'T LEFT A TRAIL LIKE THIS BEFORE. SOMETHING'S CHANGED.
IT WAS FLYING BEFORE, LEAVING NO TRACKS.
BUT NOW ITS PATH IS CLEAR.

A SCALE OF SOME KIND WAS LEFT AT ONE OF THE ATTACKS.

MY ANALYSIS SHOWED THAT IT'S FROM AN UNIDENTIFIED REPTILE.

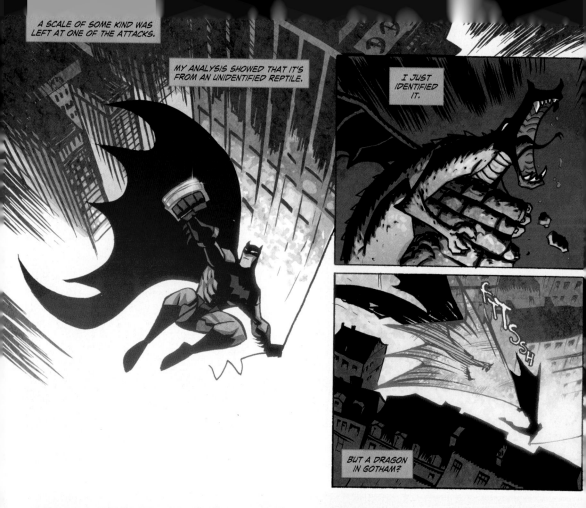

I JUST IDENTIFIED IT.

BUT A DRAGON IN GOTHAM?

THERE'S GOT TO BE MORE TO THIS RIDDLE.

I'LL FIGURE THAT OUT WHEN I BRING IT IN.

I DON'T WANT TO HURT IT.

I DOUBT THE FEELING IS MUTUAL.

FTTSSH

RRRAR!

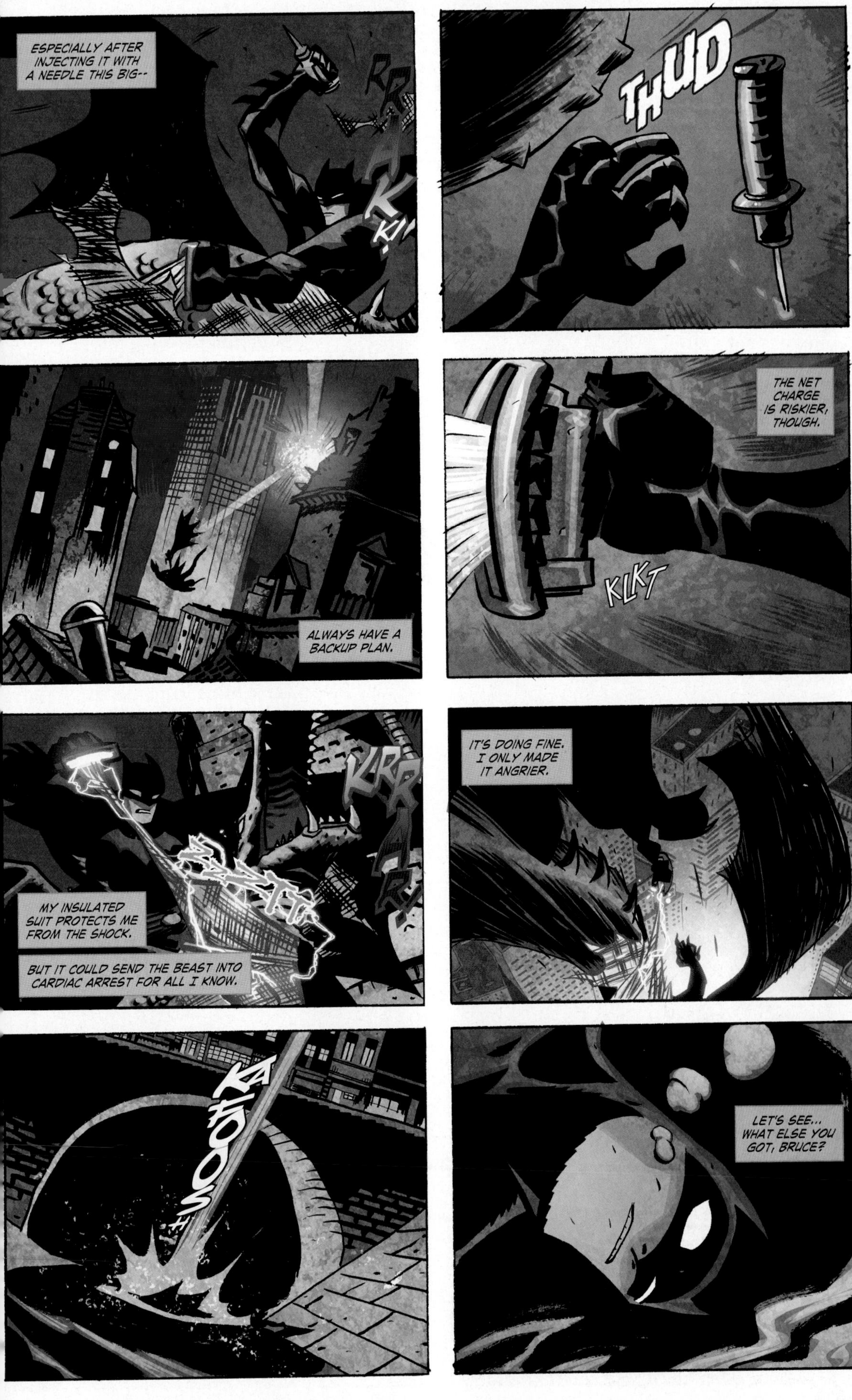
ESPECIALLY AFTER INJECTING IT WITH A NEEDLE THIS BIG--
RRAAKK!
THUD
ALWAYS HAVE A BACKUP PLAN.
THE NET CHARGE IS RISKIER, THOUGH.
KLKT
KRRR!
ZZZTT
MY INSULATED SUIT PROTECTS ME FROM THE SHOCK.
BUT IT COULD SEND THE BEAST INTO CARDIAC ARREST FOR ALL I KNOW.
IT'S DOING FINE. I ONLY MADE IT ANGRIER.
KA-FOOOSH
LET'S SEE... WHAT ELSE YOU GOT, BRUCE?

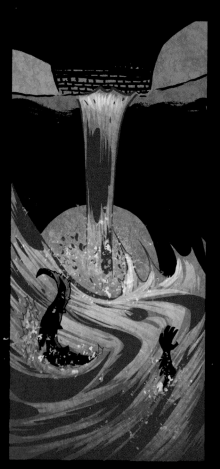

THE NETTING, TRANQUILIZERS, AND TASER ALL FAILED.

LET'S JUST DO THIS THE HARD WAY, THEN.

WHEN IT LUNGES AT ME I REALIZE SOMETHING IS WRONG.

WHATEVER THIS MONSTER IS, IT'S SICK--BURNING WITH SOME BILE DESTROYING IT FROM THE INSIDE.

I CAN SMELL IT.

THE SICKNESS IS MAKING IT WEAK, OFF-BALANCE.

I CAN TAKE ADVANTAGE OF THAT...

...THEN CAPTURE IT ALIVE.

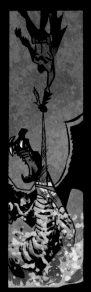

SICK OR NOT, THIS THING IS STILL FAST.

IF THE NETTING WON'T HOLD HIM...

...MAYBE THIS KEVLAR WILL.

THWACK

KRRSAAR!

OOF!

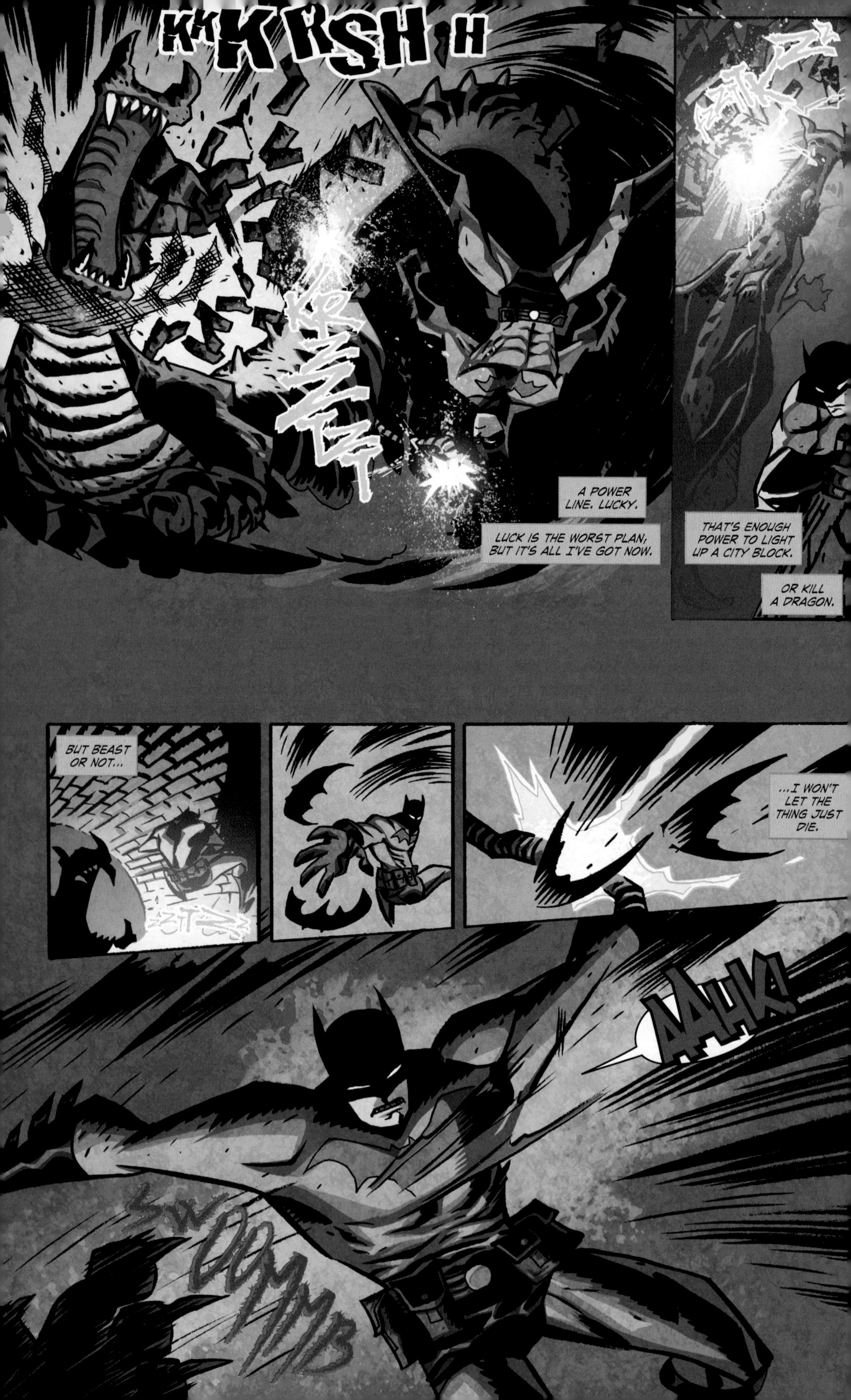
KKKRSHH
KRZZZT
A POWER LINE. LUCKY.
LUCK IS THE WORST PLAN, BUT IT'S ALL I'VE GOT NOW.
THAT'S ENOUGH POWER TO LIGHT UP A CITY BLOCK.
OR KILL A DRAGON.
BUT BEAST OR NOT...
...I WON'T LET THE THING JUST DIE.
AAHK!
SWOOMB

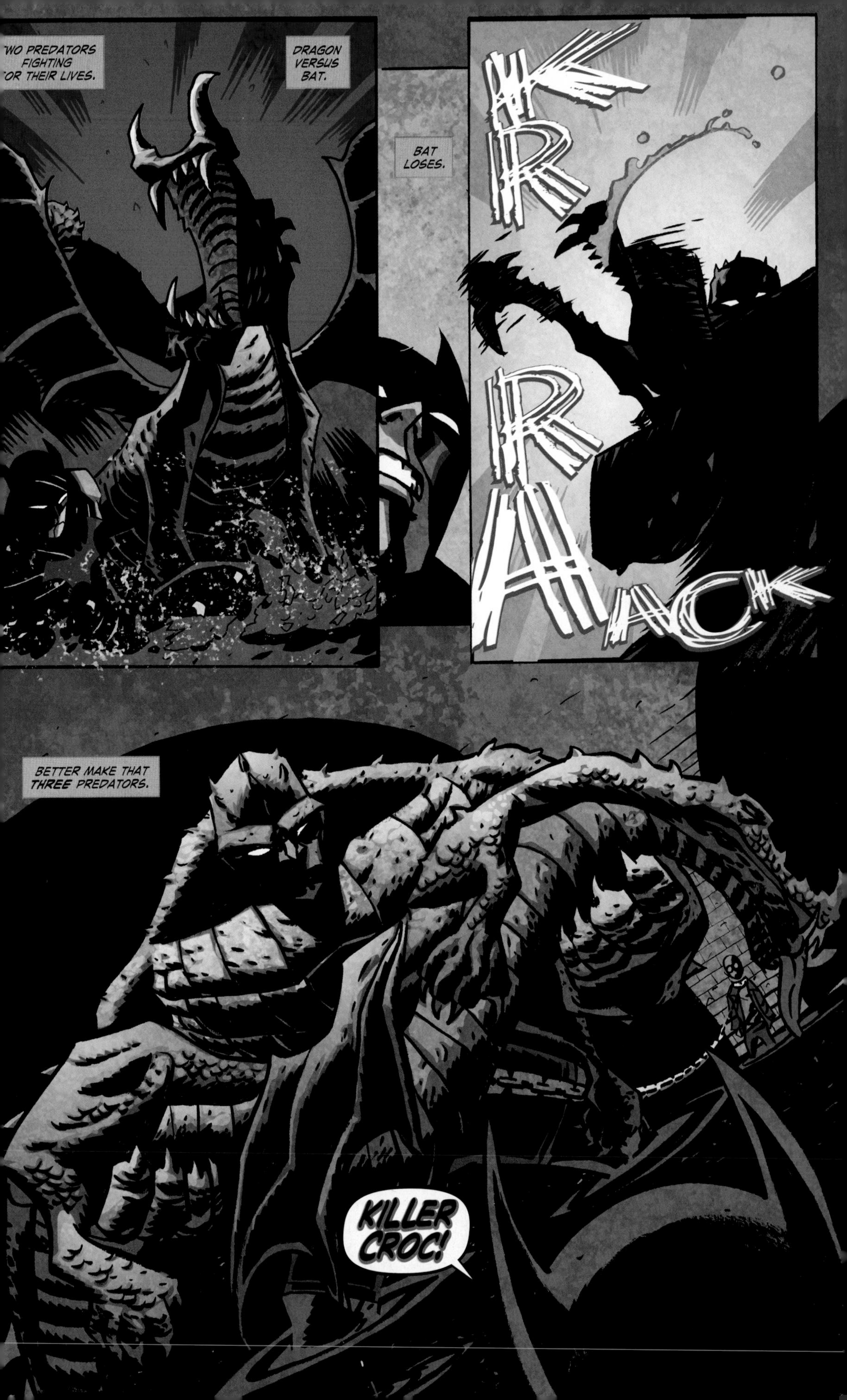

TWO PREDATORS FIGHTING FOR THEIR LIVES.
DRAGON VERSUS BAT.
BAT LOSES.
KRRAACK
BETTER MAKE THAT THREE PREDATORS.
KILLER CROC!

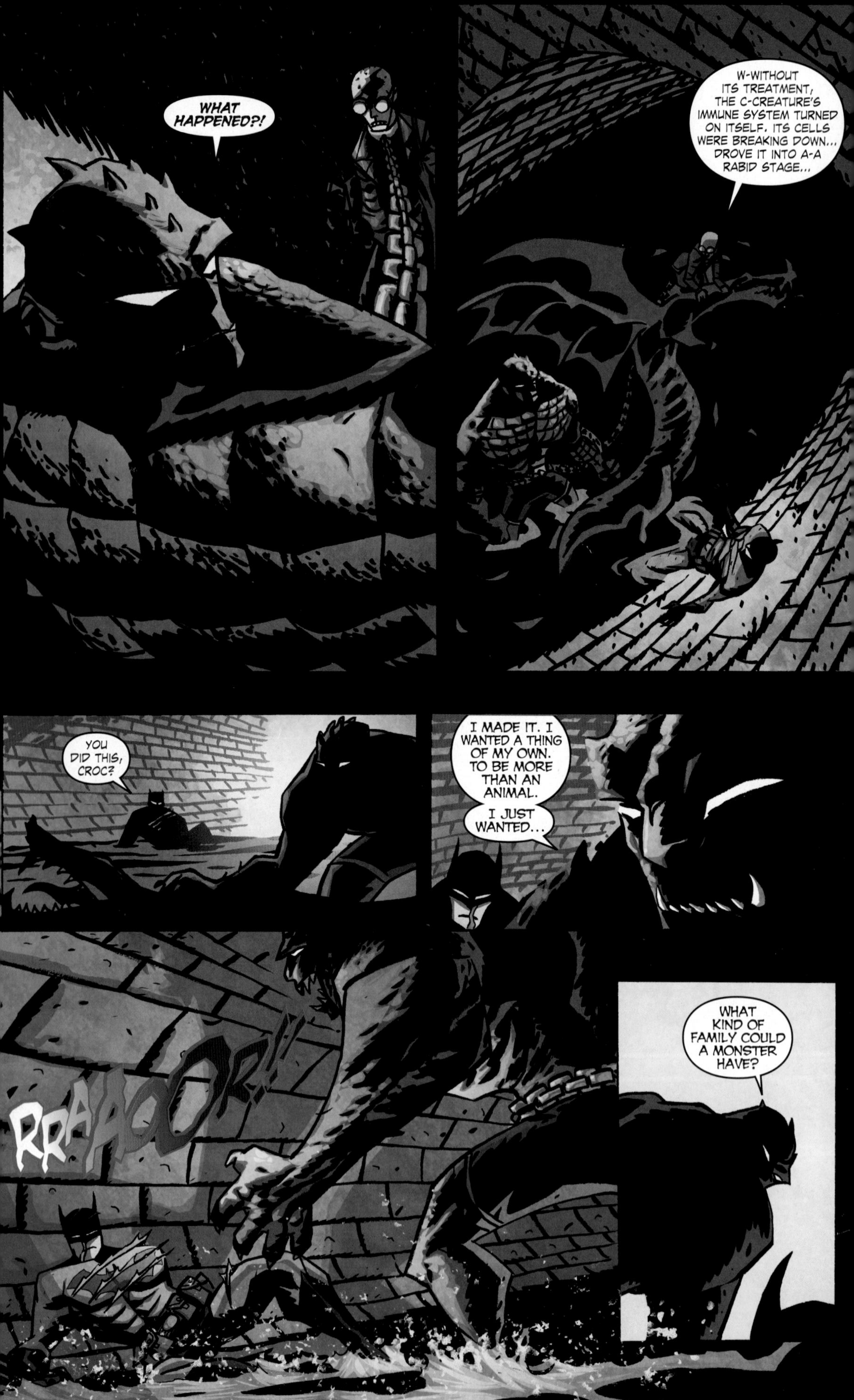
WHAT HAPPENED?!
W-WITHOUT ITS TREATMENT, THE C-CREATURE'S IMMUNE SYSTEM TURNED ON ITSELF. ITS CELLS WERE BREAKING DOWN... DROVE IT INTO A-A RABID STAGE...
YOU DID THIS, CROC?
I MADE IT. I WANTED A THING OF MY OWN. TO BE MORE THAN AN ANIMAL.
I JUST WANTED...
RRAAOOR!!
WHAT KIND OF FAMILY COULD A MONSTER HAVE?

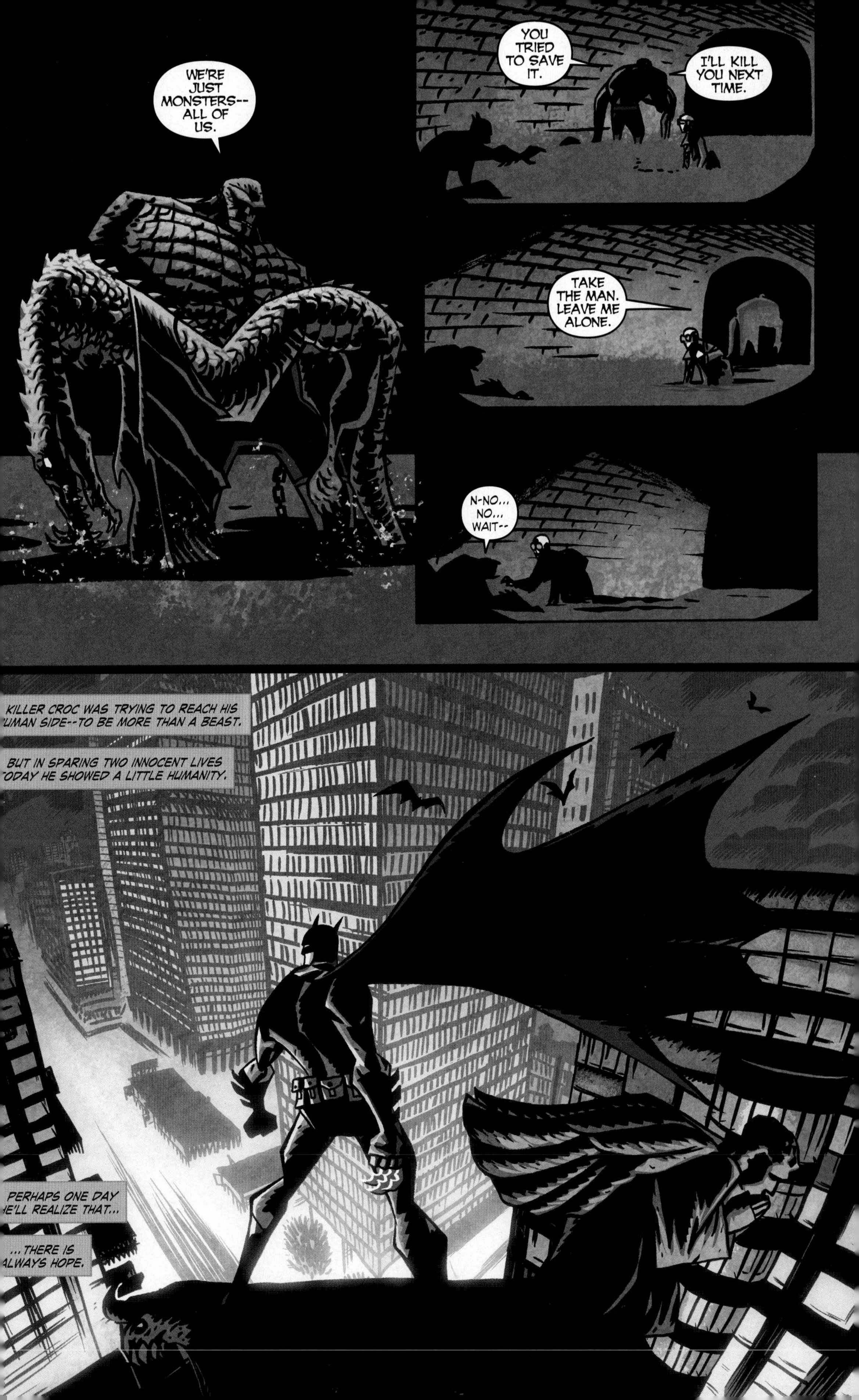
WE'RE JUST MONSTERS-- ALL OF US.
YOU TRIED TO SAVE IT.
I'LL KILL YOU NEXT TIME.
TAKE THE MAN. LEAVE ME ALONE.
N-NO... NO... WAIT--
KILLER CROC WAS TRYING TO REACH HIS HUMAN SIDE--TO BE MORE THAN A BEAST.
BUT IN SPARING TWO INNOCENT LIVES TODAY HE SHOWED A LITTLE HUMANITY.
PERHAPS ONE DAY HE'LL REALIZE THAT...
...THERE IS ALWAYS HOPE.

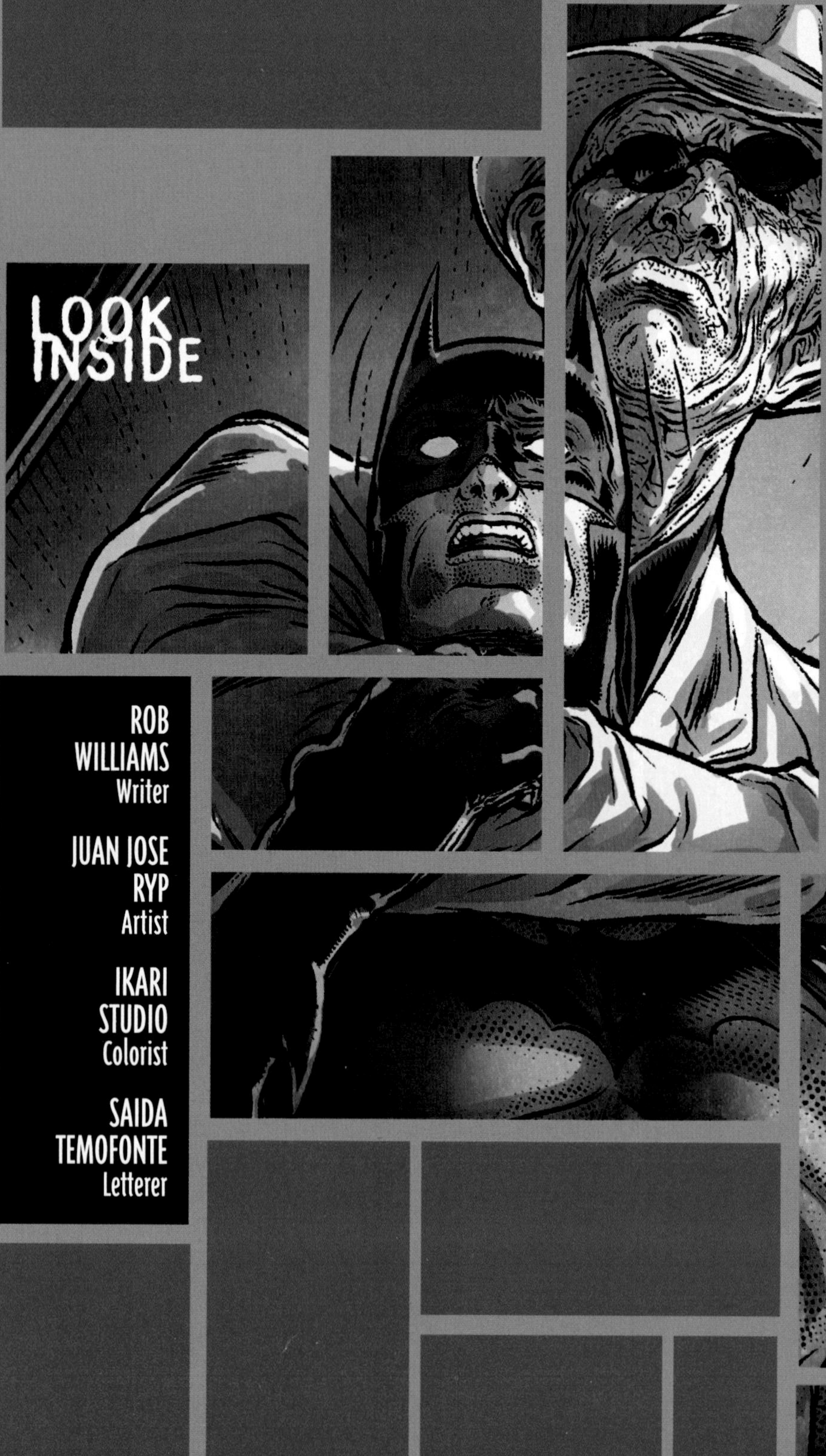
LOOK INSIDE

ROB WILLIAMS
Writer

JUAN JOSE RYP
Artist

IKARI STUDIO
Colorist

SAIDA TEMOFONTE
Letterer

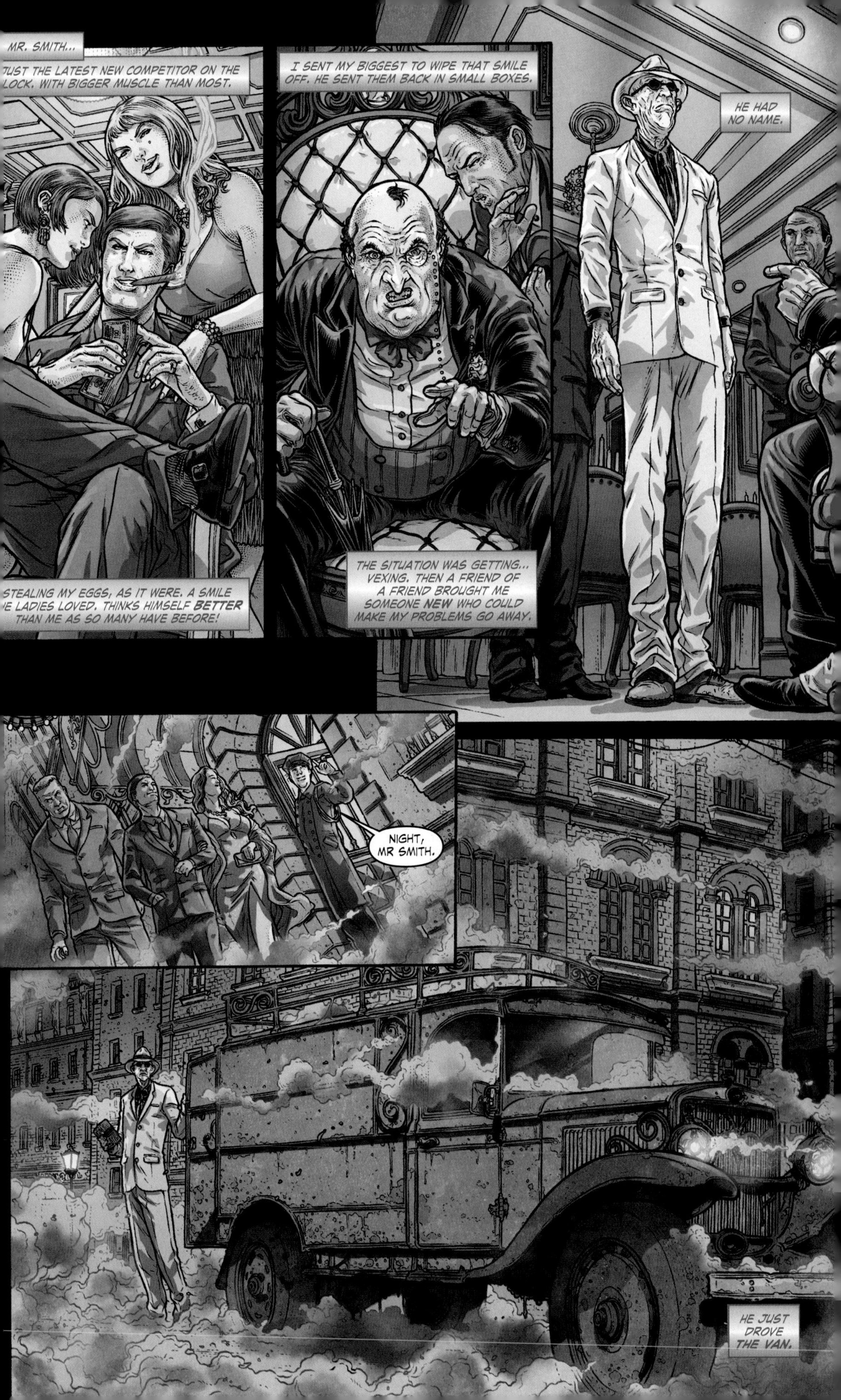
MR. SMITH...
JUST THE LATEST NEW COMPETITOR ON THE BLOCK. WITH BIGGER MUSCLE THAN MOST.
STEALING MY EGGS, AS IT WERE. A SMILE THE LADIES LOVED. THINKS HIMSELF BETTER THAN ME AS SO MANY HAVE BEFORE!
I SENT MY BIGGEST TO WIPE THAT SMILE OFF. HE SENT THEM BACK IN SMALL BOXES.
THE SITUATION WAS GETTING... VEXING. THEN A FRIEND OF A FRIEND BROUGHT ME SOMEONE NEW WHO COULD MAKE MY PROBLEMS GO AWAY.
HE HAD NO NAME.
NIGHT, MR SMITH.
HE JUST DROVE THE VAN.

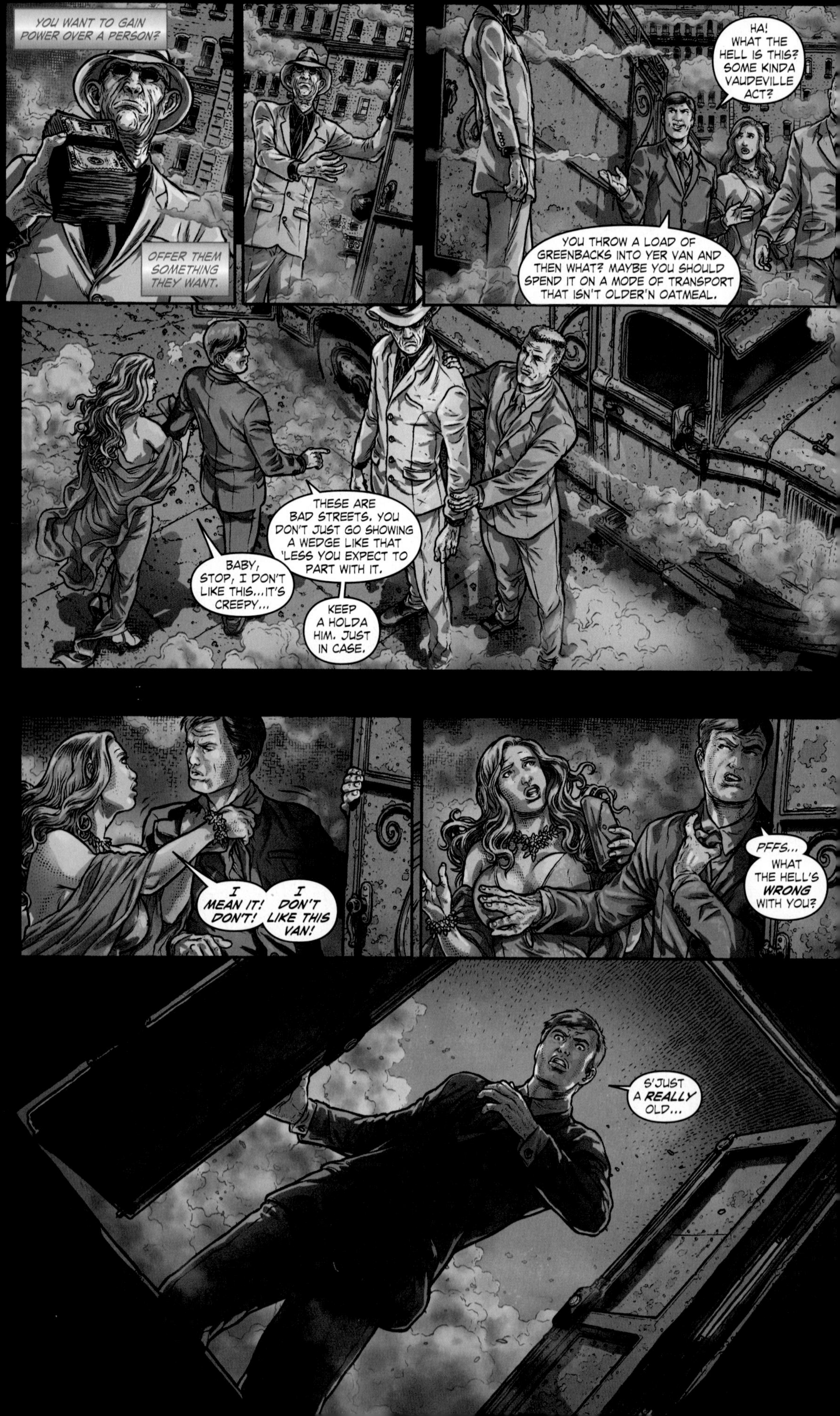
YOU WANT TO GAIN POWER OVER A PERSON?
OFFER THEM SOMETHING THEY WANT.
HA! WHAT THE HELL IS THIS? SOME KINDA VAUDEVILLE ACT?
YOU THROW A LOAD OF GREENBACKS INTO YER VAN AND THEN WHAT? MAYBE YOU SHOULD SPEND IT ON A MODE OF TRANSPORT THAT ISN'T OLDER'N OATMEAL.
THESE ARE BAD STREETS. YOU DON'T JUST GO SHOWING A WEDGE LIKE THAT 'LESS YOU EXPECT TO PART WITH IT.
BABY, STOP, I DON'T LIKE THIS...IT'S CREEPY...
KEEP A HOLDA HIM. JUST IN CASE.
I MEAN IT! DON'T!
I DON'T LIKE THIS VAN!
PFFS... WHAT THE HELL'S WRONG WITH YOU?
S'JUST A REALLY OLD...

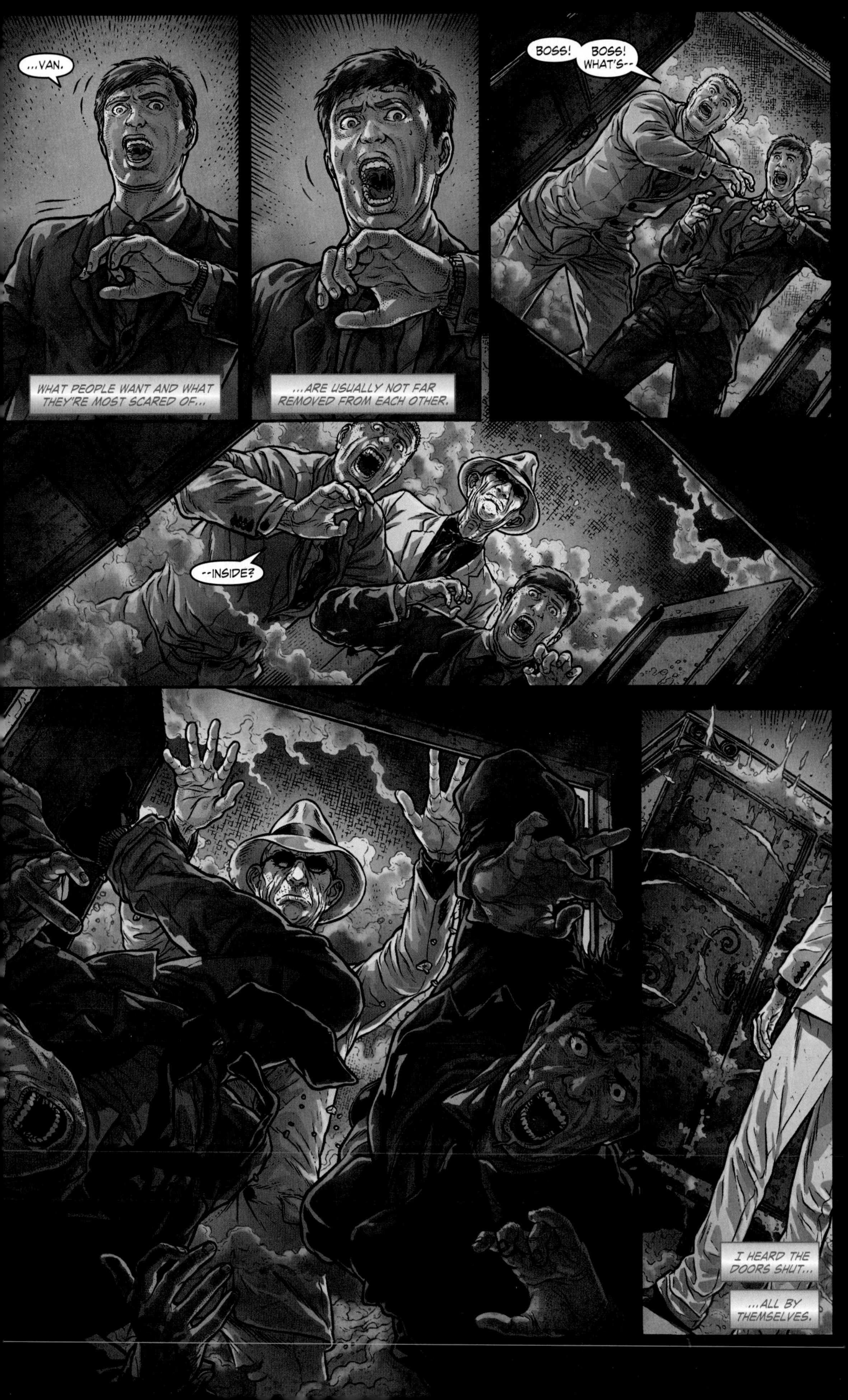
...VAN.
WHAT PEOPLE WANT AND WHAT THEY'RE MOST SCARED OF...
...ARE USUALLY NOT FAR REMOVED FROM EACH OTHER.
BOSS!
BOSS! WHAT'S--
--INSIDE?
I HEARD THE DOORS SHUT...
...ALL BY THEMSELVES.

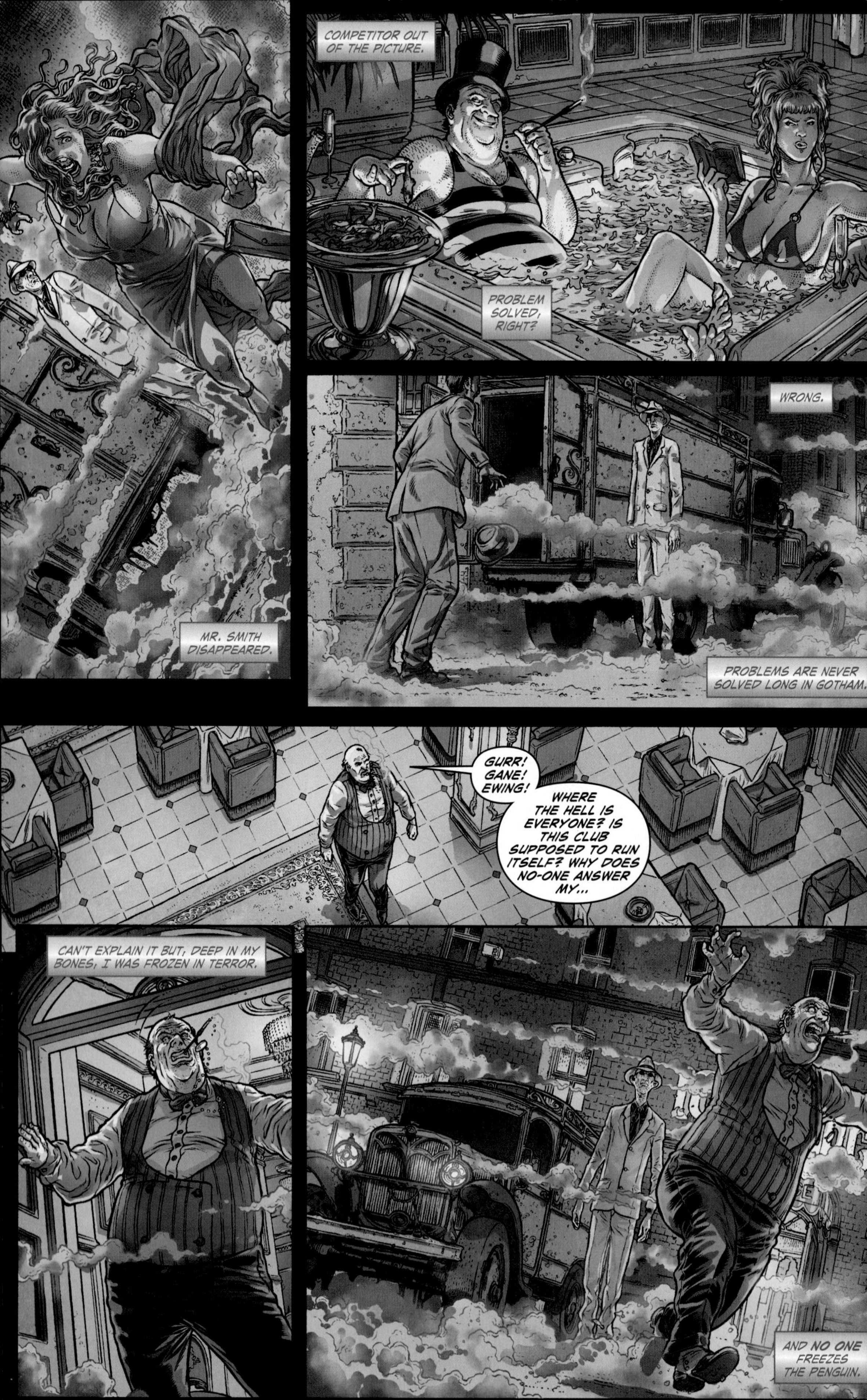
MR. SMITH DISAPPEARED.
COMPETITOR OUT OF THE PICTURE.
PROBLEM SOLVED, RIGHT?
WRONG.
PROBLEMS ARE NEVER SOLVED LONG IN GOTHAM.
GURR! GANE! EWING!
WHERE THE HELL IS EVERYONE? IS THIS CLUB SUPPOSED TO RUN ITSELF? WHY DOES NO-ONE ANSWER MY...
CAN'T EXPLAIN IT BUT, DEEP IN MY BONES, I WAS FROZEN IN TERROR.
AND NO ONE FREEZES THE PENGUIN.

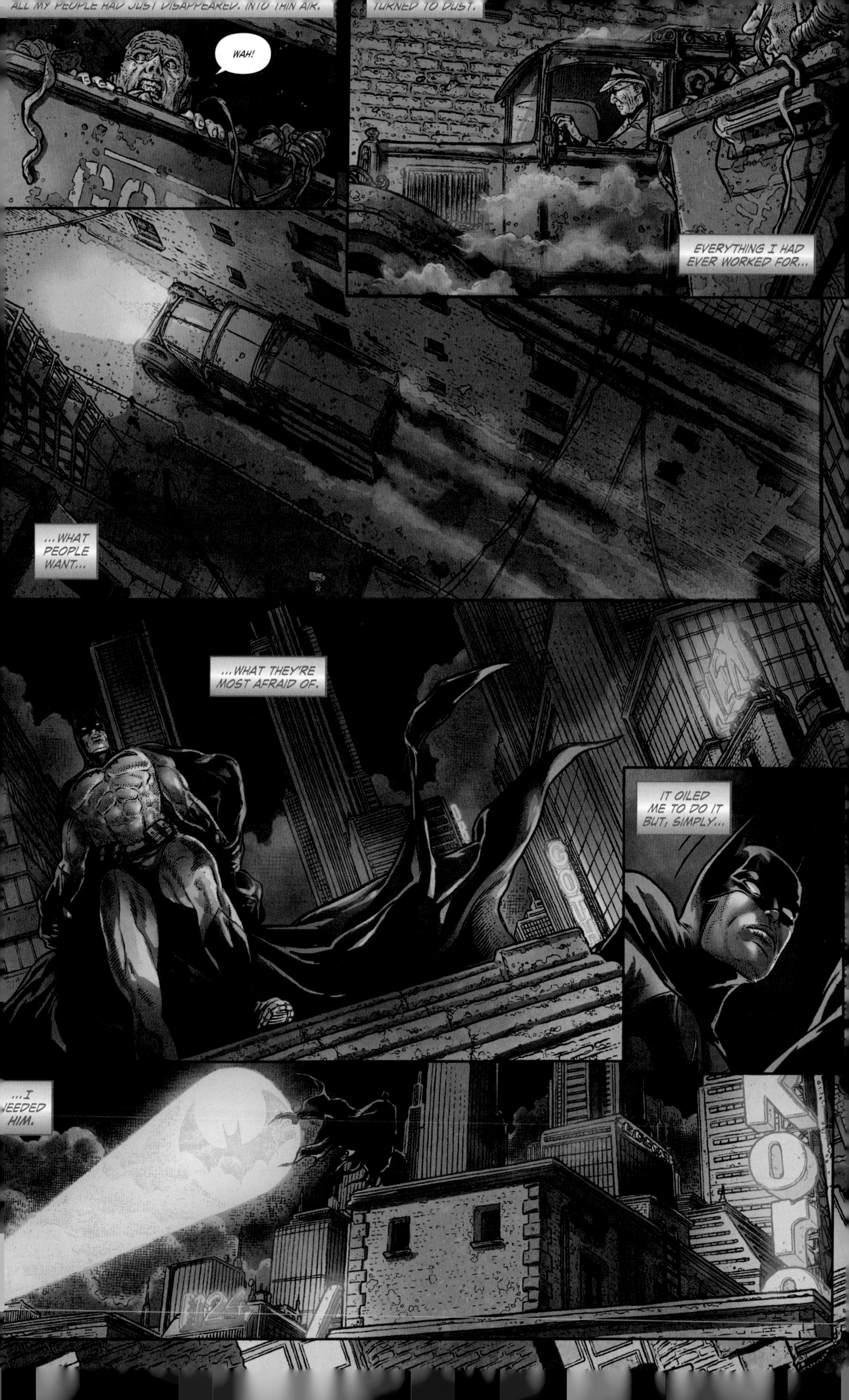
ALL MY PEOPLE HAD JUST DISAPPEARED. INTO THIN AIR.
WAH!
TURNED TO DUST.
EVERYTHING I HAD EVER WORKED FOR...
...WHAT PEOPLE WANT...
...WHAT THEY'RE MOST AFRAID OF.
IT OILED ME TO DO IT BUT, SIMPLY...
...I NEEDED HIM.

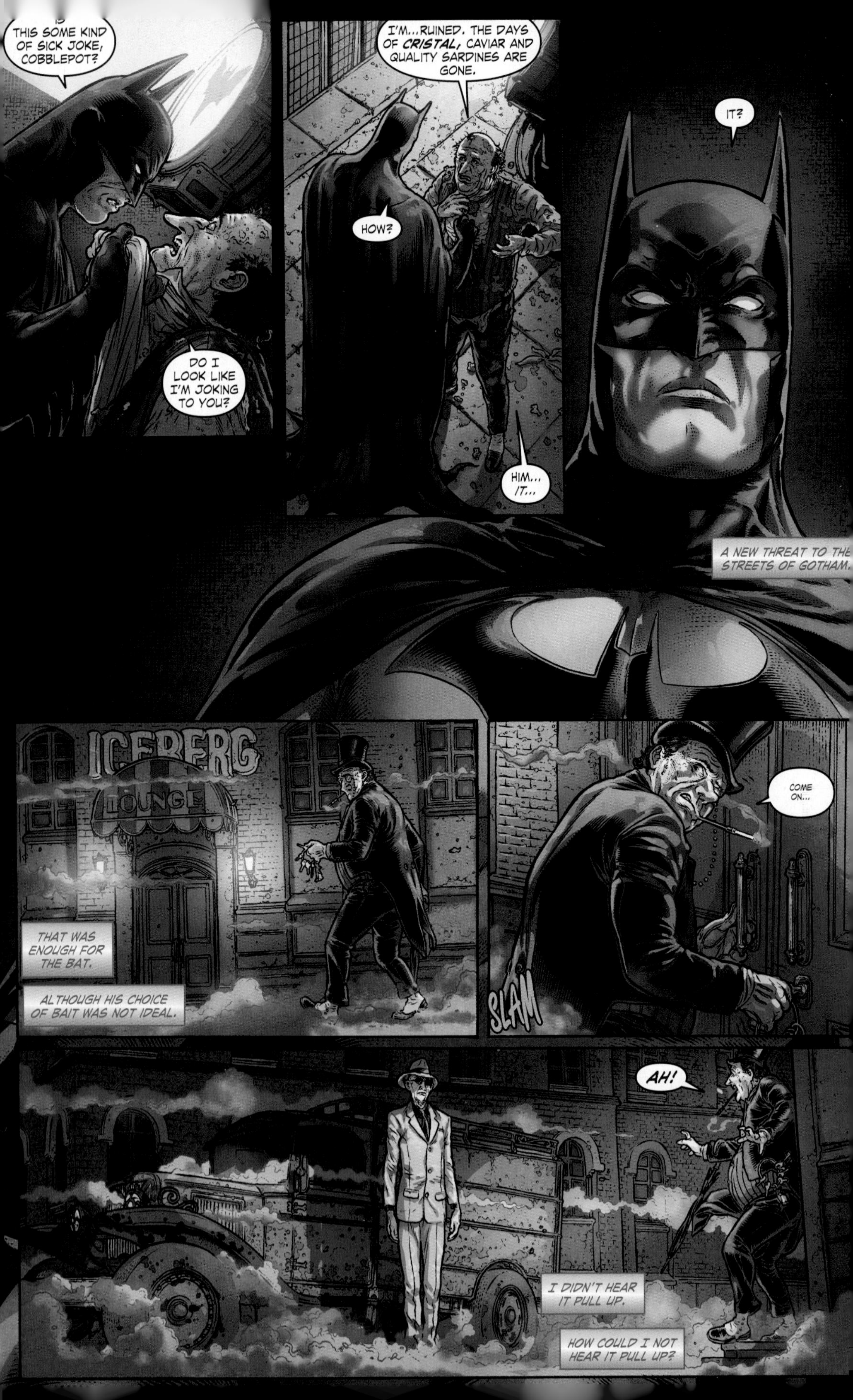
IS THIS SOME KIND OF SICK JOKE, COBBLEPOT?
DO I LOOK LIKE I'M JOKING TO YOU?
I'M...RUINED. THE DAYS OF CRISTAL, CAVIAR AND QUALITY SARDINES ARE GONE.
HOW?
HIM... IT...
IT?
A NEW THREAT TO THE STREETS OF GOTHAM.
ICEBERG
LOUNGE
THAT WAS ENOUGH FOR THE BAT.
ALTHOUGH HIS CHOICE OF BAIT WAS NOT IDEAL.
COME ON...
SLAM
AH!
I DIDN'T HEAR IT PULL UP.
HOW COULD I NOT HEAR IT PULL UP?

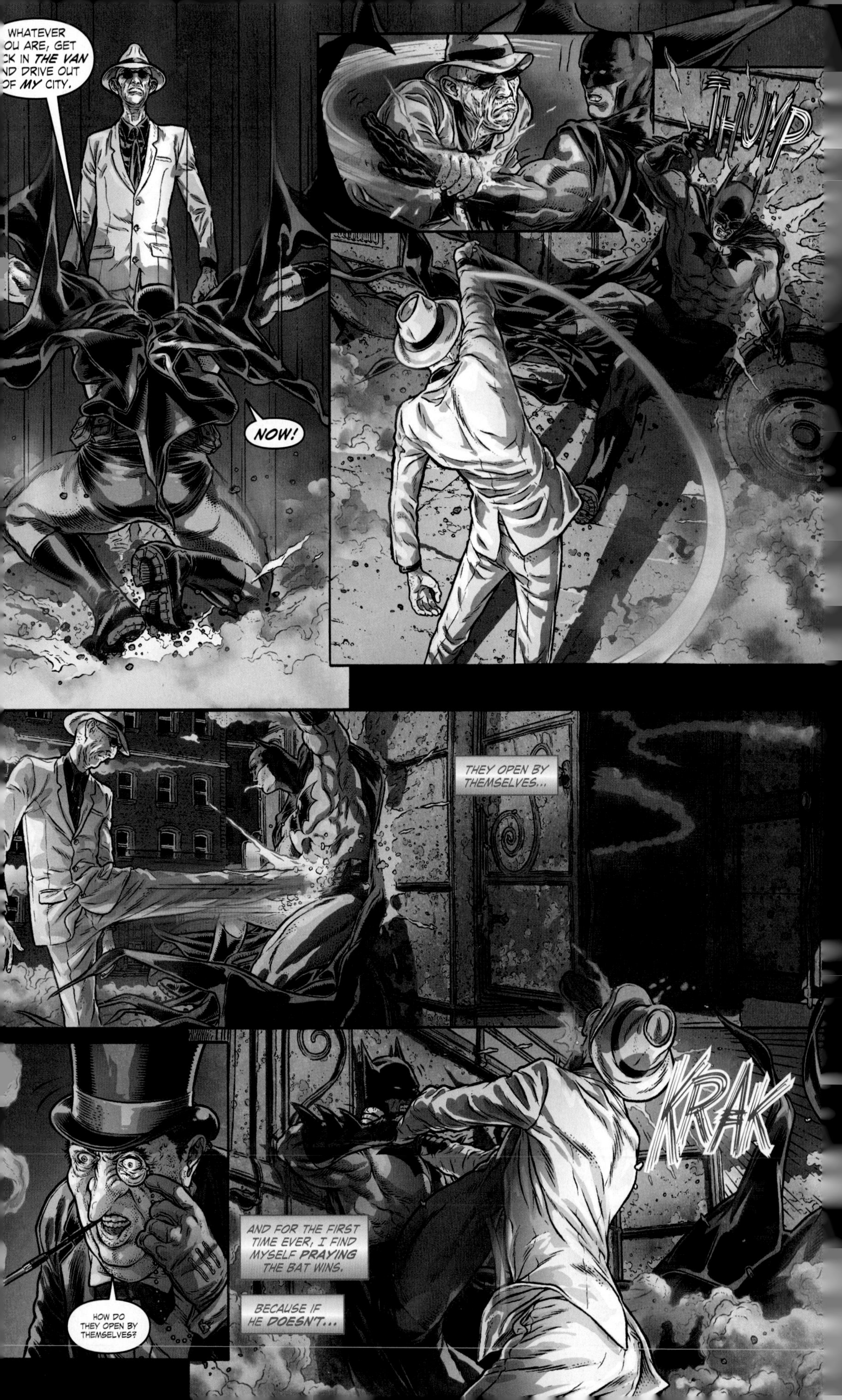

WHATEVER
OU ARE, GET
CK IN THE VAN
ND DRIVE OUT
OF MY CITY.
NOW!
THUMP
THEY OPEN BY
THEMSELVES...
HOW DO
THEY OPEN BY
THEMSELVES?
AND FOR THE FIRST
TIME EVER, I FIND
MYSELF PRAYING
THE BAT WINS.
BECAUSE IF
HE DOESN'T...
KRAK

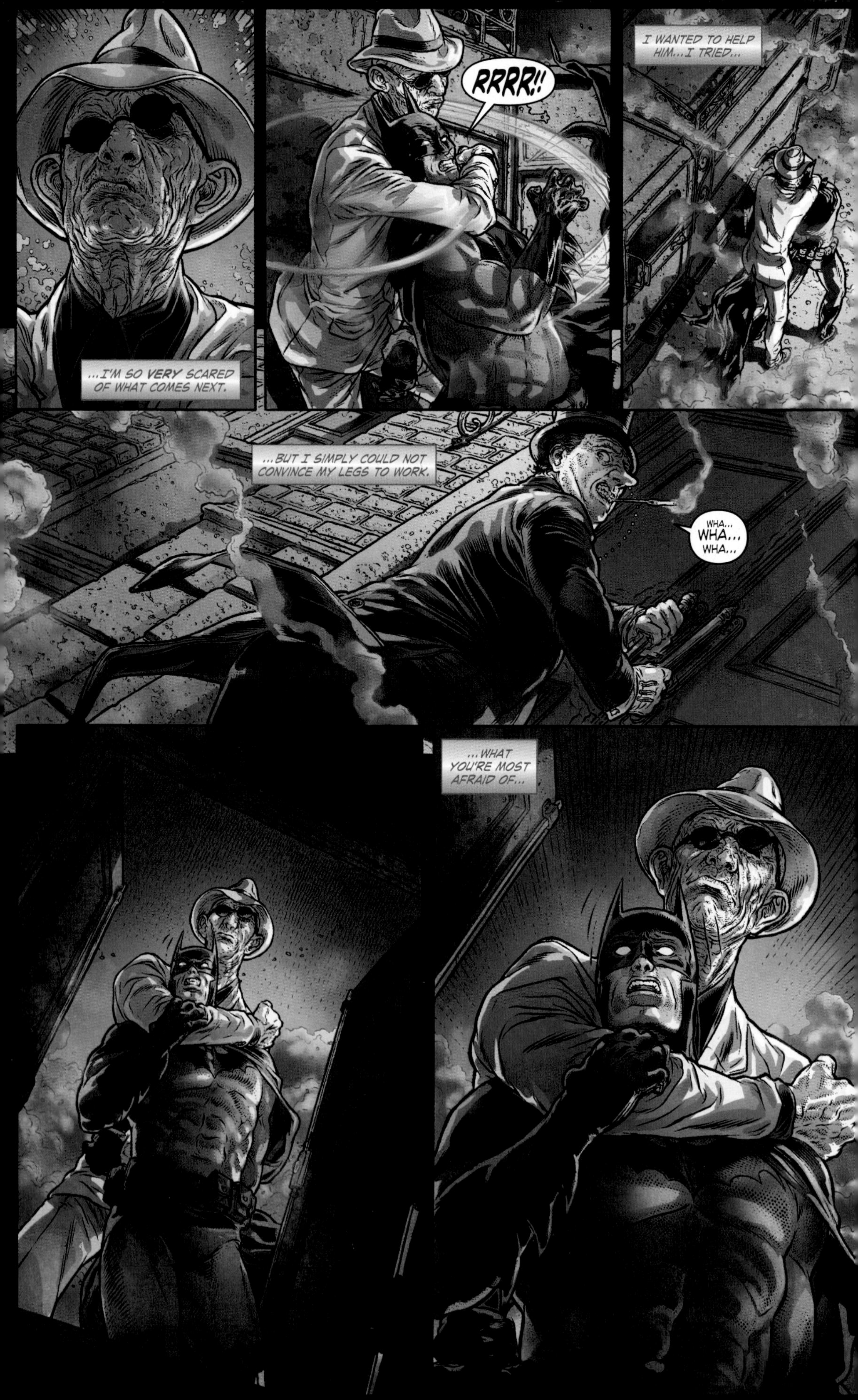
...I'M SO VERY SCARED OF WHAT COMES NEXT.
RRRR!!
I WANTED TO HELP HIM... I TRIED...
...BUT I SIMPLY COULD NOT CONVINCE MY LEGS TO WORK.
WHA... WHA... WHA...
...WHAT YOU'RE MOST AFRAID OF...

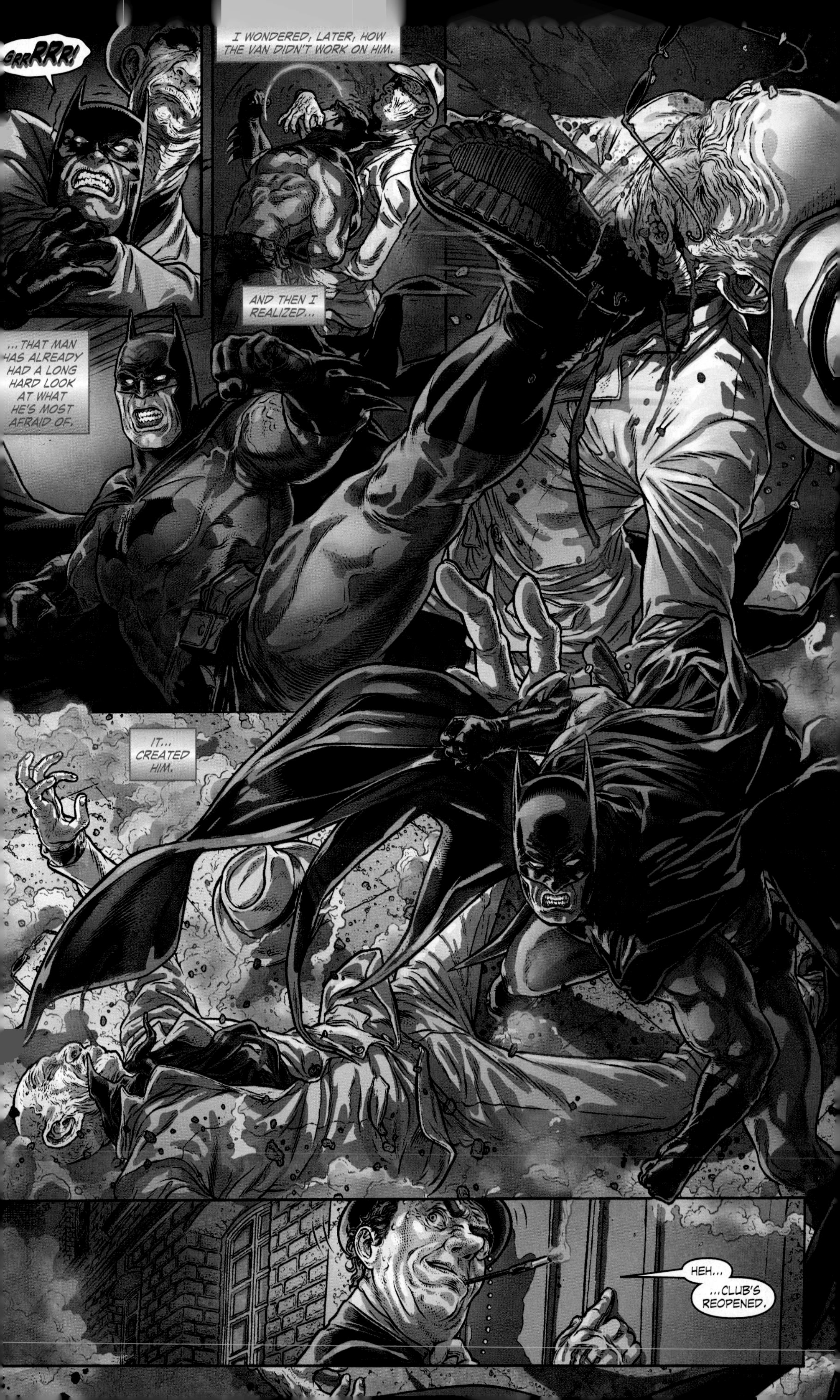

GRRRRR!
I WONDERED, LATER, HOW THE VAN DIDN'T WORK ON HIM.
AND THEN I REALIZED...
...THAT MAN HAS ALREADY HAD A LONG HARD LOOK AT WHAT HE'S MOST AFRAID OF.
IT... CREATED HIM.
HEH...
...CLUB'S REOPENED.

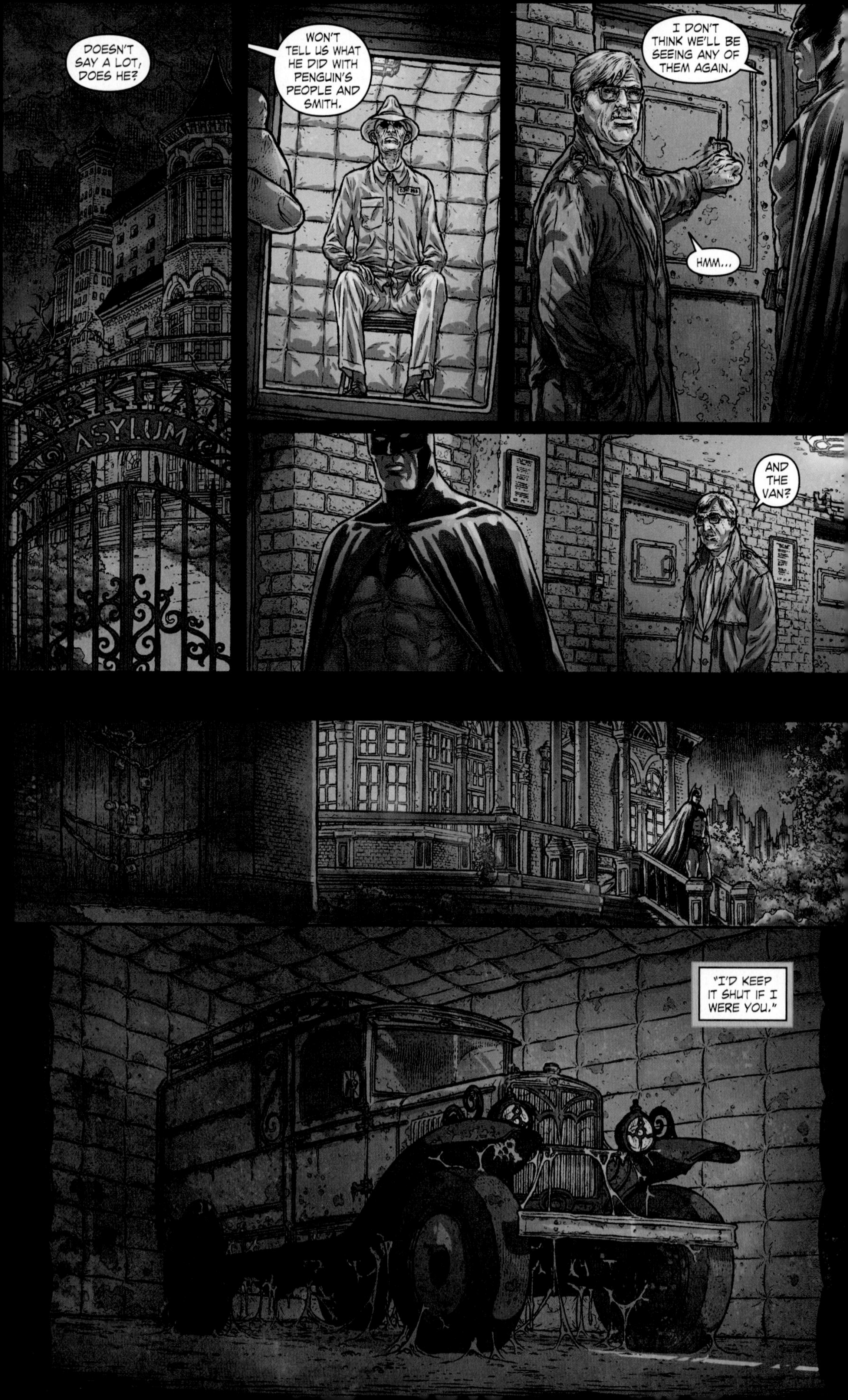
DOESN'T SAY A LOT, DOES HE?
WON'T TELL US WHAT HE DID WITH PENGUIN'S PEOPLE AND SMITH.
I DON'T THINK WE'LL BE SEEING ANY OF THEM AGAIN.
HMM...
ASYLUM
AND THE VAN?
"I'D KEEP IT SHUT IF I WERE YOU."

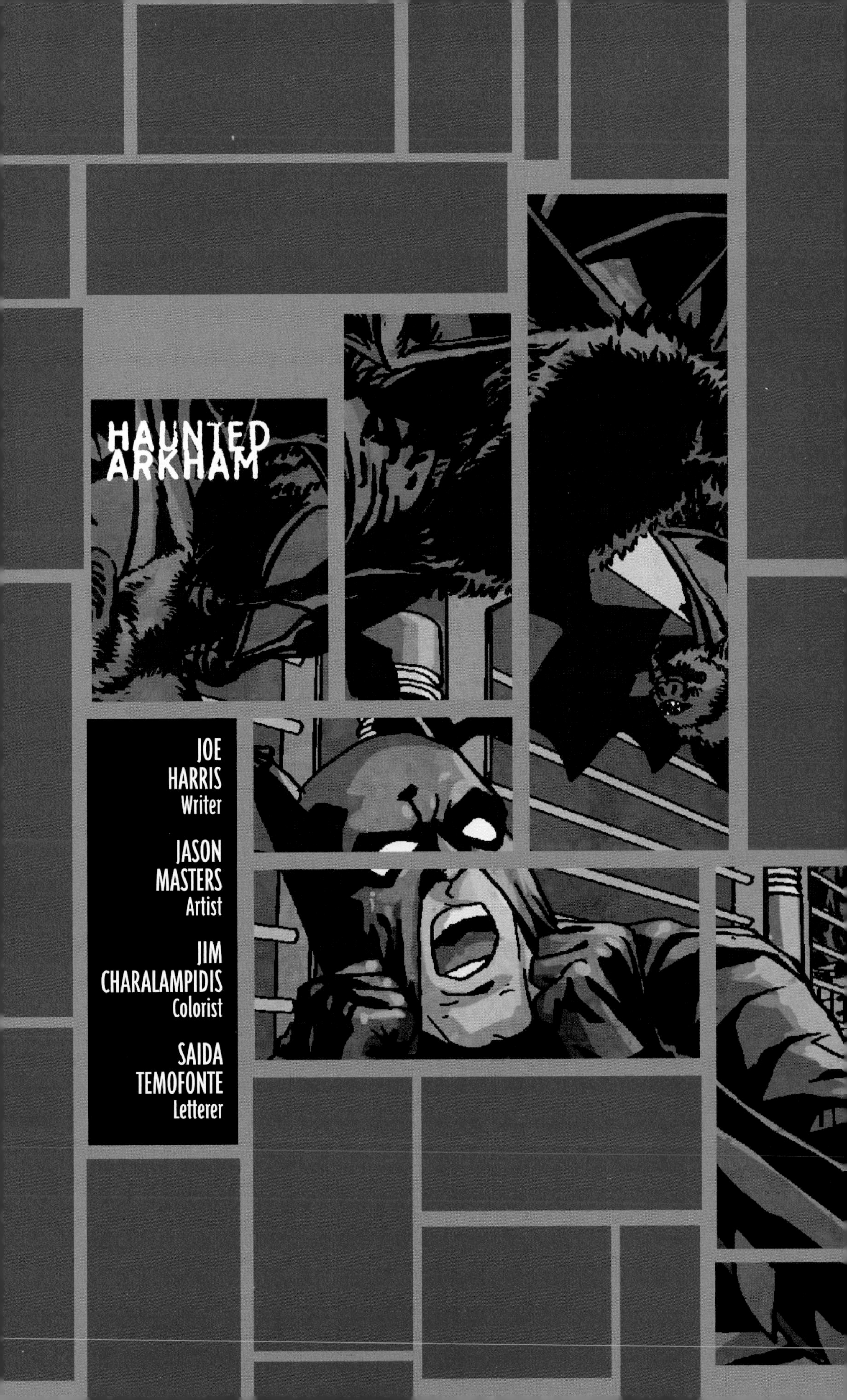
HAUNTED ARKHAM
JOE HARRIS Writer
JASON MASTERS Artist
JIM CHARALAMPIDIS Colorist
SAIDA TEMOFONTE Letterer

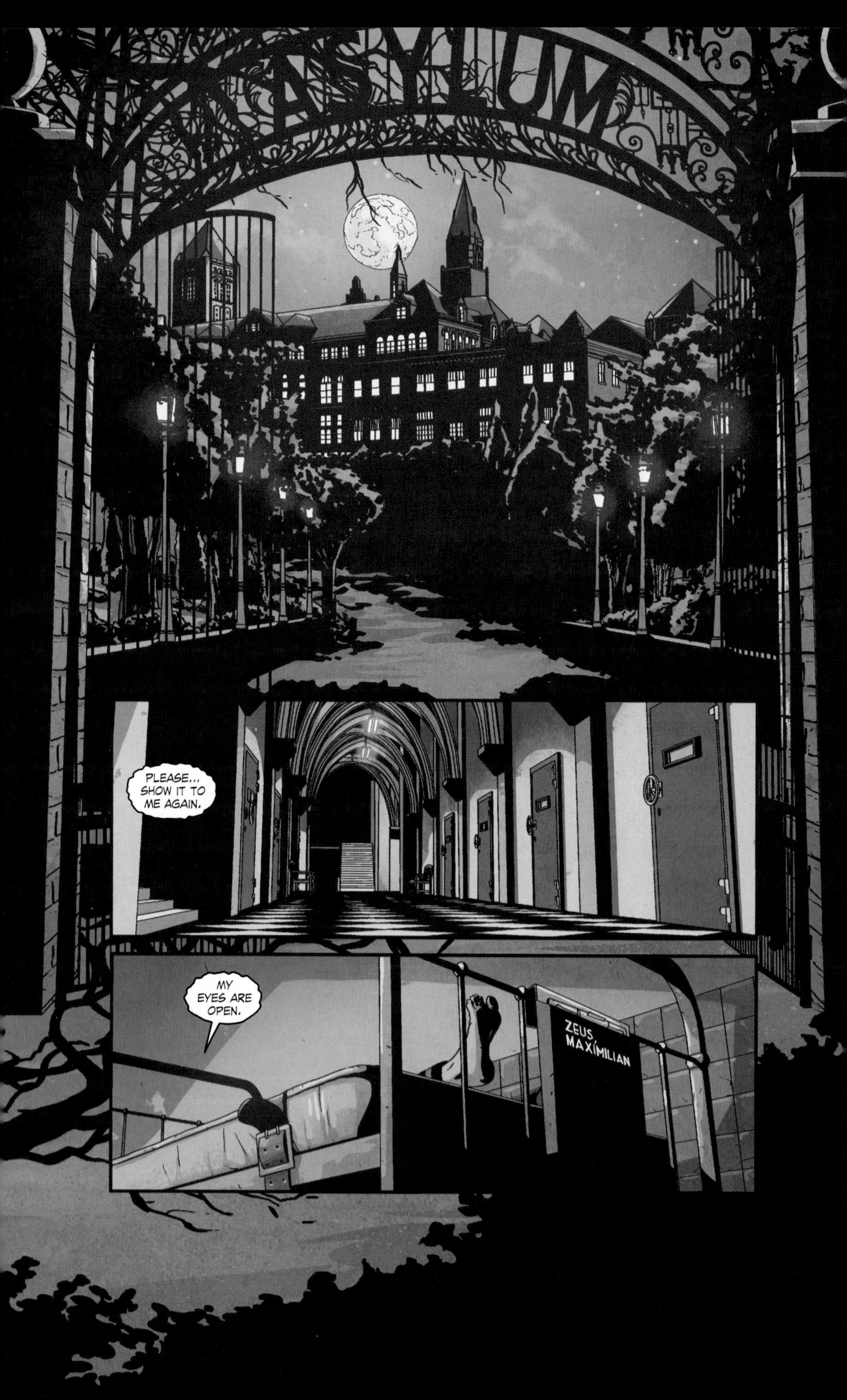
ASYLUM
PLEASE... SHOW IT TO ME AGAIN.
MY EYES ARE OPEN.
ZEUS, MAXÍMILIAN

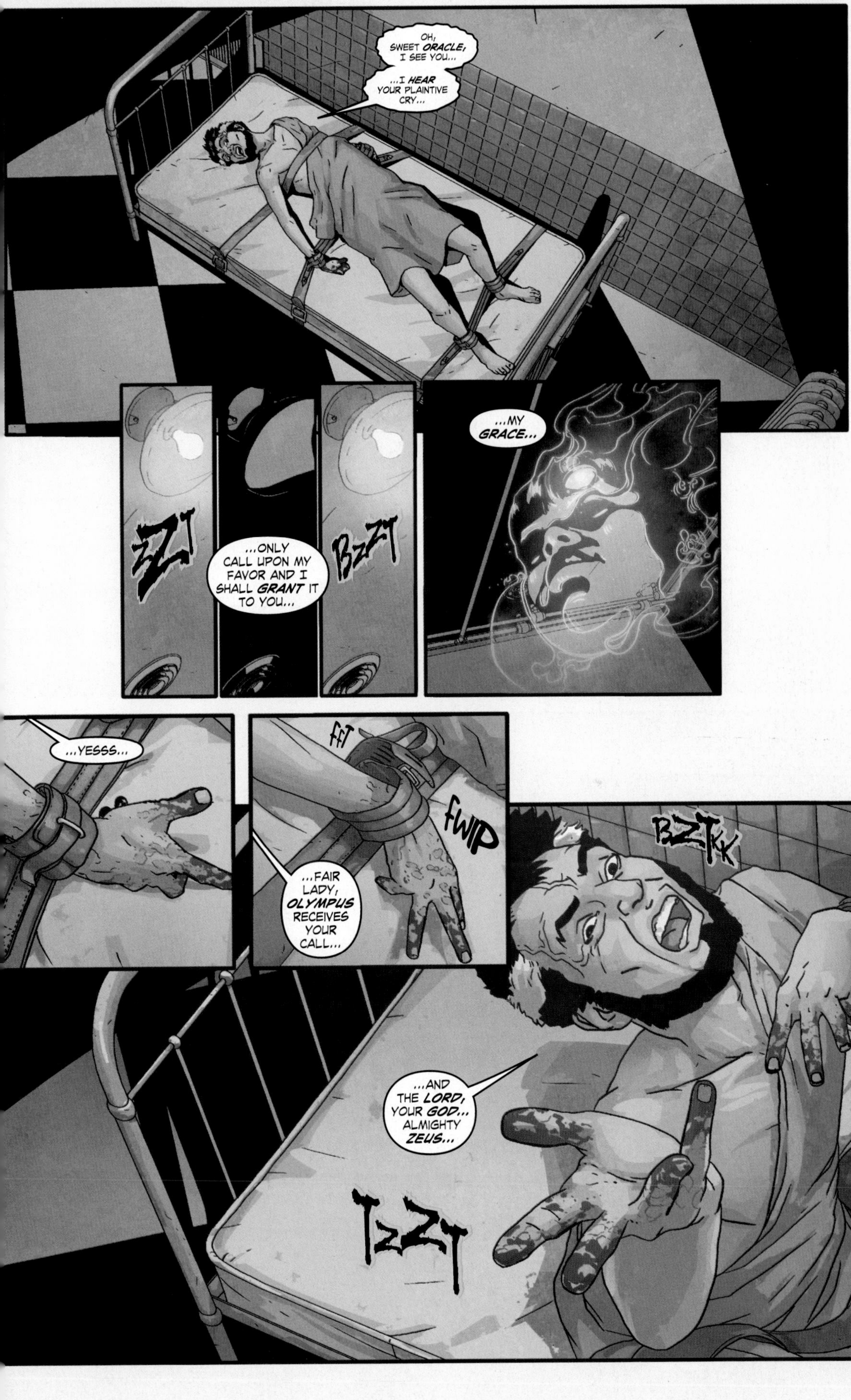
OH, SWEET ORACLE, I SEE YOU...
...I HEAR YOUR PLAINTIVE CRY...
ZZT
...ONLY CALL UPON MY FAVOR AND I SHALL GRANT IT TO YOU...
BZZT
...MY GRACE...
...YESSS...
FFT
FWIP
...FAIR LADY, OLYMPUS RECEIVES YOUR CALL...
BZTKK
...AND THE LORD, YOUR GOD... ALMIGHTY ZEUS...
TZZT

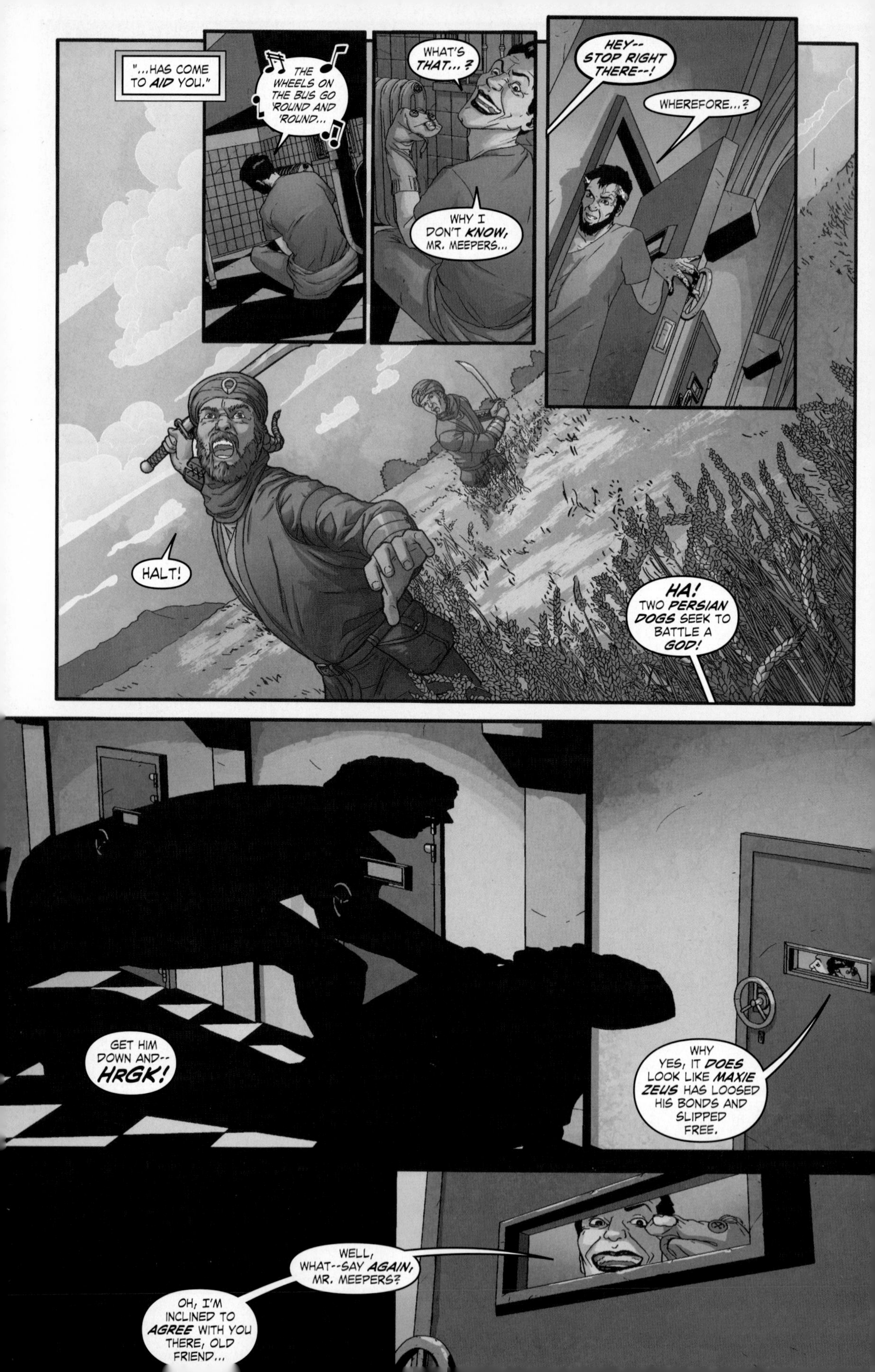
"...HAS COME TO AID YOU."
THE WHEELS ON THE BUS GO 'ROUND AND 'ROUND...
WHAT'S THAT...?
WHY I DON'T KNOW, MR. MEEPERS...
HEY-- STOP RIGHT THERE--!
WHEREFORE...?
HALT!
HA! TWO PERSIAN DOGS SEEK TO BATTLE A GOD!
GET HIM DOWN AND-- HRGK!
WHY YES, IT DOES LOOK LIKE MAXIE ZEUS HAS LOOSED HIS BONDS AND SLIPPED FREE.
WELL, WHAT--SAY AGAIN, MR. MEEPERS?
OH, I'M INCLINED TO AGREE WITH YOU THERE, OLD FRIEND...

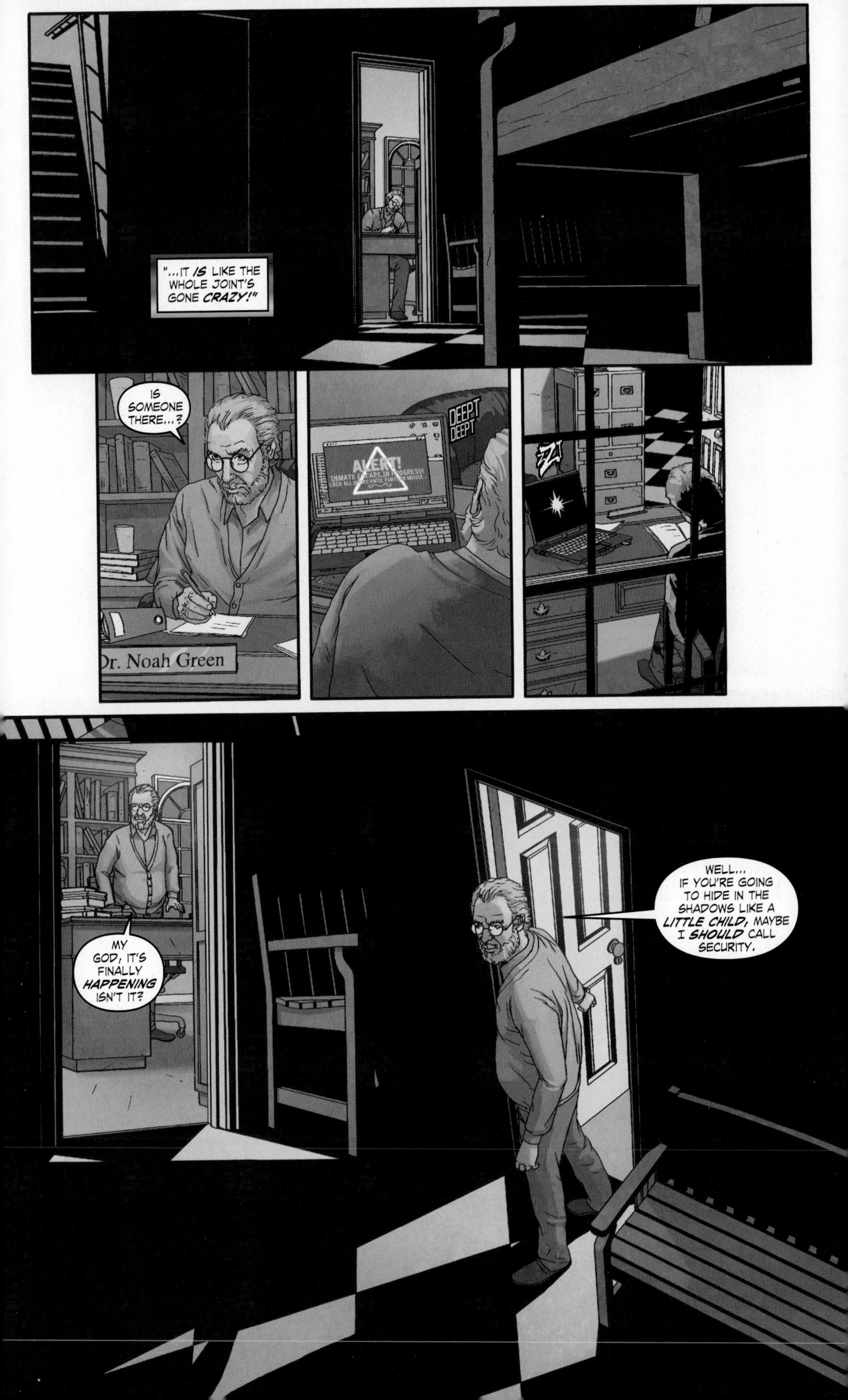
"...IT *IS* LIKE THE WHOLE JOINT'S GONE *CRAZY!*"
IS SOMEONE THERE...?
Dr. Noah Green
DEEPT DEEPT
ALERT!
INMATE ESCAPE IN PROGRESS!
ZT
MY GOD, IT'S FINALLY *HAPPENING* ISN'T IT?
WELL... IF YOU'RE GOING TO HIDE IN THE SHADOWS LIKE A *LITTLE CHILD,* MAYBE I *SHOULD* CALL SECURITY.

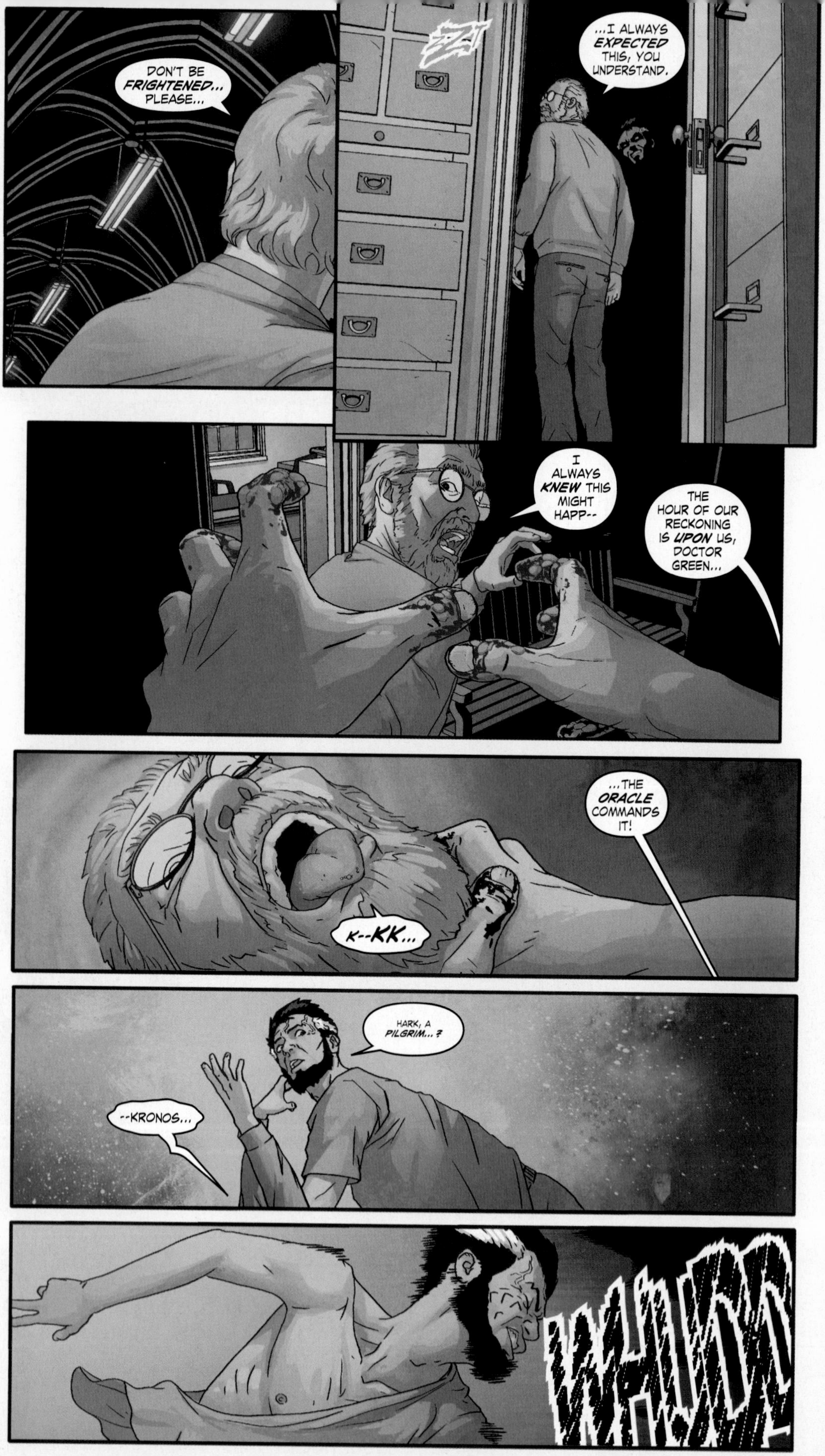
DON'T BE FRIGHTENED... PLEASE...
ZZT
...I ALWAYS EXPECTED THIS, YOU UNDERSTAND.
I ALWAYS KNEW THIS MIGHT HAPP--
THE HOUR OF OUR RECKONING IS UPON US, DOCTOR GREEN...
...THE ORACLE COMMANDS IT!
K--KK...
HARK, A PILGRIM...?
--KRONOS...

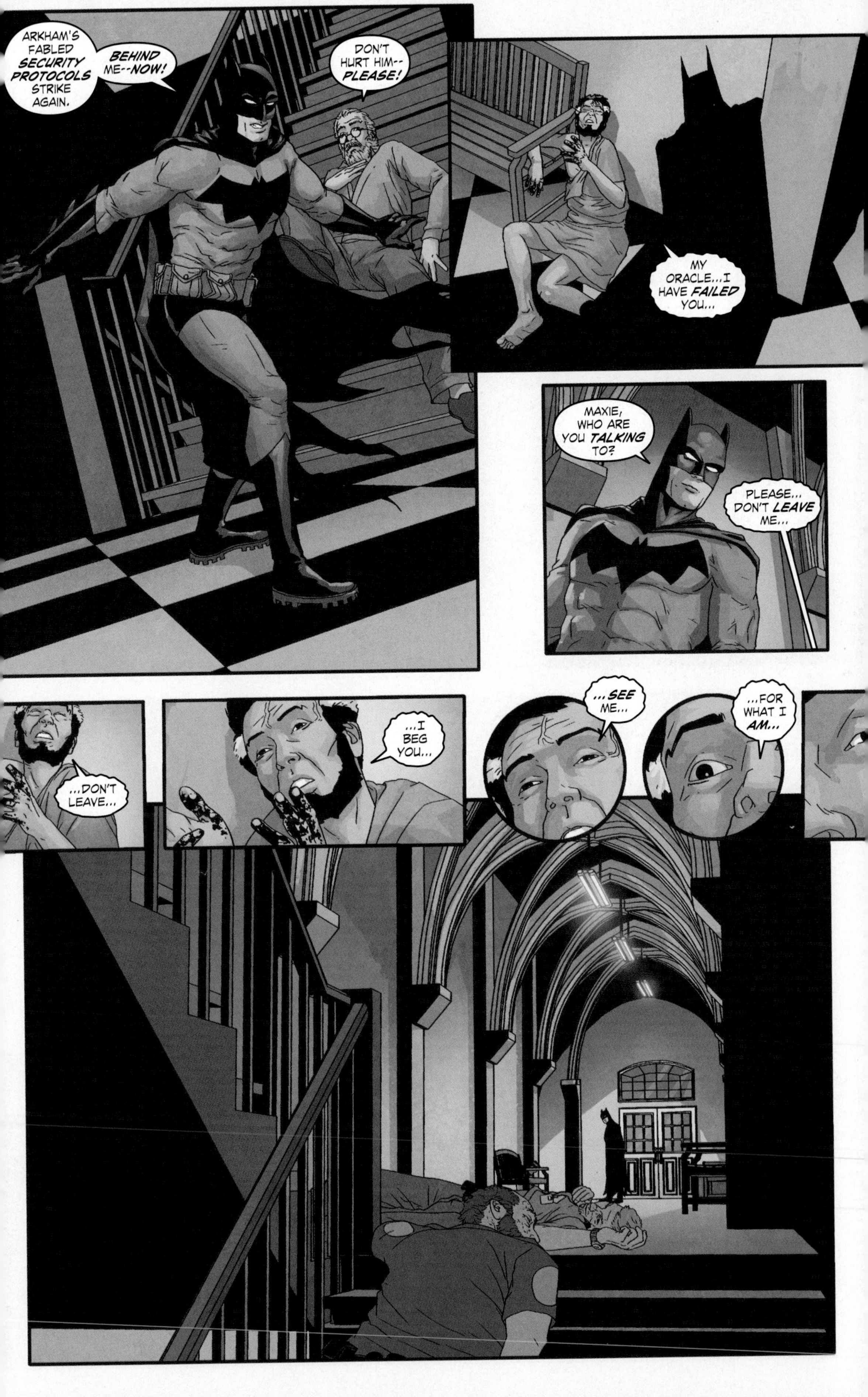
ARKHAM'S FABLED SECURITY PROTOCOLS STRIKE AGAIN.
BEHIND ME--NOW!
DON'T HURT HIM-- PLEASE!
MY ORACLE...I HAVE FAILED YOU...
MAXIE, WHO ARE YOU TALKING TO?
PLEASE... DON'T LEAVE ME...
...DON'T LEAVE...
...I BEG YOU...
...SEE ME...
...FOR WHAT I AM...

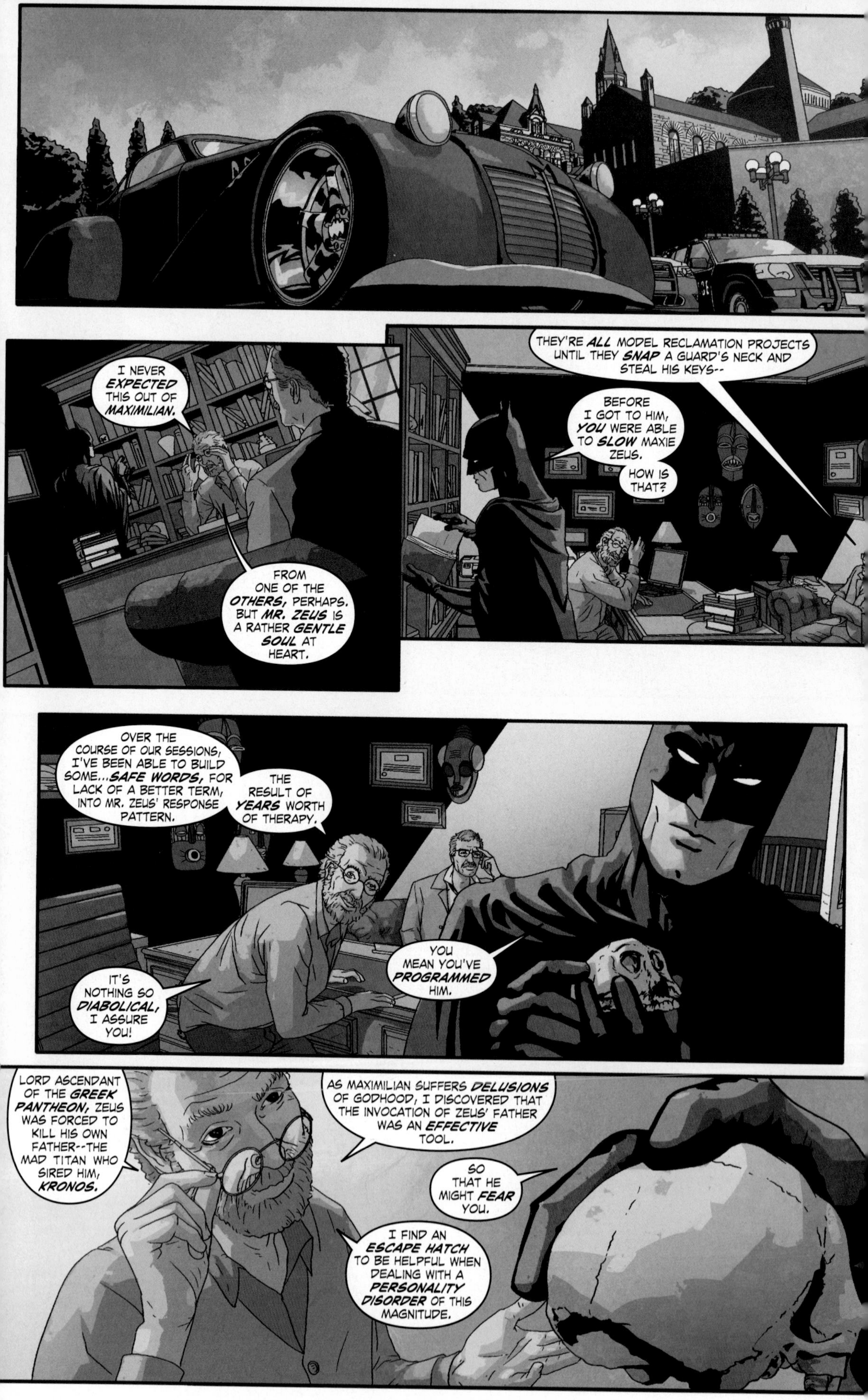

I NEVER EXPECTED THIS OUT OF MAXIMILIAN.
FROM ONE OF THE OTHERS, PERHAPS. BUT MR. ZEUS IS A RATHER GENTLE SOUL AT HEART.
THEY'RE ALL MODEL RECLAMATION PROJECTS UNTIL THEY SNAP A GUARD'S NECK AND STEAL HIS KEYS--
BEFORE I GOT TO HIM, YOU WERE ABLE TO SLOW MAXIE ZEUS.
HOW IS THAT?
OVER THE COURSE OF OUR SESSIONS, I'VE BEEN ABLE TO BUILD SOME...SAFE WORDS, FOR LACK OF A BETTER TERM, INTO MR. ZEUS' RESPONSE PATTERN.
THE RESULT OF YEARS WORTH OF THERAPY.
YOU MEAN YOU'VE PROGRAMMED HIM.
IT'S NOTHING SO DIABOLICAL, I ASSURE YOU!
LORD ASCENDANT OF THE GREEK PANTHEON, ZEUS WAS FORCED TO KILL HIS OWN FATHER--THE MAD TITAN WHO SIRED HIM, KRONOS.
AS MAXIMILIAN SUFFERS DELUSIONS OF GODHOOD, I DISCOVERED THAT THE INVOCATION OF ZEUS' FATHER WAS AN EFFECTIVE TOOL.
SO THAT HE MIGHT FEAR YOU.
I FIND AN ESCAPE HATCH TO BE HELPFUL WHEN DEALING WITH A PERSONALITY DISORDER OF THIS MAGNITUDE.

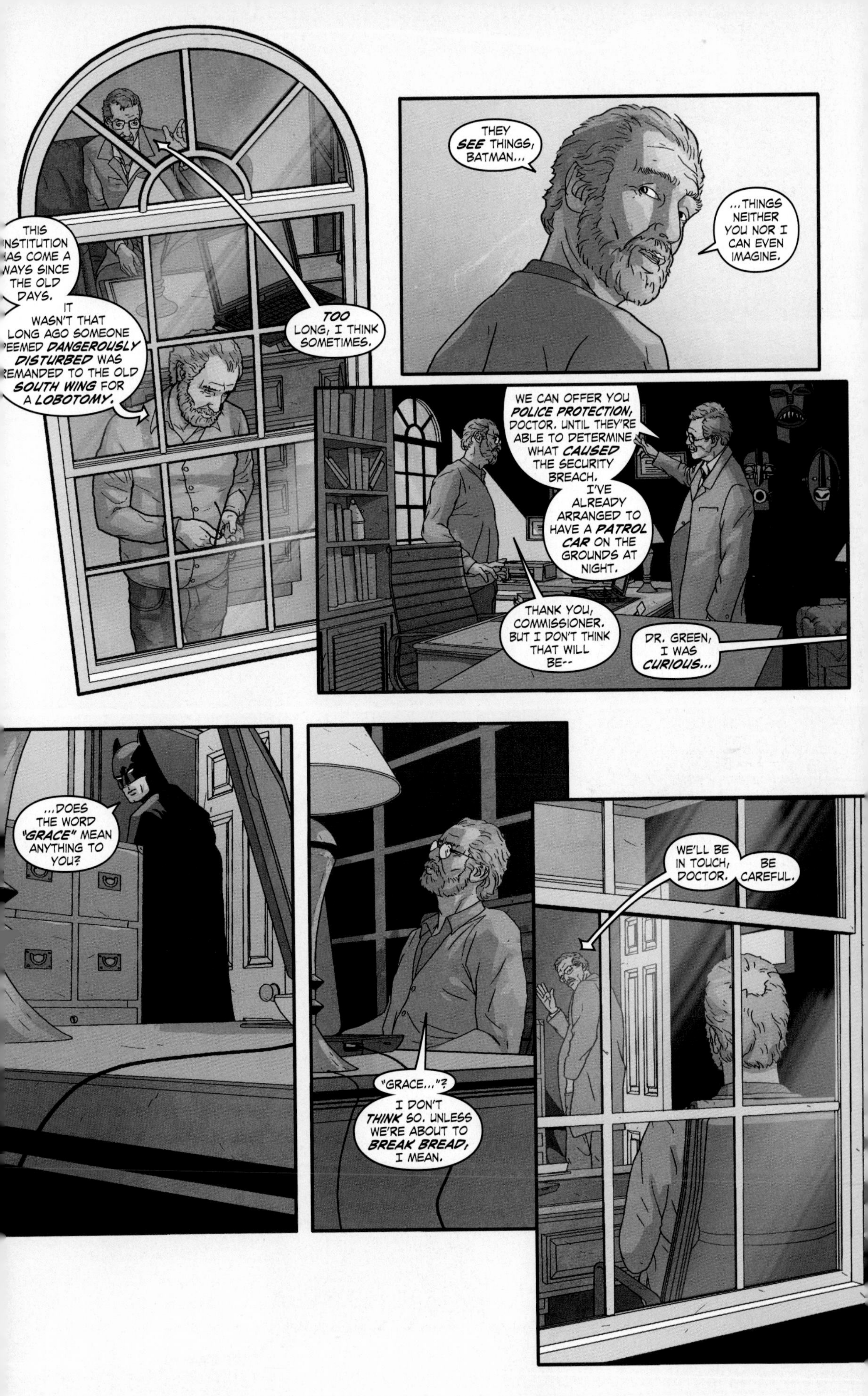
THIS INSTITUTION HAS COME A WAYS SINCE THE OLD DAYS.
IT WASN'T THAT LONG AGO SOMEONE DEEMED DANGEROUSLY DISTURBED WAS REMANDED TO THE OLD SOUTH WING FOR A LOBOTOMY.
TOO LONG, I THINK SOMETIMES.
THEY SEE THINGS, BATMAN...
...THINGS NEITHER YOU NOR I CAN EVEN IMAGINE.
WE CAN OFFER YOU POLICE PROTECTION, DOCTOR. UNTIL THEY'RE ABLE TO DETERMINE WHAT CAUSED THE SECURITY BREACH.
I'VE ALREADY ARRANGED TO HAVE A PATROL CAR ON THE GROUNDS AT NIGHT.
THANK YOU, COMMISSIONER. BUT I DON'T THINK THAT WILL BE--
DR. GREEN, I WAS CURIOUS...
...DOES THE WORD "GRACE" MEAN ANYTHING TO YOU?
"GRACE..."?
I DON'T THINK SO. UNLESS WE'RE ABOUT TO BREAK BREAD, I MEAN.
WE'LL BE IN TOUCH, DOCTOR.
BE CAREFUL.

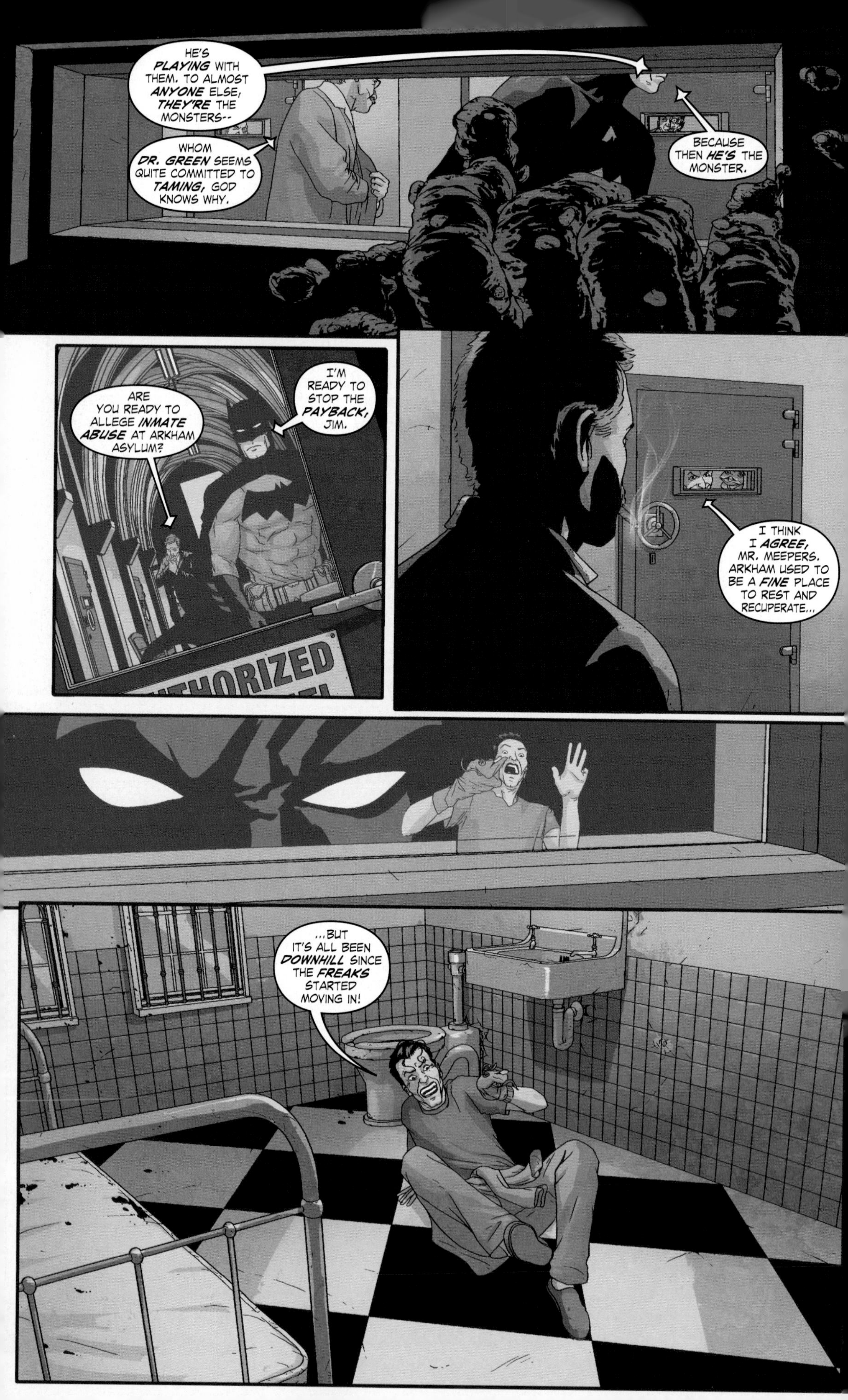
HE'S PLAYING WITH THEM. TO ALMOST ANYONE ELSE, THEY'RE THE MONSTERS--
WHOM DR. GREEN SEEMS QUITE COMMITTED TO TAMING, GOD KNOWS WHY.
BECAUSE THEN HE'S THE MONSTER.
ARE YOU READY TO ALLEGE INMATE ABUSE AT ARKHAM ASYLUM?
I'M READY TO STOP THE PAYBACK, JIM.
I THINK I AGREE, MR. MEEPERS. ARKHAM USED TO BE A FINE PLACE TO REST AND RECUPERATE...
...BUT IT'S ALL BEEN DOWNHILL SINCE THE FREAKS STARTED MOVING IN!

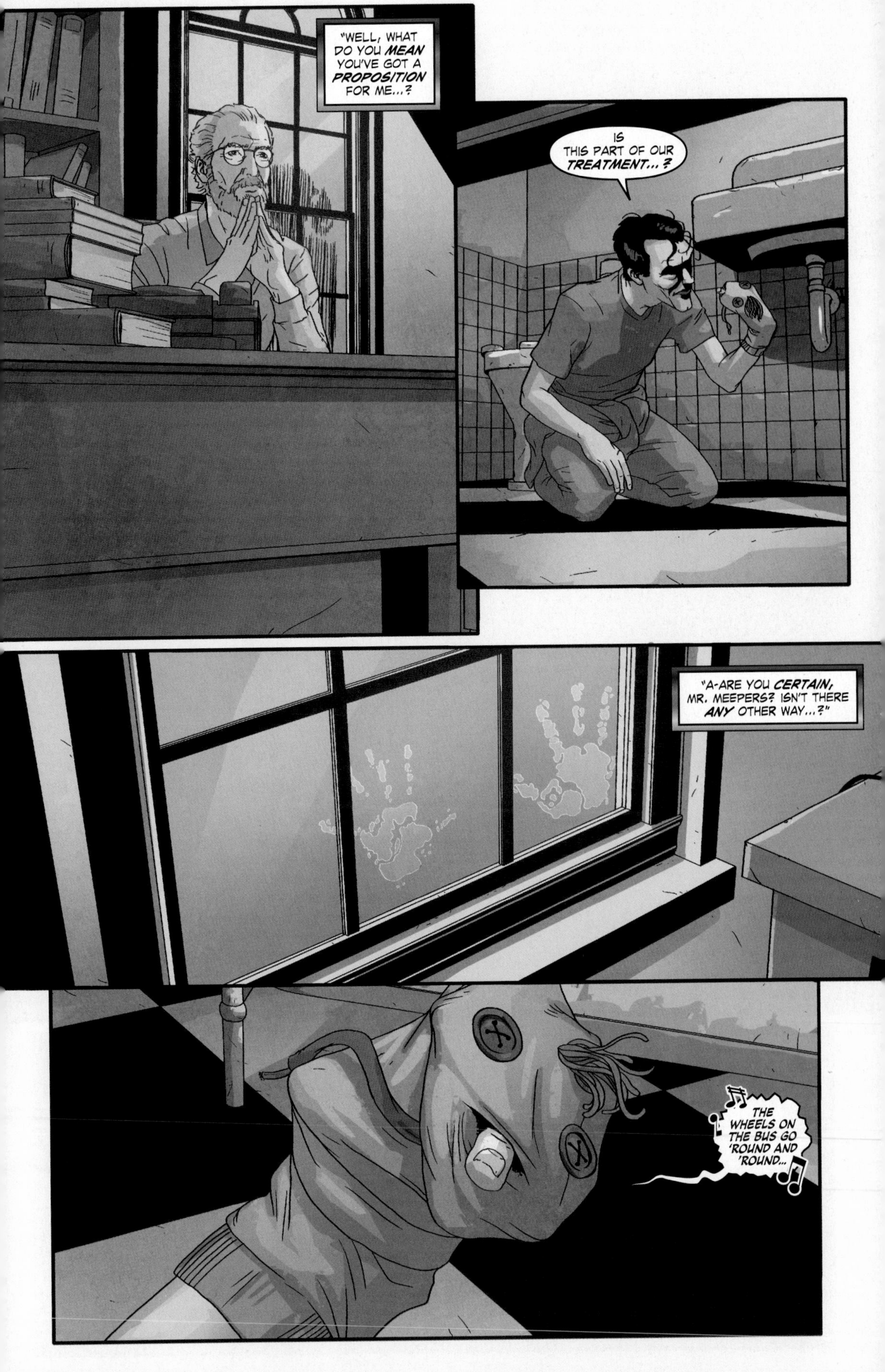
"WELL, WHAT DO YOU MEAN YOU'VE GOT A PROPOSITION FOR ME...?
IS THIS PART OF OUR TREATMENT...?
"A-ARE YOU CERTAIN, MR. MEEPERS? ISN'T THERE ANY OTHER WAY...?"
THE WHEELS ON THE BUS GO 'ROUND AND 'ROUND...

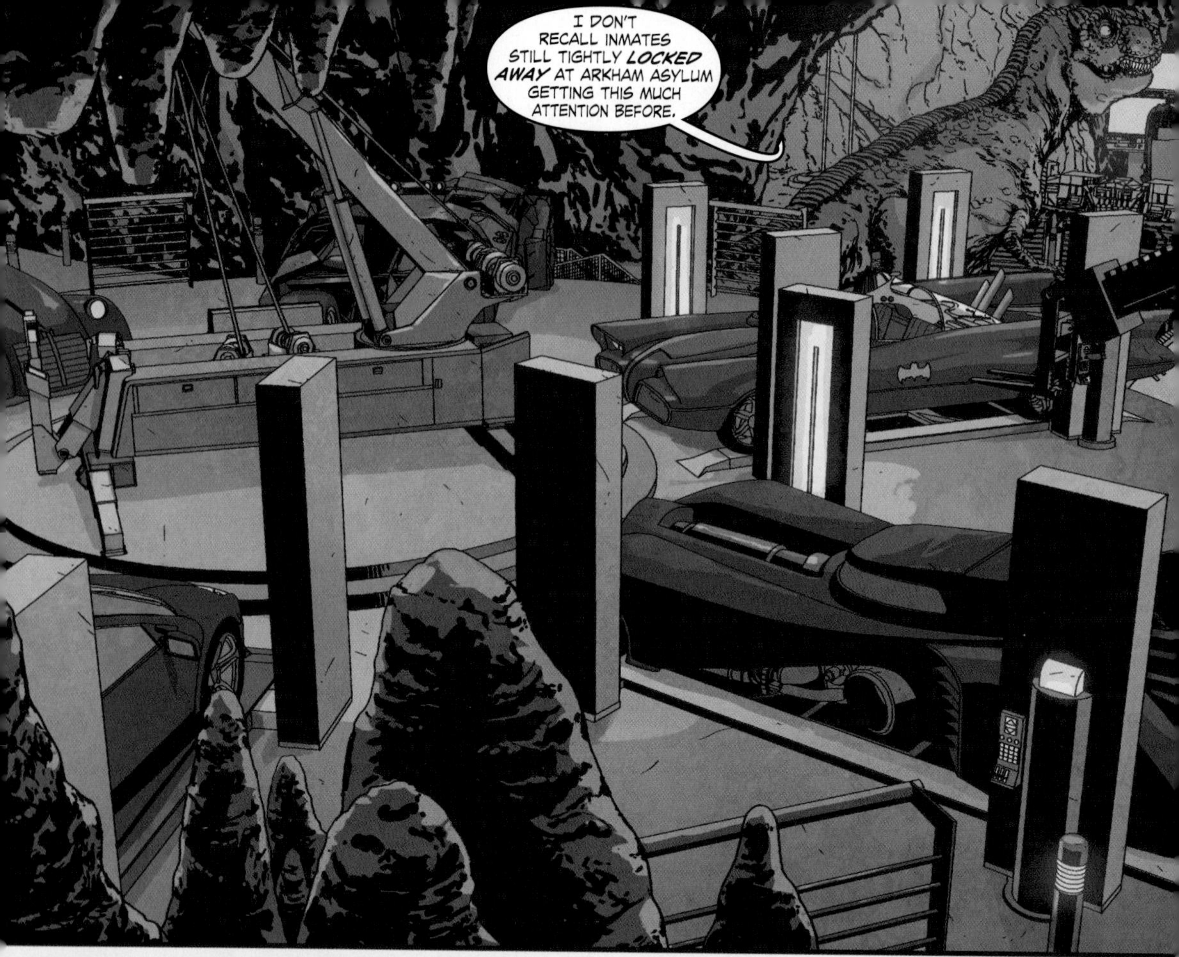
I DON'T RECALL INMATES STILL TIGHTLY LOCKED AWAY AT ARKHAM ASYLUM GETTING THIS MUCH ATTENTION BEFORE.

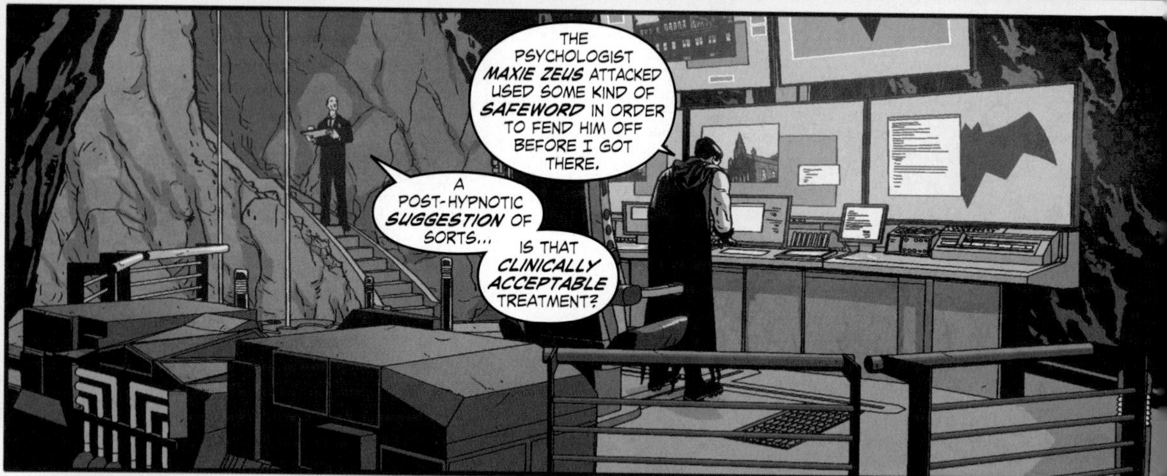
THE PSYCHOLOGIST MAXIE ZEUS ATTACKED USED SOME KIND OF SAFEWORD IN ORDER TO FEND HIM OFF BEFORE I GOT THERE.
A POST-HYPNOTIC SUGGESTION OF SORTS...
IS THAT CLINICALLY ACCEPTABLE TREATMENT?

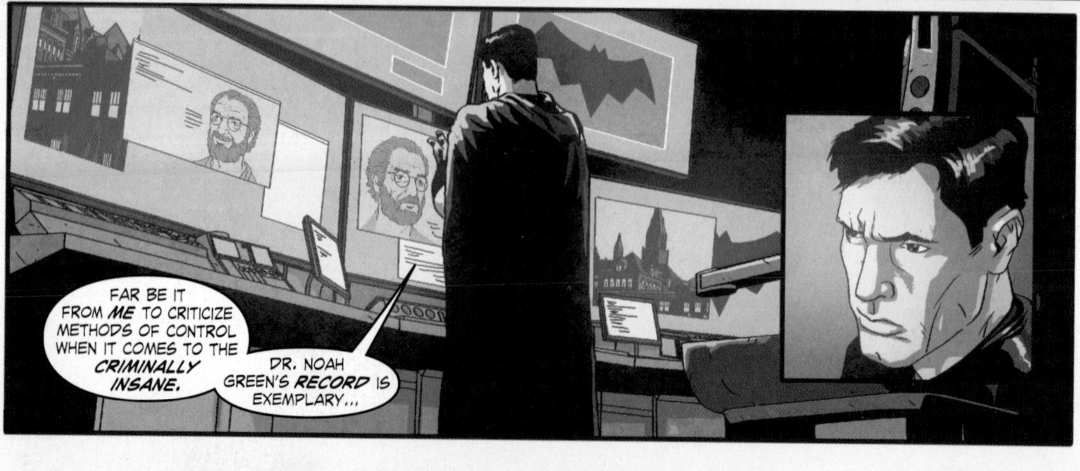
DR. NOAH GREEN'S RECORD IS EXEMPLARY...
FAR BE IT FROM ME TO CRITICIZE METHODS OF CONTROL WHEN IT COMES TO THE CRIMINALLY INSANE.

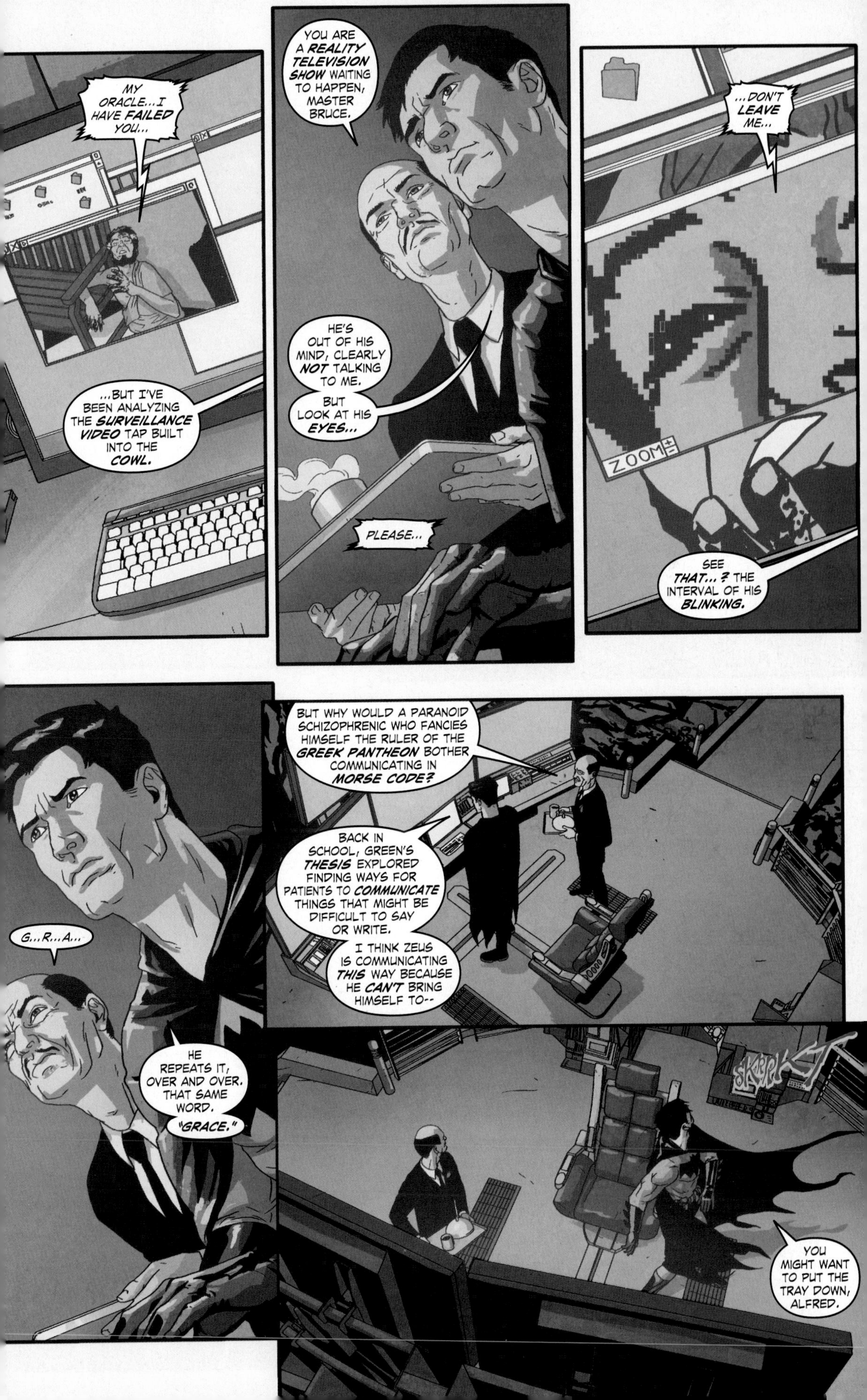
MY ORACLE... I HAVE FAILED YOU...
...BUT I'VE BEEN ANALYZING THE SURVEILLANCE VIDEO TAP BUILT INTO THE COWL.
YOU ARE A REALITY TELEVISION SHOW WAITING TO HAPPEN, MASTER BRUCE.
HE'S OUT OF HIS MIND, CLEARLY NOT TALKING TO ME.
BUT LOOK AT HIS EYES...
PLEASE...
...DON'T LEAVE ME...
ZOOM + −
SEE THAT...? THE INTERVAL OF HIS BLINKING.
G...R...A...
HE REPEATS IT, OVER AND OVER. THAT SAME WORD. "GRACE."
BUT WHY WOULD A PARANOID SCHIZOPHRENIC WHO FANCIES HIMSELF THE RULER OF THE GREEK PANTHEON BOTHER COMMUNICATING IN MORSE CODE?
BACK IN SCHOOL, GREEN'S THESIS EXPLORED FINDING WAYS FOR PATIENTS TO COMMUNICATE THINGS THAT MIGHT BE DIFFICULT TO SAY OR WRITE.
I THINK ZEUS IS COMMUNICATING THIS WAY BECAUSE HE CAN'T BRING HIMSELF TO--
YOU MIGHT WANT TO PUT THE TRAY DOWN, ALFRED.

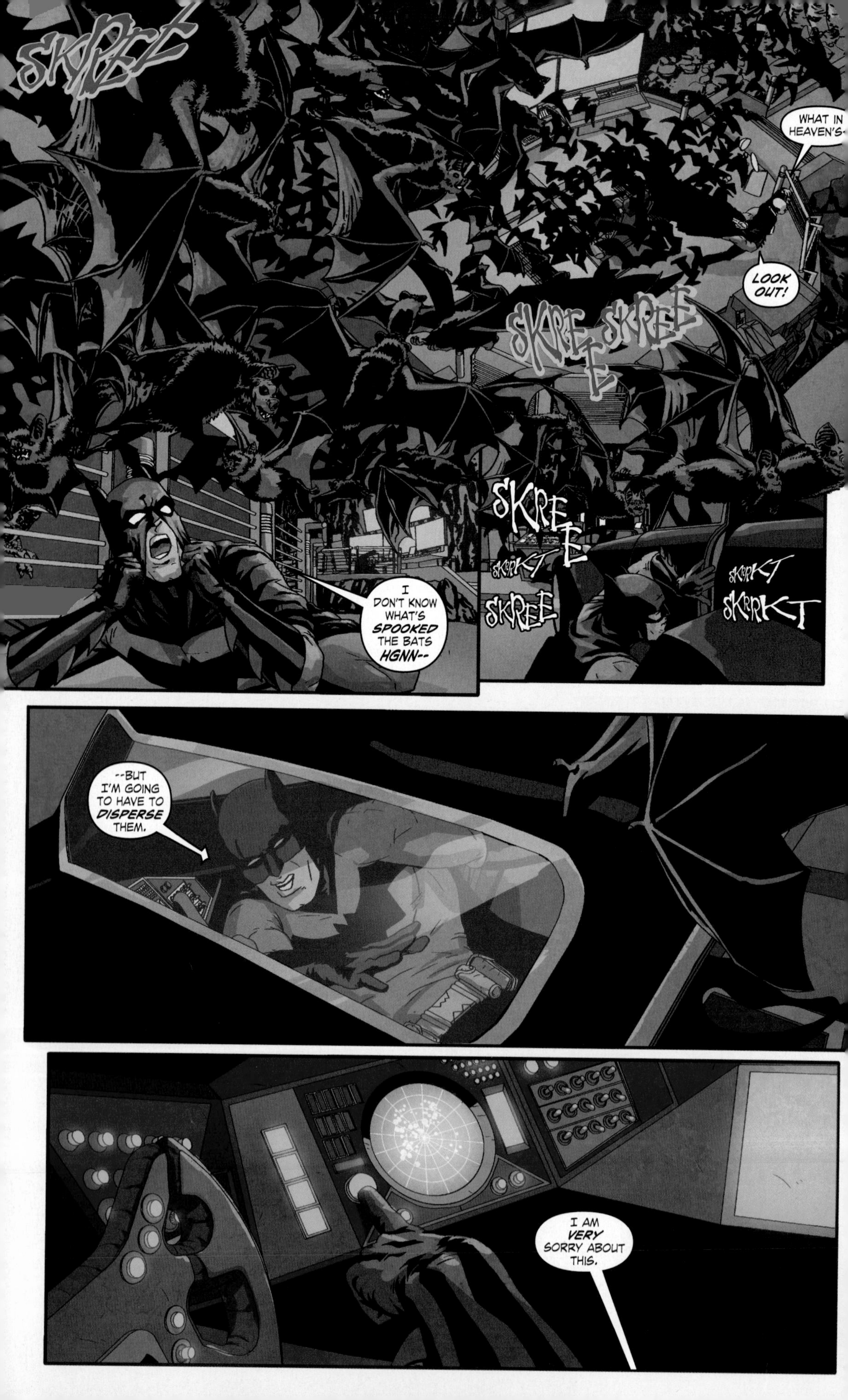
SKREE
WHAT IN HEAVEN'S--
LOOK OUT!
SKREE SKREE
I DON'T KNOW WHAT'S SPOOKED THE BATS HGNN--
SKREE
SKRRKT
SKREE
SKRRKT
SKRRKT
--BUT I'M GOING TO HAVE TO DISPERSE THEM.
I AM VERY SORRY ABOUT THIS.

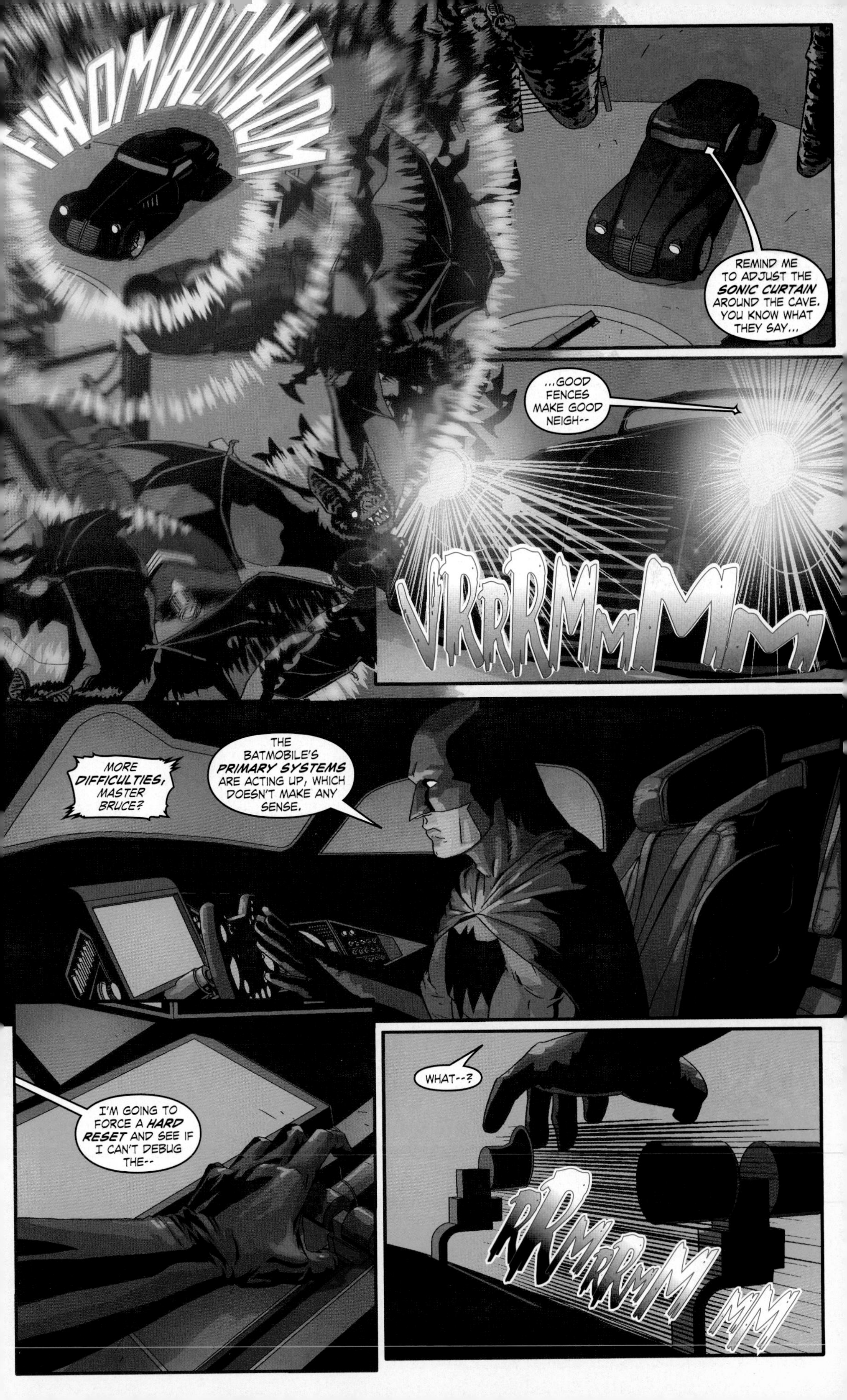
FWOMHUMHUM
REMIND ME TO ADJUST THE SONIC CURTAIN AROUND THE CAVE. YOU KNOW WHAT THEY SAY...
...GOOD FENCES MAKE GOOD NEIGH--
VRRRMMMMM
MORE DIFFICULTIES, MASTER BRUCE?
THE BATMOBILE'S PRIMARY SYSTEMS ARE ACTING UP, WHICH DOESN'T MAKE ANY SENSE.
I'M GOING TO FORCE A HARD RESET AND SEE IF I CAN'T DEBUG THE--
WHAT--?
RRRMRRMMMM

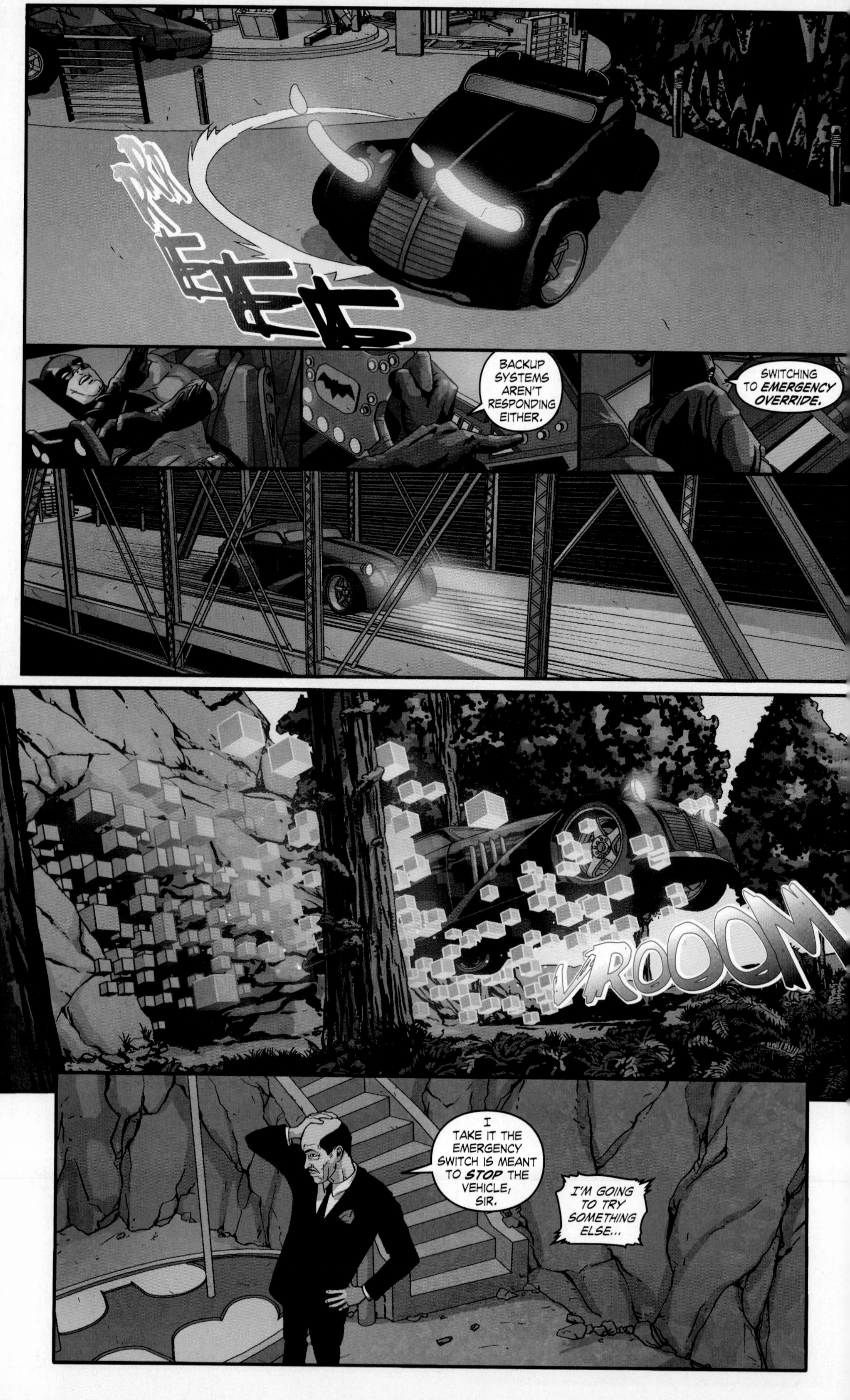
BACKUP SYSTEMS AREN'T RESPONDING EITHER.
SWITCHING TO *EMERGENCY OVERRIDE.*
VROOOM
I TAKE IT THE EMERGENCY SWITCH IS MEANT TO **STOP** THE VEHICLE, SIR.
I'M GOING TO TRY SOMETHING ELSE...

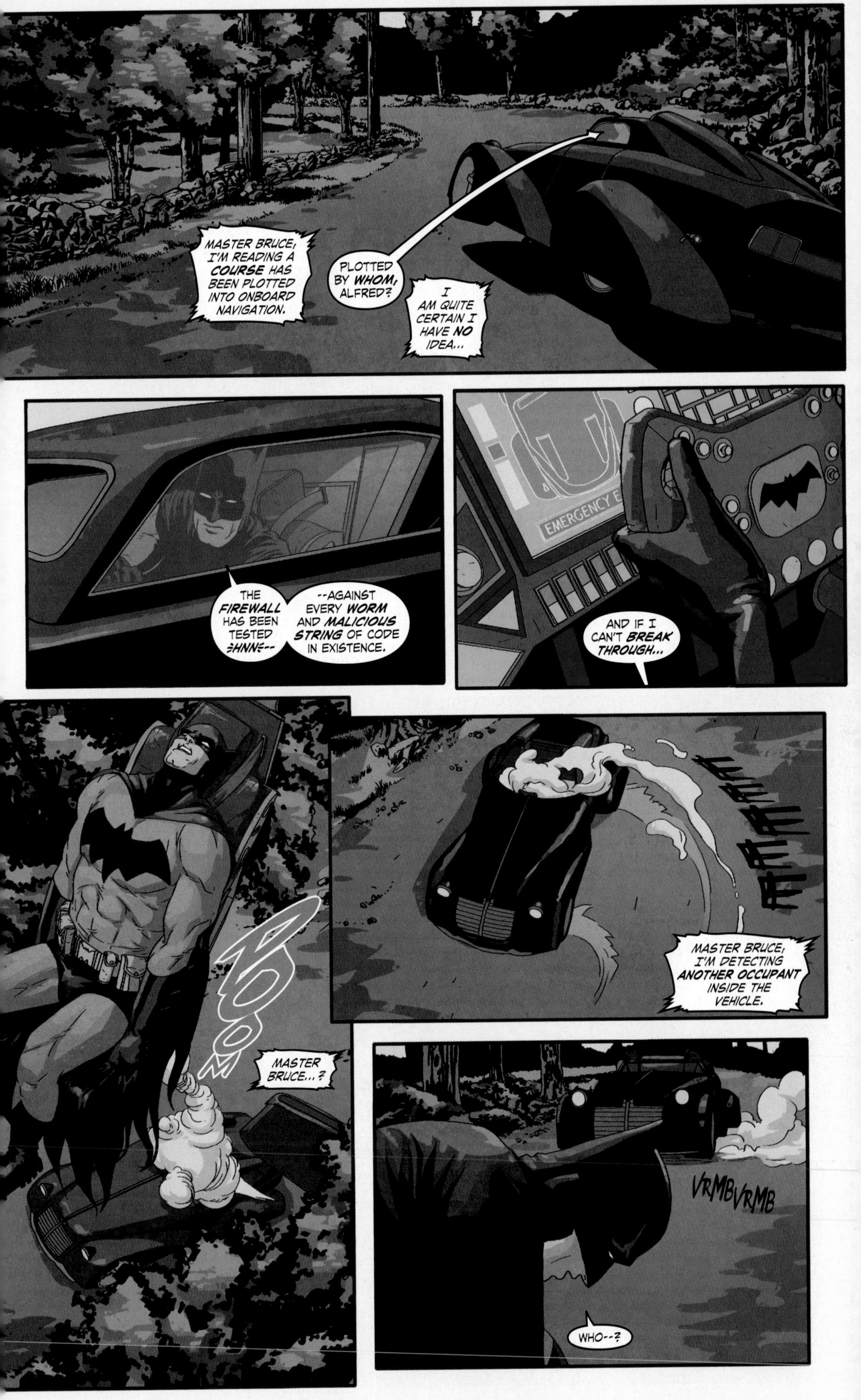
MASTER BRUCE, I'M READING A COURSE HAS BEEN PLOTTED INTO ONBOARD NAVIGATION.
PLOTTED BY WHOM, ALFRED?
I AM QUITE CERTAIN I HAVE NO IDEA...
THE FIREWALL HAS BEEN TESTED ≈HNN≈--
--AGAINST EVERY WORM AND MALICIOUS STRING OF CODE IN EXISTENCE.
EMERGENCY E
AND IF I CAN'T BREAK THROUGH...
MASTER BRUCE, I'M DETECTING ANOTHER OCCUPANT INSIDE THE VEHICLE.
MASTER BRUCE...?
VRMBVRMB
WHO--?

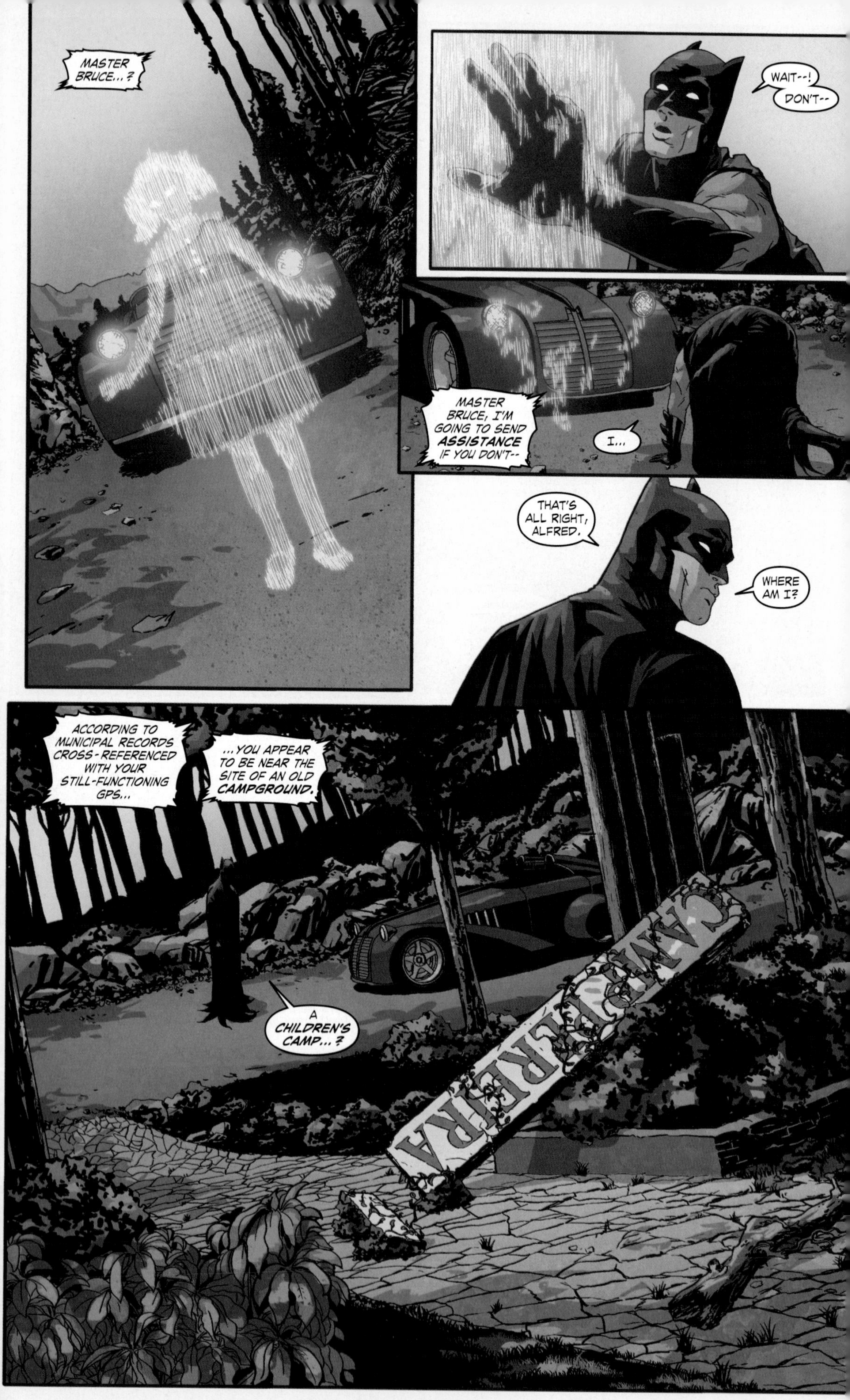
MASTER BRUCE...?
WAIT--!
DON'T--
MASTER BRUCE, I'M GOING TO SEND ASSISTANCE IF YOU DON'T--
I...
THAT'S ALL RIGHT, ALFRED.
WHERE AM I?
ACCORDING TO MUNICIPAL RECORDS CROSS-REFERENCED WITH YOUR STILL-FUNCTIONING GPS...
...YOU APPEAR TO BE NEAR THE SITE OF AN OLD CAMPGROUND.
A CHILDREN'S CAMP...?

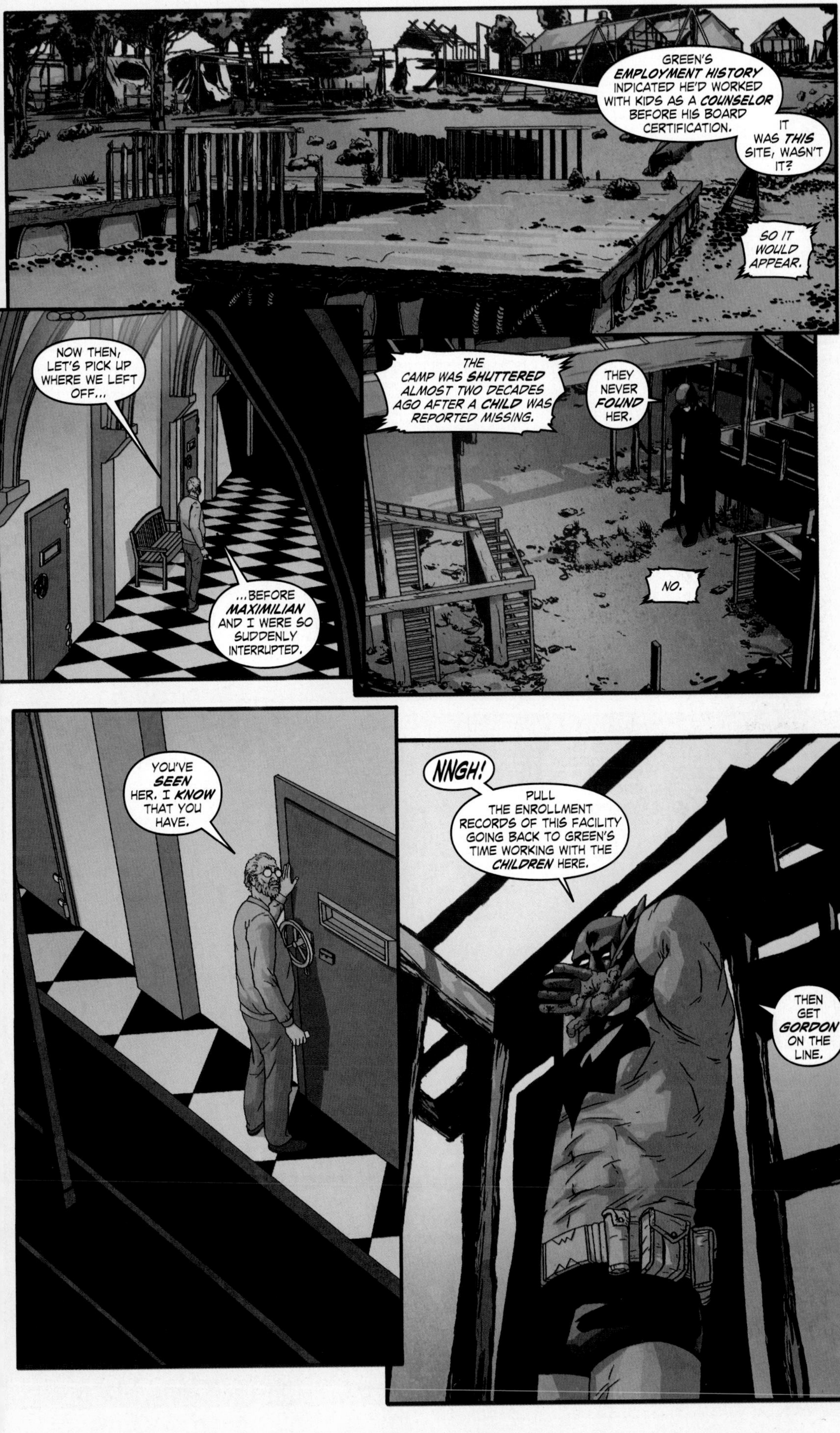
GREEN'S EMPLOYMENT HISTORY INDICATED HE'D WORKED WITH KIDS AS A COUNSELOR BEFORE HIS BOARD CERTIFICATION.
IT WAS THIS SITE, WASN'T IT?
SO IT WOULD APPEAR.
NOW THEN, LET'S PICK UP WHERE WE LEFT OFF...
...BEFORE MAXIMILIAN AND I WERE SO SUDDENLY INTERRUPTED.
THE CAMP WAS SHUTTERED ALMOST TWO DECADES AGO AFTER A CHILD WAS REPORTED MISSING.
THEY NEVER FOUND HER.
NO.
YOU'VE SEEN HER. I KNOW THAT YOU HAVE.
NNGH!
PULL THE ENROLLMENT RECORDS OF THIS FACILITY GOING BACK TO GREEN'S TIME WORKING WITH THE CHILDREN HERE.
THEN GET GORDON ON THE LINE.

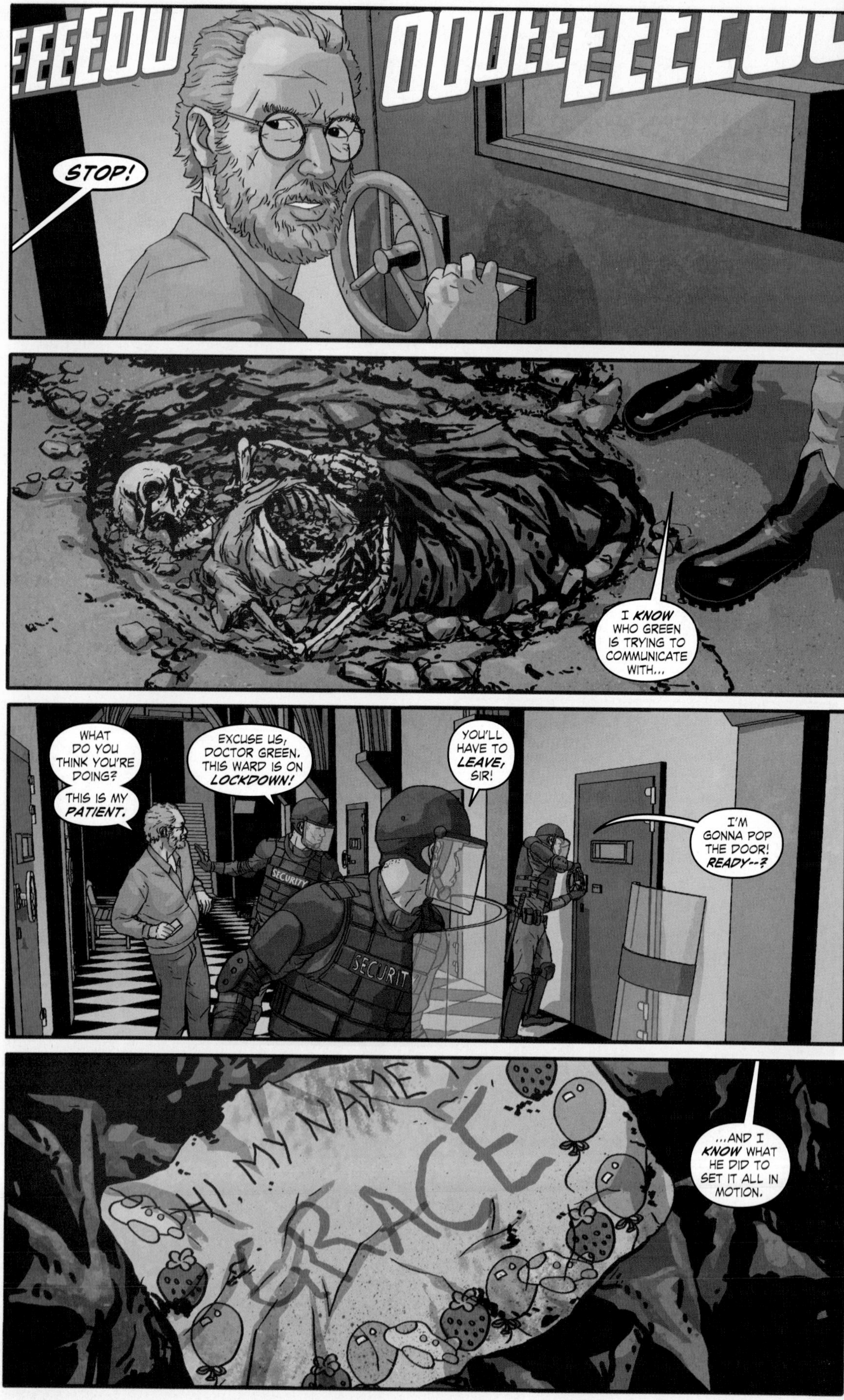

EEEEOU
OOOEEEEEOO
STOP!
I KNOW WHO GREEN IS TRYING TO COMMUNICATE WITH...
WHAT DO YOU THINK YOU'RE DOING?
THIS IS MY PATIENT.
EXCUSE US, DOCTOR GREEN. THIS WARD IS ON LOCKDOWN!
YOU'LL HAVE TO LEAVE, SIR!
I'M GONNA POP THE DOOR! READY--?
SECURITY
SECURITY
HI! MY NAME IS GRACE
...AND I KNOW WHAT HE DID TO SET IT ALL IN MOTION.

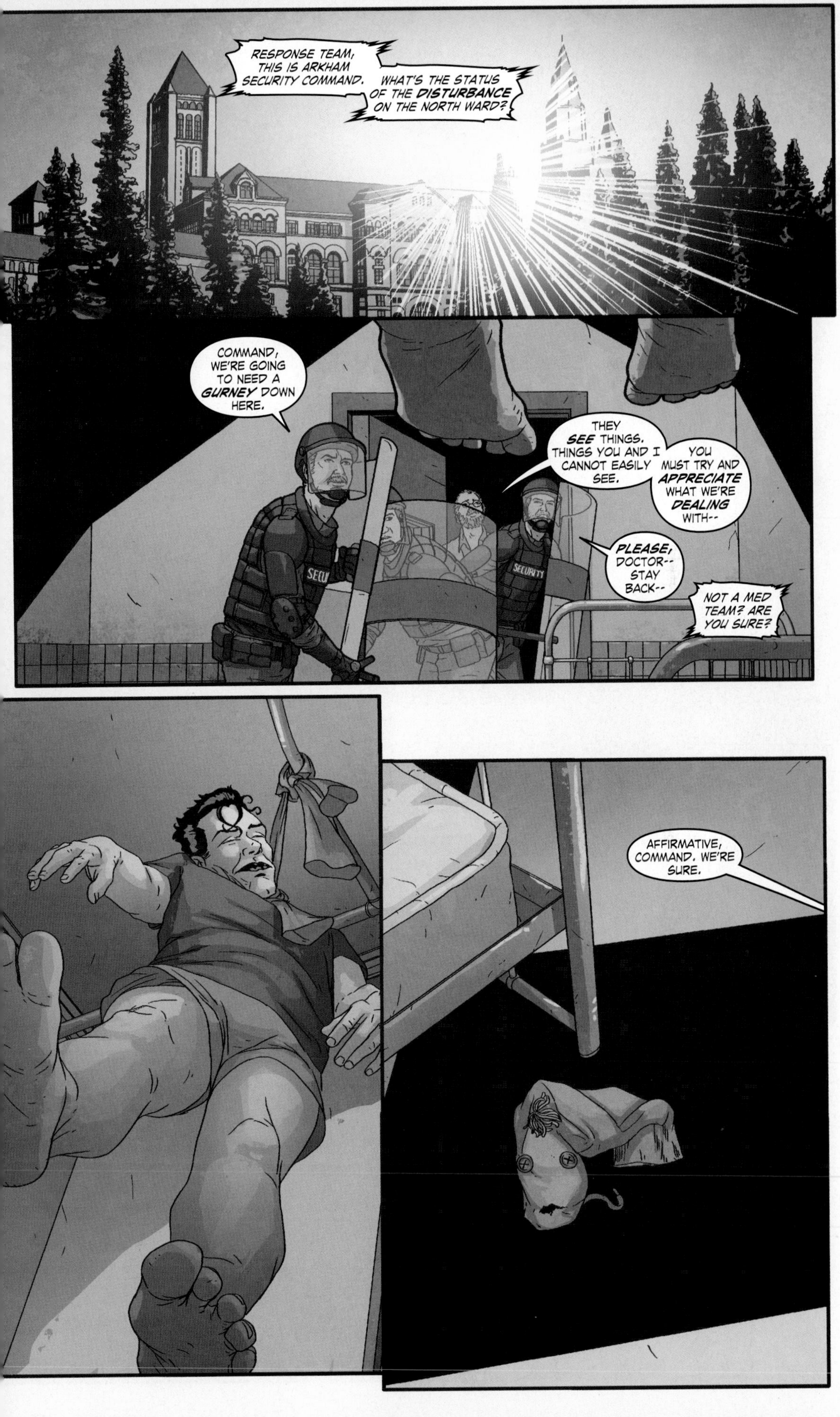
RESPONSE TEAM, THIS IS ARKHAM SECURITY COMMAND.
WHAT'S THE STATUS OF THE DISTURBANCE ON THE NORTH WARD?
COMMAND, WE'RE GOING TO NEED A GURNEY DOWN HERE.
THEY SEE THINGS. THINGS YOU AND I CANNOT EASILY SEE.
YOU MUST TRY AND APPRECIATE WHAT WE'RE DEALING WITH--
PLEASE, DOCTOR-- STAY BACK--
NOT A MED TEAM? ARE YOU SURE?
AFFIRMATIVE, COMMAND. WE'RE SURE.

YOU BELIEVE HE *DID* IT?

YEAH, BUT...HE WAS, LIKE, THE *NUMBER ONE* AROUND HERE.

Arkham Asylum
Case# 9987-18
Cell #32
Name JOKER

WHAT DO YOU MEAN, DO I *BELIEVE* IT? I'M *PUSHING* HIM ALONG, AIN'T I?

NUMBER ONE *PSYCHOPATH,* YOU MEAN.

I GOT A CALL LATE LAST NIGHT FROM THE *CORONER'S* OFFICE...

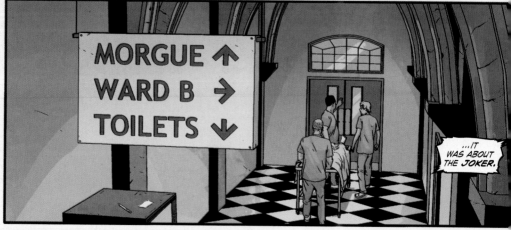

MORGUE ↑
WARD B →
TOILETS ↓

...IT WAS ABOUT THE *JOKER.*

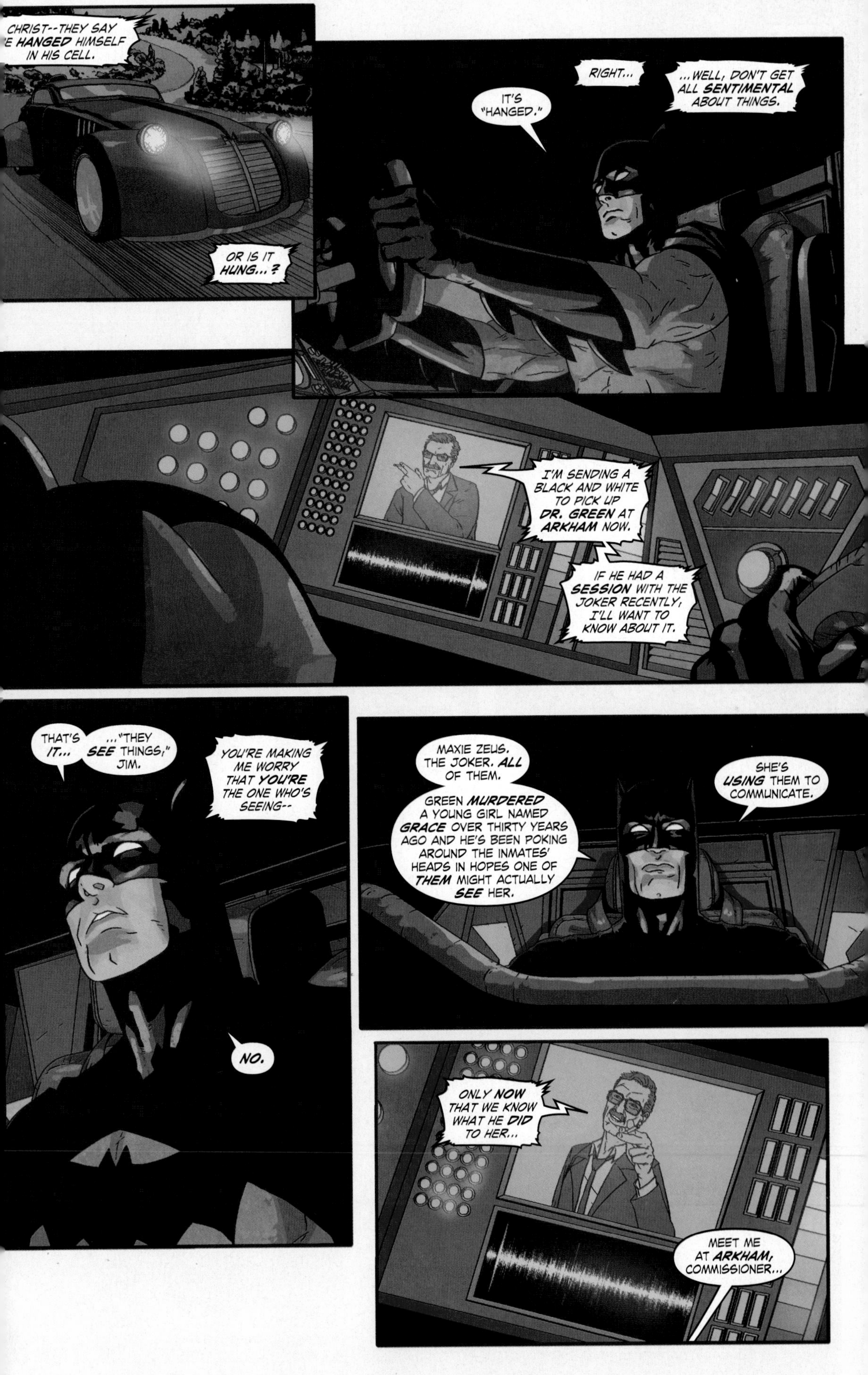

CHRIST--THEY SAY
E HANGED HIMSELF
IN HIS CELL.
OR IS IT
HUNG...?
IT'S "HANGED."
RIGHT...
...WELL, DON'T GET ALL SENTIMENTAL ABOUT THINGS.
I'M SENDING A BLACK AND WHITE TO PICK UP DR. GREEN AT ARKHAM NOW.
IF HE HAD A SESSION WITH THE JOKER RECENTLY, I'LL WANT TO KNOW ABOUT IT.
THAT'S IT...
..."THEY SEE THINGS," JIM.
YOU'RE MAKING ME WORRY THAT YOU'RE THE ONE WHO'S SEEING--
NO.
MAXIE ZEUS. THE JOKER. ALL OF THEM.
GREEN MURDERED A YOUNG GIRL NAMED GRACE OVER THIRTY YEARS AGO AND HE'S BEEN POKING AROUND THE INMATES' HEADS IN HOPES ONE OF THEM MIGHT ACTUALLY SEE HER.
SHE'S USING THEM TO COMMUNICATE.
ONLY NOW THAT WE KNOW WHAT HE DID TO HER...
MEET ME AT ARKHAM, COMMISSIONER...

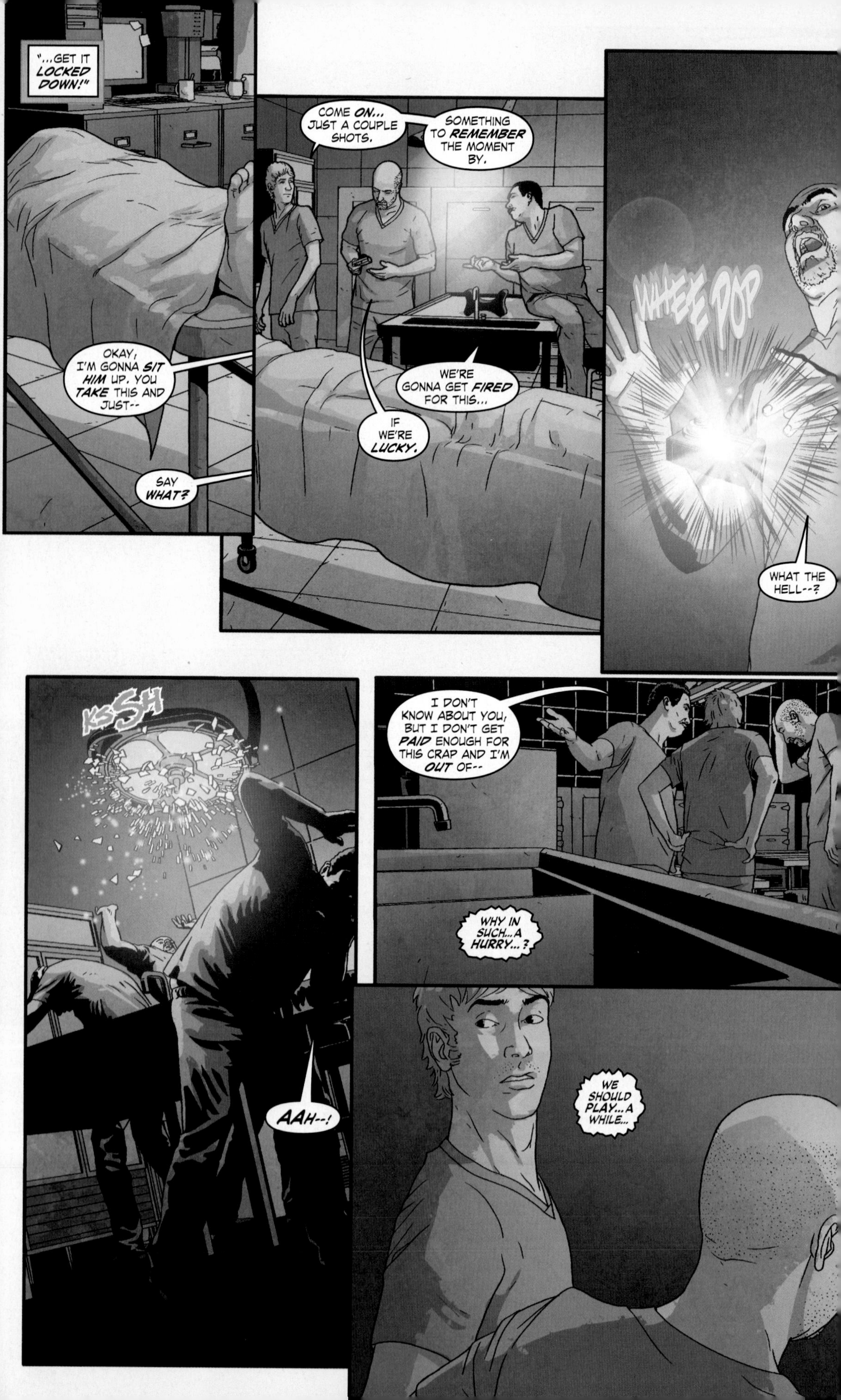
"...GET IT LOCKED DOWN!"
OKAY, I'M GONNA SIT HIM UP. YOU TAKE THIS AND JUST--
SAY WHAT?
COME ON... JUST A COUPLE SHOTS.
SOMETHING TO REMEMBER THE MOMENT BY.
WE'RE GONNA GET FIRED FOR THIS...
IF WE'RE LUCKY.
WHEEE POP
WHAT THE HELL--?
KSSH
AAH--!
I DON'T KNOW ABOUT YOU, BUT I DON'T GET PAID ENOUGH FOR THIS CRAP AND I'M OUT OF--
WHY IN SUCH... A HURRY...?
WE SHOULD PLAY... A WHILE...

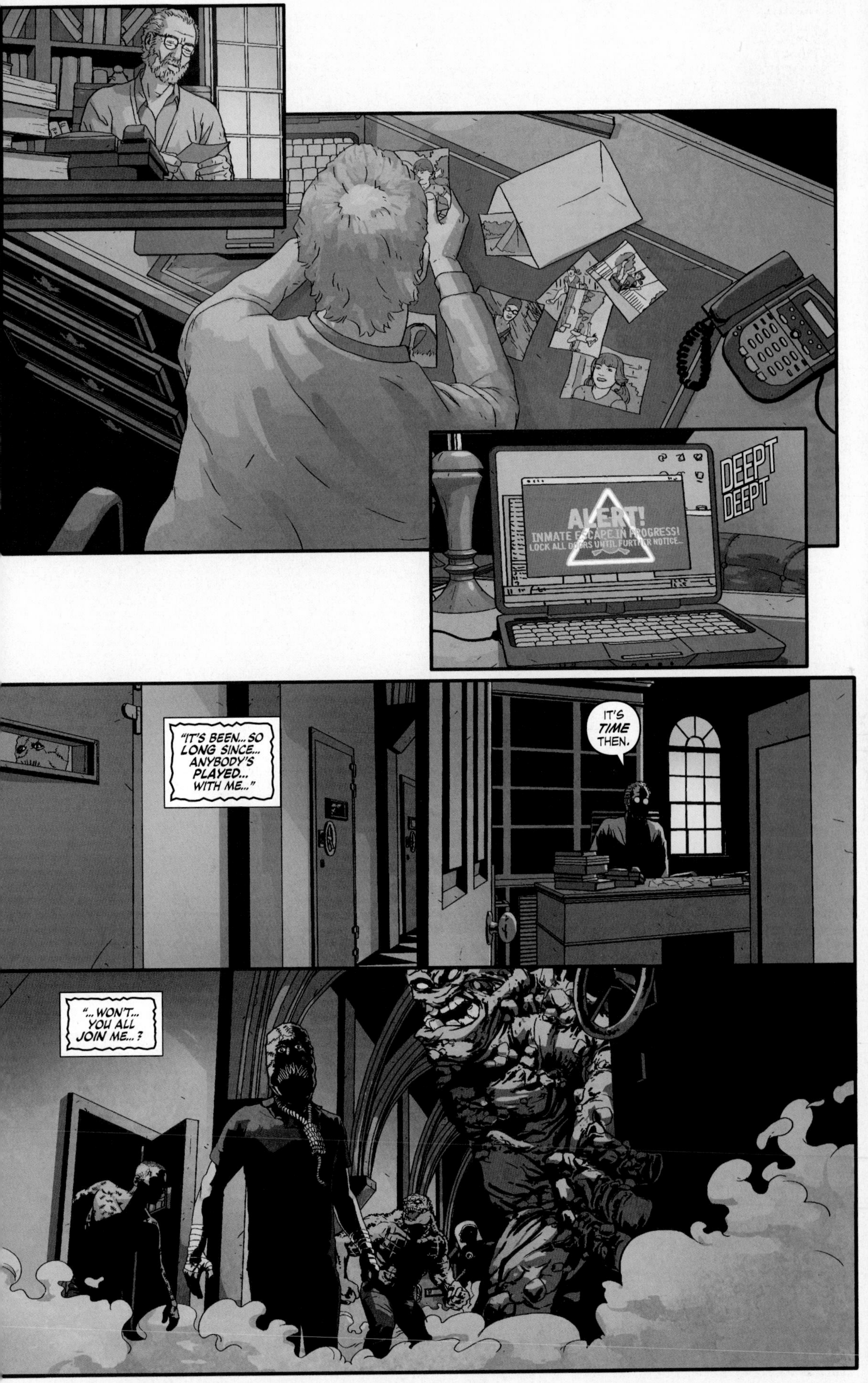
DEEPT
DEEPT
ALERT!
INMATE ESCAPE IN PROGRESS!
LOCK ALL DOORS UNTIL FURTHER NOTICE...
"IT'S BEEN... SO LONG SINCE... ANYBODY'S PLAYED... WITH ME..."
IT'S TIME THEN.
"...WON'T... YOU ALL JOIN ME...?

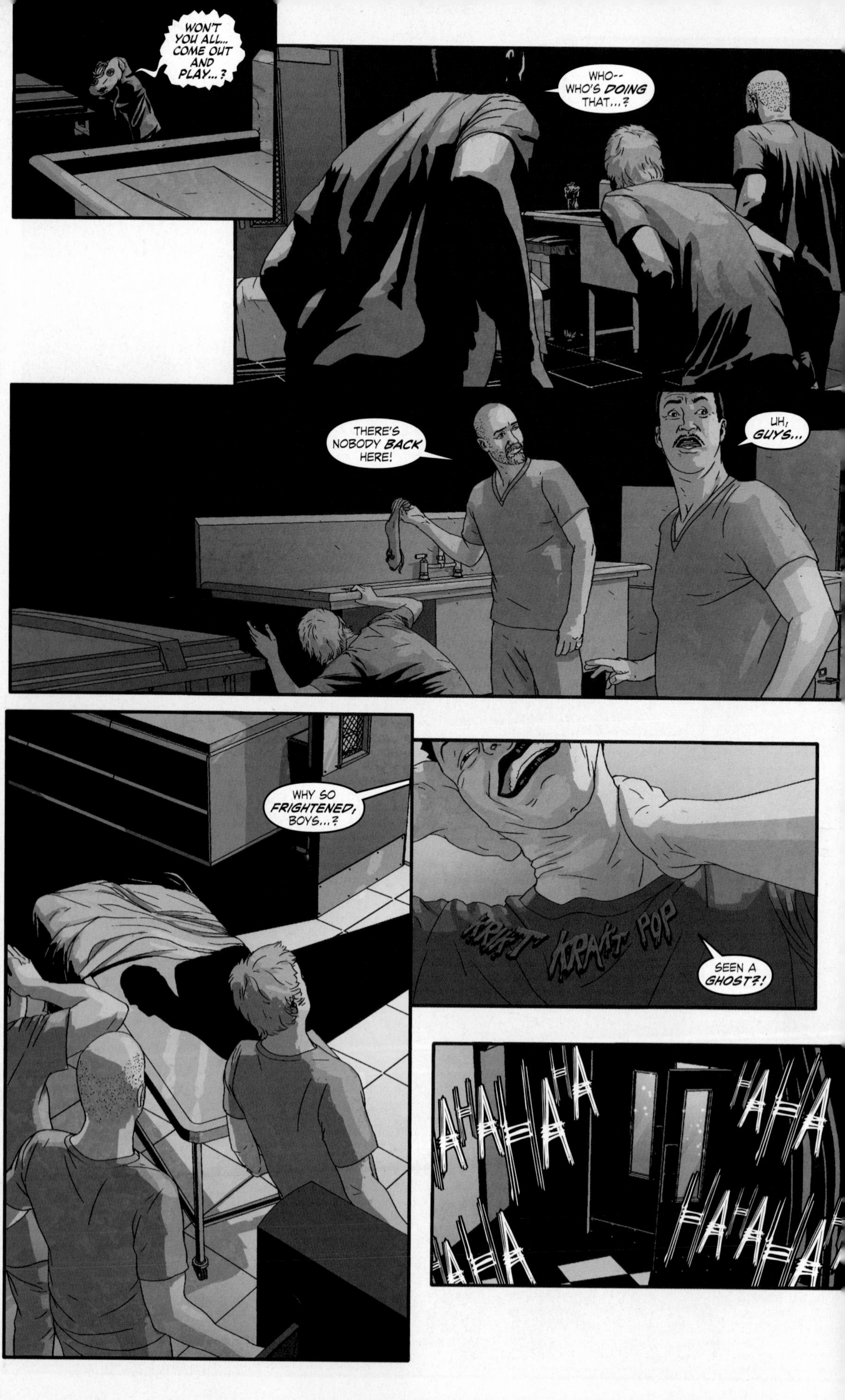
WON'T YOU ALL... COME OUT AND PLAY...?
WHO-- WHO'S DOING THAT...?
THERE'S NOBODY BACK HERE!
UH, GUYS...
WHY SO FRIGHTENED, BOYS...?
KRIKT KRAKT POP
SEEN A GHOST?!
HAHAHAHA
HAHA
HAHAHAHAHA
HAHAHA

MY MEN COULDN'T GET *THROUGH* THE MAIN CORRIDOR. THE LINE TO *GREEN'S* OFFICE IS DEAD, BUT AN *ORDERLY* SAID THE GOOD DOCTOR WAS LOOKING FOR ANOTHER EXIT TO THE *SOUTH.*

THE SOUTH *WING?*

I DON'T KNOW. CAN YOU *GET* THERE?

THAT'S THE *THING,* COMMISSIONER...

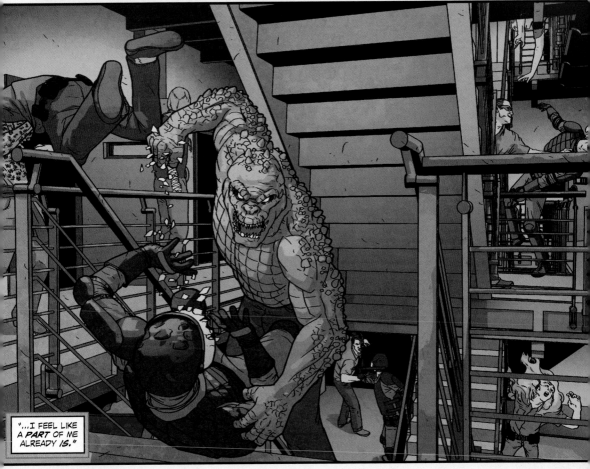

"...I FEEL LIKE A *PART* OF ME ALREADY *IS.*"

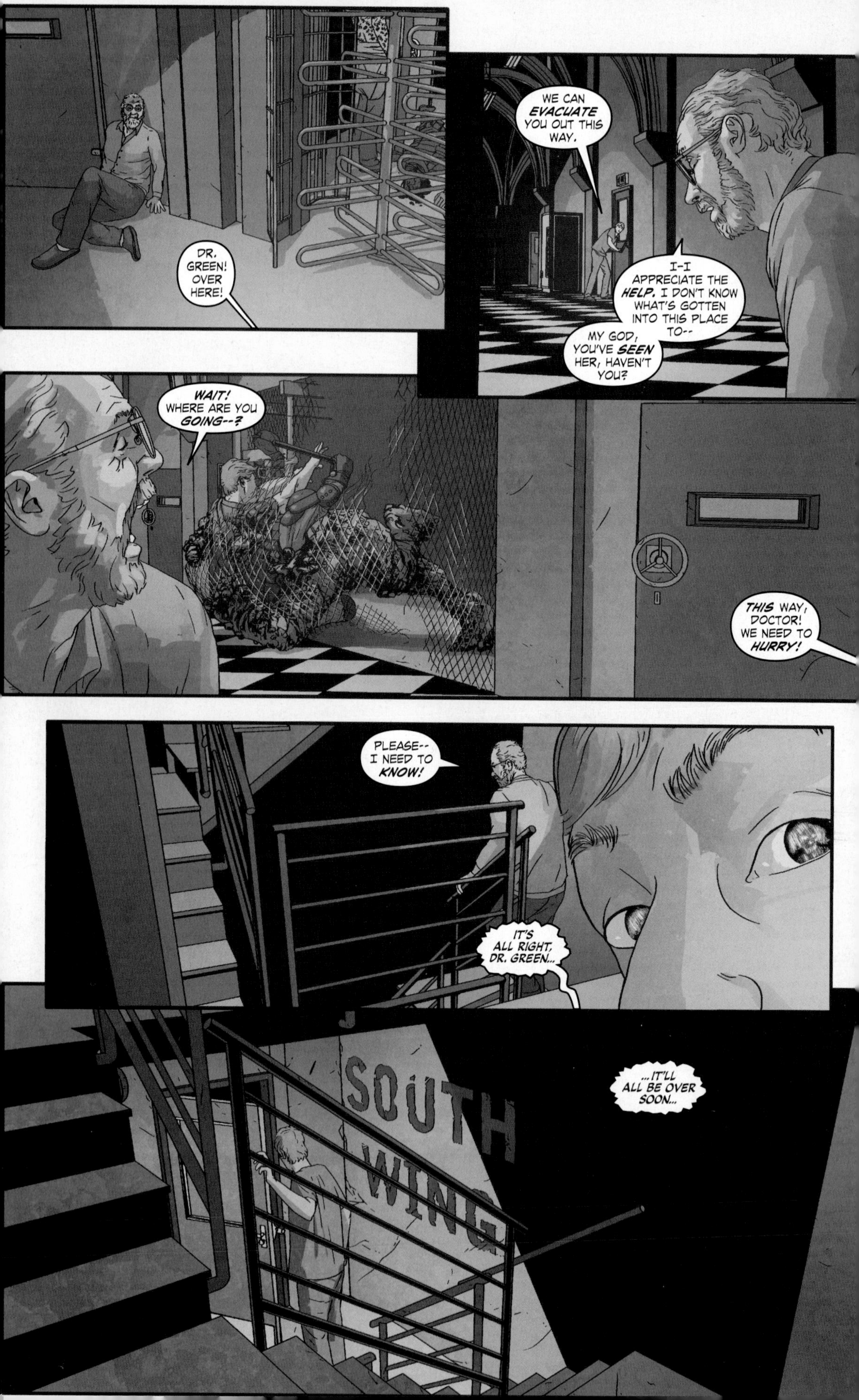
DR. GREEN! OVER HERE!
WE CAN EVACUATE YOU OUT THIS WAY.
I-I APPRECIATE THE HELP. I DON'T KNOW WHAT'S GOTTEN INTO THIS PLACE TO--
MY GOD, YOU'VE SEEN HER, HAVEN'T YOU?
WAIT! WHERE ARE YOU GOING--?
THIS WAY, DOCTOR! WE NEED TO HURRY!
PLEASE-- I NEED TO KNOW!
IT'S ALL RIGHT, DR. GREEN...
...IT'LL ALL BE OVER SOON...
SOUTH WING

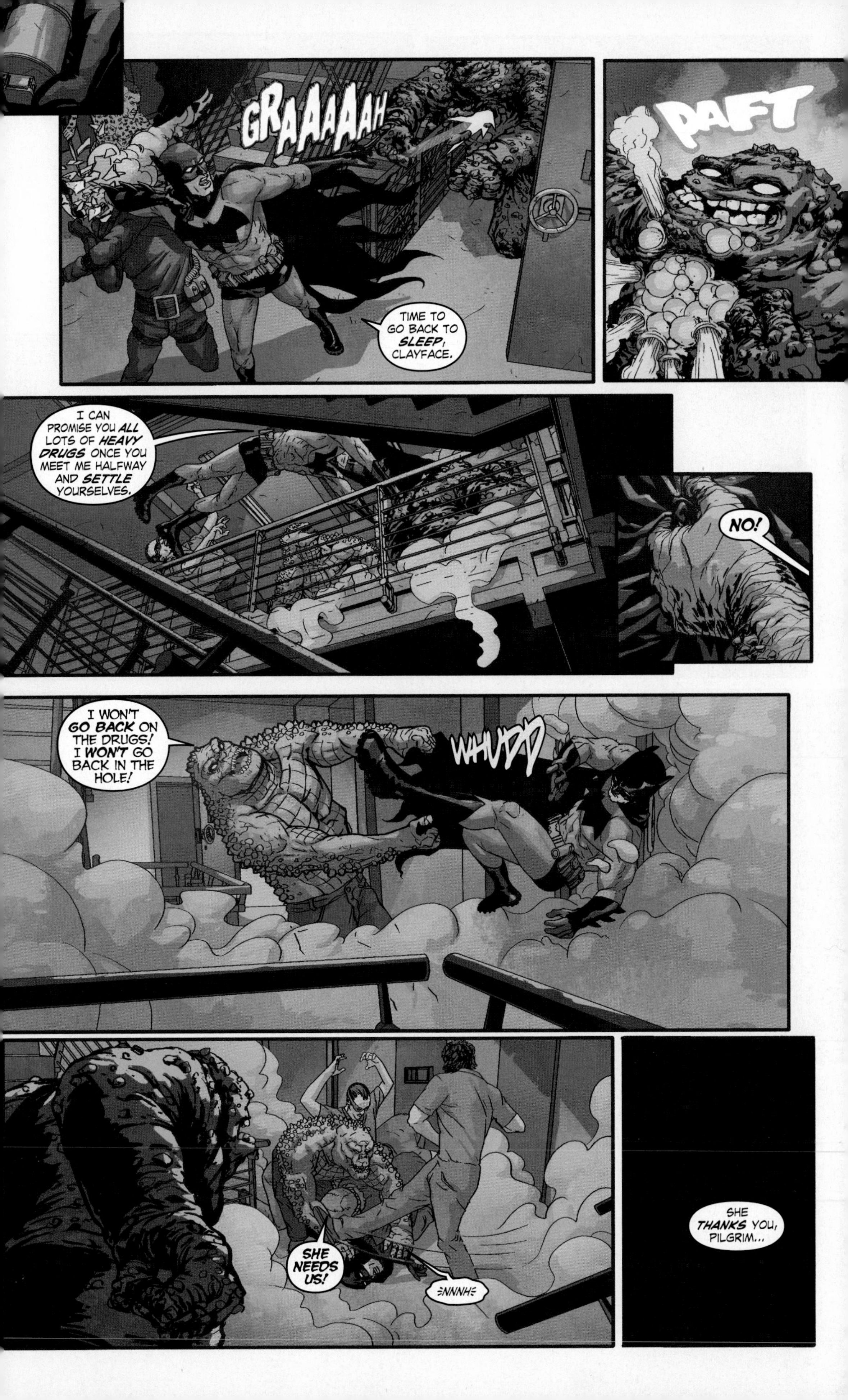
GRAAAAAH
TIME TO GO BACK TO SLEEP, CLAYFACE.
PAFT
I CAN PROMISE YOU ALL LOTS OF HEAVY DRUGS ONCE YOU MEET ME HALFWAY AND SETTLE YOURSELVES.
NO!
I WON'T GO BACK ON THE DRUGS! I WON'T GO BACK IN THE HOLE!
WHUDD
SHE NEEDS US!
NNNH
SHE THANKS YOU, PILGRIM...

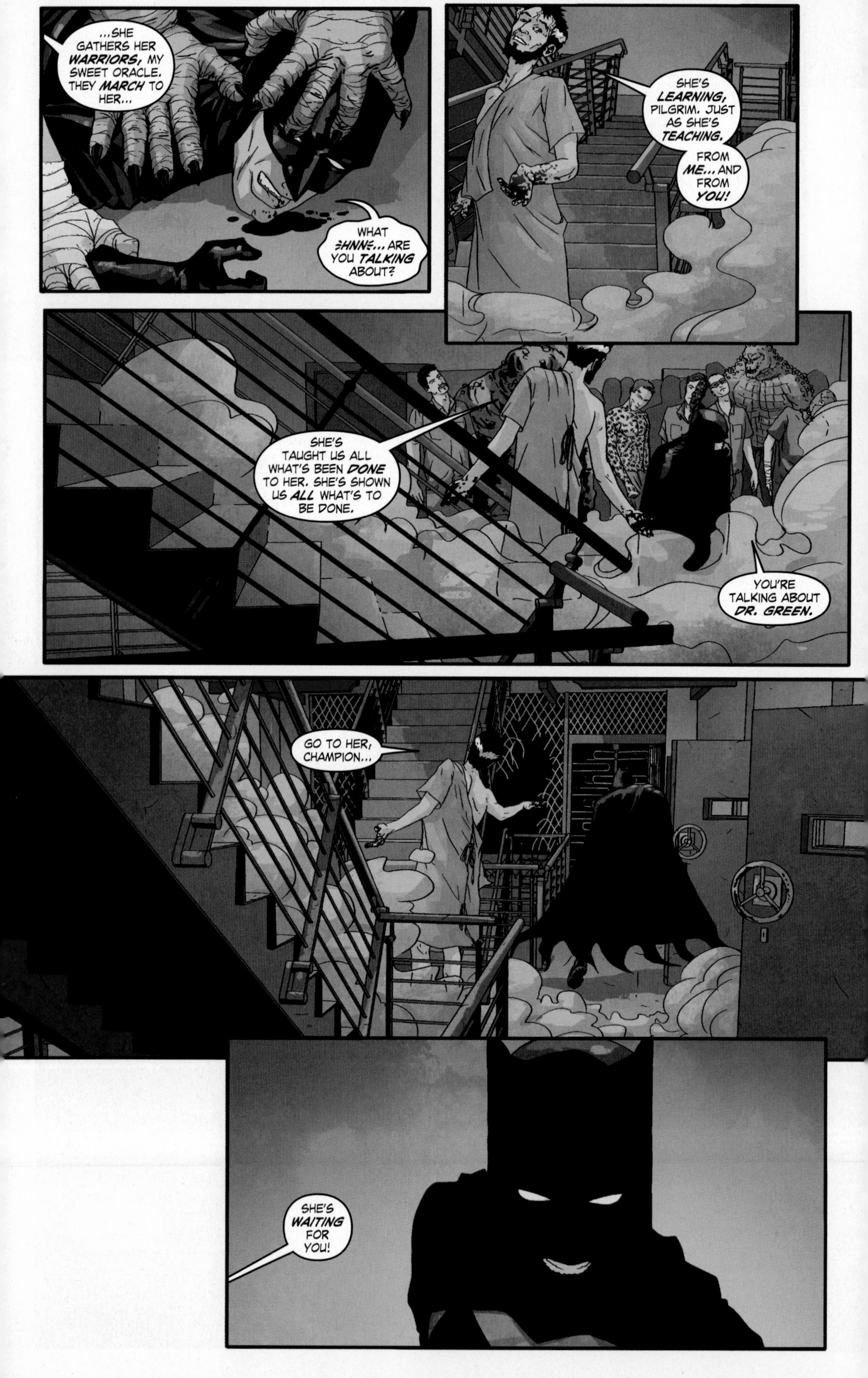
...SHE GATHERS HER WARRIORS, MY SWEET ORACLE. THEY MARCH TO HER...
WHAT -HNN-... ARE YOU TALKING ABOUT?
SHE'S LEARNING, PILGRIM. JUST AS SHE'S TEACHING.
FROM ME... AND FROM YOU!
SHE'S TAUGHT US ALL WHAT'S BEEN DONE TO HER. SHE'S SHOWN US ALL WHAT'S TO BE DONE.
YOU'RE TALKING ABOUT DR. GREEN.
GO TO HER, CHAMPION...
SHE'S WAITING FOR YOU!

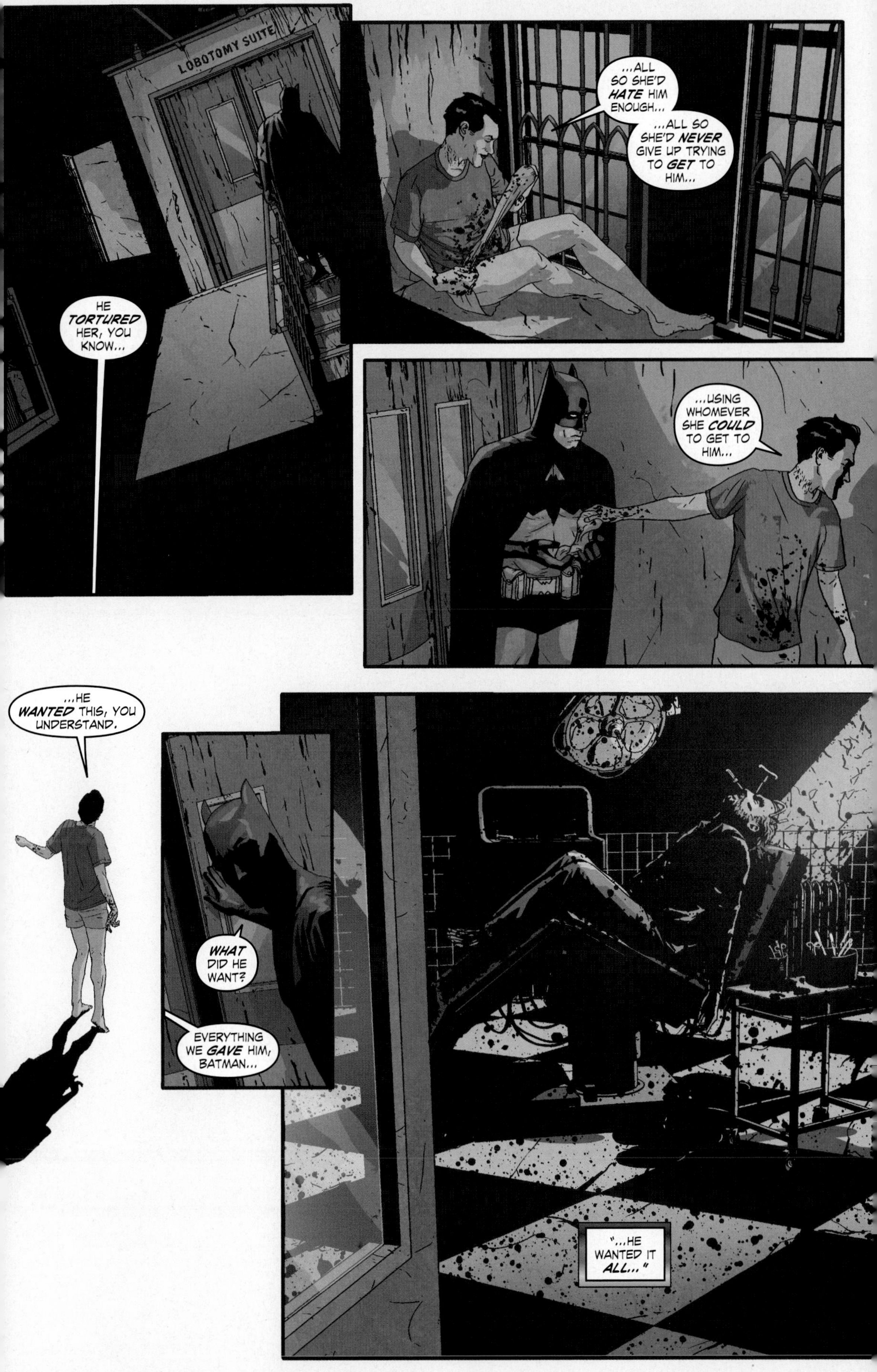
LOBOTOMY SUITE
HE TORTURED HER, YOU KNOW...
...ALL SO SHE'D HATE HIM ENOUGH...
...ALL SO SHE'D NEVER GIVE UP TRYING TO GET TO HIM...
...USING WHOMEVER SHE COULD TO GET TO HIM...
...HE WANTED THIS, YOU UNDERSTAND.
WHAT DID HE WANT?
EVERYTHING WE GAVE HIM, BATMAN...
"...HE WANTED IT ALL..."

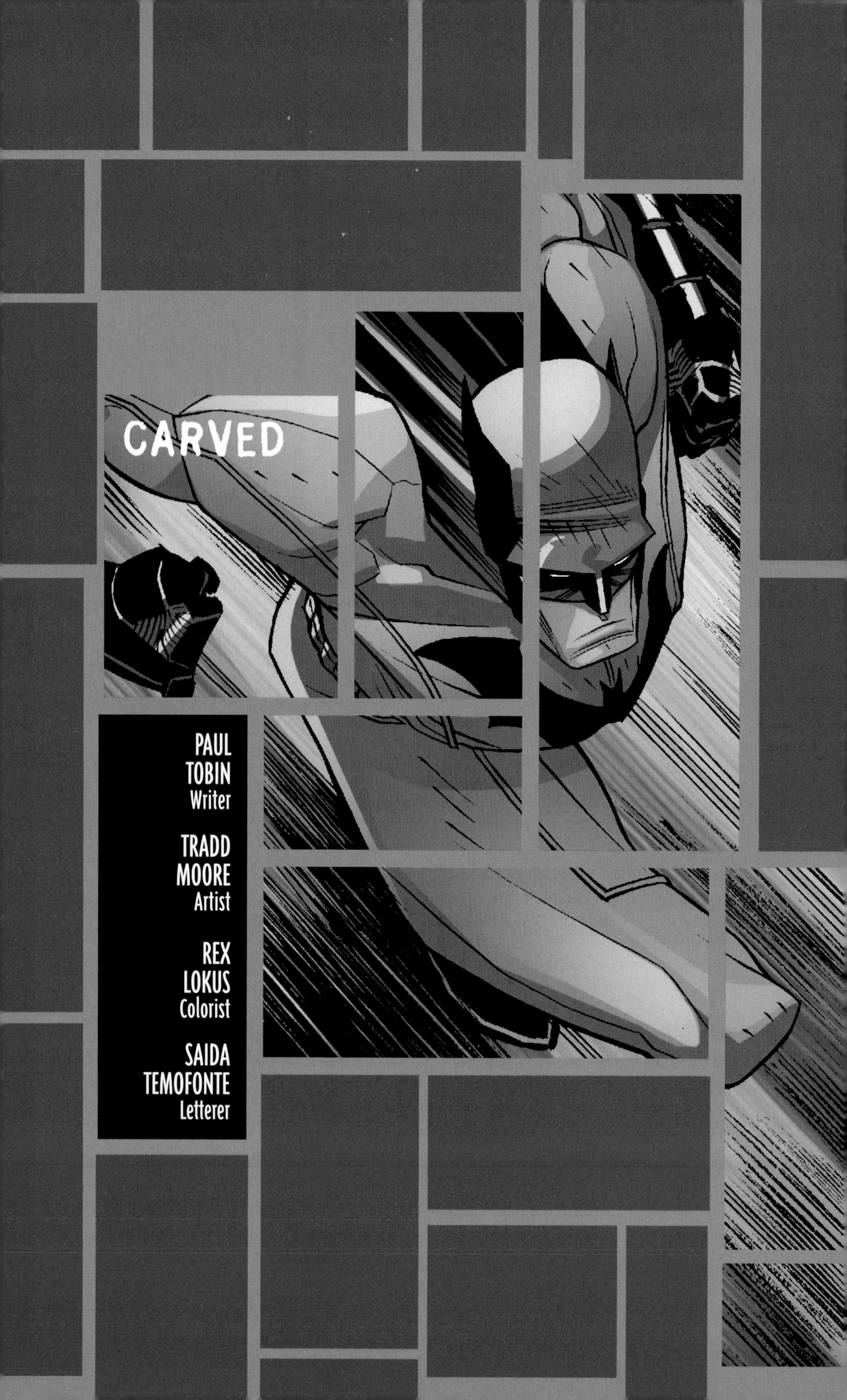
CARVED
PAUL TOBIN
Writer
TRADD MOORE
Artist
REX LOKUS
Colorist
SAIDA TEMOFONTE
Letterer

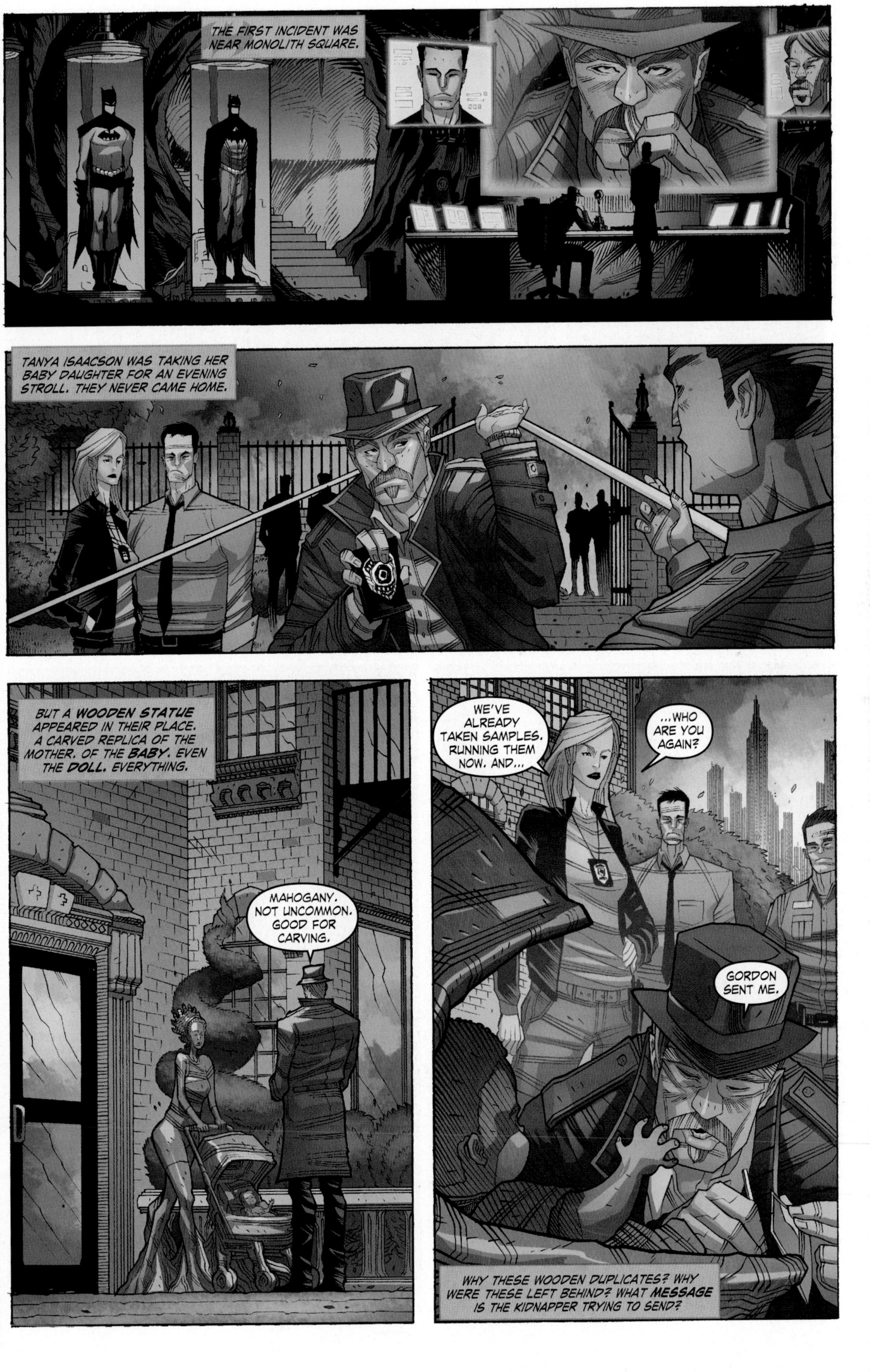
THE FIRST INCIDENT WAS NEAR MONOLITH SQUARE.
TANYA ISAACSON WAS TAKING HER BABY DAUGHTER FOR AN EVENING STROLL. THEY NEVER CAME HOME.
BUT A WOODEN STATUE APPEARED IN THEIR PLACE. A CARVED REPLICA OF THE MOTHER. OF THE BABY. EVEN THE DOLL. EVERYTHING.
MAHOGANY. NOT UNCOMMON. GOOD FOR CARVING.
WE'VE ALREADY TAKEN SAMPLES. RUNNING THEM NOW. AND...
...WHO ARE YOU AGAIN?
GORDON SENT ME.
WHY THESE WOODEN DUPLICATES? WHY WERE THESE LEFT BEHIND? WHAT MESSAGE IS THE KIDNAPPER TRYING TO SEND?

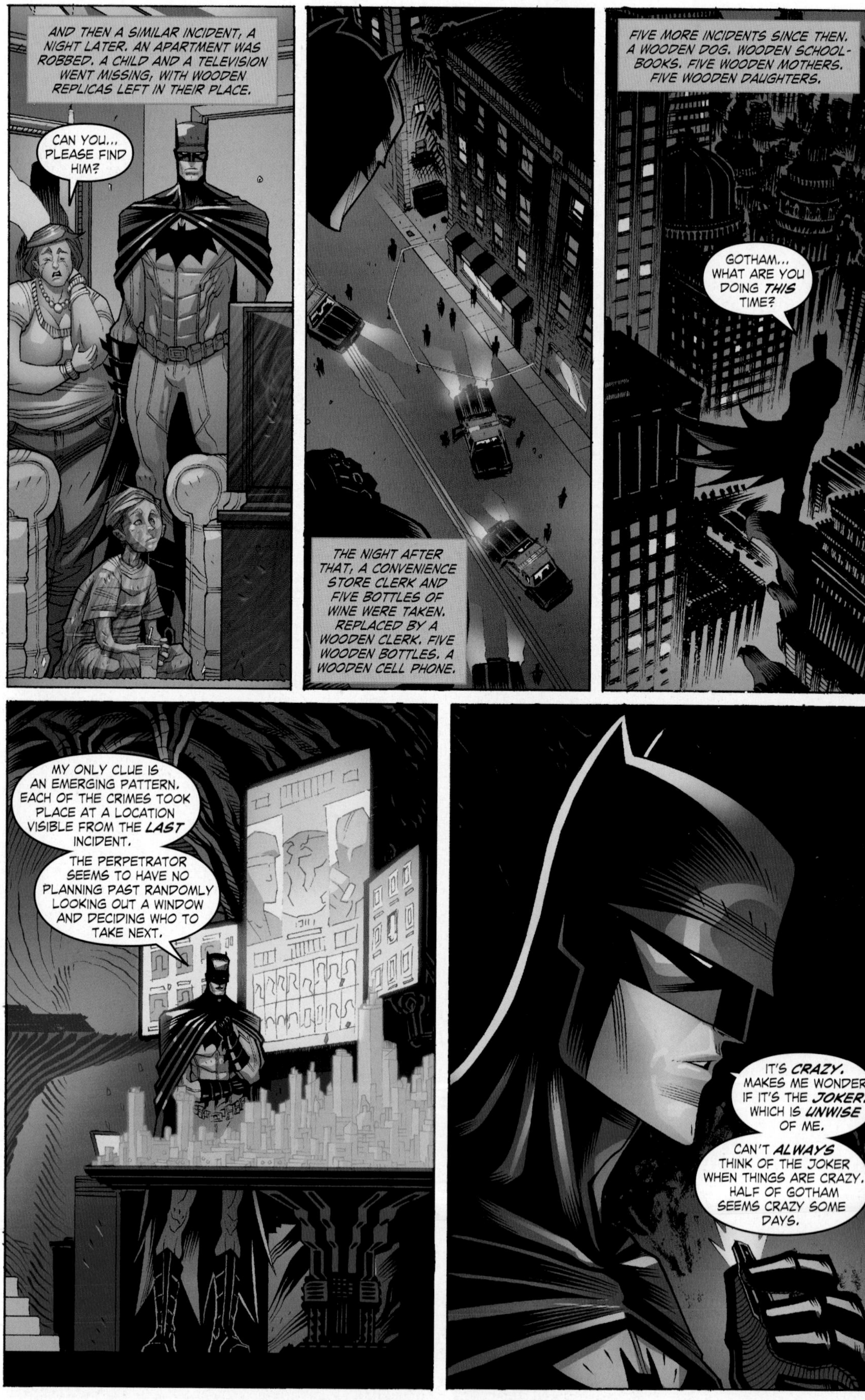
AND THEN A SIMILAR INCIDENT, A NIGHT LATER. AN APARTMENT WAS ROBBED. A CHILD AND A TELEVISION WENT MISSING, WITH WOODEN REPLICAS LEFT IN THEIR PLACE.
CAN YOU... PLEASE FIND HIM?
THE NIGHT AFTER THAT, A CONVENIENCE STORE CLERK AND FIVE BOTTLES OF WINE WERE TAKEN. REPLACED BY A WOODEN CLERK. FIVE WOODEN BOTTLES. A WOODEN CELL PHONE.
FIVE MORE INCIDENTS SINCE THEN. A WOODEN DOG. WOODEN SCHOOL-BOOKS. FIVE WOODEN MOTHERS. FIVE WOODEN DAUGHTERS.
GOTHAM... WHAT ARE YOU DOING *THIS* TIME?
MY ONLY CLUE IS AN EMERGING PATTERN. EACH OF THE CRIMES TOOK PLACE AT A LOCATION VISIBLE FROM THE *LAST* INCIDENT.
THE PERPETRATOR SEEMS TO HAVE NO PLANNING PAST RANDOMLY LOOKING OUT A WINDOW AND DECIDING WHO TO TAKE NEXT.
IT'S *CRAZY.* MAKES ME WONDER IF IT'S THE *JOKER.* WHICH IS *UNWISE* OF ME.
CAN'T *ALWAYS* THINK OF THE JOKER WHEN THINGS ARE CRAZY. HALF OF GOTHAM SEEMS CRAZY SOME DAYS.

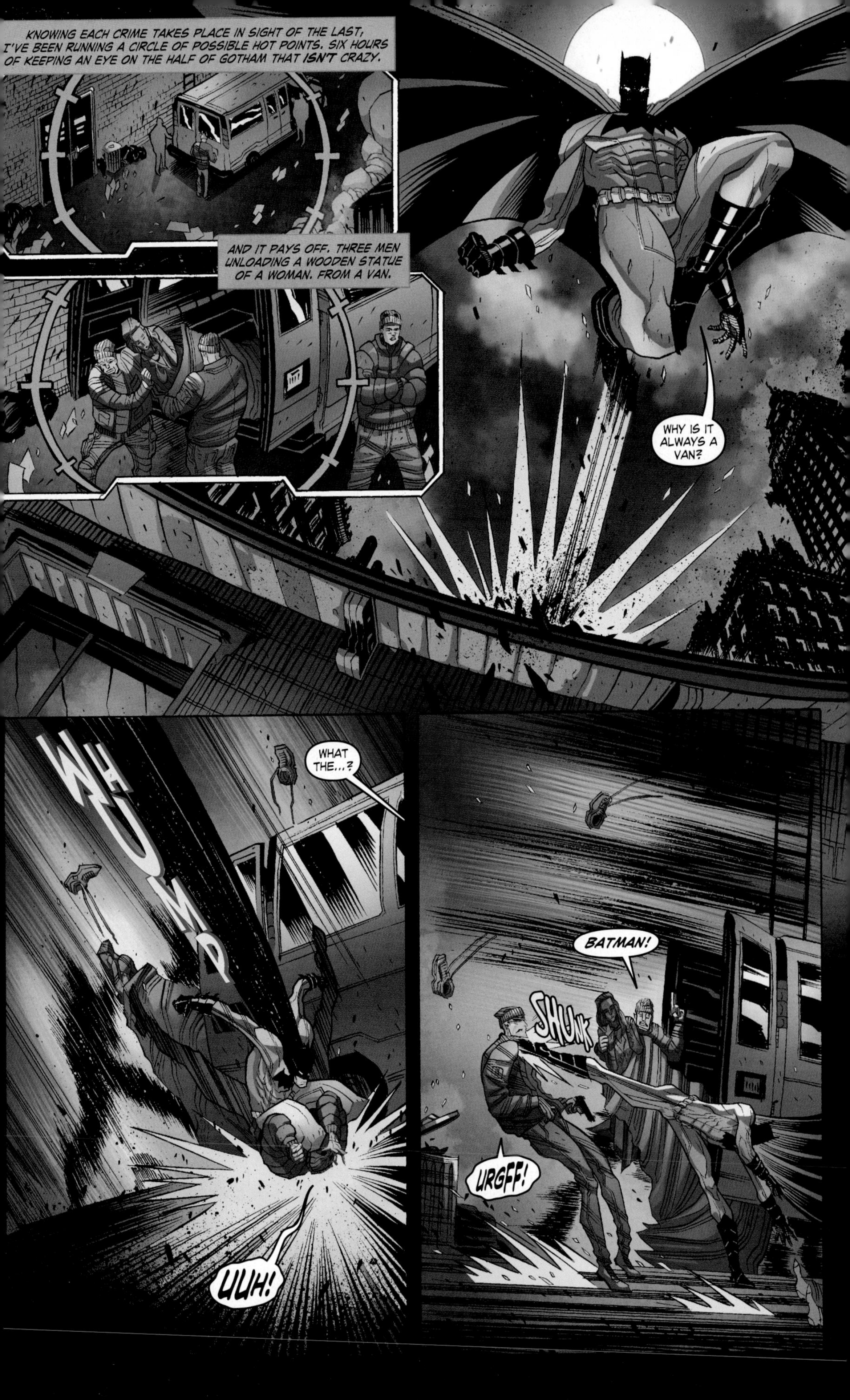
KNOWING EACH CRIME TAKES PLACE IN SIGHT OF THE LAST, I'VE BEEN RUNNING A CIRCLE OF POSSIBLE HOT POINTS. SIX HOURS OF KEEPING AN EYE ON THE HALF OF GOTHAM THAT ISN'T CRAZY.
AND IT PAYS OFF. THREE MEN UNLOADING A WOODEN STATUE OF A WOMAN. FROM A VAN.
WHY IS IT ALWAYS A VAN?
WHUMP
WHAT THE...?
UUH!
BATMAN!
SHUNK
URGFF!

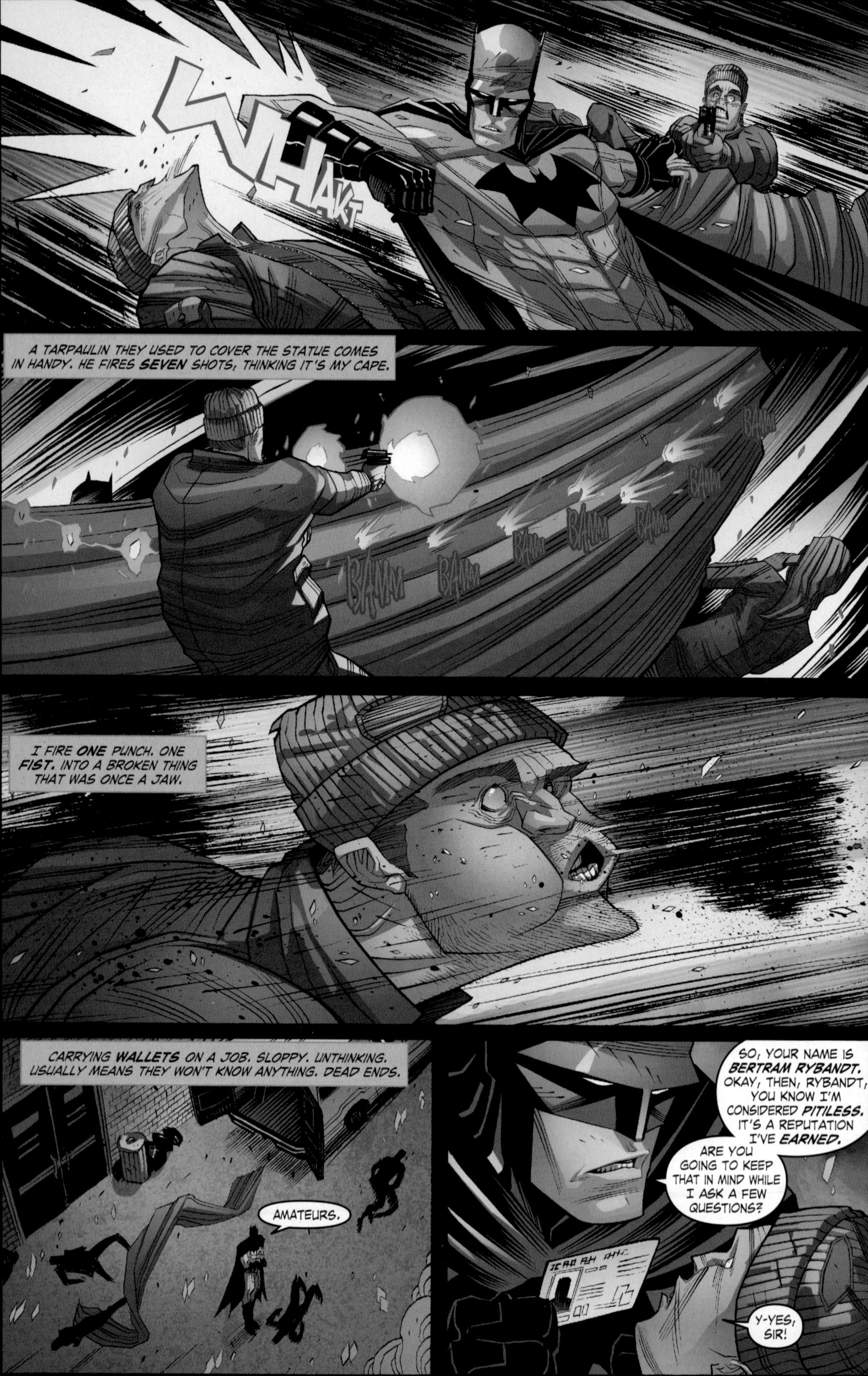
WHAKT
A TARPAULIN THEY USED TO COVER THE STATUE COMES IN HANDY. HE FIRES SEVEN SHOTS, THINKING IT'S MY CAPE.
BAMM
BAMM
BAMM
BAMM
BAMM
BAMM
BAMM
I FIRE ONE PUNCH. ONE FIST. INTO A BROKEN THING THAT WAS ONCE A JAW.
CARRYING WALLETS ON A JOB. SLOPPY. UNTHINKING. USUALLY MEANS THEY WON'T KNOW ANYTHING. DEAD ENDS.
AMATEURS.
SO, YOUR NAME IS BERTRAM RYBANDT. OKAY, THEN, RYBANDT, YOU KNOW I'M CONSIDERED PITILESS. IT'S A REPUTATION I'VE EARNED.
ARE YOU GOING TO KEEP THAT IN MIND WHILE I ASK A FEW QUESTIONS?
Y-YES, SIR!

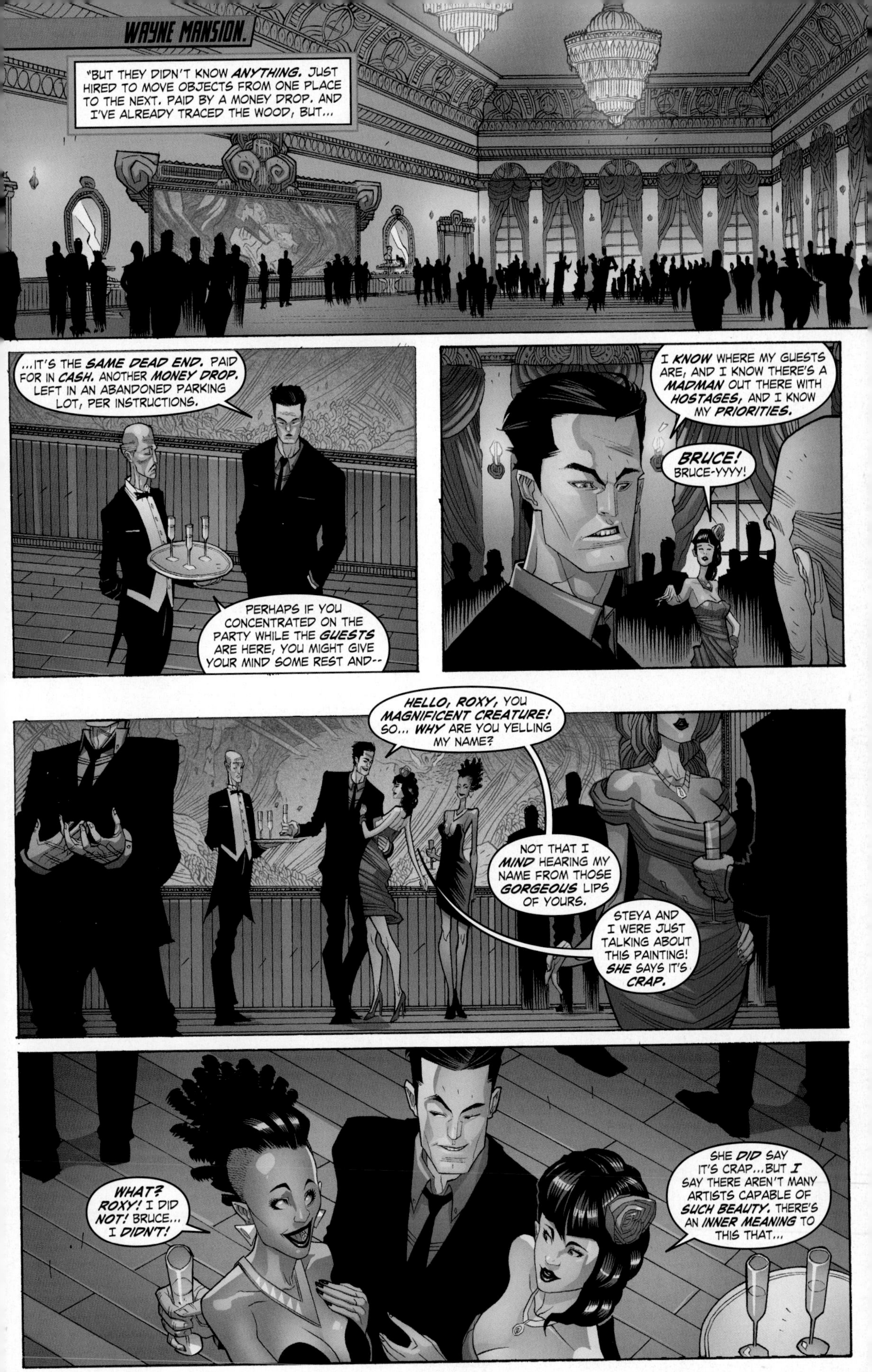
WAYNE MANSION.
"BUT THEY DIDN'T KNOW ANYTHING. JUST HIRED TO MOVE OBJECTS FROM ONE PLACE TO THE NEXT. PAID BY A MONEY DROP. AND I'VE ALREADY TRACED THE WOOD, BUT...
...IT'S THE SAME DEAD END. PAID FOR IN CASH. ANOTHER MONEY DROP. LEFT IN AN ABANDONED PARKING LOT, PER INSTRUCTIONS.
PERHAPS IF YOU CONCENTRATED ON THE PARTY WHILE THE GUESTS ARE HERE, YOU MIGHT GIVE YOUR MIND SOME REST AND--
I KNOW WHERE MY GUESTS ARE, AND I KNOW THERE'S A MADMAN OUT THERE WITH HOSTAGES, AND I KNOW MY PRIORITIES.
BRUCE! BRUCE-YYYY!
HELLO, ROXY, YOU MAGNIFICENT CREATURE! SO... WHY ARE YOU YELLING MY NAME?
NOT THAT I MIND HEARING MY NAME FROM THOSE GORGEOUS LIPS OF YOURS.
STEYA AND I WERE JUST TALKING ABOUT THIS PAINTING! SHE SAYS IT'S CRAP.
WHAT? ROXY! I DID NOT! BRUCE... I DIDN'T!
SHE DID SAY IT'S CRAP...BUT I SAY THERE AREN'T MANY ARTISTS CAPABLE OF SUCH BEAUTY. THERE'S AN INNER MEANING TO THIS THAT...

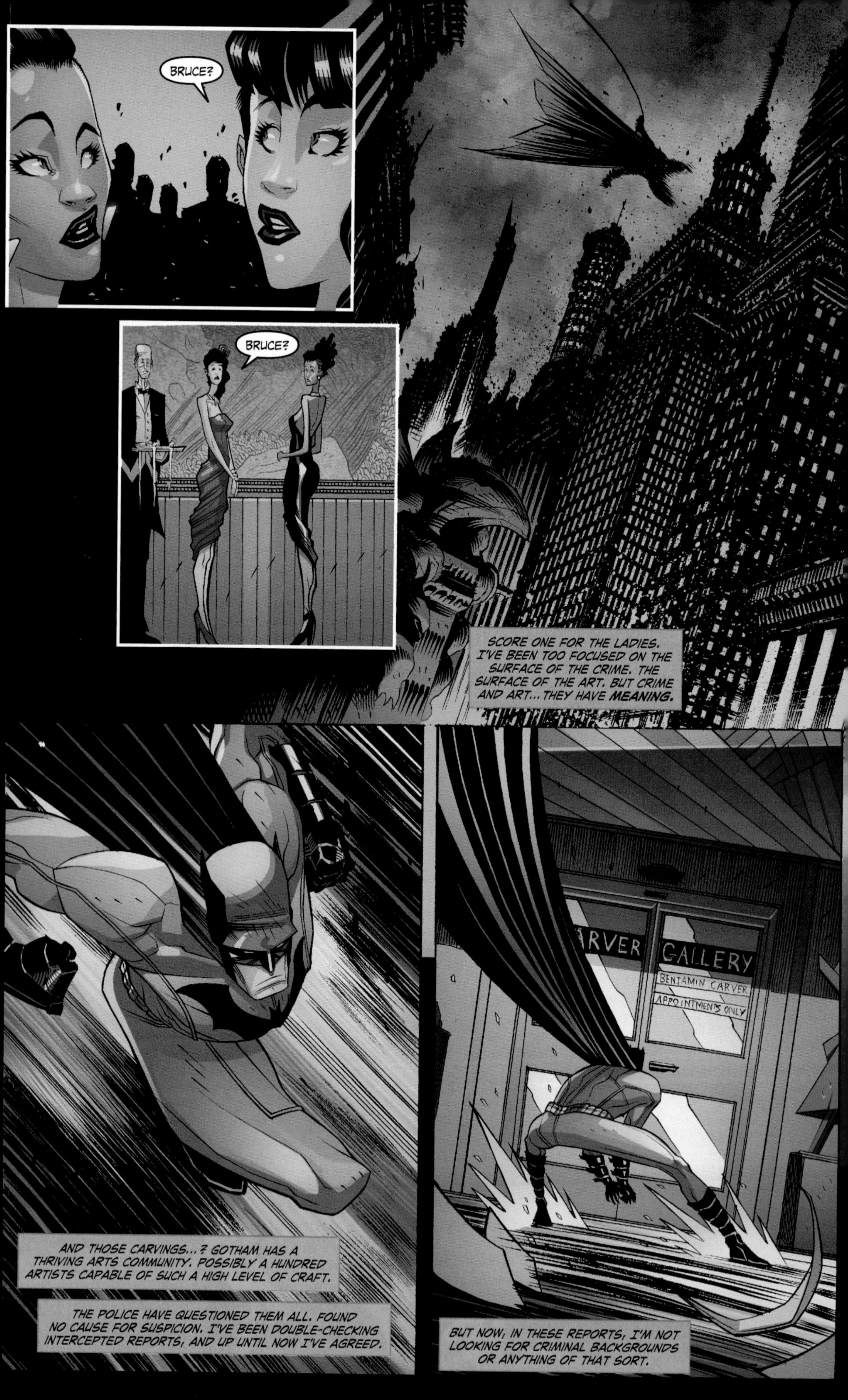

BRUCE?
BRUCE?
SCORE ONE FOR THE LADIES. I'VE BEEN TOO FOCUSED ON THE SURFACE OF THE CRIME. THE SURFACE OF THE ART. BUT CRIME AND ART...THEY HAVE MEANING.
AND THOSE CARVINGS...? GOTHAM HAS A THRIVING ARTS COMMUNITY. POSSIBLY A HUNDRED ARTISTS CAPABLE OF SUCH A HIGH LEVEL OF CRAFT.
THE POLICE HAVE QUESTIONED THEM ALL. FOUND NO CAUSE FOR SUSPICION. I'VE BEEN DOUBLE-CHECKING INTERCEPTED REPORTS, AND UP UNTIL NOW I'VE AGREED.
ARVER GALLERY
BENJAMIN CARVER
APPOINTMENTS ONLY
BUT NOW, IN THESE REPORTS, I'M NOT LOOKING FOR CRIMINAL BACKGROUNDS OR ANYTHING OF THAT SORT.

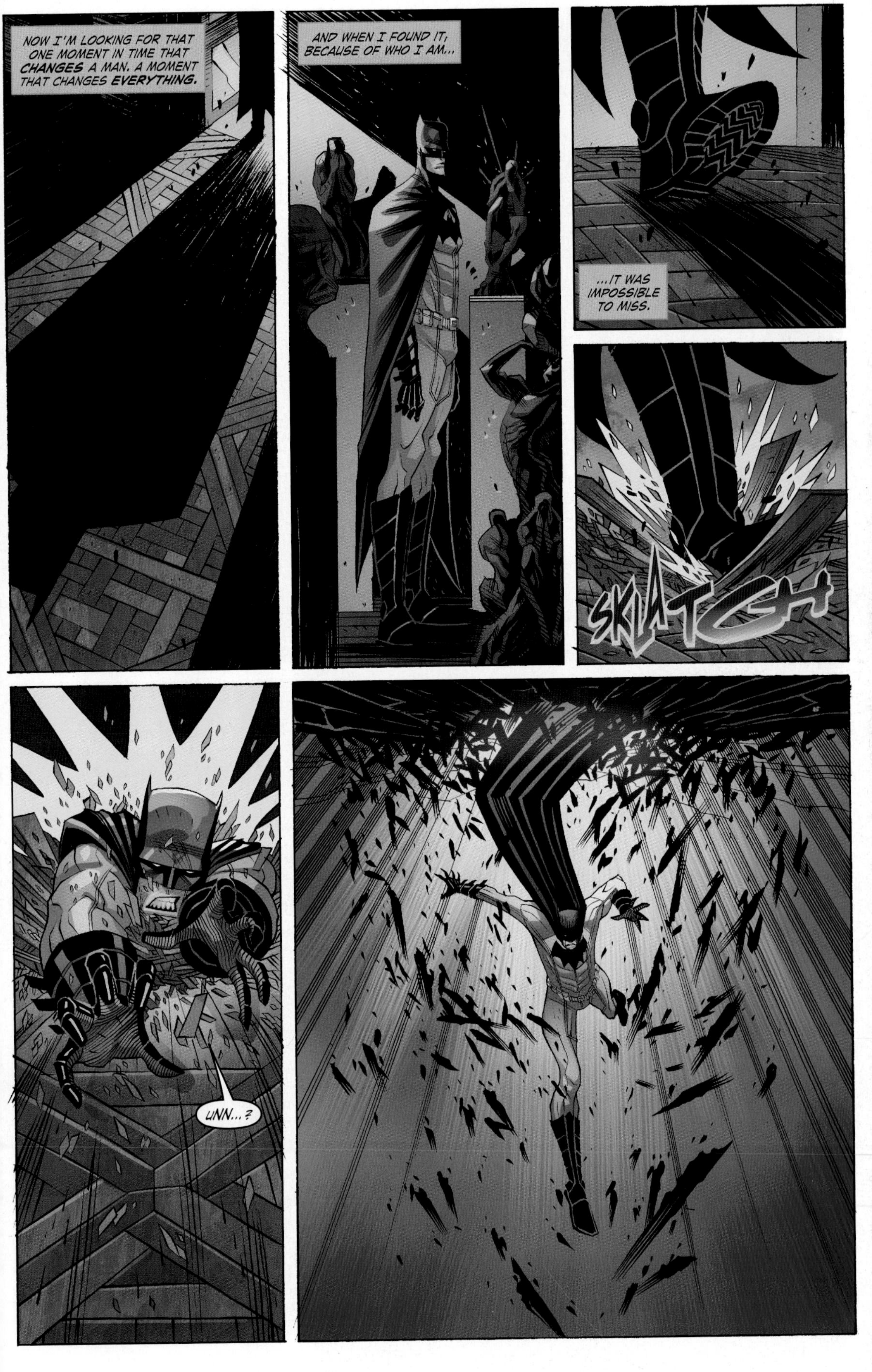
NOW I'M LOOKING FOR THAT ONE MOMENT IN TIME THAT CHANGES A MAN. A MOMENT THAT CHANGES EVERYTHING.
AND WHEN I FOUND IT, BECAUSE OF WHO I AM...
...IT WAS IMPOSSIBLE TO MISS.
SKLATCH
UNN...?

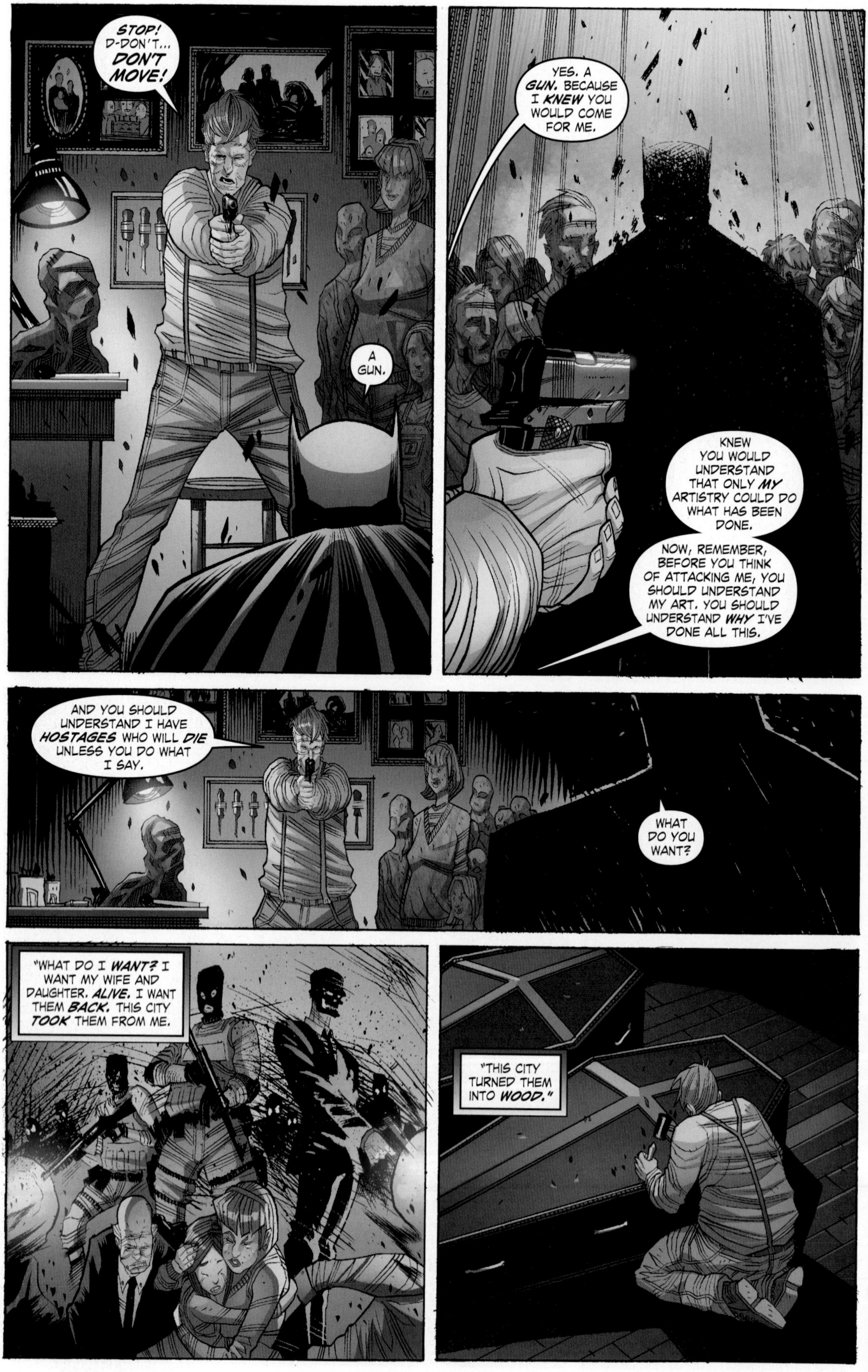
STOP! D-DON'T... DON'T MOVE!
A GUN.
YES. A GUN. BECAUSE I KNEW YOU WOULD COME FOR ME.
KNEW YOU WOULD UNDERSTAND THAT ONLY MY ARTISTRY COULD DO WHAT HAS BEEN DONE.
NOW, REMEMBER, BEFORE YOU THINK OF ATTACKING ME, YOU SHOULD UNDERSTAND MY ART. YOU SHOULD UNDERSTAND WHY I'VE DONE ALL THIS.
AND YOU SHOULD UNDERSTAND I HAVE HOSTAGES WHO WILL DIE UNLESS YOU DO WHAT I SAY.
WHAT DO YOU WANT?
"WHAT DO I WANT? I WANT MY WIFE AND DAUGHTER. ALIVE. I WANT THEM BACK. THIS CITY TOOK THEM FROM ME.
"THIS CITY TURNED THEM INTO WOOD."

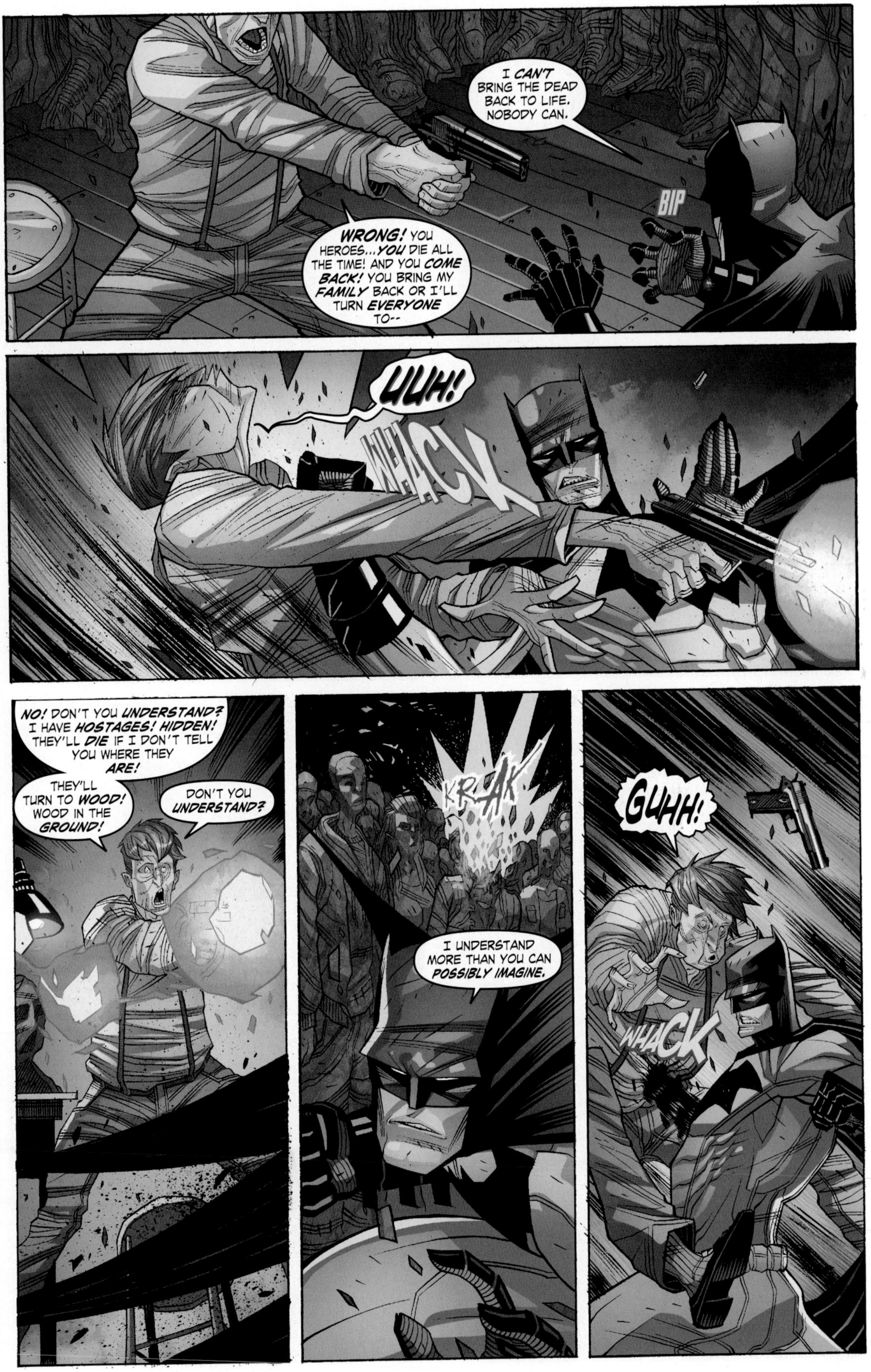
I CAN'T BRING THE DEAD BACK TO LIFE. NOBODY CAN.
BIP
WRONG! YOU HEROES...YOU DIE ALL THE TIME! AND YOU COME BACK! YOU BRING MY FAMILY BACK OR I'LL TURN EVERYONE TO--
UUH!
WHACK
NO! DON'T YOU UNDERSTAND? I HAVE HOSTAGES! HIDDEN! THEY'LL DIE IF I DON'T TELL YOU WHERE THEY ARE!
THEY'LL TURN TO WOOD! WOOD IN THE GROUND!
DON'T YOU UNDERSTAND?
KRAK
I UNDERSTAND MORE THAN YOU CAN POSSIBLY IMAGINE.
GUHH!
WHACK

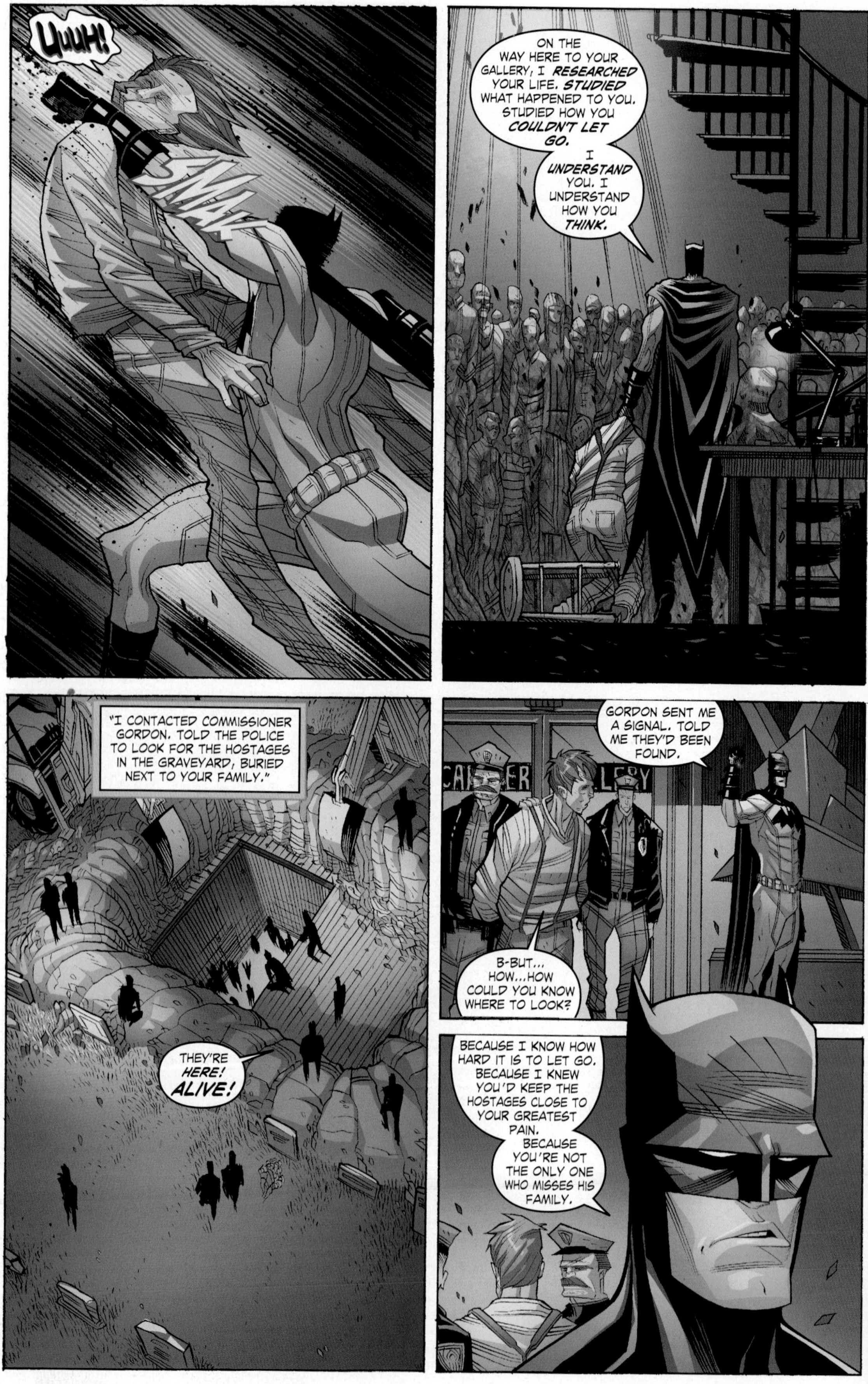
UUUH!
SMAK
ON THE WAY HERE TO YOUR GALLERY, I RESEARCHED YOUR LIFE. STUDIED WHAT HAPPENED TO YOU. STUDIED HOW YOU COULDN'T LET GO.
I UNDERSTAND YOU. I UNDERSTAND HOW YOU THINK.
"I CONTACTED COMMISSIONER GORDON. TOLD THE POLICE TO LOOK FOR THE HOSTAGES IN THE GRAVEYARD, BURIED NEXT TO YOUR FAMILY."
THEY'RE HERE! ALIVE!
GORDON SENT ME A SIGNAL. TOLD ME THEY'D BEEN FOUND.
B-BUT... HOW...HOW COULD YOU KNOW WHERE TO LOOK?
BECAUSE I KNOW HOW HARD IT IS TO LET GO. BECAUSE I KNEW YOU'D KEEP THE HOSTAGES CLOSE TO YOUR GREATEST PAIN.
BECAUSE YOU'RE NOT THE ONLY ONE WHO MISSES HIS FAMILY.

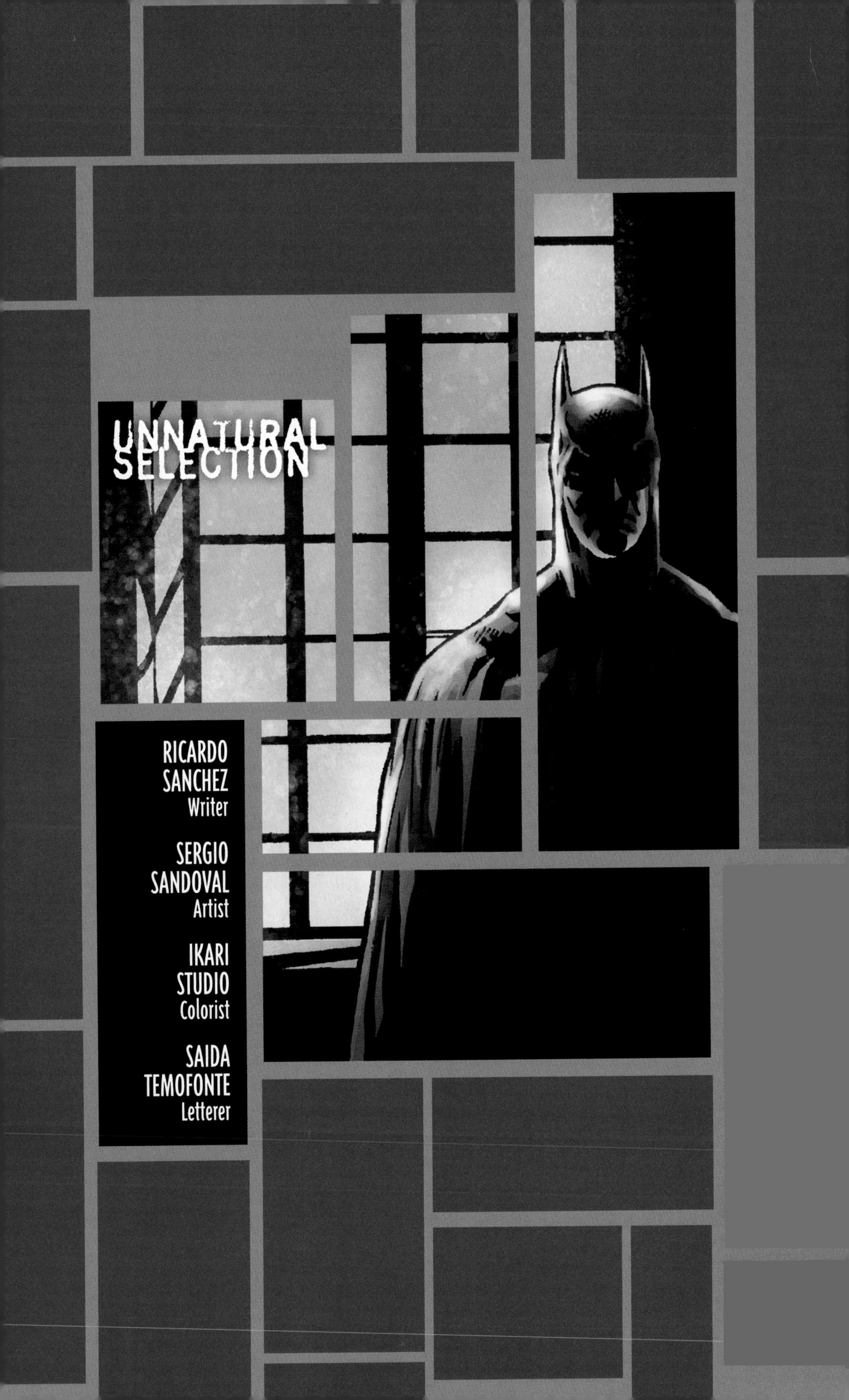
UNNATURAL SELECTION
RICARDO SANCHEZ Writer
SERGIO SANDOVAL Artist
IKARI STUDIO Colorist
SAIDA TEMOFONTE Letterer

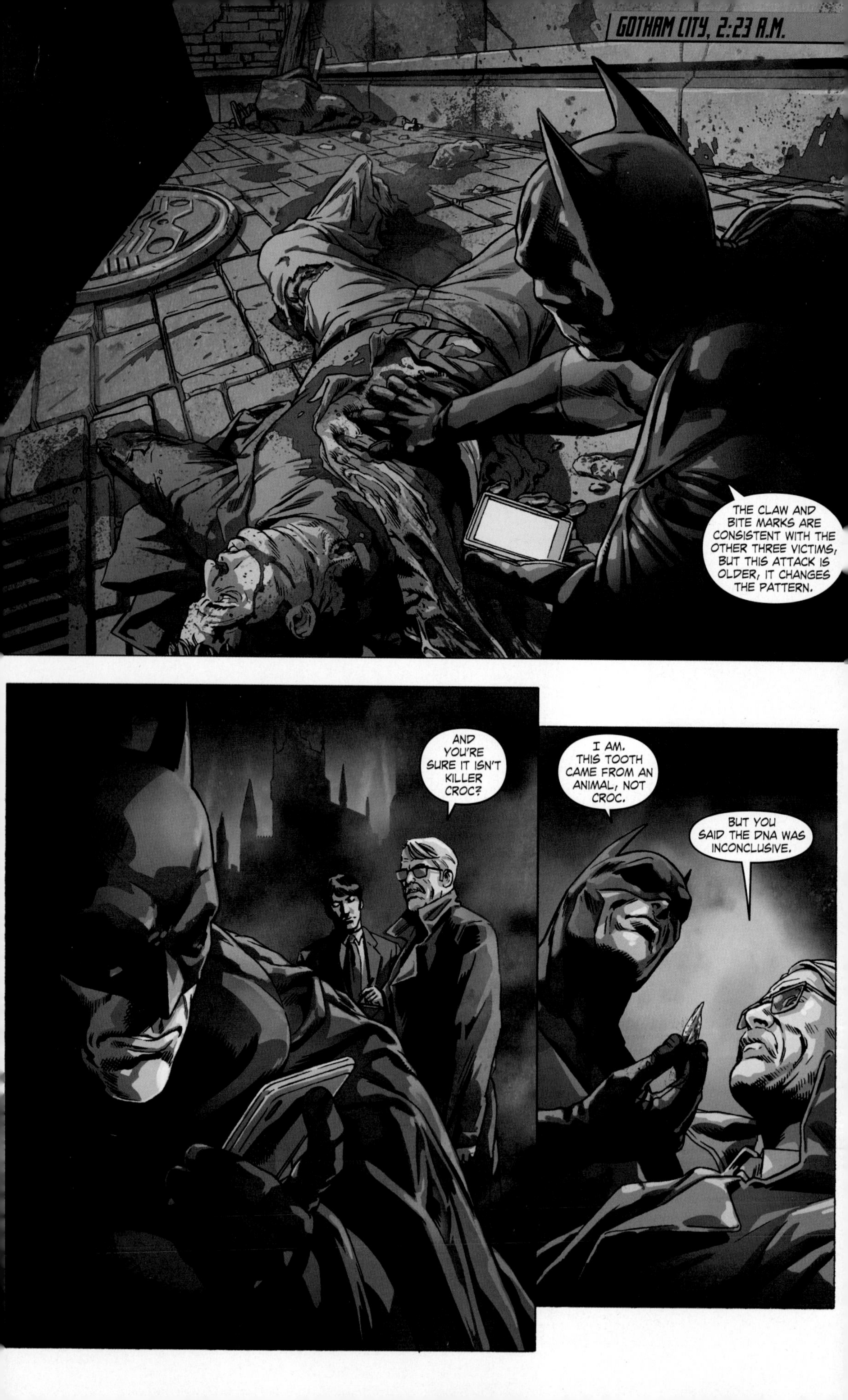
GOTHAM CITY, 2:23 A.M.
THE CLAW AND BITE MARKS ARE CONSISTENT WITH THE OTHER THREE VICTIMS, BUT THIS ATTACK IS OLDER, IT CHANGES THE PATTERN.
AND YOU'RE SURE IT ISN'T KILLER CROC?
I AM. THIS TOOTH CAME FROM AN ANIMAL, NOT CROC.
BUT YOU SAID THE DNA WAS INCONCLUSIVE.

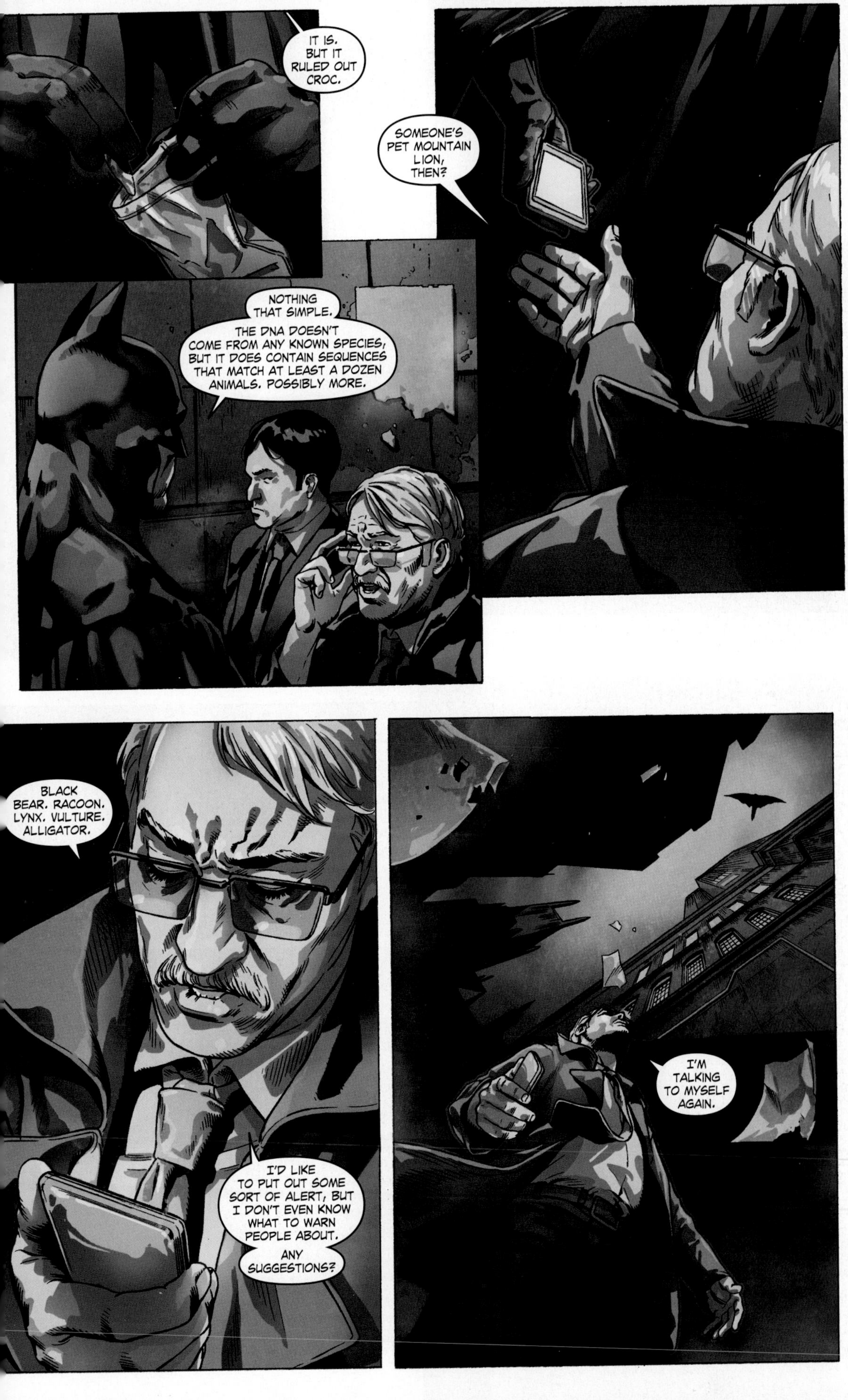
IT IS. BUT IT RULED OUT CROC.
SOMEONE'S PET MOUNTAIN LION, THEN?
NOTHING THAT SIMPLE.
THE DNA DOESN'T COME FROM ANY KNOWN SPECIES, BUT IT DOES CONTAIN SEQUENCES THAT MATCH AT LEAST A DOZEN ANIMALS. POSSIBLY MORE.
BLACK BEAR. RACOON. LYNX. VULTURE. ALLIGATOR.
I'D LIKE TO PUT OUT SOME SORT OF ALERT, BUT I DON'T EVEN KNOW WHAT TO WARN PEOPLE ABOUT.
ANY SUGGESTIONS?
I'M TALKING TO MYSELF AGAIN.

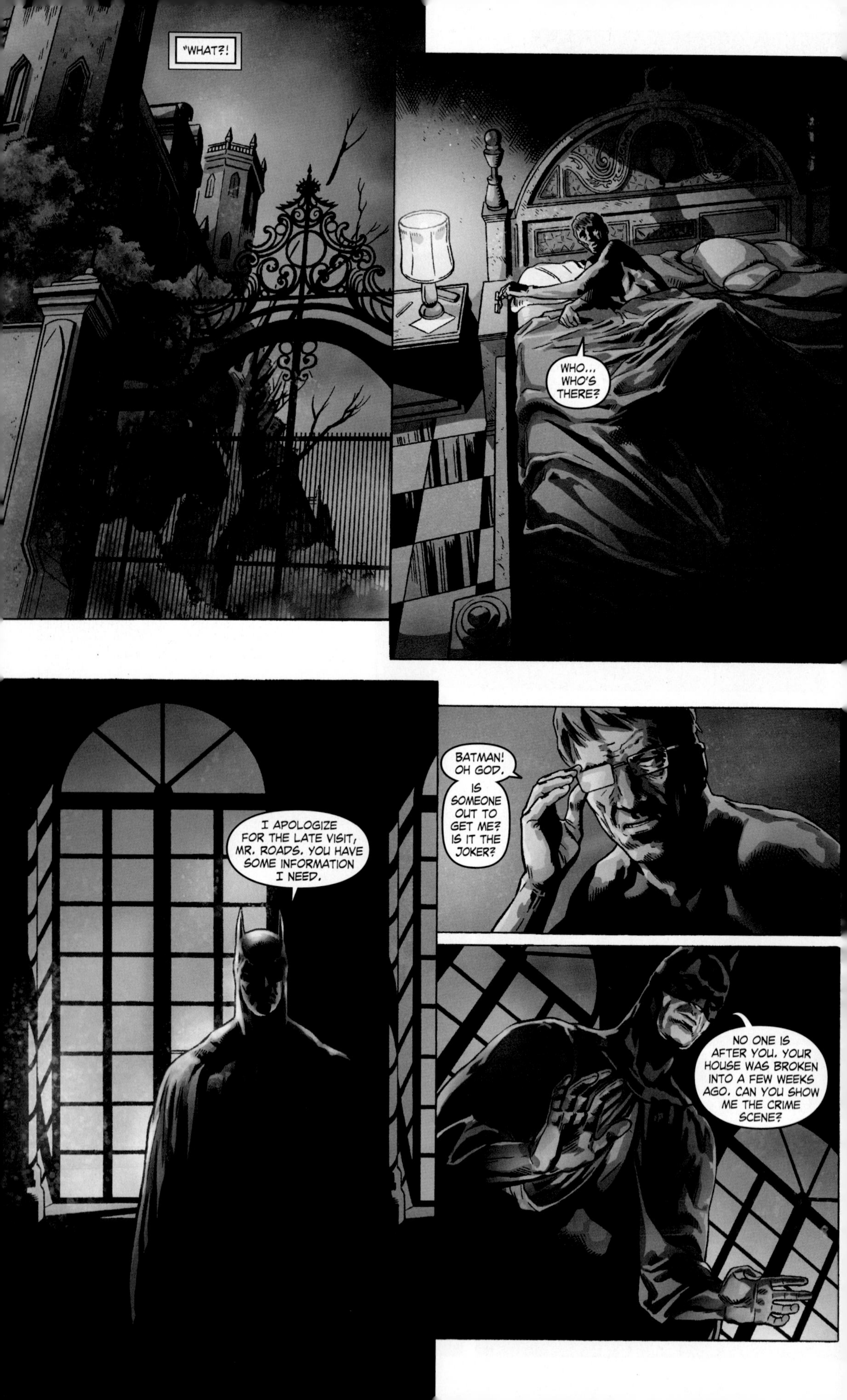
"WHAT?!
WHO... WHO'S THERE?
I APOLOGIZE FOR THE LATE VISIT, MR. ROADS. YOU HAVE SOME INFORMATION I NEED.
BATMAN! OH GOD.
IS SOMEONE OUT TO GET ME? IS IT THE JOKER?
NO ONE IS AFTER YOU. YOUR HOUSE WAS BROKEN INTO A FEW WEEKS AGO. CAN YOU SHOW ME THE CRIME SCENE?

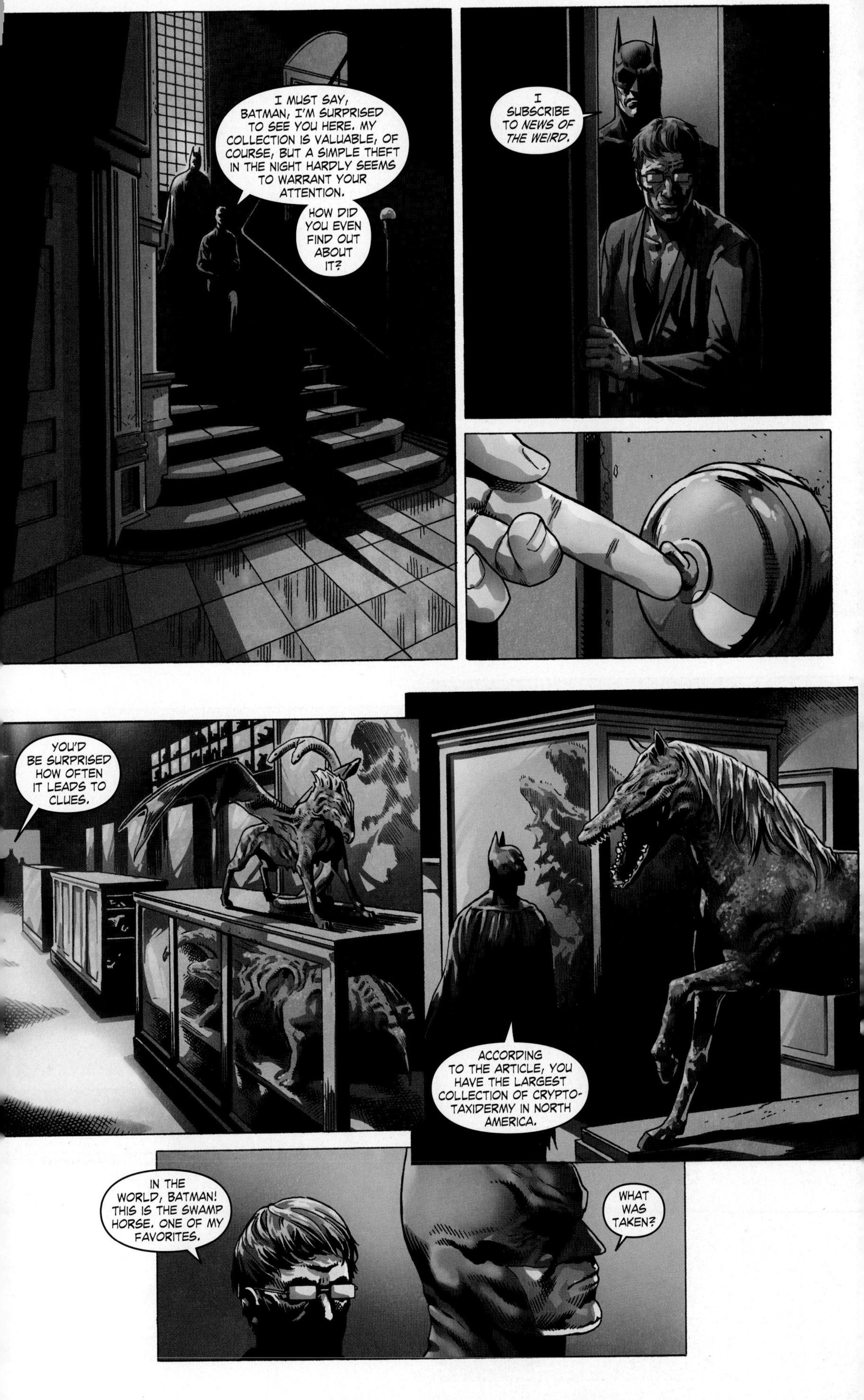
I MUST SAY, BATMAN, I'M SURPRISED TO SEE YOU HERE. MY COLLECTION IS VALUABLE, OF COURSE, BUT A SIMPLE THEFT IN THE NIGHT HARDLY SEEMS TO WARRANT YOUR ATTENTION.
HOW DID YOU EVEN FIND OUT ABOUT IT?
I SUBSCRIBE TO *NEWS OF THE WEIRD*.
YOU'D BE SURPRISED HOW OFTEN IT LEADS TO CLUES.
ACCORDING TO THE ARTICLE, YOU HAVE THE LARGEST COLLECTION OF CRYPTO-TAXIDERMY IN NORTH AMERICA.
IN THE WORLD, BATMAN! THIS IS THE SWAMP HORSE. ONE OF MY FAVORITES.
WHAT WAS TAKEN?

THE BARGHEST. THE PRIDE OF MY COLLECTION.

NOTHING ELSE?

NO, JUST THAT.

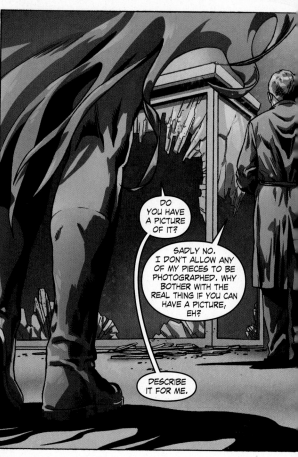

DO YOU HAVE A PICTURE OF IT?

SADLY NO. I DON'T ALLOW ANY OF MY PIECES TO BE PHOTOGRAPHED. WHY BOTHER WITH THE REAL THING IF YOU CAN HAVE A PICTURE, EH?

DESCRIBE IT FOR ME.

WELL, IT'S ABOUT EIGHT FEET TALL, LONG TALONS, HUGE JAWS, AN ALMOST REPTILIAN FACE.

THE THING ABOUT CRYPTO IS YOU CAN USUALLY IDENTIFY THE INDIVIDUAL PIECES. BUT NOT WITH THIS ONE.

WHERE DID YOU GET IT?

THAT'S THE TRULY AMAZING THING! JOEL GARFIELD MADE IT. HE WAS A LAUGHING STOCK A YEAR AGO WITH HIS PATHETIC LITTLE JACKALOPES AND WINGED CATS.

BUT THE BARGHEST! A MASTERPIECE.

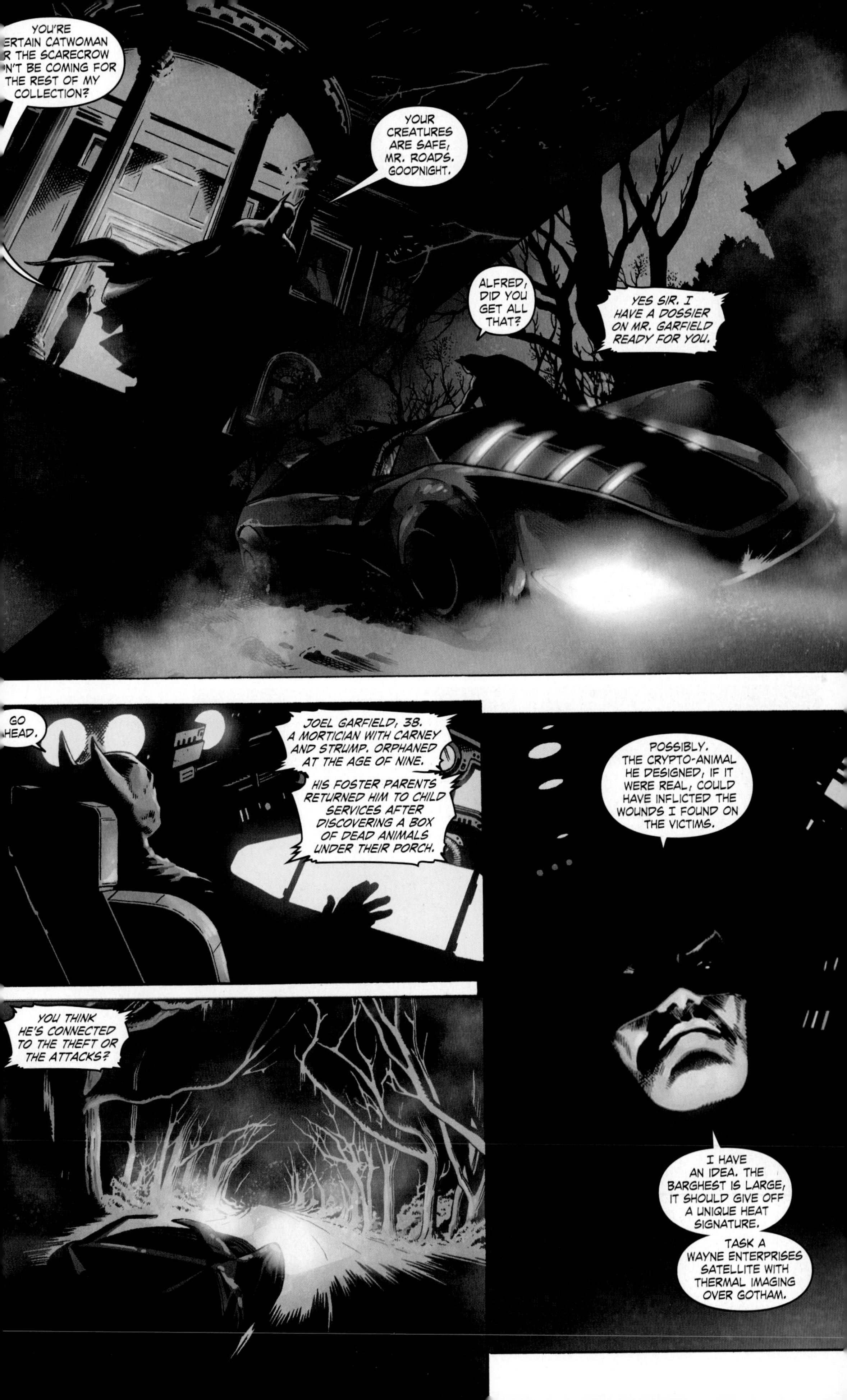
YOU'RE ERTAIN CATWOMAN R THE SCARECROW N'T BE COMING FOR THE REST OF MY COLLECTION?
YOUR CREATURES ARE SAFE, MR. ROADS. GOODNIGHT.
ALFRED, DID YOU GET ALL THAT?
YES SIR. I HAVE A DOSSIER ON MR. GARFIELD READY FOR YOU.
GO HEAD.
JOEL GARFIELD, 38. A MORTICIAN WITH CARNEY AND STRUMP. ORPHANED AT THE AGE OF NINE.
HIS FOSTER PARENTS RETURNED HIM TO CHILD SERVICES AFTER DISCOVERING A BOX OF DEAD ANIMALS UNDER THEIR PORCH.
YOU THINK HE'S CONNECTED TO THE THEFT OR THE ATTACKS?
POSSIBLY. THE CRYPTO-ANIMAL HE DESIGNED, IF IT WERE REAL, COULD HAVE INFLICTED THE WOUNDS I FOUND ON THE VICTIMS.
I HAVE AN IDEA. THE BARGHEST IS LARGE, IT SHOULD GIVE OFF A UNIQUE HEAT SIGNATURE.
TASK A WAYNE ENTERPRISES SATELLITE WITH THERMAL IMAGING OVER GOTHAM.

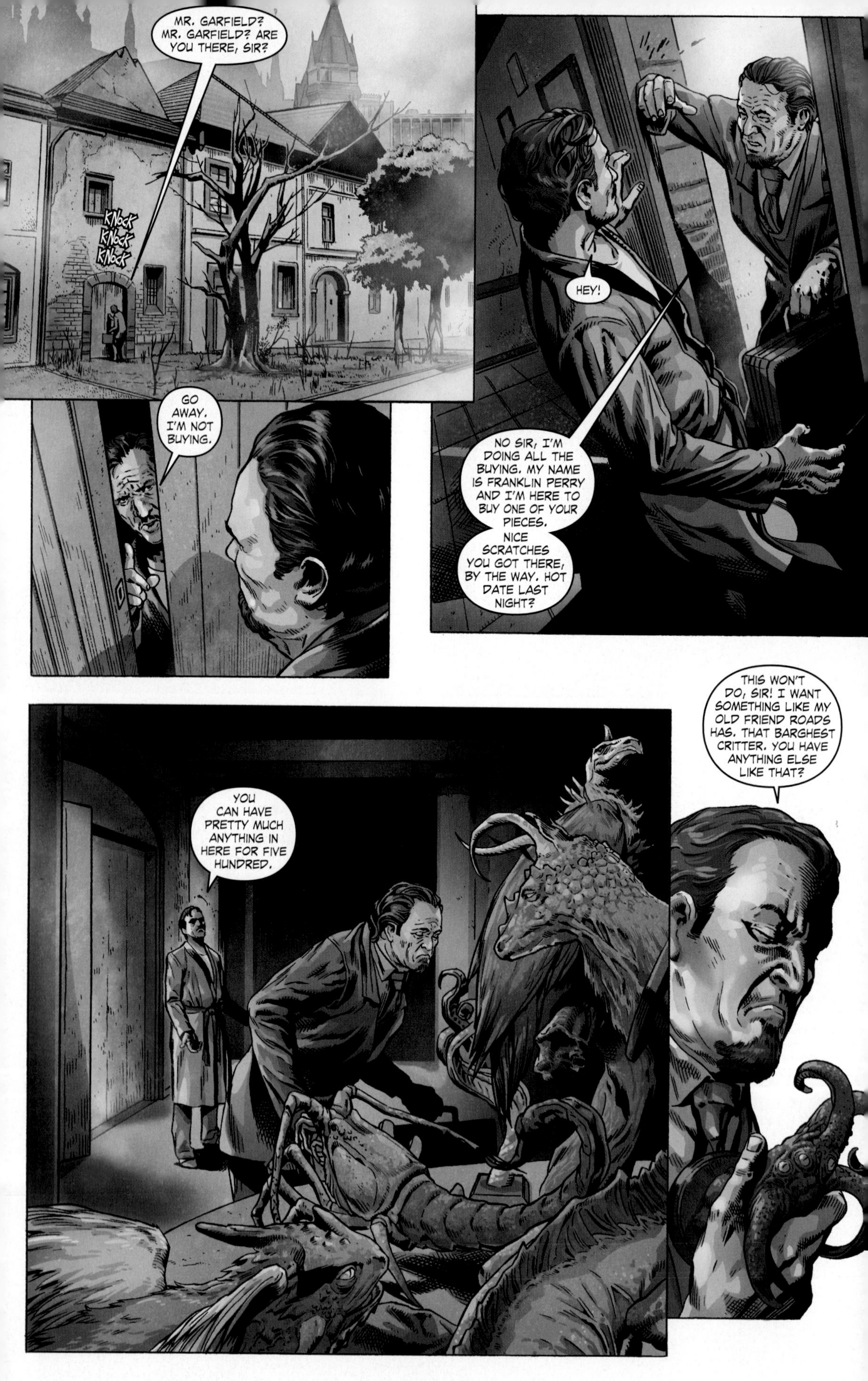
MR. GARFIELD? MR. GARFIELD? ARE YOU THERE, SIR?
KNOCK KNOCK KNOCK
GO AWAY. I'M NOT BUYING.
HEY!
NO SIR, I'M DOING ALL THE BUYING. MY NAME IS FRANKLIN PERRY AND I'M HERE TO BUY ONE OF YOUR PIECES.
NICE SCRATCHES YOU GOT THERE, BY THE WAY. HOT DATE LAST NIGHT?
YOU CAN HAVE PRETTY MUCH ANYTHING IN HERE FOR FIVE HUNDRED.
THIS WON'T DO, SIR! I WANT SOMETHING LIKE MY OLD FRIEND ROADS HAS. THAT BARGHEST CRITTER. YOU HAVE ANYTHING ELSE LIKE THAT?

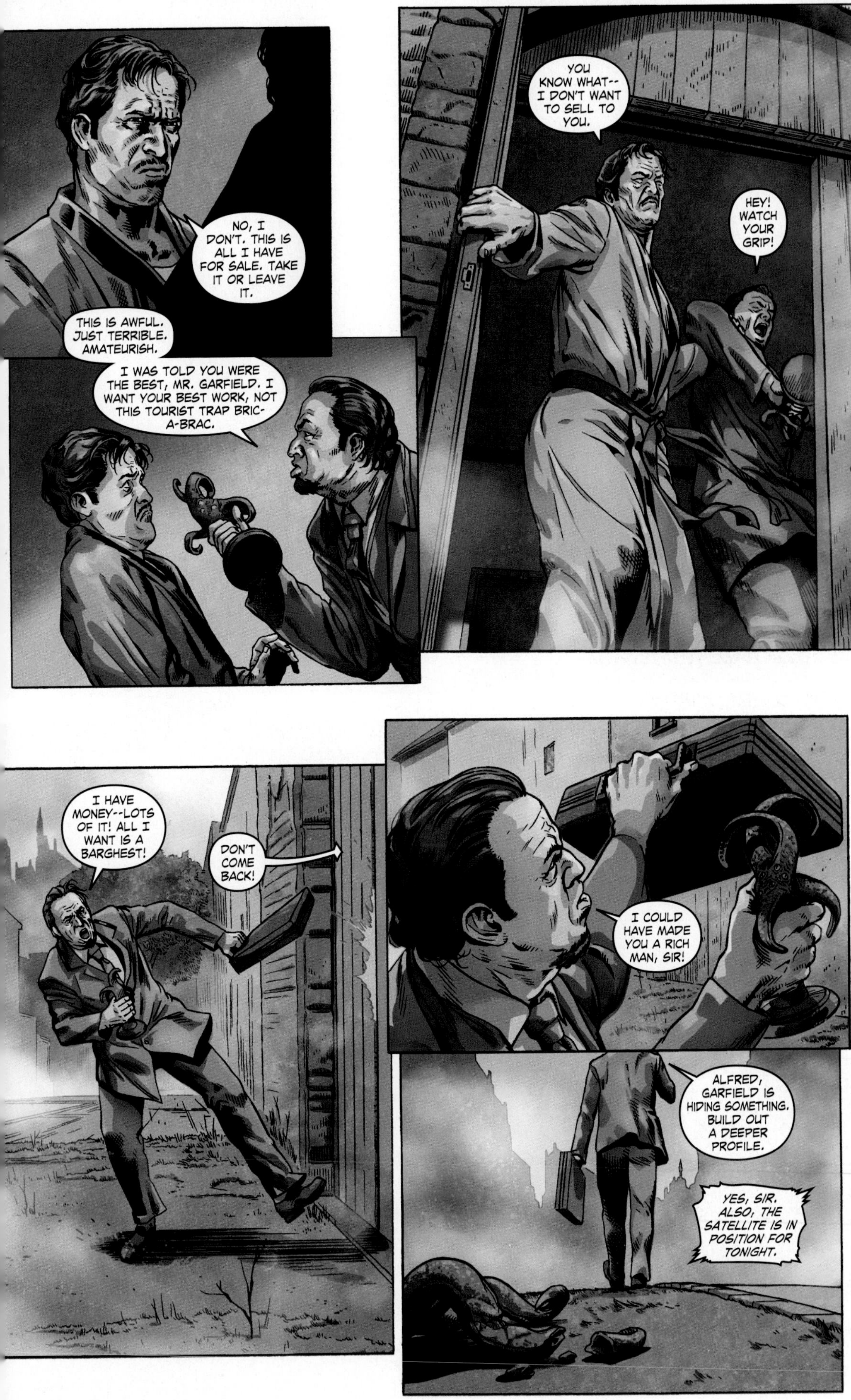
NO, I DON'T. THIS IS ALL I HAVE FOR SALE. TAKE IT OR LEAVE IT.
THIS IS AWFUL. JUST TERRIBLE. AMATEURISH.
I WAS TOLD YOU WERE THE BEST, MR. GARFIELD. I WANT YOUR BEST WORK, NOT THIS TOURIST TRAP BRIC-A-BRAC.
YOU KNOW WHAT--I DON'T WANT TO SELL TO YOU.
HEY! WATCH YOUR GRIP!
I HAVE MONEY--LOTS OF IT! ALL I WANT IS A BARGHEST!
DON'T COME BACK!
I COULD HAVE MADE YOU A RICH MAN, SIR!
ALFRED, GARFIELD IS HIDING SOMETHING. BUILD OUT A DEEPER PROFILE.
YES, SIR. ALSO, THE SATELLITE IS IN POSITION FOR TONIGHT.

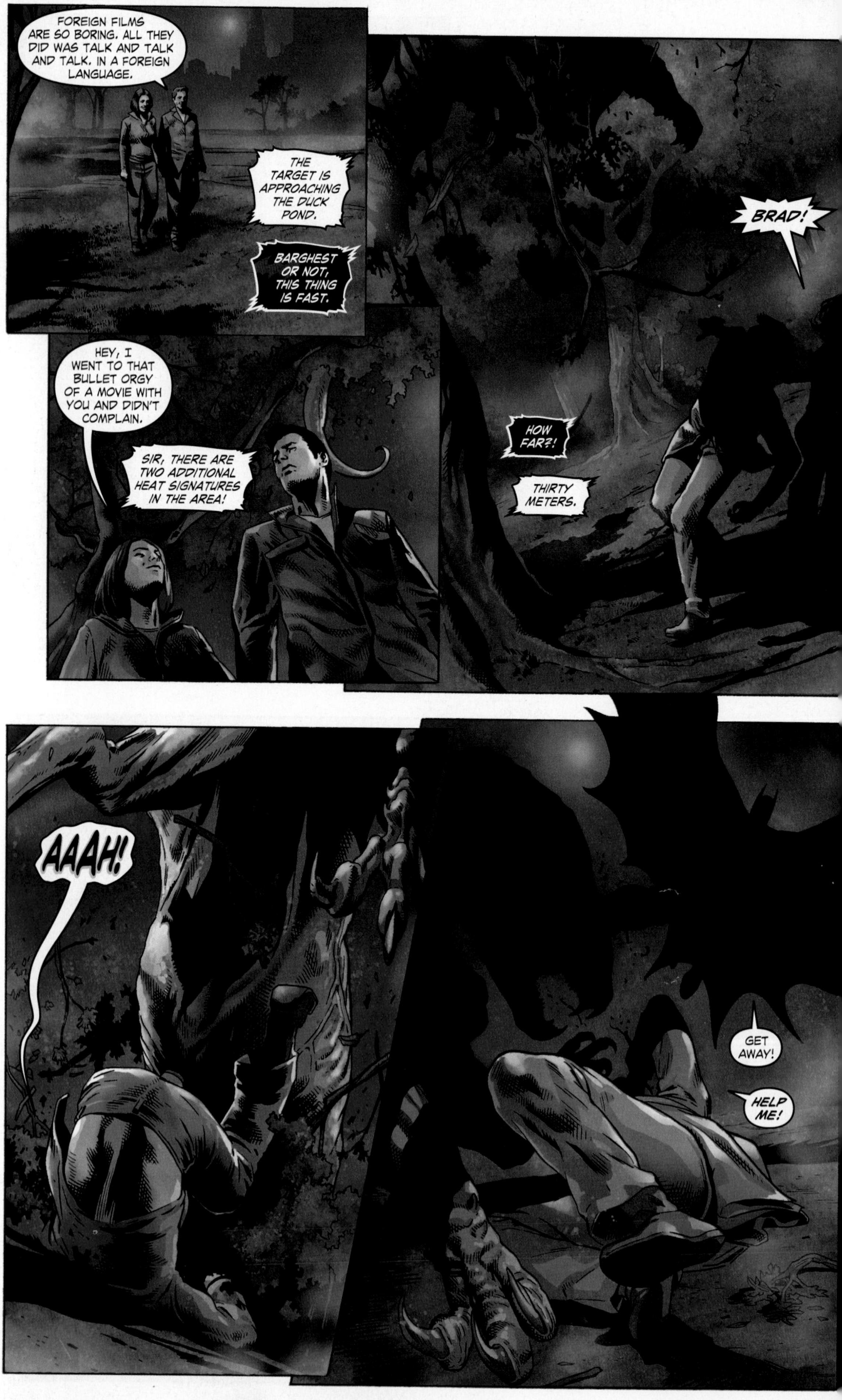
FOREIGN FILMS ARE SO BORING. ALL THEY DID WAS TALK AND TALK AND TALK. IN A FOREIGN LANGUAGE.
THE TARGET IS APPROACHING THE DUCK POND.
BARGHEST OR NOT, THIS THING IS FAST.
BRAD!
HEY, I WENT TO THAT BULLET ORGY OF A MOVIE WITH YOU AND DIDN'T COMPLAIN.
SIR, THERE ARE TWO ADDITIONAL HEAT SIGNATURES IN THE AREA!
HOW FAR?!
THIRTY METERS.
AAAH!
GET AWAY!
HELP ME!

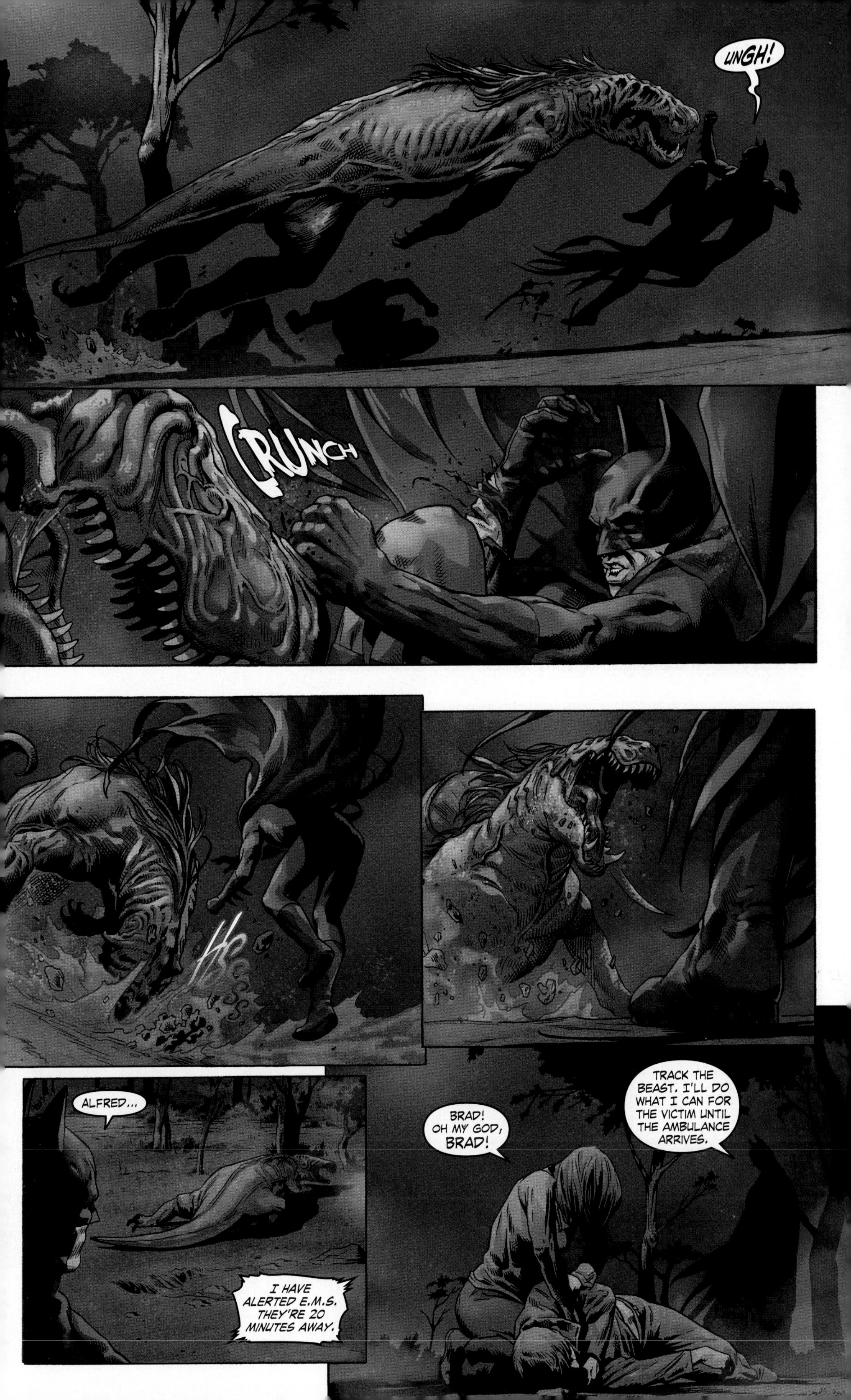
UNGH!
CRUNCH
HSSSSS
ALFRED...
I HAVE ALERTED E.M.S. THEY'RE 20 MINUTES AWAY.
BRAD! OH MY GOD, BRAD!
TRACK THE BEAST. I'LL DO WHAT I CAN FOR THE VICTIM UNTIL THE AMBULANCE ARRIVES.

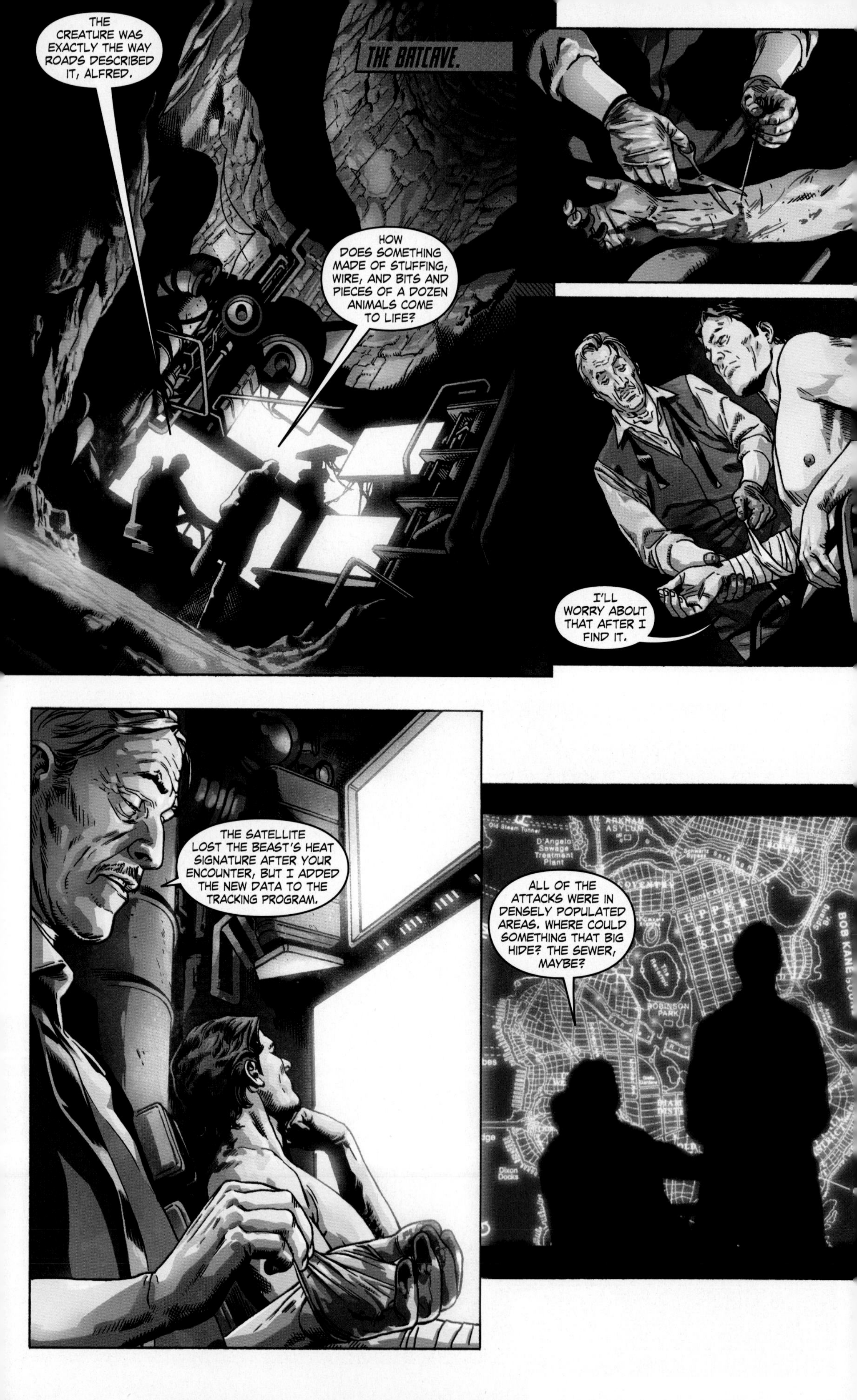
THE BATCAVE.
THE CREATURE WAS EXACTLY THE WAY ROADS DESCRIBED IT, ALFRED.
HOW DOES SOMETHING MADE OF STUFFING, WIRE, AND BITS AND PIECES OF A DOZEN ANIMALS COME TO LIFE?
I'LL WORRY ABOUT THAT AFTER I FIND IT.
THE SATELLITE LOST THE BEAST'S HEAT SIGNATURE AFTER YOUR ENCOUNTER, BUT I ADDED THE NEW DATA TO THE TRACKING PROGRAM.
ALL OF THE ATTACKS WERE IN DENSELY POPULATED AREAS. WHERE COULD SOMETHING THAT BIG HIDE? THE SEWER, MAYBE?
ARKHAM ASYLUM
Old Steam Tunnel
D'Angelo Sewage Treatment Plant
ROBINSON PARK
Dixon Docks

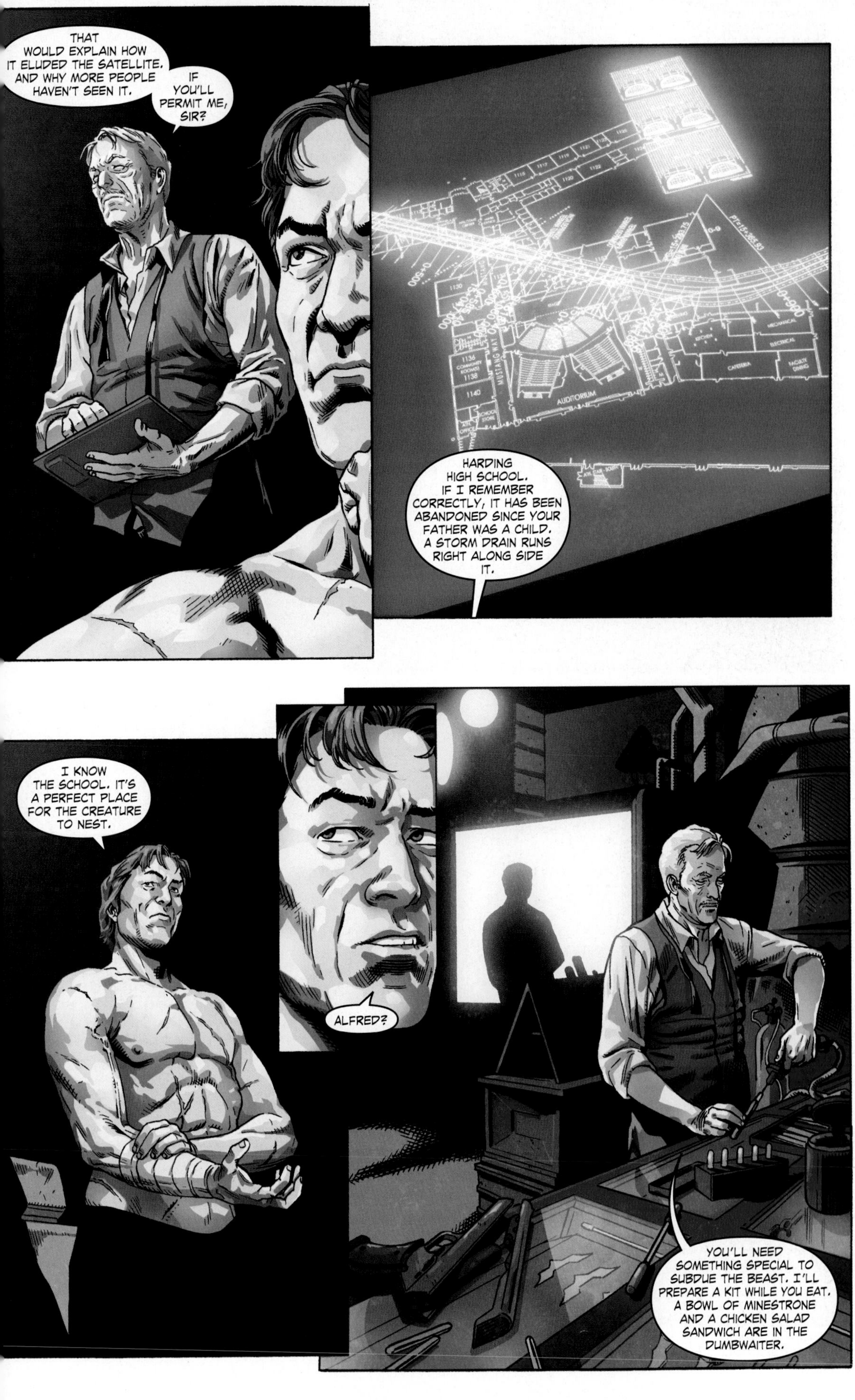
THAT WOULD EXPLAIN HOW IT ELUDED THE SATELLITE. AND WHY MORE PEOPLE HAVEN'T SEEN IT.
IF YOU'LL PERMIT ME, SIR?
MUSTANG WAY
AUDITORIUM
HARDING HIGH SCHOOL. IF I REMEMBER CORRECTLY, IT HAS BEEN ABANDONED SINCE YOUR FATHER WAS A CHILD. A STORM DRAIN RUNS RIGHT ALONG SIDE IT.
I KNOW THE SCHOOL. IT'S A PERFECT PLACE FOR THE CREATURE TO NEST.
ALFRED?
YOU'LL NEED SOMETHING SPECIAL TO SUBDUE THE BEAST. I'LL PREPARE A KIT WHILE YOU EAT. A BOWL OF MINESTRONE AND A CHICKEN SALAD SANDWICH ARE IN THE DUMBWAITER.

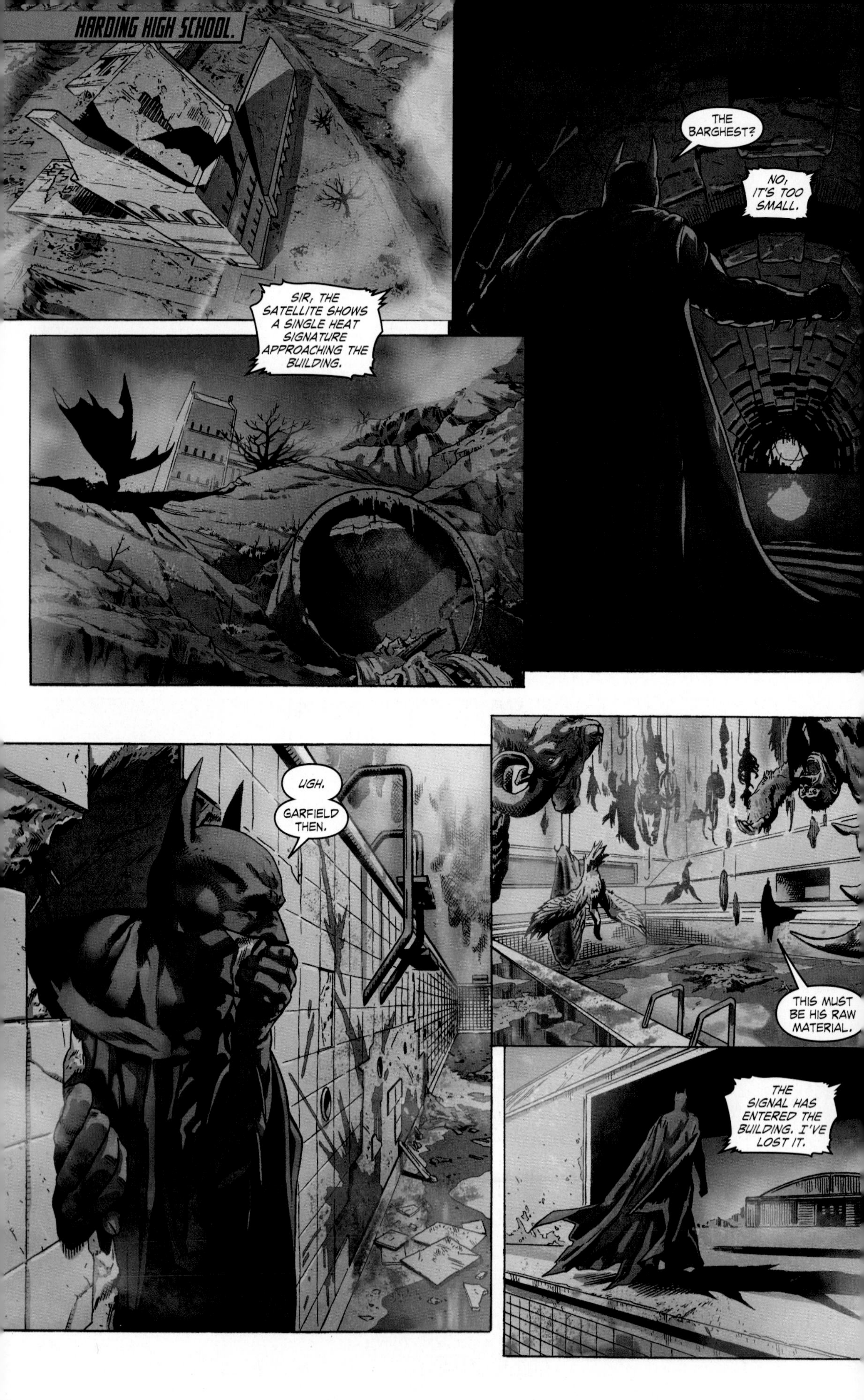
HARDING HIGH SCHOOL.
THE BARGHEST?
NO, IT'S TOO SMALL.
SIR, THE SATELLITE SHOWS A SINGLE HEAT SIGNATURE APPROACHING THE BUILDING.
UGH.
GARFIELD THEN.
THIS MUST BE HIS RAW MATERIAL.
THE SIGNAL HAS ENTERED THE BUILDING. I'VE LOST IT.

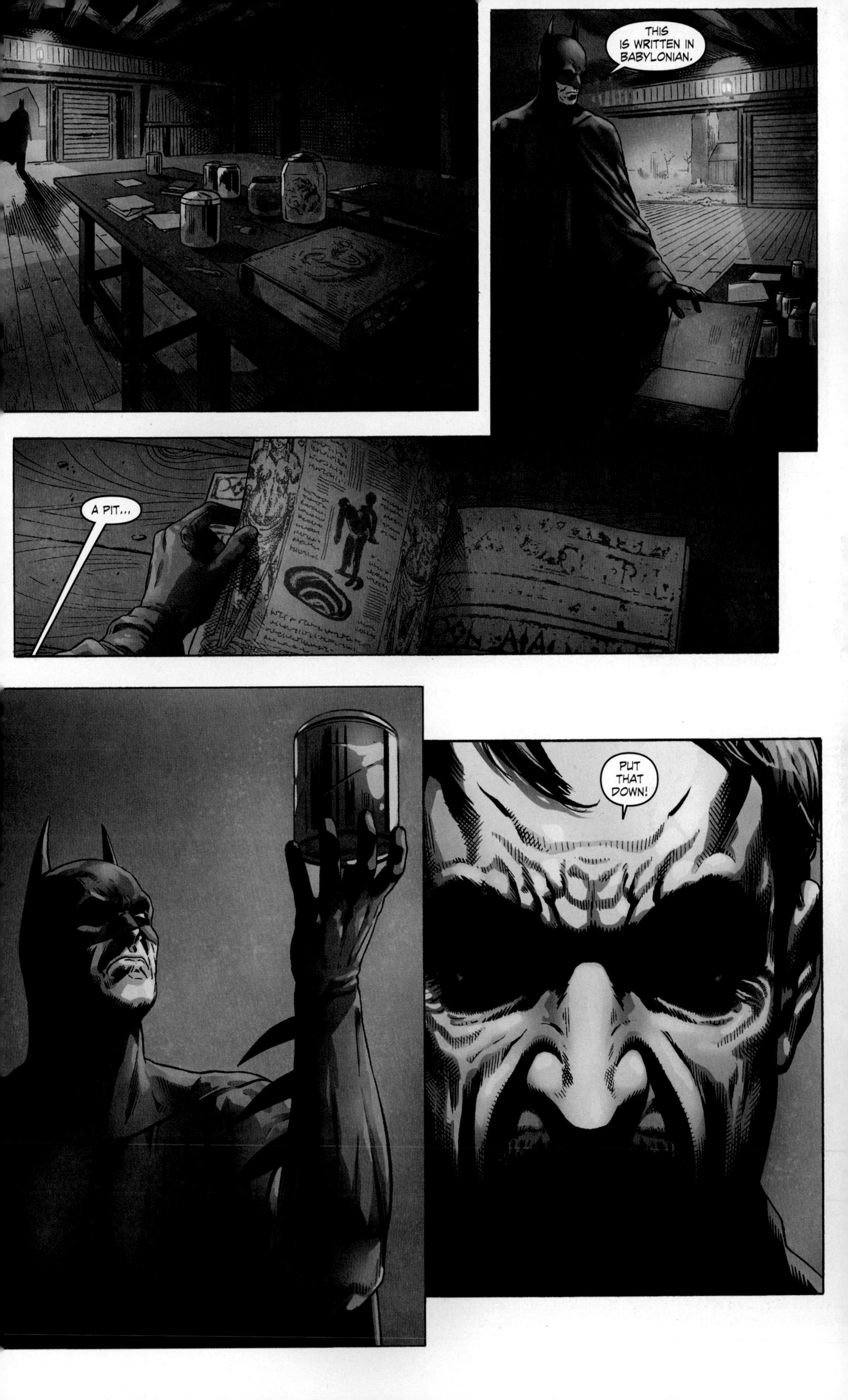
THIS IS WRITTEN IN BABYLONIAN.
A PIT...
PUT THAT DOWN!

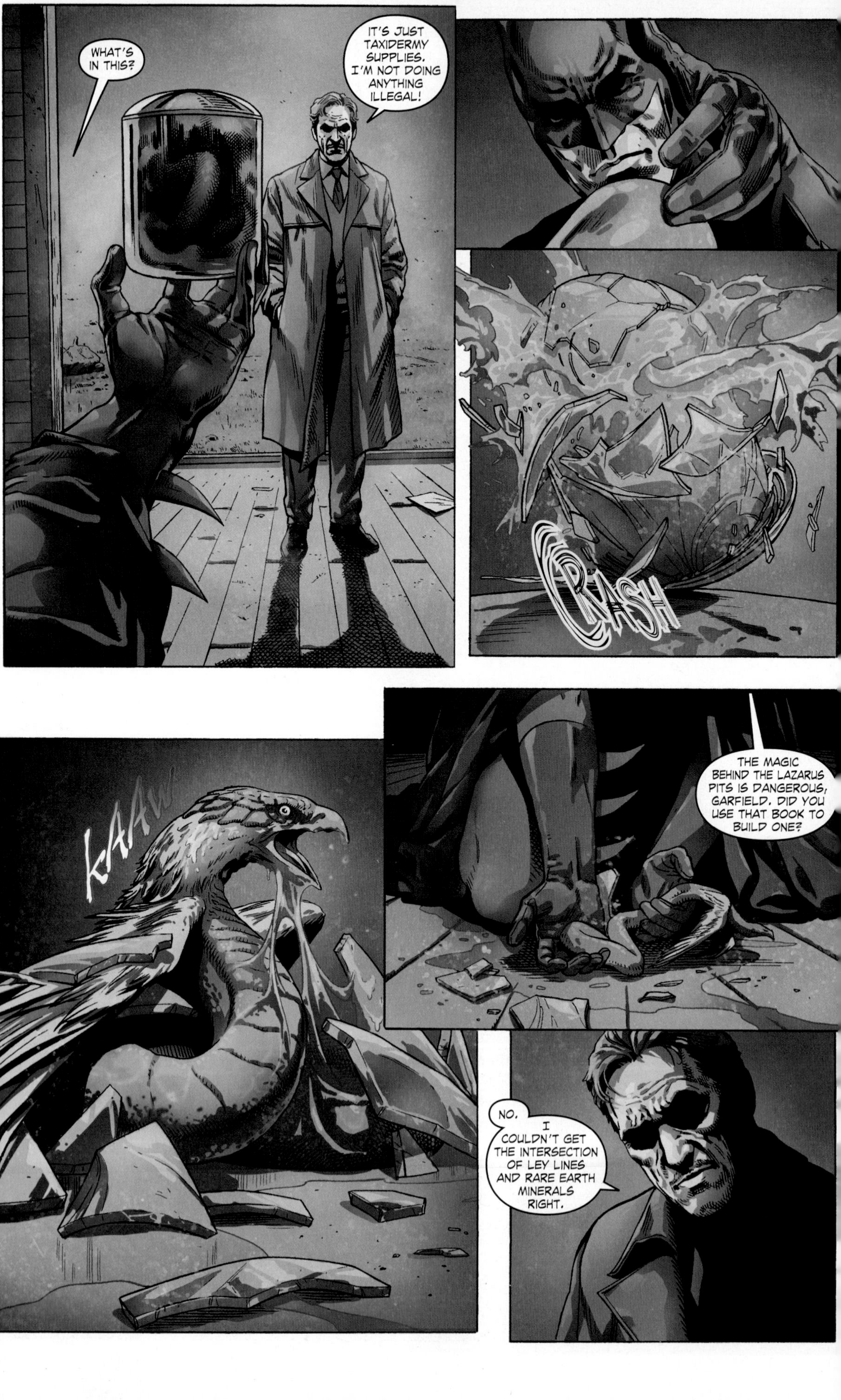
WHAT'S IN THIS?
IT'S JUST TAXIDERMY SUPPLIES. I'M NOT DOING ANYTHING ILLEGAL!
CRASH
KAAW
THE MAGIC BEHIND THE LAZARUS PITS IS DANGEROUS, GARFIELD. DID YOU USE THAT BOOK TO BUILD ONE?
NO.
I COULDN'T GET THE INTERSECTION OF LEY LINES AND RARE EARTH MINERALS RIGHT.

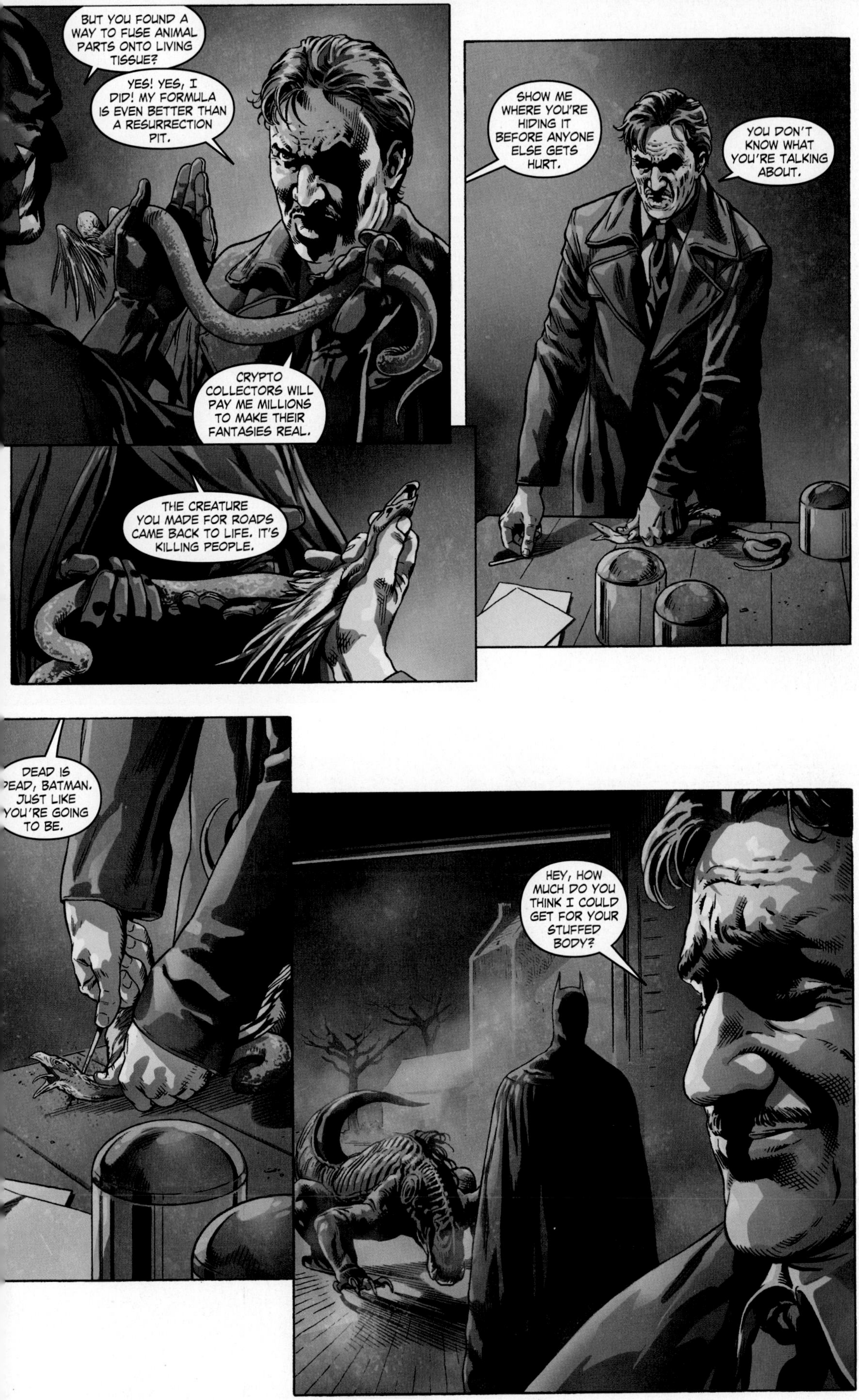
BUT YOU FOUND A WAY TO FUSE ANIMAL PARTS ONTO LIVING TISSUE?
YES! YES, I DID! MY FORMULA IS EVEN BETTER THAN A RESURRECTION PIT.
CRYPTO COLLECTORS WILL PAY ME MILLIONS TO MAKE THEIR FANTASIES REAL.
SHOW ME WHERE YOU'RE HIDING IT BEFORE ANYONE ELSE GETS HURT.
YOU DON'T KNOW WHAT YOU'RE TALKING ABOUT.
THE CREATURE YOU MADE FOR ROADS CAME BACK TO LIFE. IT'S KILLING PEOPLE.
DEAD IS DEAD, BATMAN. JUST LIKE YOU'RE GOING TO BE.
HEY, HOW MUCH DO YOU THINK I COULD GET FOR YOUR STUFFED BODY?

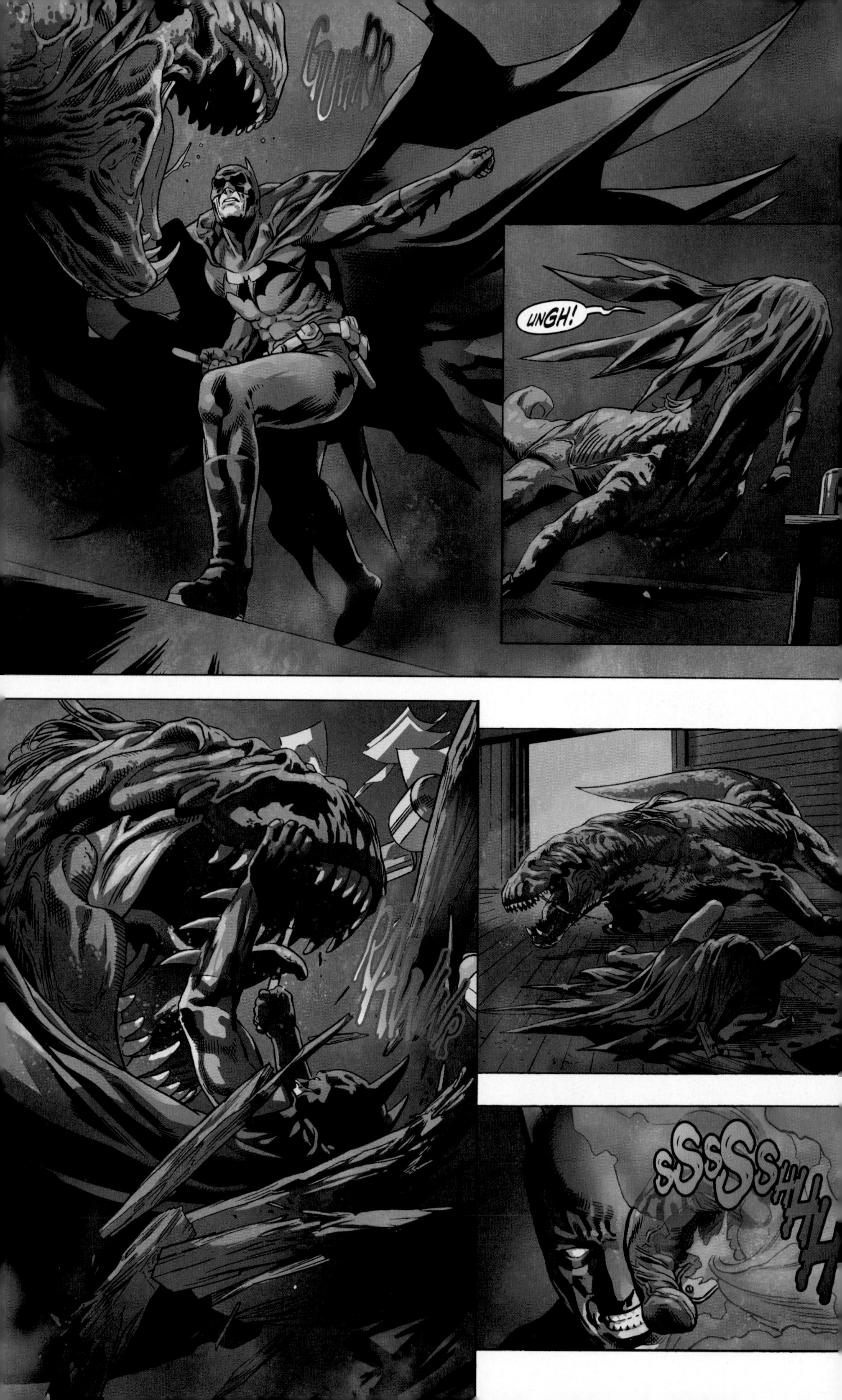

UNGH!
sSSSSHHHH

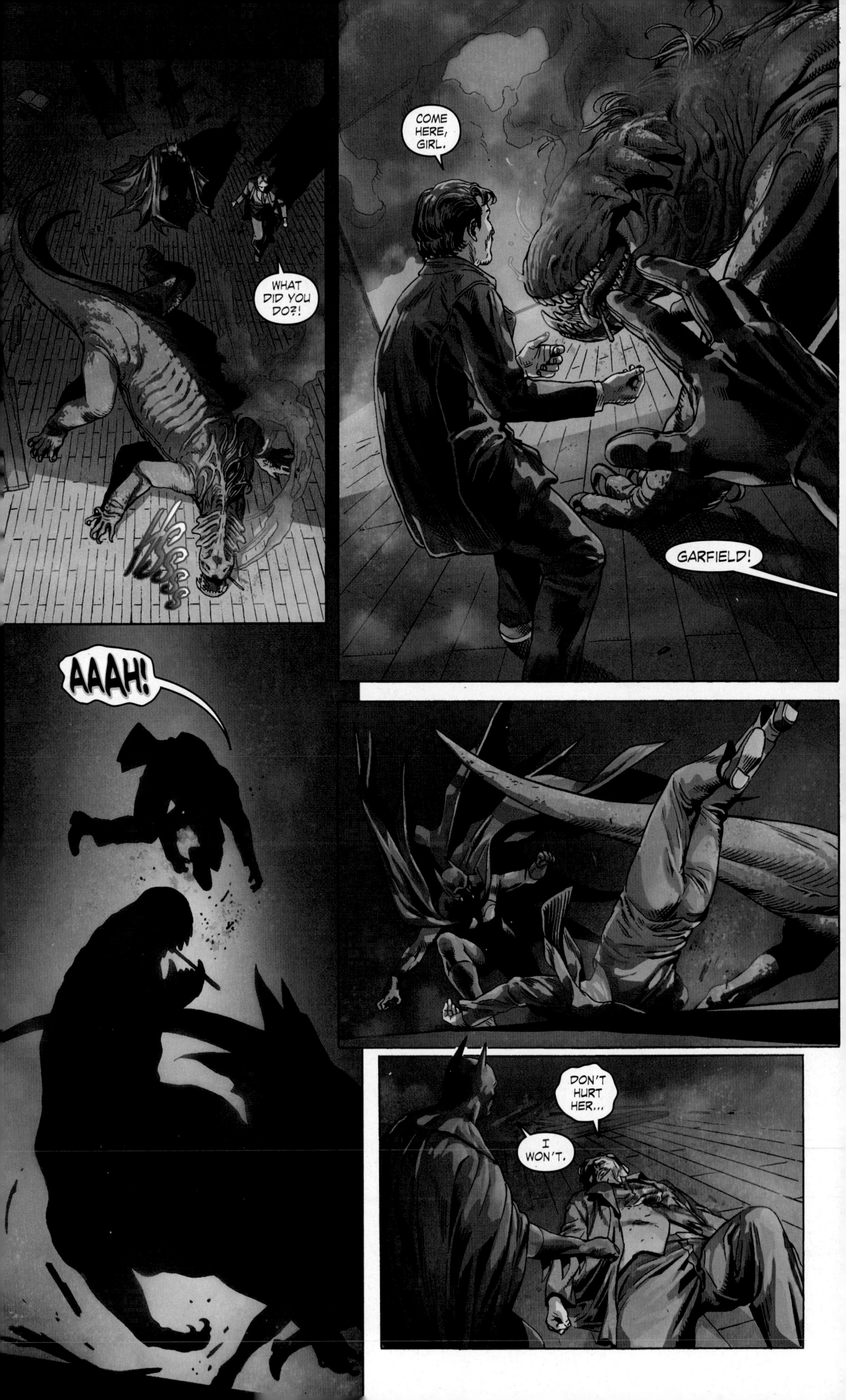
WHAT DID YOU DO?!
COME HERE, GIRL.
GARFIELD!
AAAH!
DON'T HURT HER...
I WON'T.

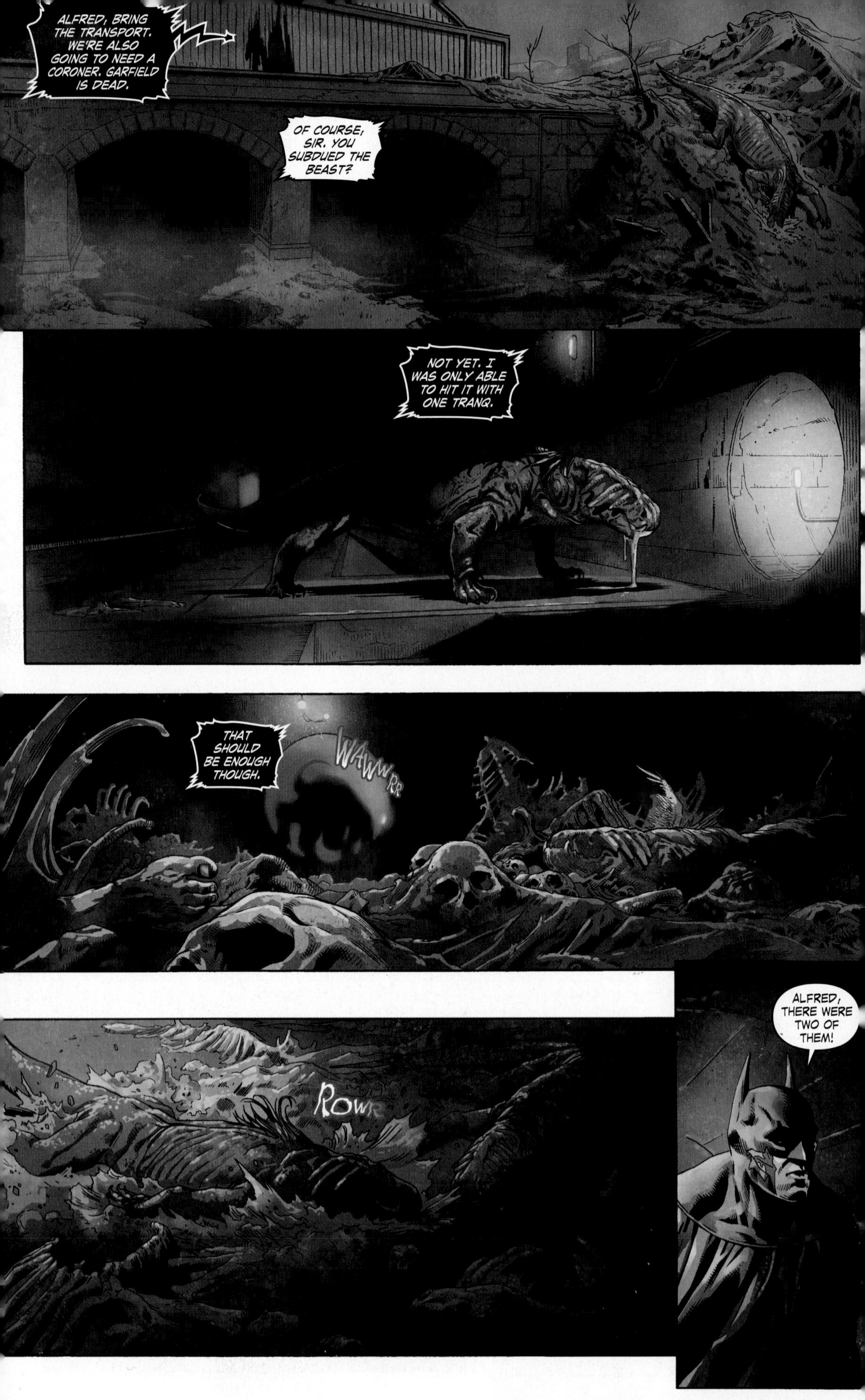

ALFRED, BRING THE TRANSPORT. WE'RE ALSO GOING TO NEED A CORONER. GARFIELD IS DEAD.
OF COURSE, SIR. YOU SUBDUED THE BEAST?
NOT YET. I WAS ONLY ABLE TO HIT IT WITH ONE TRANQ.
THAT SHOULD BE ENOUGH THOUGH.
WAWWRR
ROWR
ALFRED, THERE WERE TWO OF THEM!

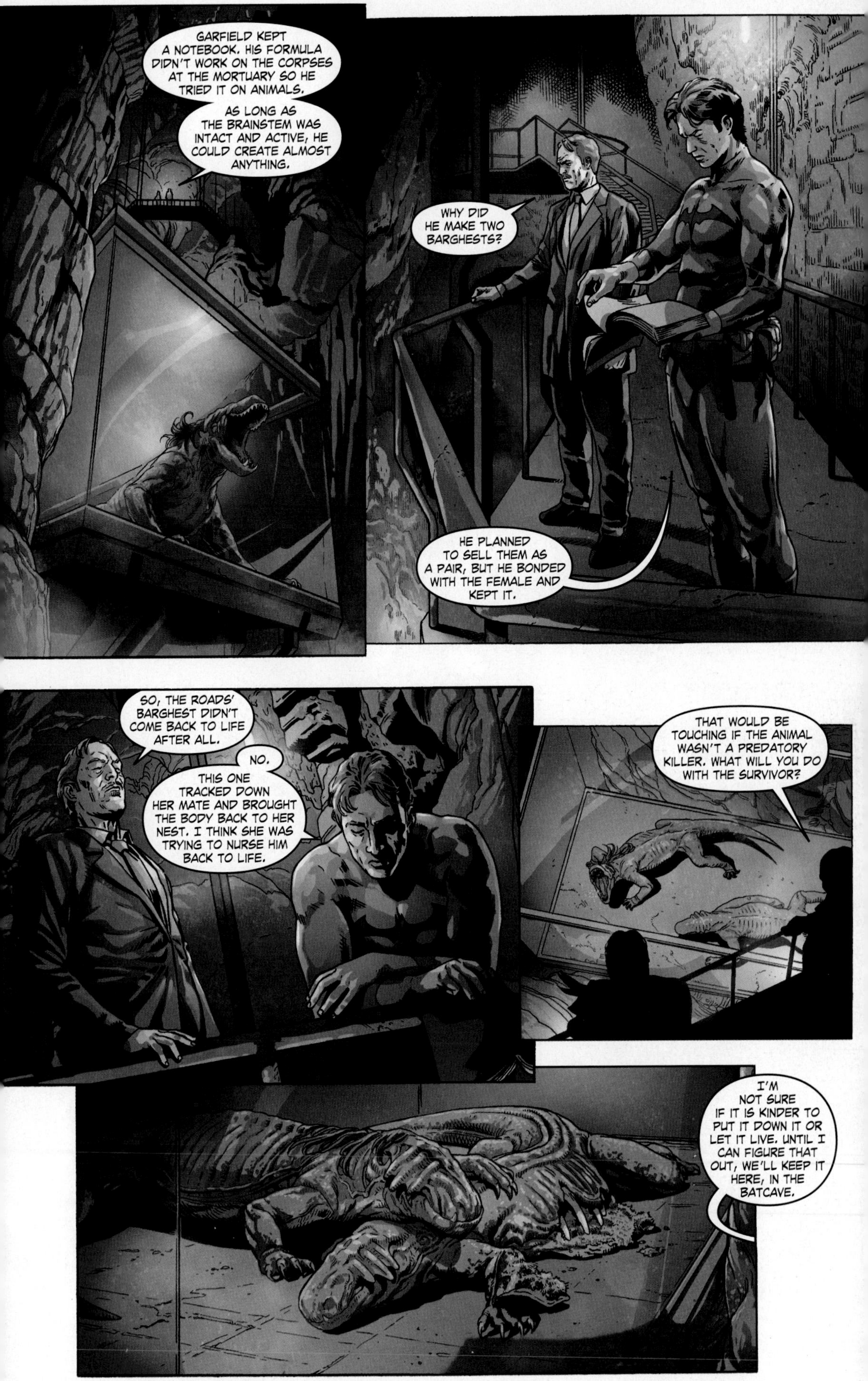
GARFIELD KEPT A NOTEBOOK. HIS FORMULA DIDN'T WORK ON THE CORPSES AT THE MORTUARY SO HE TRIED IT ON ANIMALS.
AS LONG AS THE BRAINSTEM WAS INTACT AND ACTIVE, HE COULD CREATE ALMOST ANYTHING.
WHY DID HE MAKE TWO BARGHESTS?
HE PLANNED TO SELL THEM AS A PAIR, BUT HE BONDED WITH THE FEMALE AND KEPT IT.
SO, THE ROADS' BARGHEST DIDN'T COME BACK TO LIFE AFTER ALL.
NO.
THIS ONE TRACKED DOWN HER MATE AND BROUGHT THE BODY BACK TO HER NEST. I THINK SHE WAS TRYING TO NURSE HIM BACK TO LIFE.
THAT WOULD BE TOUCHING IF THE ANIMAL WASN'T A PREDATORY KILLER. WHAT WILL YOU DO WITH THE SURVIVOR?
I'M NOT SURE IF IT IS KINDER TO PUT IT DOWN IT OR LET IT LIVE. UNTIL I CAN FIGURE THAT OUT, WE'LL KEEP IT HERE, IN THE BATCAVE.

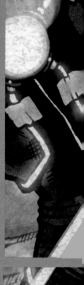

DREAMING HE IS A BUTTERFLY

CHRISTOS GAGE
Writer

JHEREMY RAAPACK
Artist

CARRIE STRACHAN
Colorist

SAIDA TEMOFONTE
Letterer

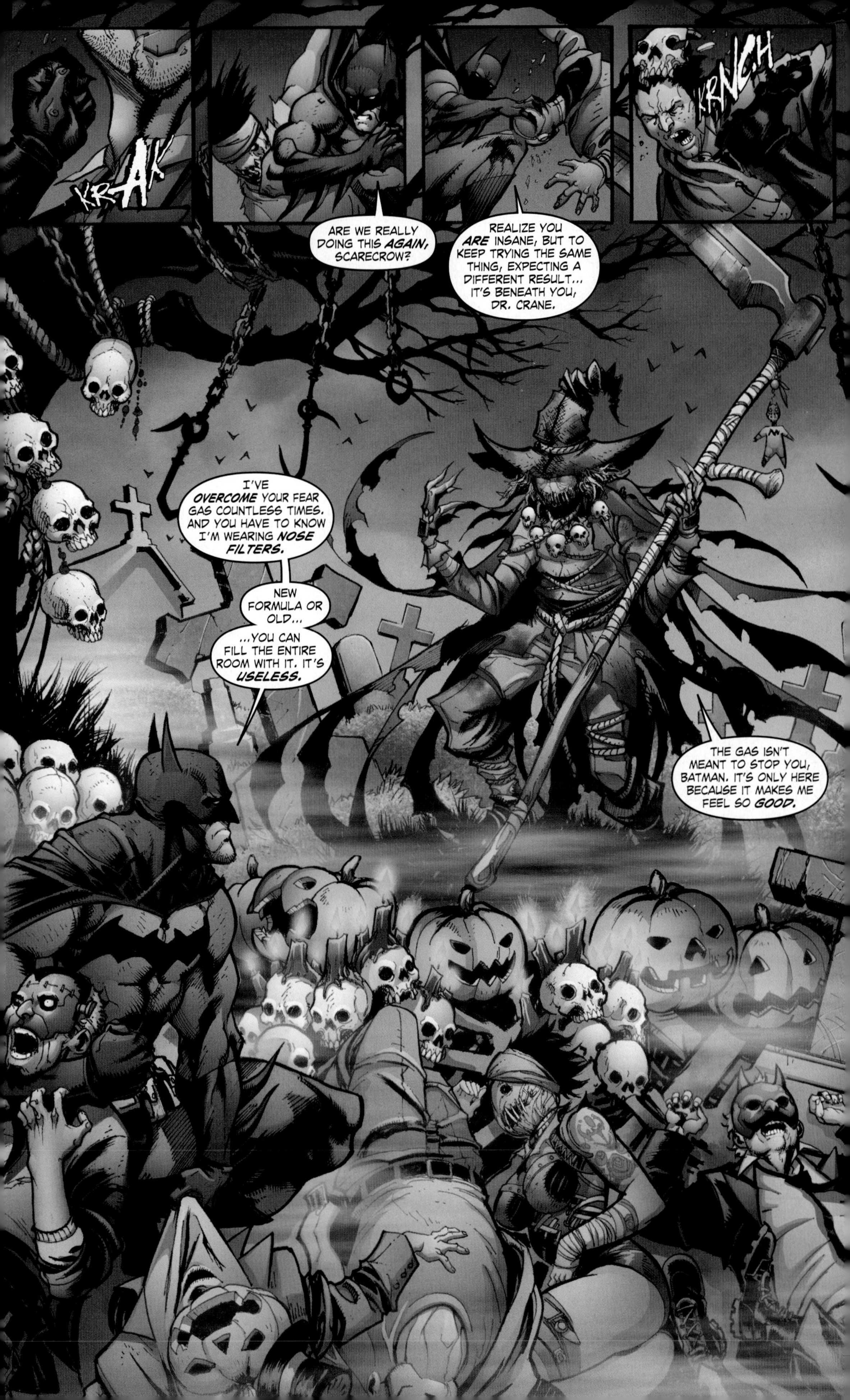
KR-AK
KRNCH
ARE WE REALLY DOING THIS AGAIN, SCARECROW?
REALIZE YOU ARE INSANE, BUT TO KEEP TRYING THE SAME THING, EXPECTING A DIFFERENT RESULT... IT'S BENEATH YOU, DR. CRANE.
I'VE OVERCOME YOUR FEAR GAS COUNTLESS TIMES. AND YOU HAVE TO KNOW I'M WEARING NOSE FILTERS.
NEW FORMULA OR OLD...
...YOU CAN FILL THE ENTIRE ROOM WITH IT. IT'S USELESS.
THE GAS ISN'T MEANT TO STOP YOU, BATMAN. IT'S ONLY HERE BECAUSE IT MAKES ME FEEL SO GOOD.

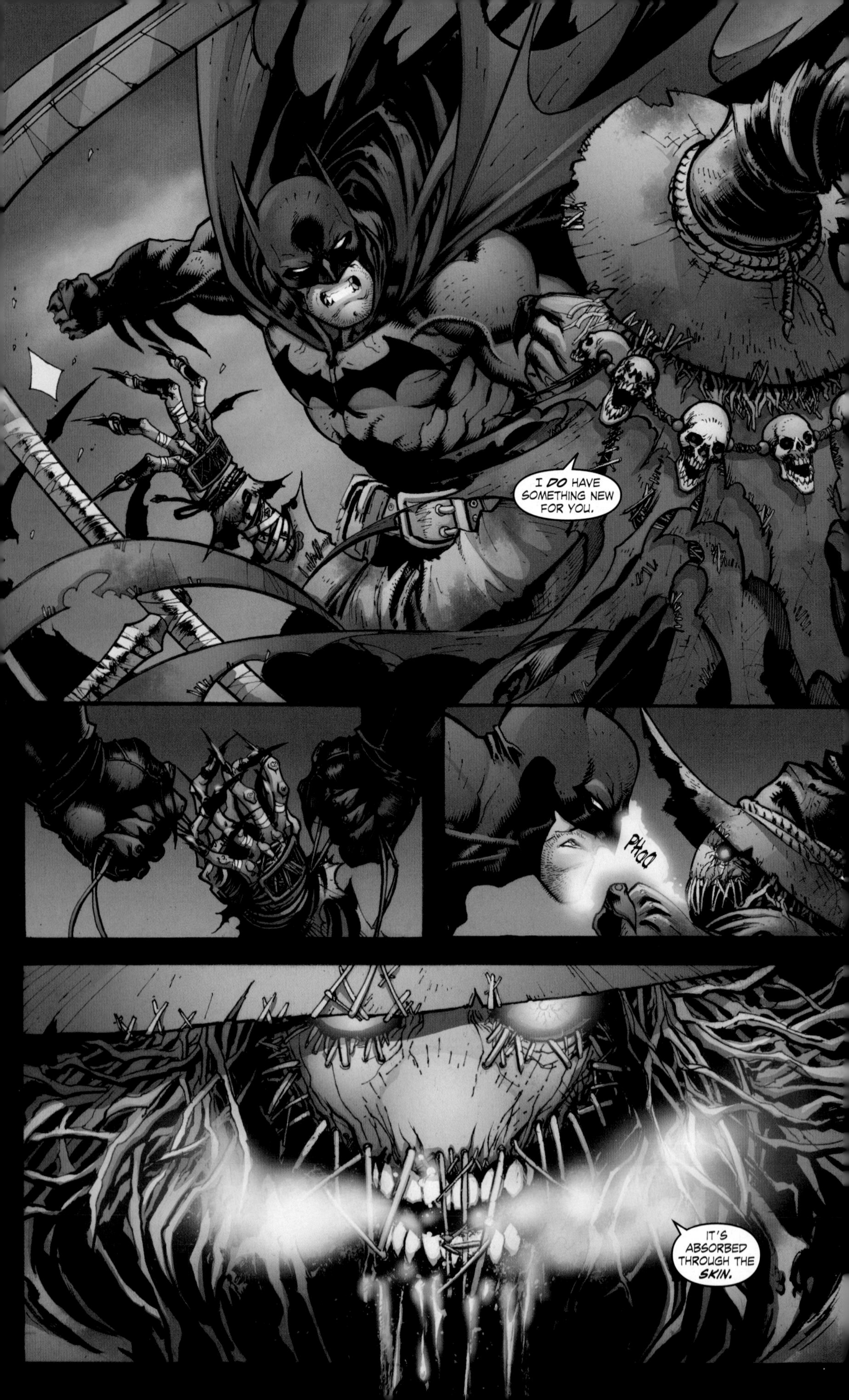
I DO HAVE SOMETHING NEW FOR YOU.
PHOO
IT'S ABSORBED THROUGH THE SKIN.

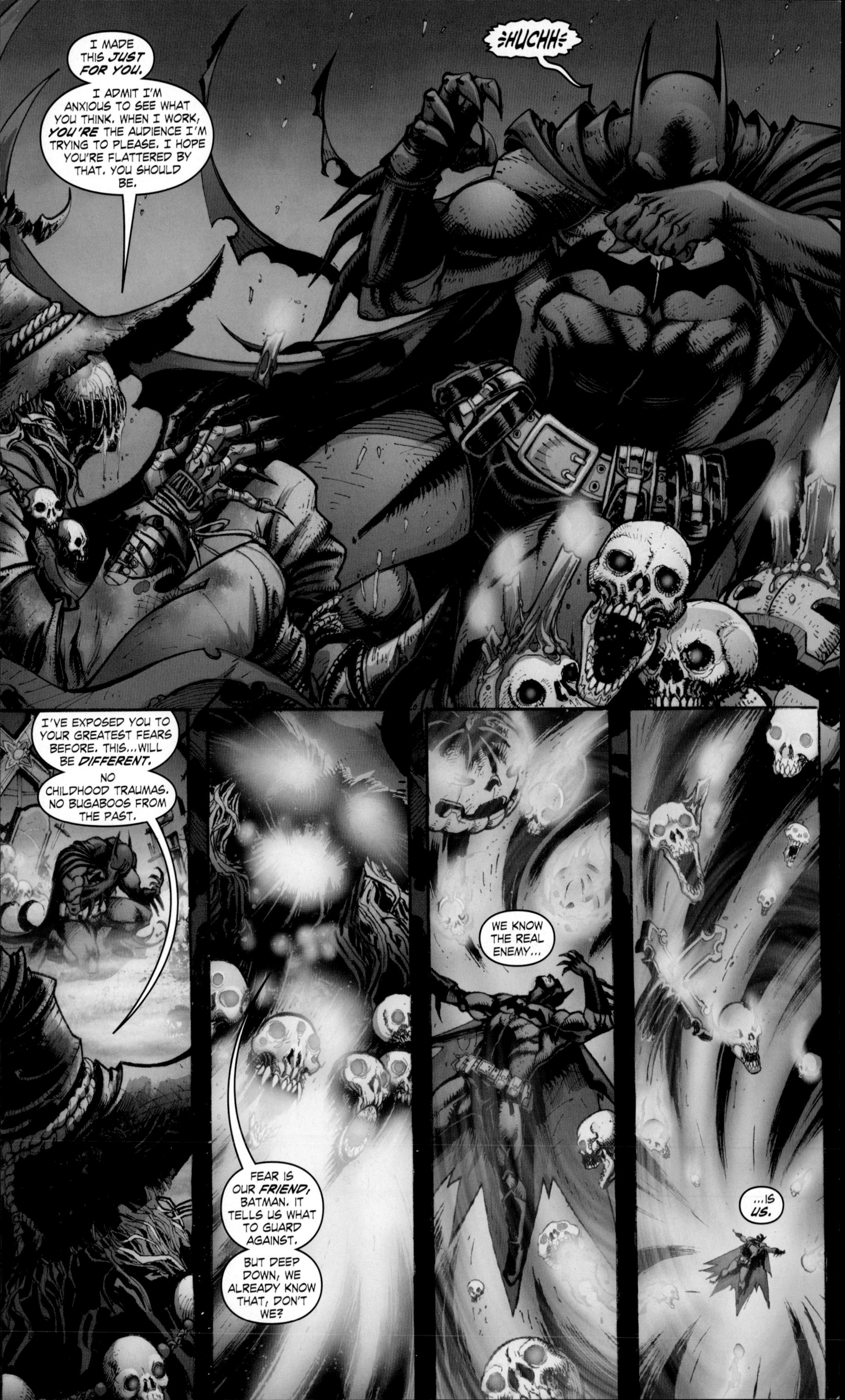

I MADE THIS JUST FOR YOU.
I ADMIT I'M ANXIOUS TO SEE WHAT YOU THINK. WHEN I WORK, YOU'RE THE AUDIENCE I'M TRYING TO PLEASE. I HOPE YOU'RE FLATTERED BY THAT. YOU SHOULD BE.
HUCHH
I'VE EXPOSED YOU TO YOUR GREATEST FEARS BEFORE. THIS...WILL BE DIFFERENT.
NO CHILDHOOD TRAUMAS. NO BUGABOOS FROM THE PAST.
FEAR IS OUR FRIEND, BATMAN. IT TELLS US WHAT TO GUARD AGAINST.
BUT DEEP DOWN, WE ALREADY KNOW THAT, DON'T WE?
WE KNOW THE REAL ENEMY...
...IS US.

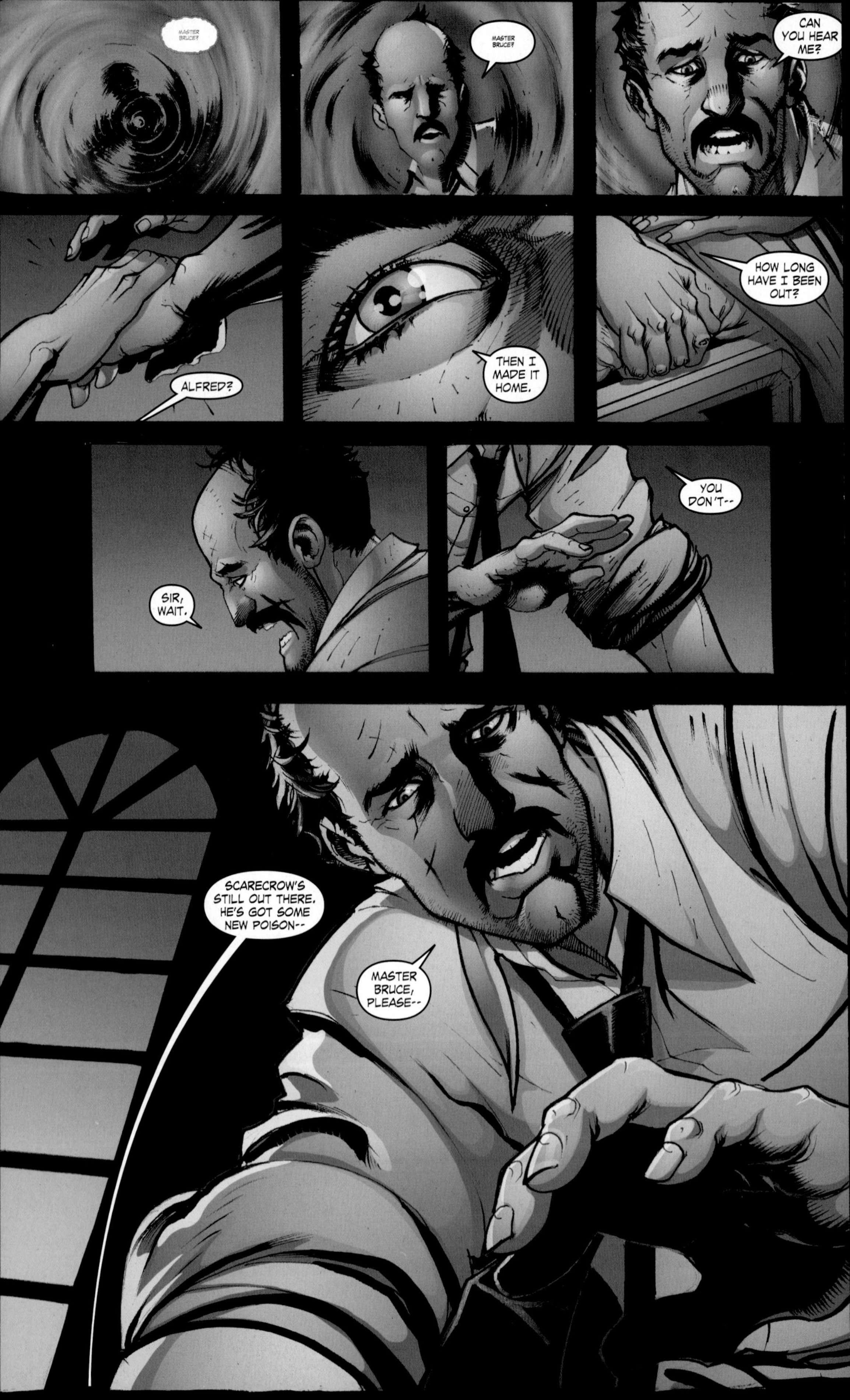
MASTER BRUCE?
MASTER BRUCE?
CAN YOU HEAR ME?
ALFRED?
THEN I MADE IT HOME.
HOW LONG HAVE I BEEN OUT?
SIR, WAIT.
YOU DON'T--
SCARECROW'S STILL OUT THERE. HE'S GOT SOME NEW POISON--
MASTER BRUCE, PLEASE--

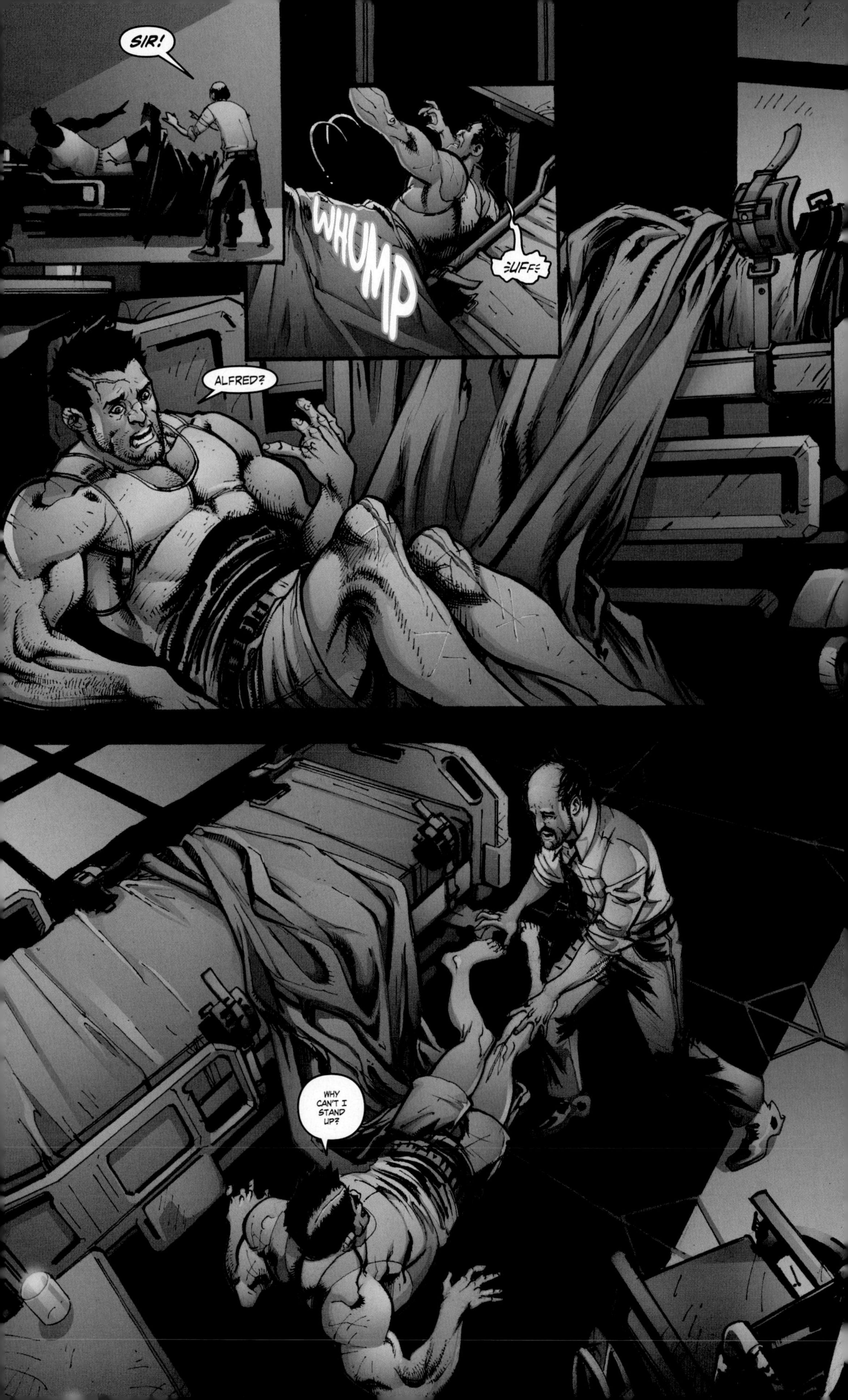
SIR!
WHUMP
UFF
ALFRED?
WHY CAN'T I STAND UP?

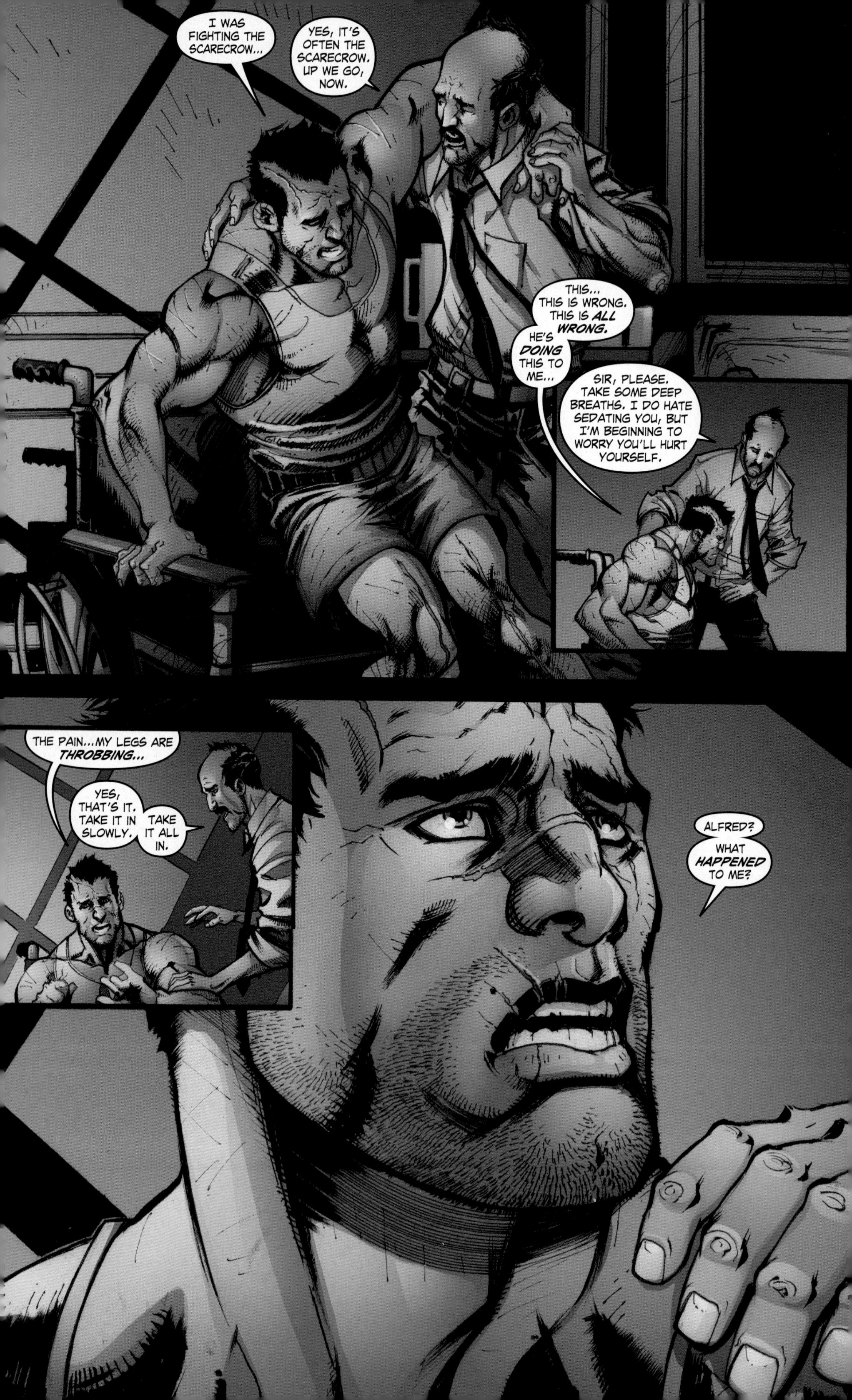
I WAS FIGHTING THE SCARECROW...
YES, IT'S OFTEN THE SCARECROW. UP WE GO, NOW.
THIS... THIS IS WRONG. THIS IS **ALL WRONG.**
HE'S ***DOING*** THIS TO ME...
SIR, PLEASE. TAKE SOME DEEP BREATHS. I DO HATE SEDATING YOU, BUT I'M BEGINNING TO WORRY YOU'LL HURT YOURSELF.
THE PAIN...MY LEGS ARE ***THROBBING...***
YES, THAT'S IT. TAKE IT IN SLOWLY.
TAKE IT ALL IN.
ALFRED? WHAT ***HAPPENED*** TO ME?

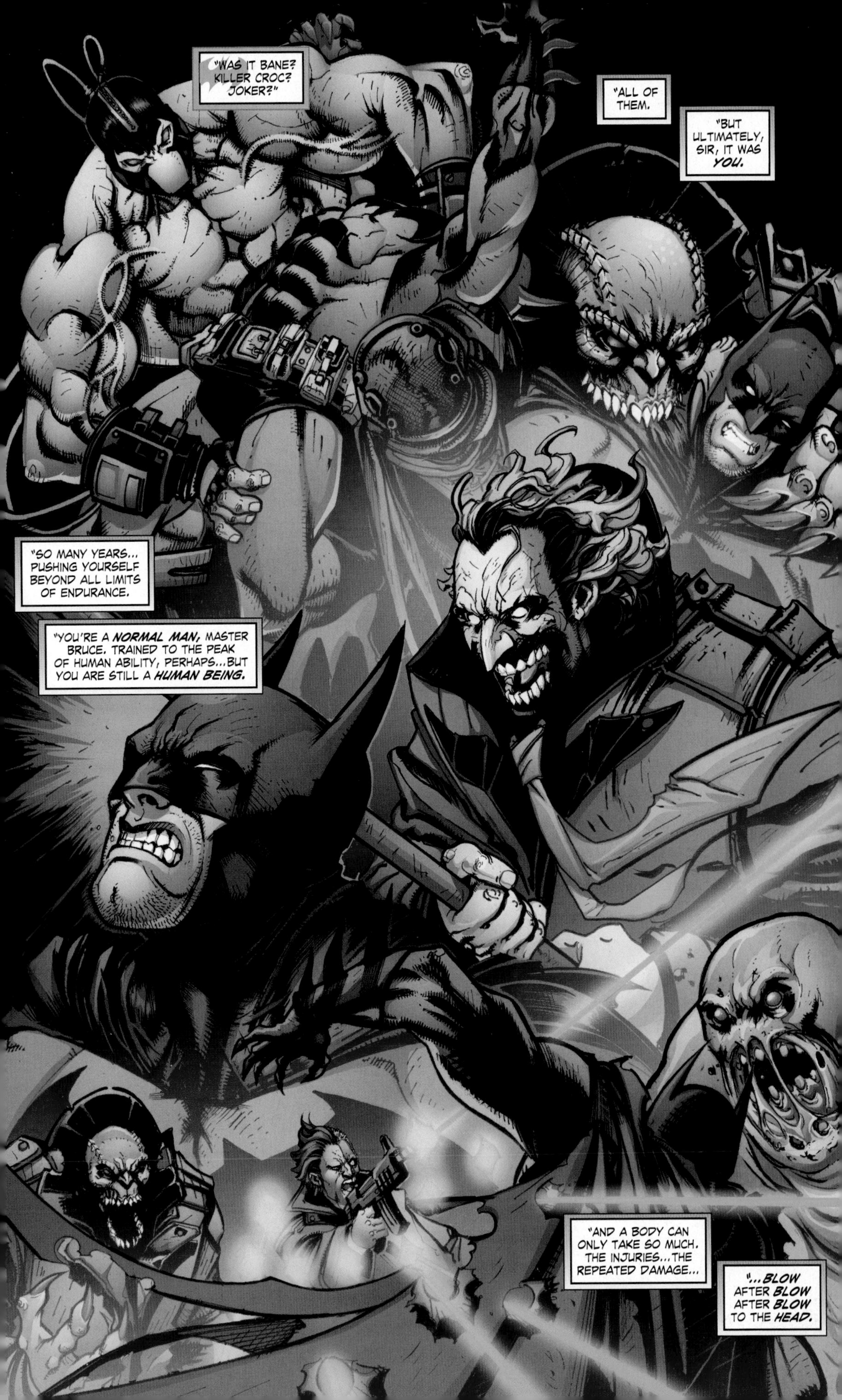
"WAS IT BANE? KILLER CROC? JOKER?"
"ALL OF THEM.
"BUT ULTIMATELY, SIR, IT WAS *YOU*.
"SO MANY YEARS... PUSHING YOURSELF BEYOND ALL LIMITS OF ENDURANCE.
"YOU'RE A *NORMAL MAN*, MASTER BRUCE. TRAINED TO THE PEAK OF HUMAN ABILITY, PERHAPS...BUT YOU ARE STILL A *HUMAN BEING*.
"AND A BODY CAN ONLY TAKE SO MUCH. THE INJURIES...THE REPEATED DAMAGE...
"...*BLOW* AFTER *BLOW* AFTER *BLOW* TO THE *HEAD*.

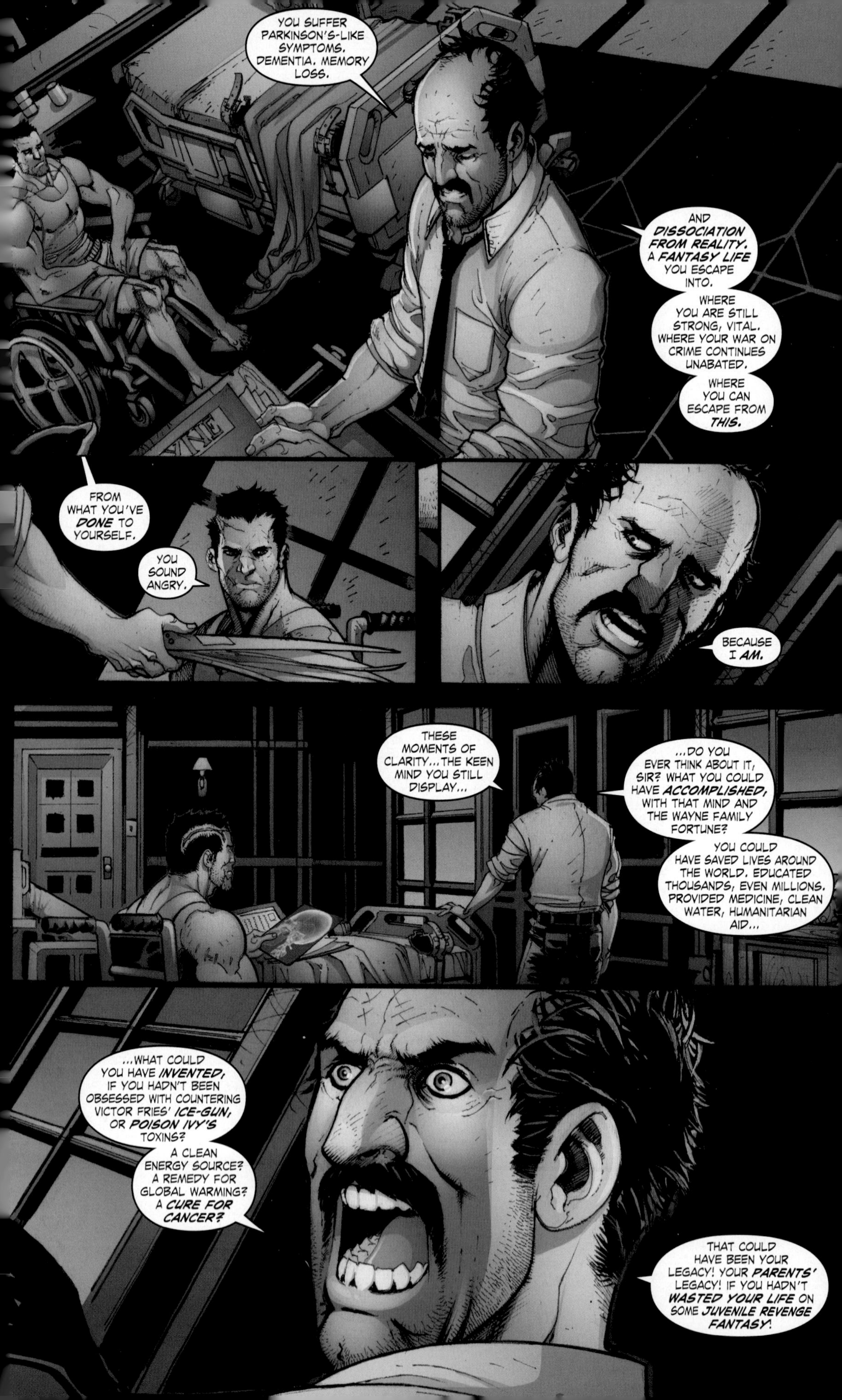

YOU SUFFER PARKINSON'S-LIKE SYMPTOMS. DEMENTIA. MEMORY LOSS.
AND DISSOCIATION FROM REALITY. A FANTASY LIFE YOU ESCAPE INTO.
WHERE YOU ARE STILL STRONG, VITAL. WHERE YOUR WAR ON CRIME CONTINUES UNABATED.
WHERE YOU CAN ESCAPE FROM THIS.
FROM WHAT YOU'VE DONE TO YOURSELF.
YOU SOUND ANGRY.
BECAUSE I AM.
THESE MOMENTS OF CLARITY...THE KEEN MIND YOU STILL DISPLAY...
...DO YOU EVER THINK ABOUT IT, SIR? WHAT YOU COULD HAVE ACCOMPLISHED, WITH THAT MIND AND THE WAYNE FAMILY FORTUNE?
YOU COULD HAVE SAVED LIVES AROUND THE WORLD. EDUCATED THOUSANDS, EVEN MILLIONS. PROVIDED MEDICINE, CLEAN WATER, HUMANITARIAN AID...
...WHAT COULD YOU HAVE INVENTED, IF YOU HADN'T BEEN OBSESSED WITH COUNTERING VICTOR FRIES' ICE-GUN, OR POISON IVY'S TOXINS?
A CLEAN ENERGY SOURCE? A REMEDY FOR GLOBAL WARMING? A CURE FOR CANCER?
THAT COULD HAVE BEEN YOUR LEGACY! YOUR PARENTS' LEGACY! IF YOU HADN'T WASTED YOUR LIFE ON SOME JUVENILE REVENGE FANTASY!

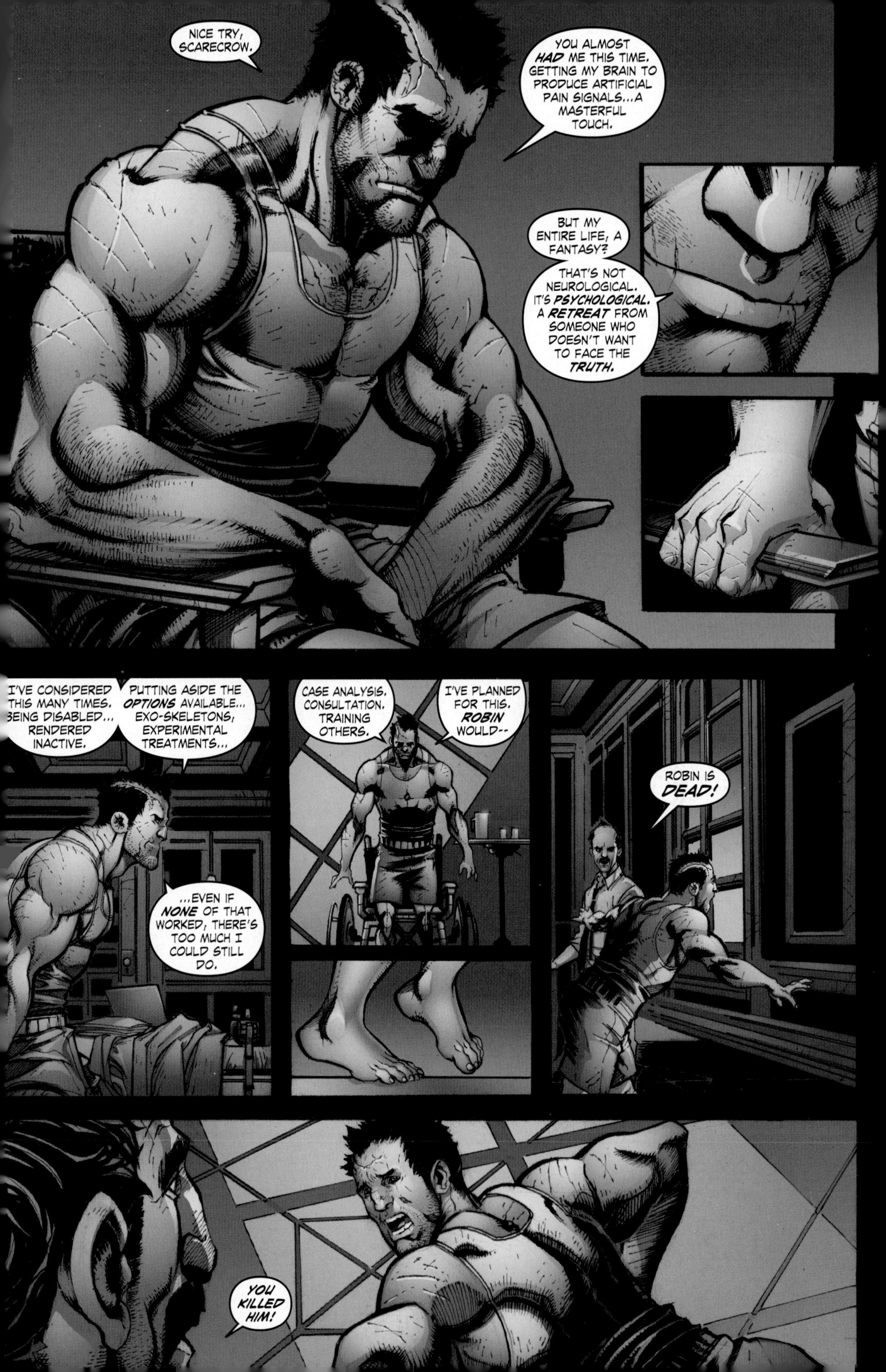
NICE TRY, SCARECROW.
YOU ALMOST HAD ME THIS TIME. GETTING MY BRAIN TO PRODUCE ARTIFICIAL PAIN SIGNALS...A MASTERFUL TOUCH.
BUT MY ENTIRE LIFE, A FANTASY?
THAT'S NOT NEUROLOGICAL. IT'S PSYCHOLOGICAL. A RETREAT FROM SOMEONE WHO DOESN'T WANT TO FACE THE TRUTH.
I'VE CONSIDERED THIS MANY TIMES. BEING DISABLED... RENDERED INACTIVE.
PUTTING ASIDE THE OPTIONS AVAILABLE... EXO-SKELETONS, EXPERIMENTAL TREATMENTS...
...EVEN IF NONE OF THAT WORKED, THERE'S TOO MUCH I COULD STILL DO.
CASE ANALYSIS. CONSULTATION. TRAINING OTHERS.
I'VE PLANNED FOR THIS. ROBIN WOULD--
ROBIN IS DEAD!
YOU KILLED HIM!

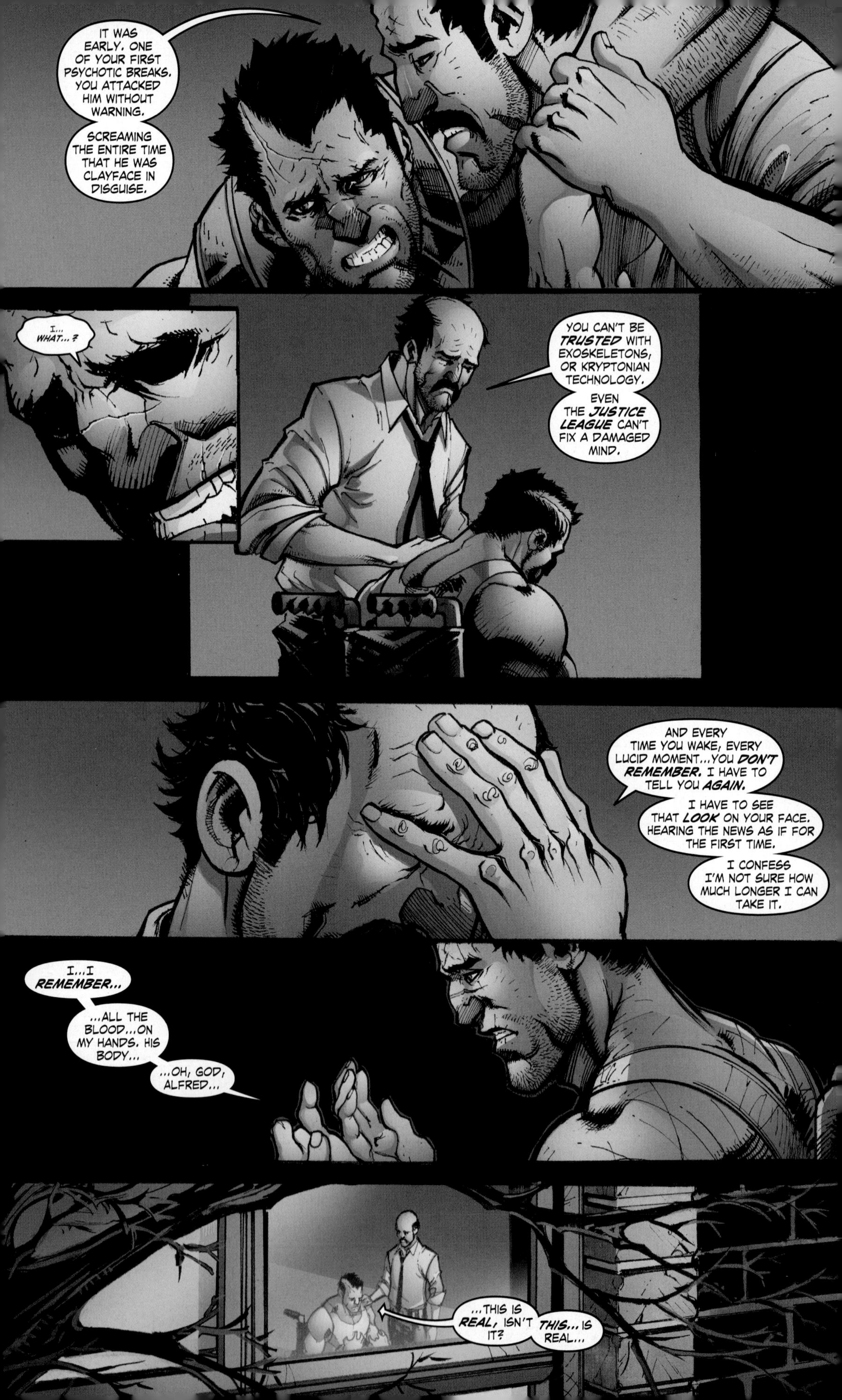

IT WAS EARLY. ONE OF YOUR FIRST PSYCHOTIC BREAKS. YOU ATTACKED HIM WITHOUT WARNING.
SCREAMING THE ENTIRE TIME THAT HE WAS CLAYFACE IN DISGUISE.
I... WHAT...?
YOU CAN'T BE TRUSTED WITH EXOSKELETONS, OR KRYPTONIAN TECHNOLOGY.
EVEN THE JUSTICE LEAGUE CAN'T FIX A DAMAGED MIND.
AND EVERY TIME YOU WAKE, EVERY LUCID MOMENT...YOU DON'T REMEMBER. I HAVE TO TELL YOU AGAIN.
I HAVE TO SEE THAT LOOK ON YOUR FACE. HEARING THE NEWS AS IF FOR THE FIRST TIME.
I CONFESS I'M NOT SURE HOW MUCH LONGER I CAN TAKE IT.
I...I REMEMBER...
...ALL THE BLOOD...ON MY HANDS. HIS BODY...
...OH, GOD, ALFRED...
...THIS IS REAL, ISN'T IT?
THIS... IS REAL...

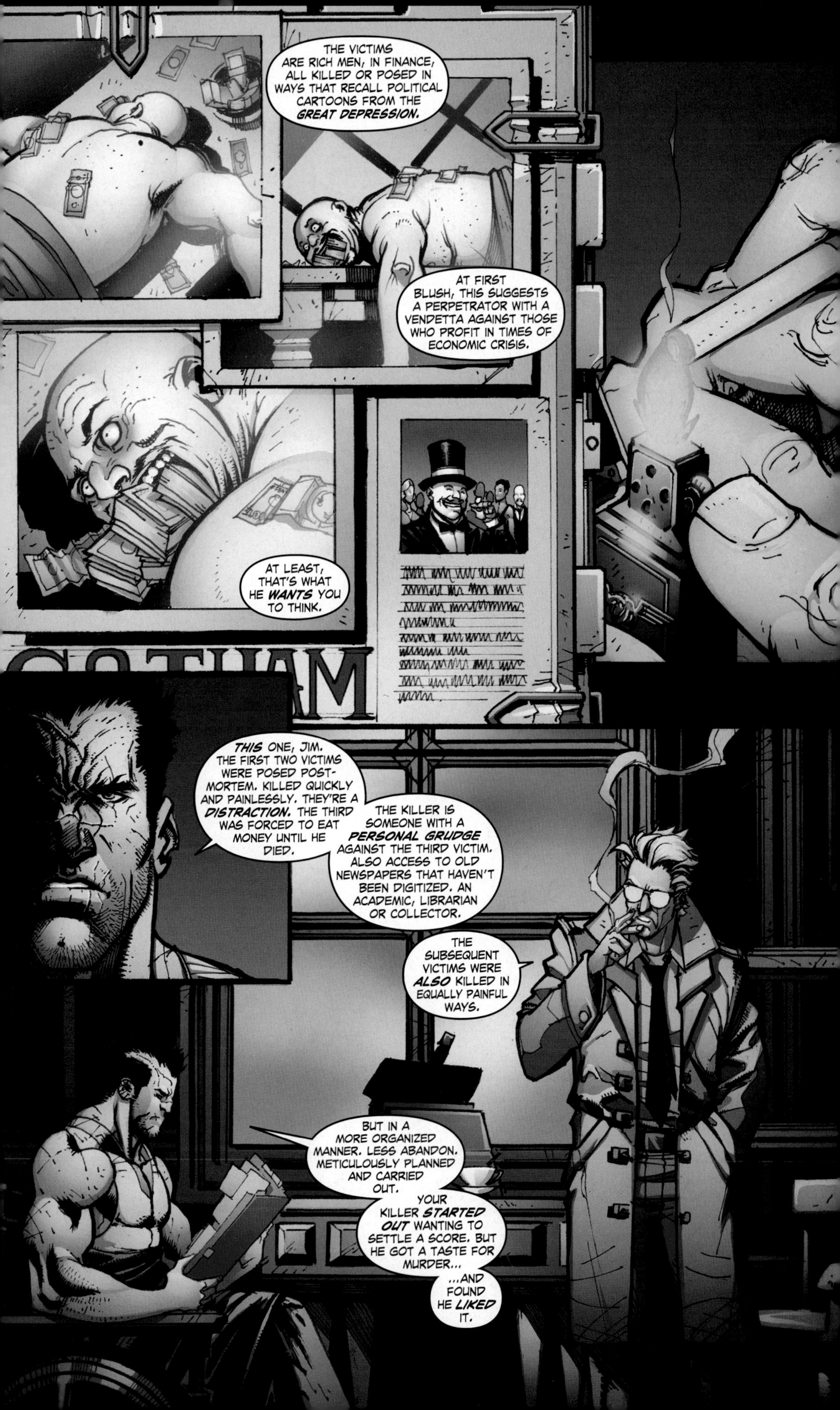
THE VICTIMS ARE RICH MEN, IN FINANCE, ALL KILLED OR POSED IN WAYS THAT RECALL POLITICAL CARTOONS FROM THE GREAT DEPRESSION.
AT FIRST BLUSH, THIS SUGGESTS A PERPETRATOR WITH A VENDETTA AGAINST THOSE WHO PROFIT IN TIMES OF ECONOMIC CRISIS.
AT LEAST, THAT'S WHAT HE WANTS YOU TO THINK.
GOTHAM
THIS ONE, JIM. THE FIRST TWO VICTIMS WERE POSED POST-MORTEM. KILLED QUICKLY AND PAINLESSLY. THEY'RE A DISTRACTION. THE THIRD WAS FORCED TO EAT MONEY UNTIL HE DIED.
THE KILLER IS SOMEONE WITH A PERSONAL GRUDGE AGAINST THE THIRD VICTIM. ALSO ACCESS TO OLD NEWSPAPERS THAT HAVEN'T BEEN DIGITIZED. AN ACADEMIC, LIBRARIAN OR COLLECTOR.
THE SUBSEQUENT VICTIMS WERE ALSO KILLED IN EQUALLY PAINFUL WAYS.
BUT IN A MORE ORGANIZED MANNER. LESS ABANDON. METICULOUSLY PLANNED AND CARRIED OUT.
YOUR KILLER STARTED OUT WANTING TO SETTLE A SCORE. BUT HE GOT A TASTE FOR MURDER...
...AND FOUND HE LIKED IT.

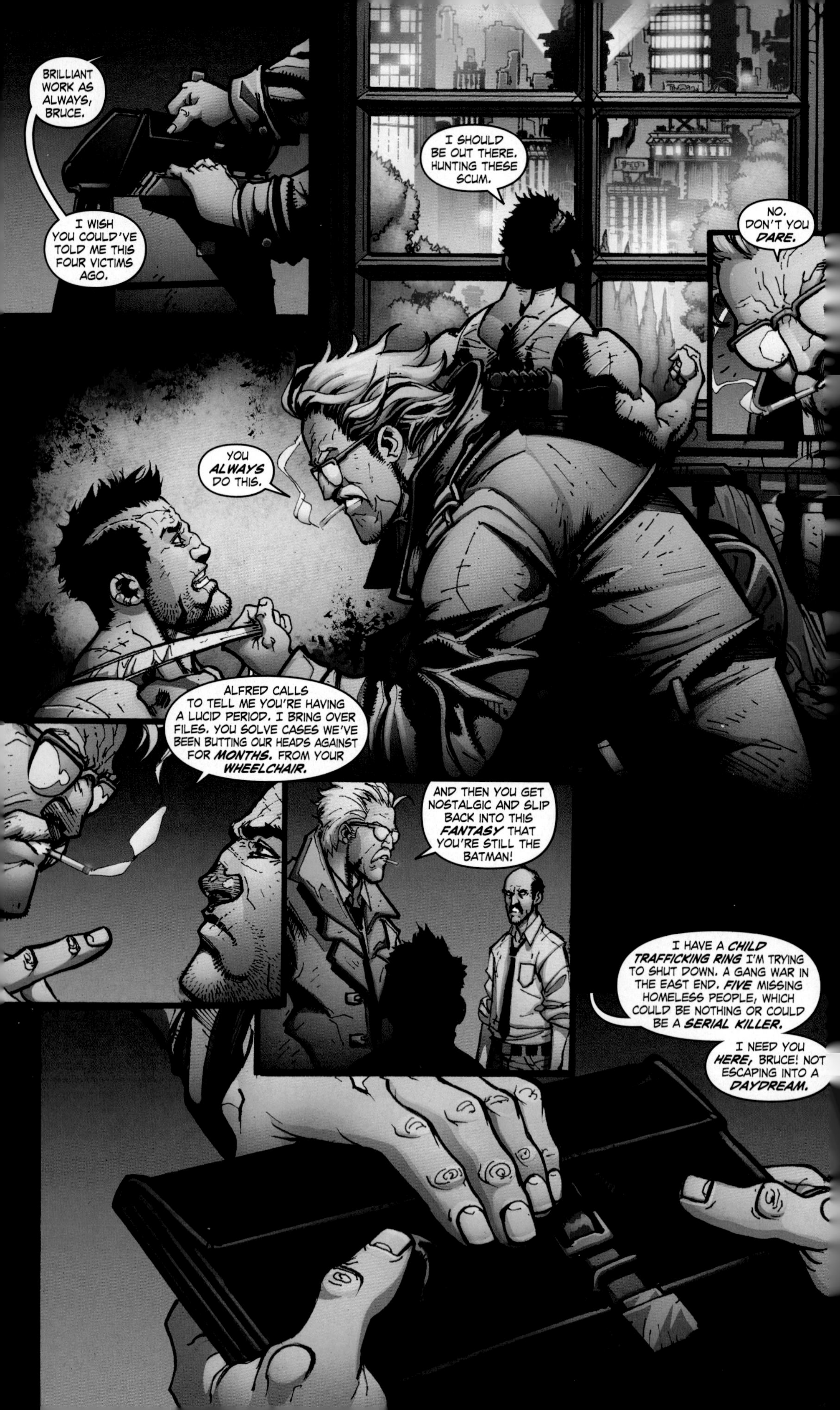
BRILLIANT WORK AS ALWAYS, BRUCE.
I WISH YOU COULD'VE TOLD ME THIS FOUR VICTIMS AGO.
I SHOULD BE OUT THERE. HUNTING THESE SCUM.
NO. DON'T YOU DARE.
YOU ALWAYS DO THIS.
ALFRED CALLS TO TELL ME YOU'RE HAVING A LUCID PERIOD. I BRING OVER FILES. YOU SOLVE CASES WE'VE BEEN BUTTING OUR HEADS AGAINST FOR MONTHS. FROM YOUR WHEELCHAIR.
AND THEN YOU GET NOSTALGIC AND SLIP BACK INTO THIS FANTASY THAT YOU'RE STILL THE BATMAN!
I HAVE A CHILD TRAFFICKING RING I'M TRYING TO SHUT DOWN. A GANG WAR IN THE EAST END. FIVE MISSING HOMELESS PEOPLE, WHICH COULD BE NOTHING OR COULD BE A SERIAL KILLER.
I NEED YOU HERE, BRUCE! NOT ESCAPING INTO A DAYDREAM.

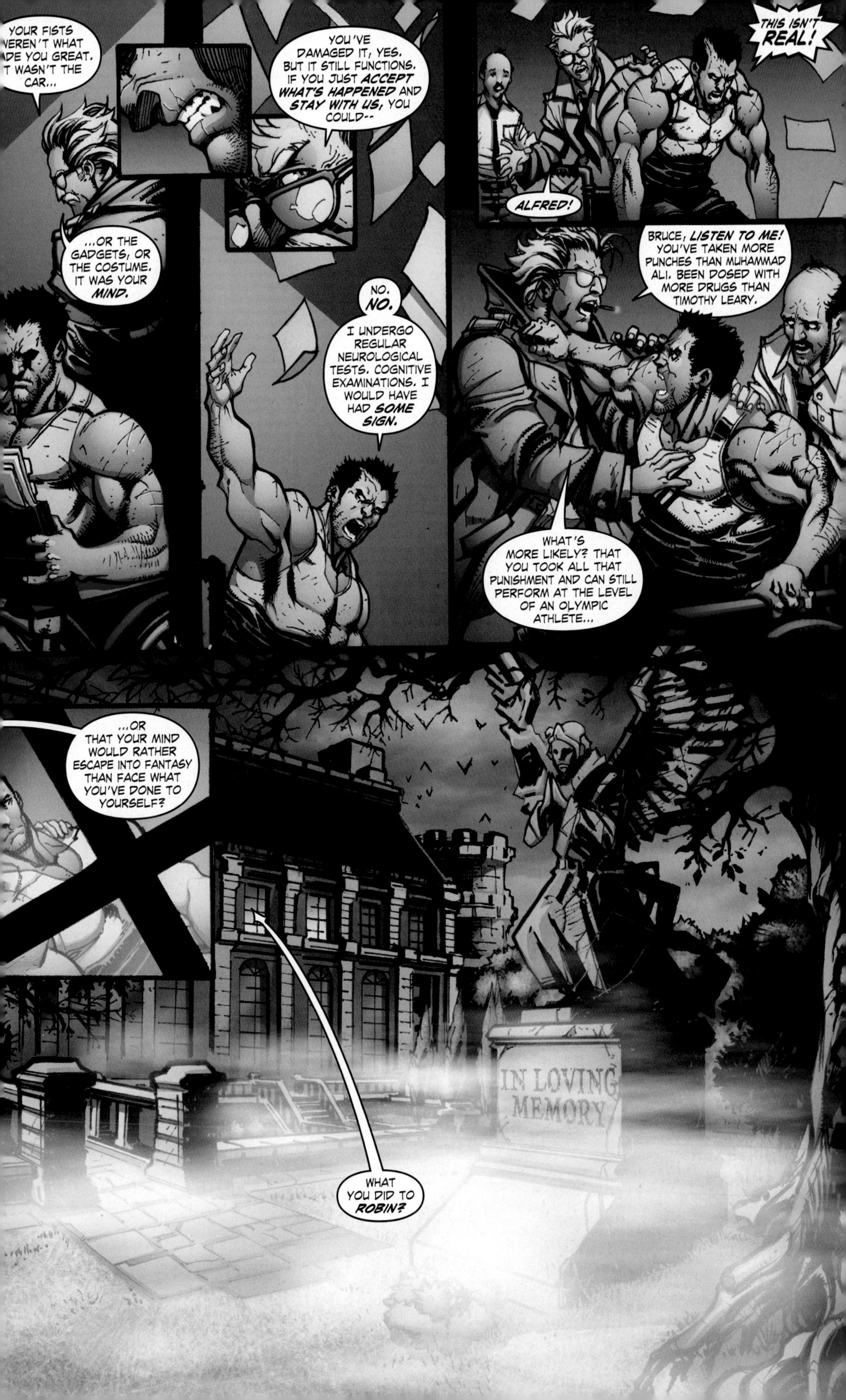

YOUR FISTS WEREN'T WHAT ADE YOU GREAT. T WASN'T THE CAR...
YOU'VE DAMAGED IT, YES. BUT IT STILL FUNCTIONS. IF YOU JUST ACCEPT WHAT'S HAPPENED AND STAY WITH US, YOU COULD--
THIS ISN'T REAL!
ALFRED!
...OR THE GADGETS, OR THE COSTUME. IT WAS YOUR MIND.
NO. NO.
I UNDERGO REGULAR NEUROLOGICAL TESTS. COGNITIVE EXAMINATIONS. I WOULD HAVE HAD SOME SIGN.
BRUCE, LISTEN TO ME! YOU'VE TAKEN MORE PUNCHES THAN MUHAMMAD ALI. BEEN DOSED WITH MORE DRUGS THAN TIMOTHY LEARY.
WHAT'S MORE LIKELY? THAT YOU TOOK ALL THAT PUNISHMENT AND CAN STILL PERFORM AT THE LEVEL OF AN OLYMPIC ATHLETE...
...OR THAT YOUR MIND WOULD RATHER ESCAPE INTO FANTASY THAN FACE WHAT YOU'VE DONE TO YOURSELF?
IN LOVING MEMORY
WHAT YOU DID TO ROBIN?

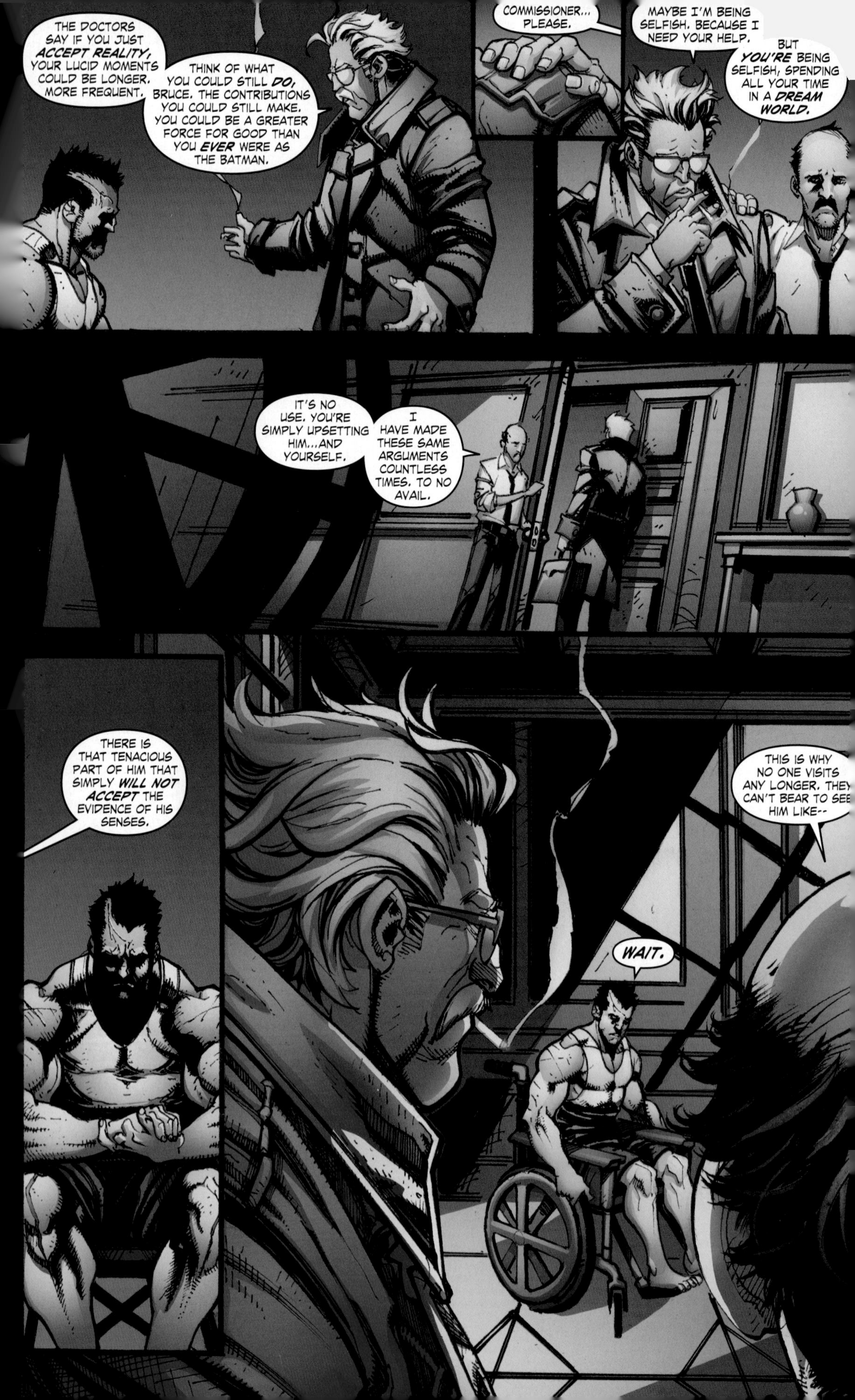
THE DOCTORS SAY IF YOU JUST ACCEPT REALITY, YOUR LUCID MOMENTS COULD BE LONGER. MORE FREQUENT.
THINK OF WHAT YOU COULD STILL DO, BRUCE. THE CONTRIBUTIONS YOU COULD STILL MAKE. YOU COULD BE A GREATER FORCE FOR GOOD THAN YOU EVER WERE AS THE BATMAN.
COMMISSIONER... PLEASE.
MAYBE I'M BEING SELFISH. BECAUSE I NEED YOUR HELP.
BUT YOU'RE BEING SELFISH, SPENDING ALL YOUR TIME IN A DREAM WORLD.
IT'S NO USE. YOU'RE SIMPLY UPSETTING HIM...AND YOURSELF.
I HAVE MADE THESE SAME ARGUMENTS COUNTLESS TIMES. TO NO AVAIL.
THERE IS THAT TENACIOUS PART OF HIM THAT SIMPLY WILL NOT ACCEPT THE EVIDENCE OF HIS SENSES.
THIS IS WHY NO ONE VISITS ANY LONGER. THEY CAN'T BEAR TO SEE HIM LIKE--
WAIT.

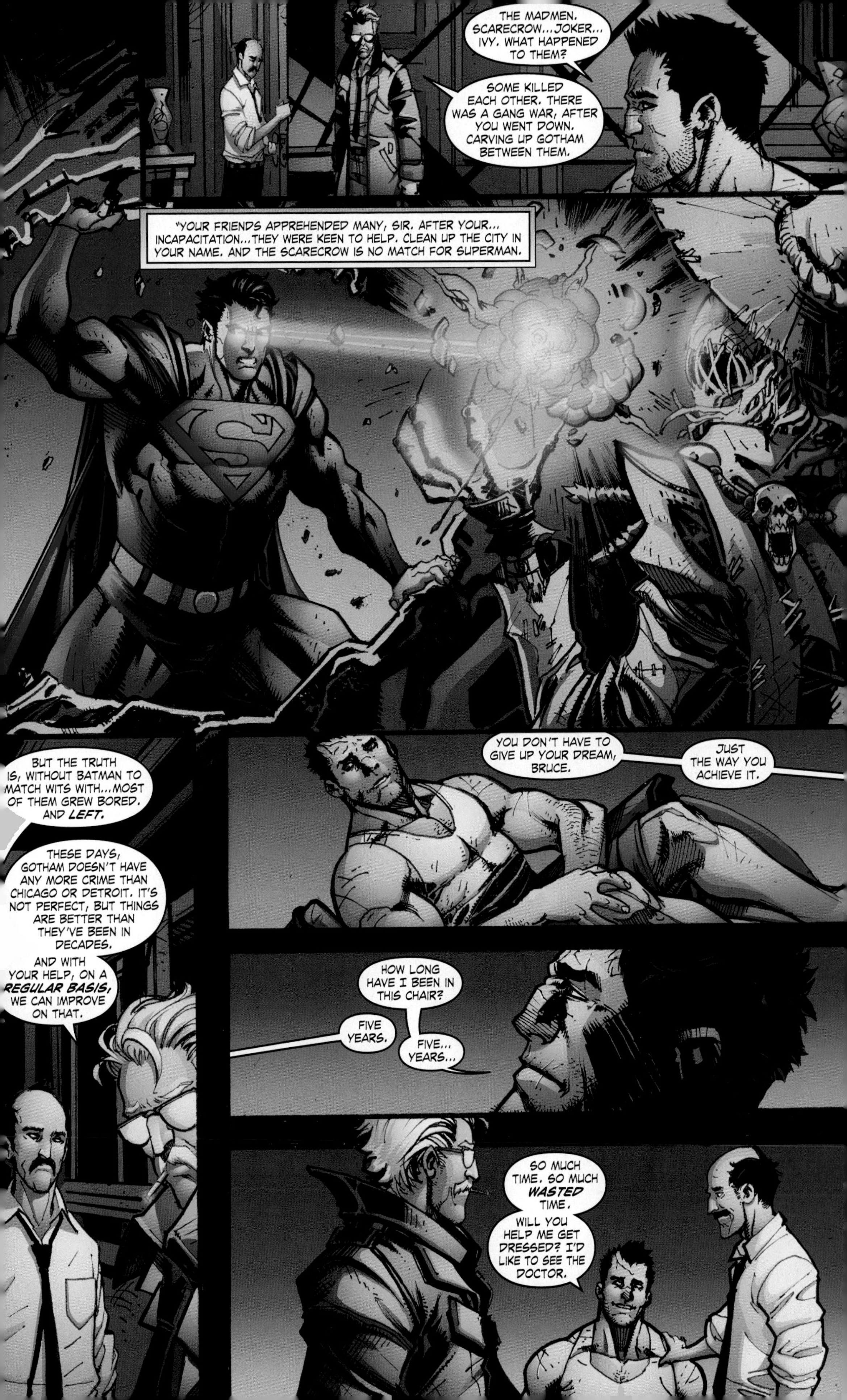
THE MADMEN. SCARECROW... JOKER... IVY. WHAT HAPPENED TO THEM?
SOME KILLED EACH OTHER. THERE WAS A GANG WAR, AFTER YOU WENT DOWN. CARVING UP GOTHAM BETWEEN THEM.
"YOUR FRIENDS APPREHENDED MANY, SIR. AFTER YOUR... INCAPACITATION... THEY WERE KEEN TO HELP. CLEAN UP THE CITY IN YOUR NAME. AND THE SCARECROW IS NO MATCH FOR SUPERMAN.
BUT THE TRUTH IS, WITHOUT BATMAN TO MATCH WITS WITH... MOST OF THEM GREW BORED. AND *LEFT.*
THESE DAYS, GOTHAM DOESN'T HAVE ANY MORE CRIME THAN CHICAGO OR DETROIT. IT'S NOT PERFECT, BUT THINGS ARE BETTER THAN THEY'VE BEEN IN DECADES.
AND WITH YOUR HELP, ON A *REGULAR BASIS,* WE CAN IMPROVE ON THAT.
YOU DON'T HAVE TO GIVE UP YOUR DREAM, BRUCE.
JUST THE WAY YOU ACHIEVE IT.
HOW LONG HAVE I BEEN IN THIS CHAIR?
FIVE YEARS.
FIVE... YEARS...
SO MUCH TIME. SO MUCH *WASTED* TIME.
WILL YOU HELP ME GET DRESSED? I'D LIKE TO SEE THE DOCTOR.

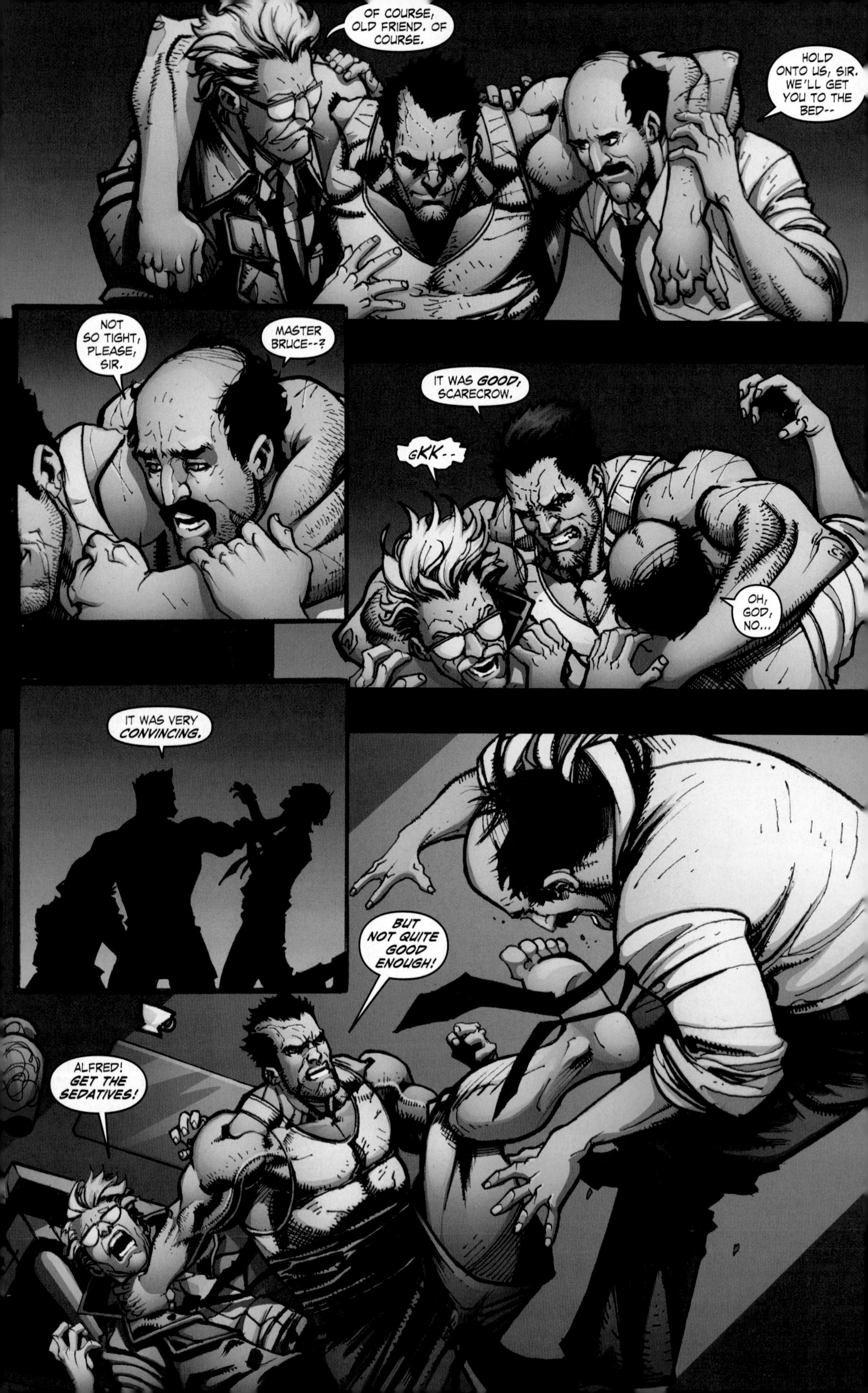
OF COURSE, OLD FRIEND. OF COURSE.
HOLD ONTO US, SIR. WE'LL GET YOU TO THE BED--
NOT SO TIGHT, PLEASE, SIR.
MASTER BRUCE--?
IT WAS *GOOD,* SCARECROW.
GKK--
OH, GOD, NO...
IT WAS VERY *CONVINCING.*
BUT NOT QUITE GOOD ENOUGH!
ALFRED! *GET THE SEDATIVES!*

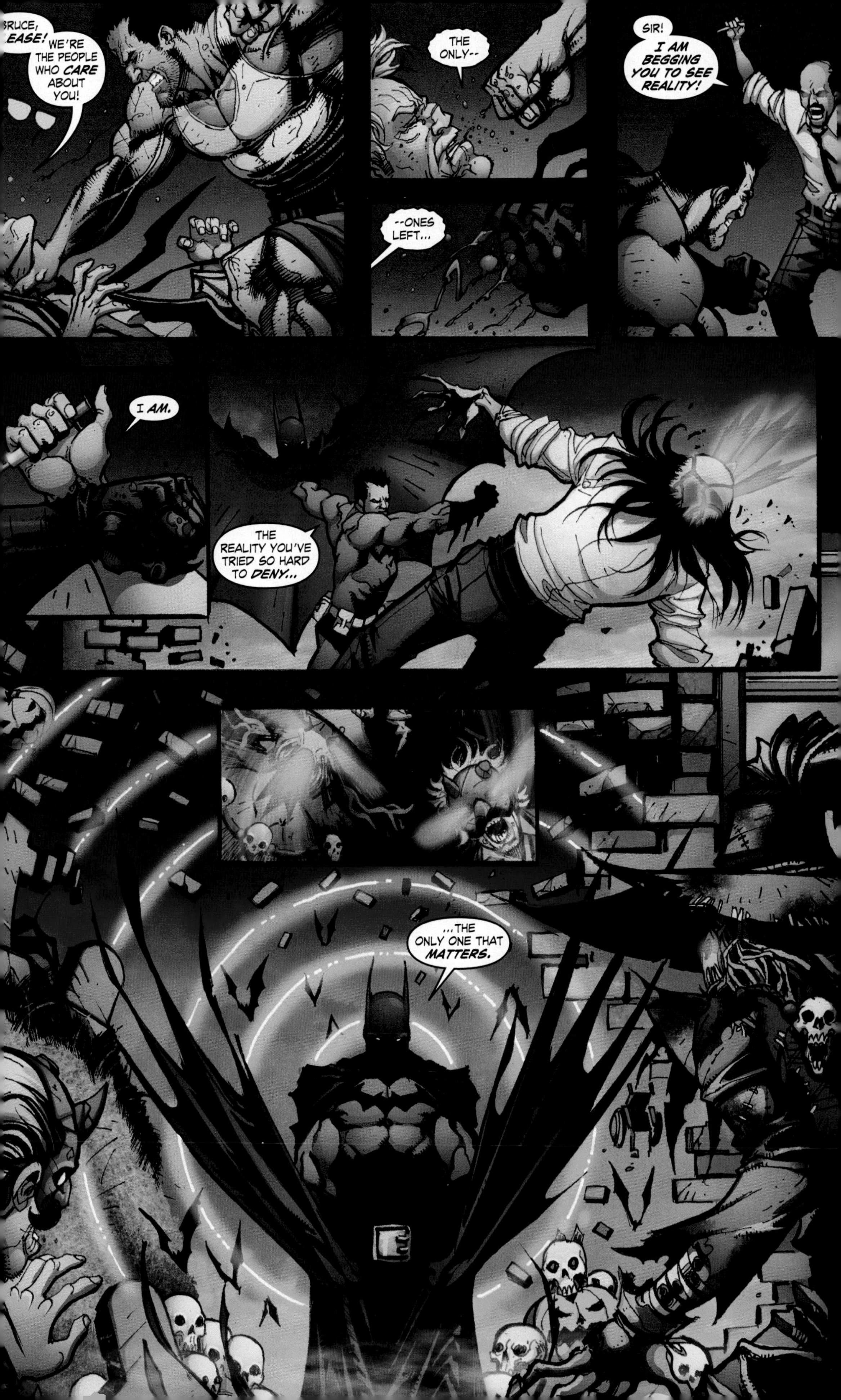
BRUCE, EASE! WE'RE THE PEOPLE WHO CARE ABOUT YOU!
THE ONLY--
--ONES LEFT...
SIR! I AM BEGGING YOU TO SEE REALITY!
I AM.
THE REALITY YOU'VE TRIED SO HARD TO DENY...
...THE ONLY ONE THAT MATTERS.

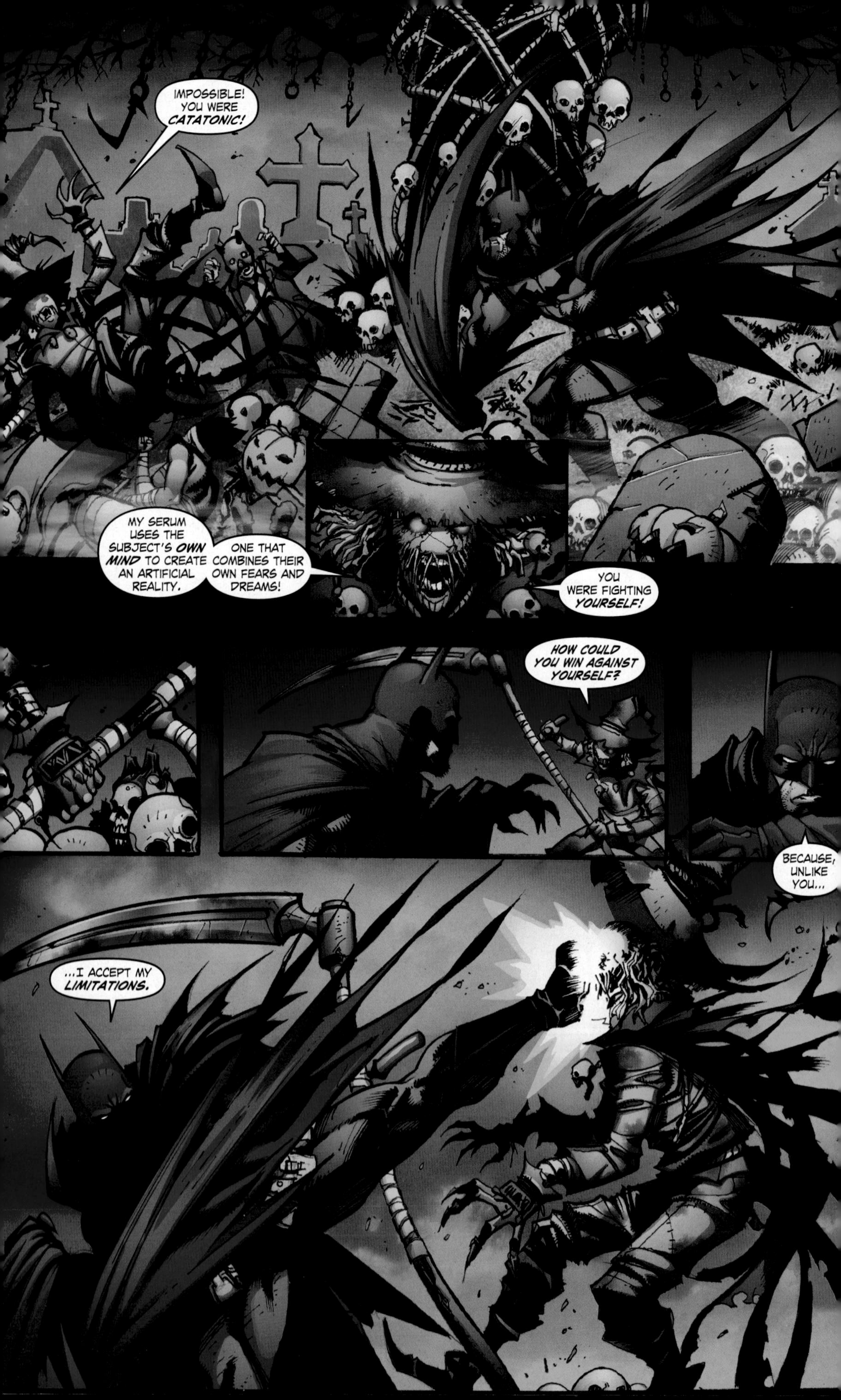
IMPOSSIBLE! YOU WERE CATATONIC!
MY SERUM USES THE SUBJECT'S OWN MIND TO CREATE AN ARTIFICIAL REALITY.
ONE THAT COMBINES THEIR OWN FEARS AND DREAMS!
YOU WERE FIGHTING YOURSELF!
HOW COULD YOU WIN AGAINST YOURSELF?
BECAUSE, UNLIKE YOU...
...I ACCEPT MY LIMITATIONS.

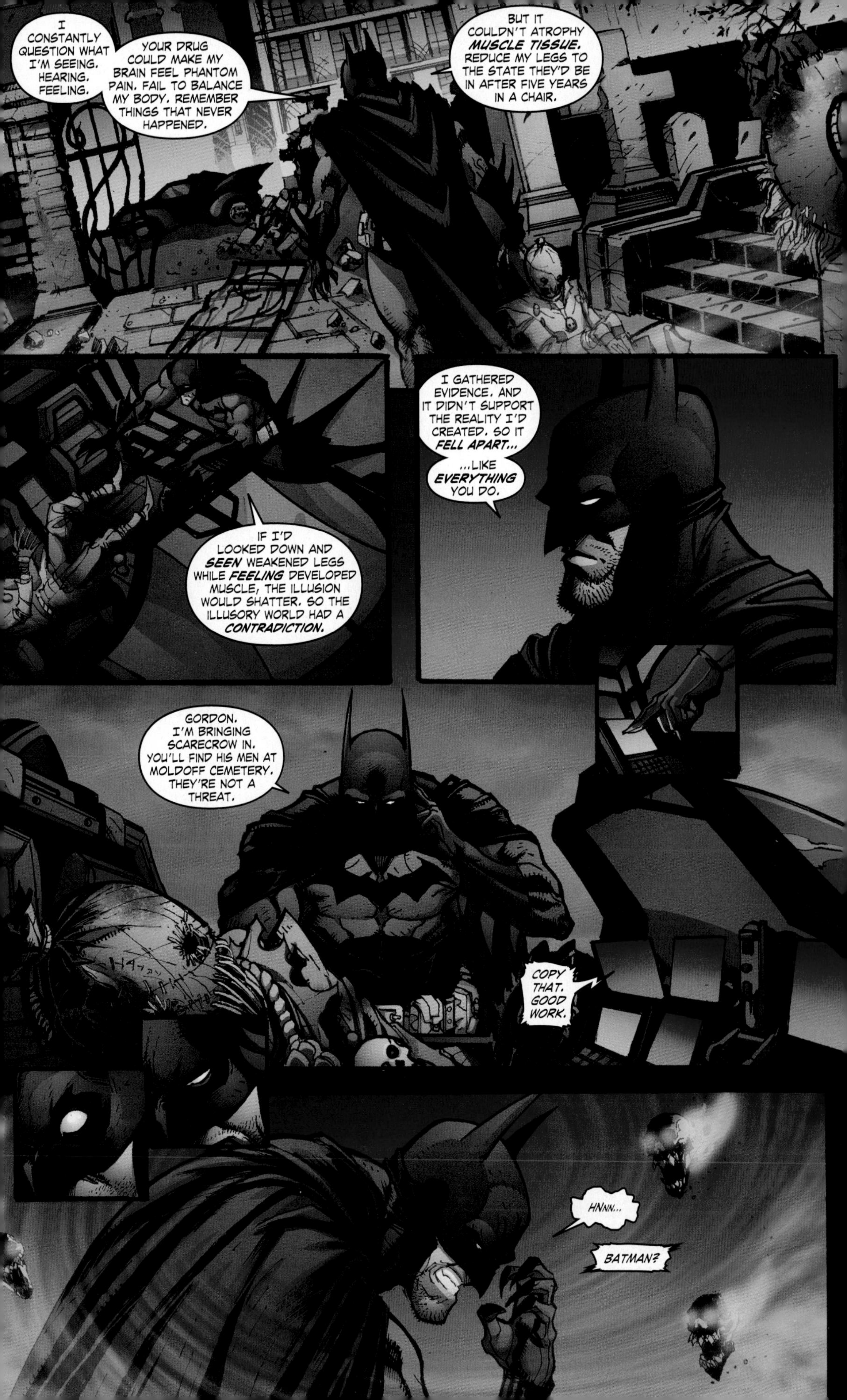
I CONSTANTLY QUESTION WHAT I'M SEEING. HEARING. FEELING.
YOUR DRUG COULD MAKE MY BRAIN FEEL PHANTOM PAIN. FAIL TO BALANCE MY BODY. REMEMBER THINGS THAT NEVER HAPPENED.
BUT IT COULDN'T ATROPHY MUSCLE TISSUE. REDUCE MY LEGS TO THE STATE THEY'D BE IN AFTER FIVE YEARS IN A CHAIR.
IF I'D LOOKED DOWN AND SEEN WEAKENED LEGS WHILE FEELING DEVELOPED MUSCLE, THE ILLUSION WOULD SHATTER. SO THE ILLUSORY WORLD HAD A CONTRADICTION.
I GATHERED EVIDENCE. AND IT DIDN'T SUPPORT THE REALITY I'D CREATED. SO IT FELL APART...
...LIKE EVERYTHING YOU DO.
GORDON. I'M BRINGING SCARECROW IN. YOU'LL FIND HIS MEN AT MOLDOFF CEMETERY. THEY'RE NOT A THREAT.
COPY THAT. GOOD WORK.
HNNN...
BATMAN?

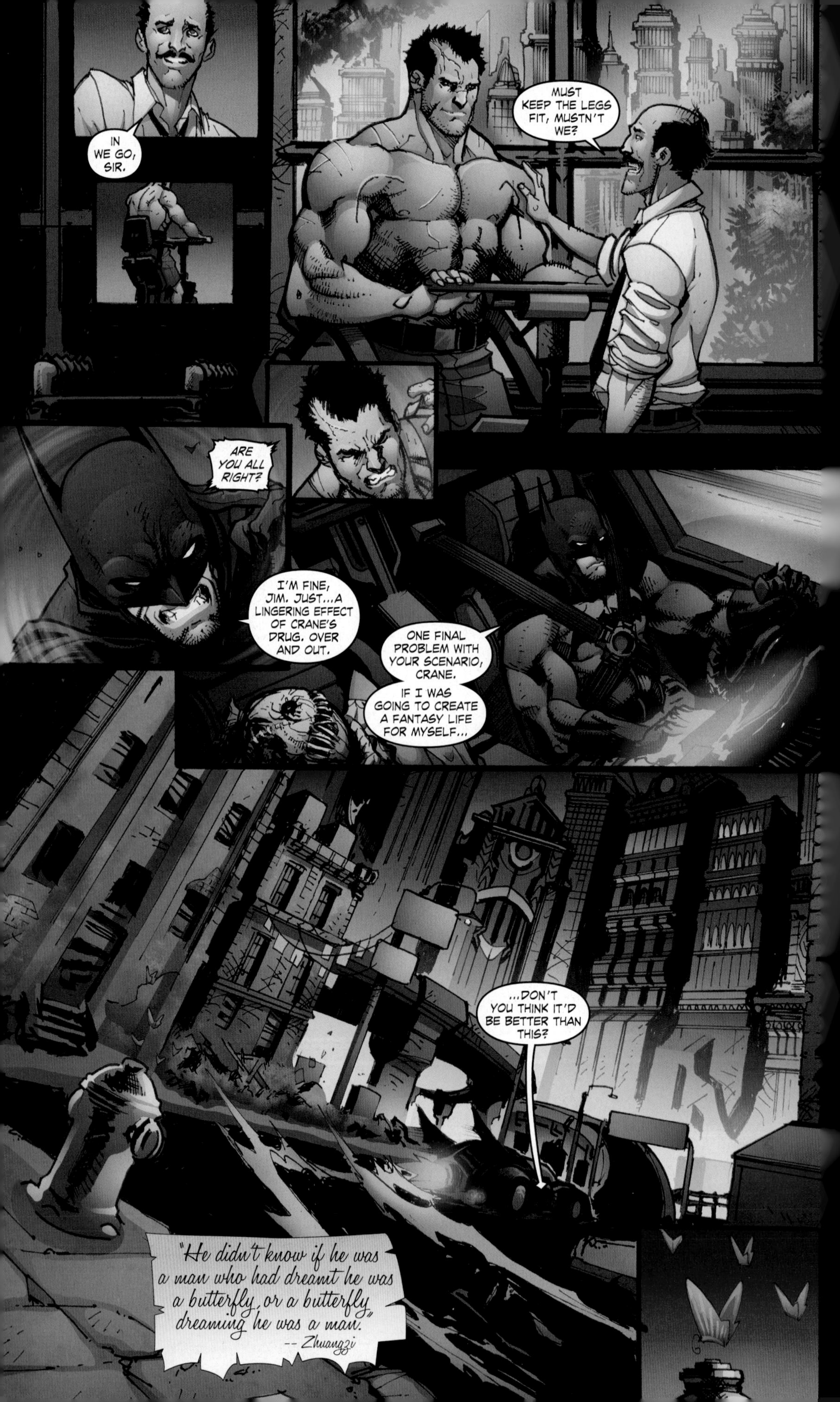
IN WE GO, SIR.
MUST KEEP THE LEGS FIT, MUSTN'T WE?
ARE YOU ALL RIGHT?
I'M FINE, JIM. JUST...A LINGERING EFFECT OF CRANE'S DRUG. OVER AND OUT.
ONE FINAL PROBLEM WITH YOUR SCENARIO, CRANE.
IF I WAS GOING TO CREATE A FANTASY LIFE FOR MYSELF...
...DON'T YOU THINK IT'D BE BETTER THAN THIS?
"He didn't know if he was a man who had dreamt he was a butterfly, or a butterfly dreaming he was a man."
-- Zhuangzi

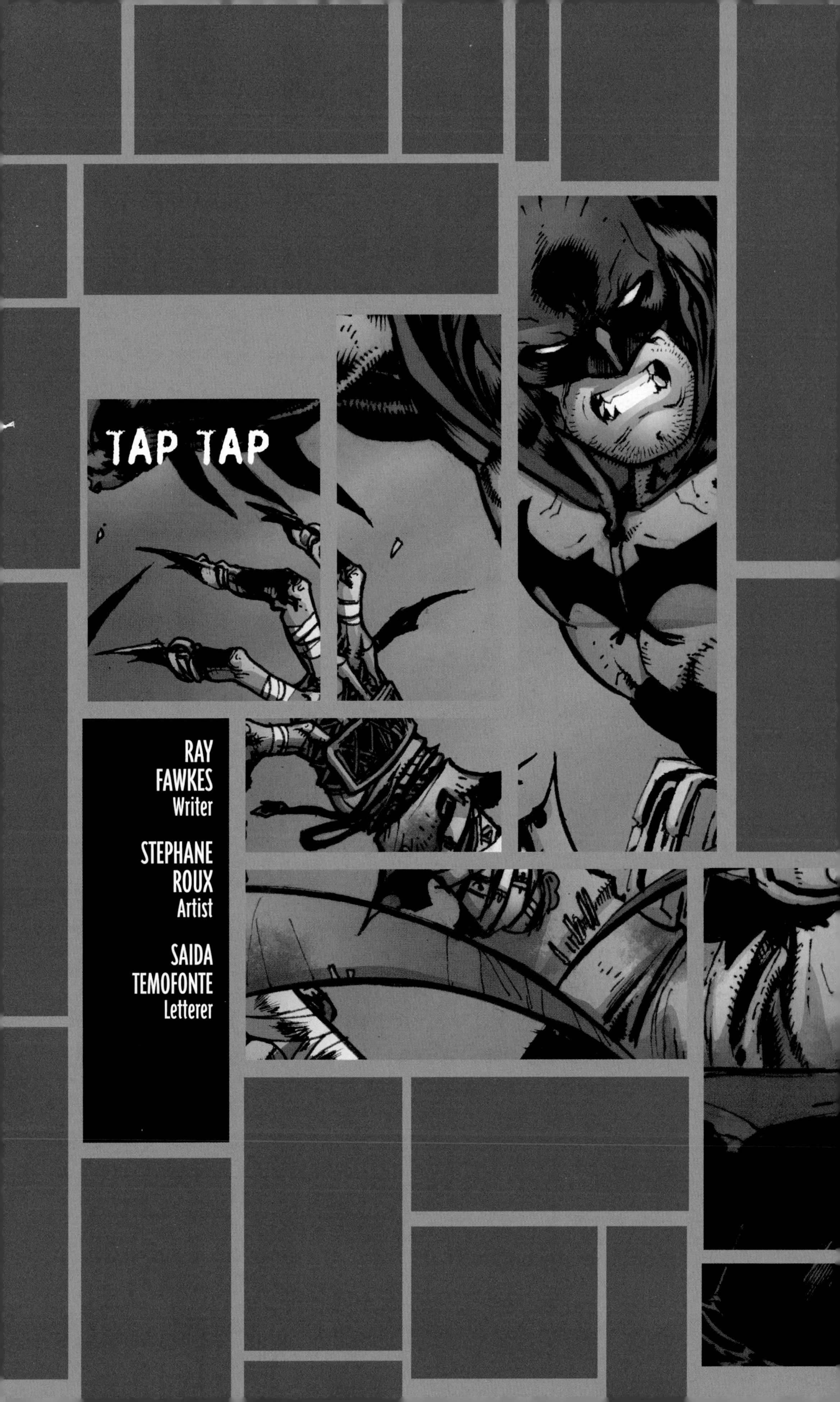

TAP TAP
RAY FAWKES Writer
STEPHANE ROUX Artist
SAIDA TEMOFONTE Letterer

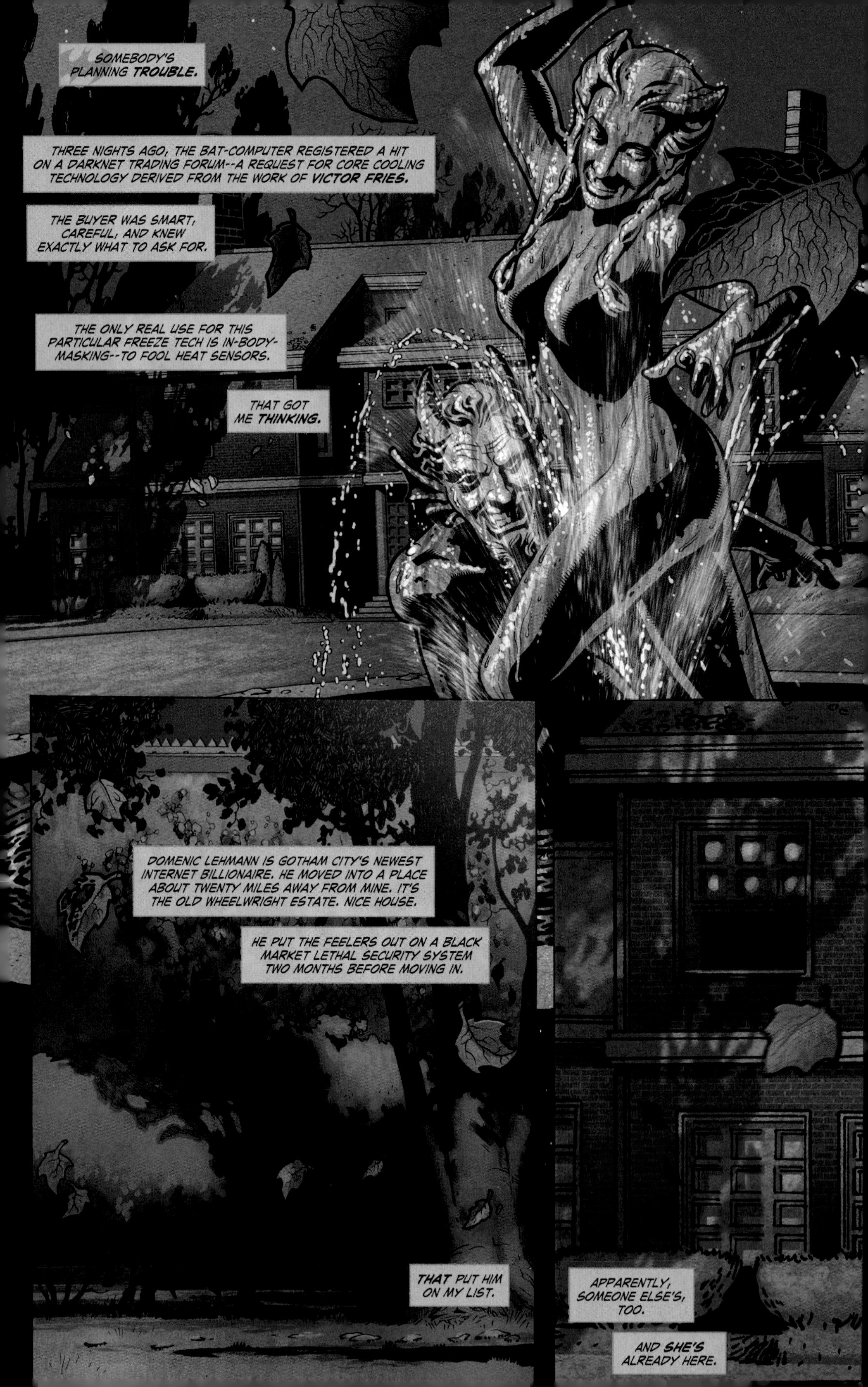
SOMEBODY'S PLANNING TROUBLE.
THREE NIGHTS AGO, THE BAT-COMPUTER REGISTERED A HIT ON A DARKNET TRADING FORUM--A REQUEST FOR CORE COOLING TECHNOLOGY DERIVED FROM THE WORK OF VICTOR FRIES.
THE BUYER WAS SMART, CAREFUL, AND KNEW EXACTLY WHAT TO ASK FOR.
THE ONLY REAL USE FOR THIS PARTICULAR FREEZE TECH IS IN-BODY-MASKING--TO FOOL HEAT SENSORS.
THAT GOT ME THINKING.
DOMENIC LEHMANN IS GOTHAM CITY'S NEWEST INTERNET BILLIONAIRE. HE MOVED INTO A PLACE ABOUT TWENTY MILES AWAY FROM MINE. IT'S THE OLD WHEELWRIGHT ESTATE. NICE HOUSE.
HE PUT THE FEELERS OUT ON A BLACK MARKET LETHAL SECURITY SYSTEM TWO MONTHS BEFORE MOVING IN.
THAT PUT HIM ON MY LIST.
APPARENTLY, SOMEONE ELSE'S, TOO.
AND SHE'S ALREADY HERE.

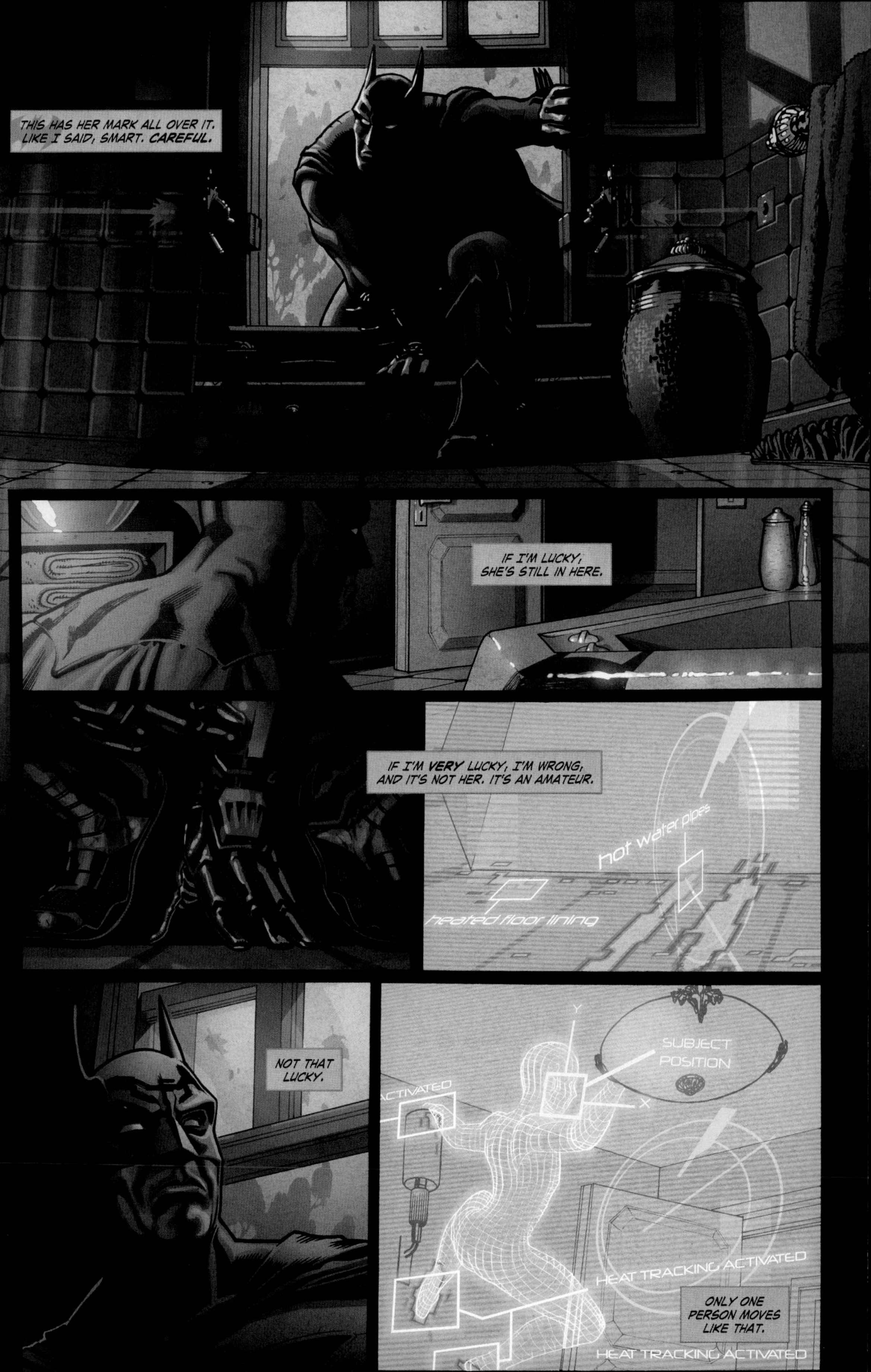
THIS HAS HER MARK ALL OVER IT. LIKE I SAID; SMART. CAREFUL.
IF I'M LUCKY, SHE'S STILL IN HERE.
IF I'M VERY LUCKY, I'M WRONG, AND IT'S NOT HER. IT'S AN AMATEUR.
hot water pipes
heated floor lining
NOT THAT LUCKY.
Y
SUBJECT POSITION
X
ACTIVATED
HEAT TRACKING ACTIVATED
ONLY ONE PERSON MOVES LIKE THAT.
HEAT TRACKING ACTIVATED

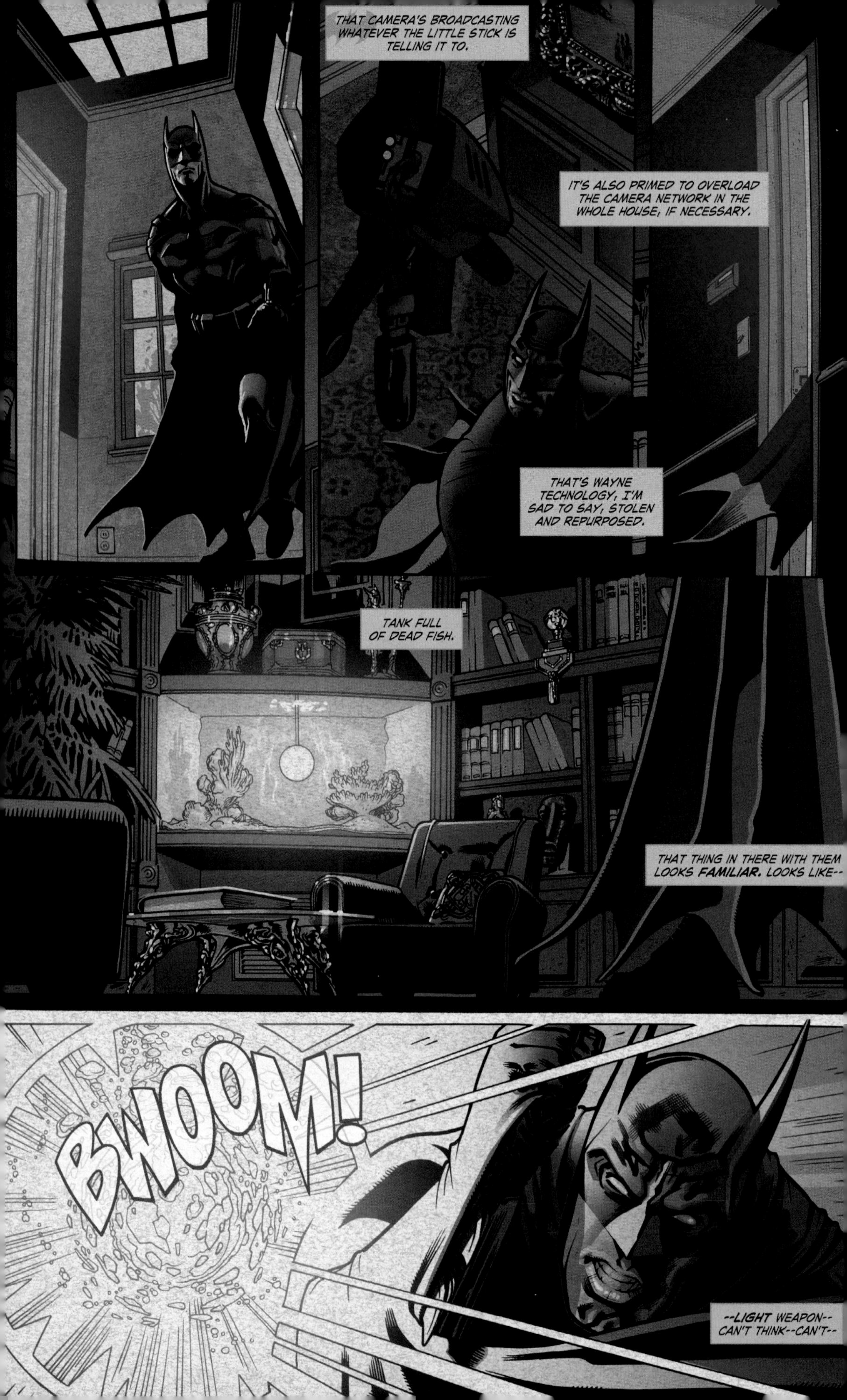
THAT CAMERA'S BROADCASTING WHATEVER THE LITTLE STICK IS TELLING IT TO.
IT'S ALSO PRIMED TO OVERLOAD THE CAMERA NETWORK IN THE WHOLE HOUSE, IF NECESSARY.
THAT'S WAYNE TECHNOLOGY, I'M SAD TO SAY, STOLEN AND REPURPOSED.
TANK FULL OF DEAD FISH.
THAT THING IN THERE WITH THEM LOOKS **FAMILIAR**. LOOKS LIKE--
BWOOM!
--**LIGHT** WEAPON-- CAN'T THINK--CAN'T--

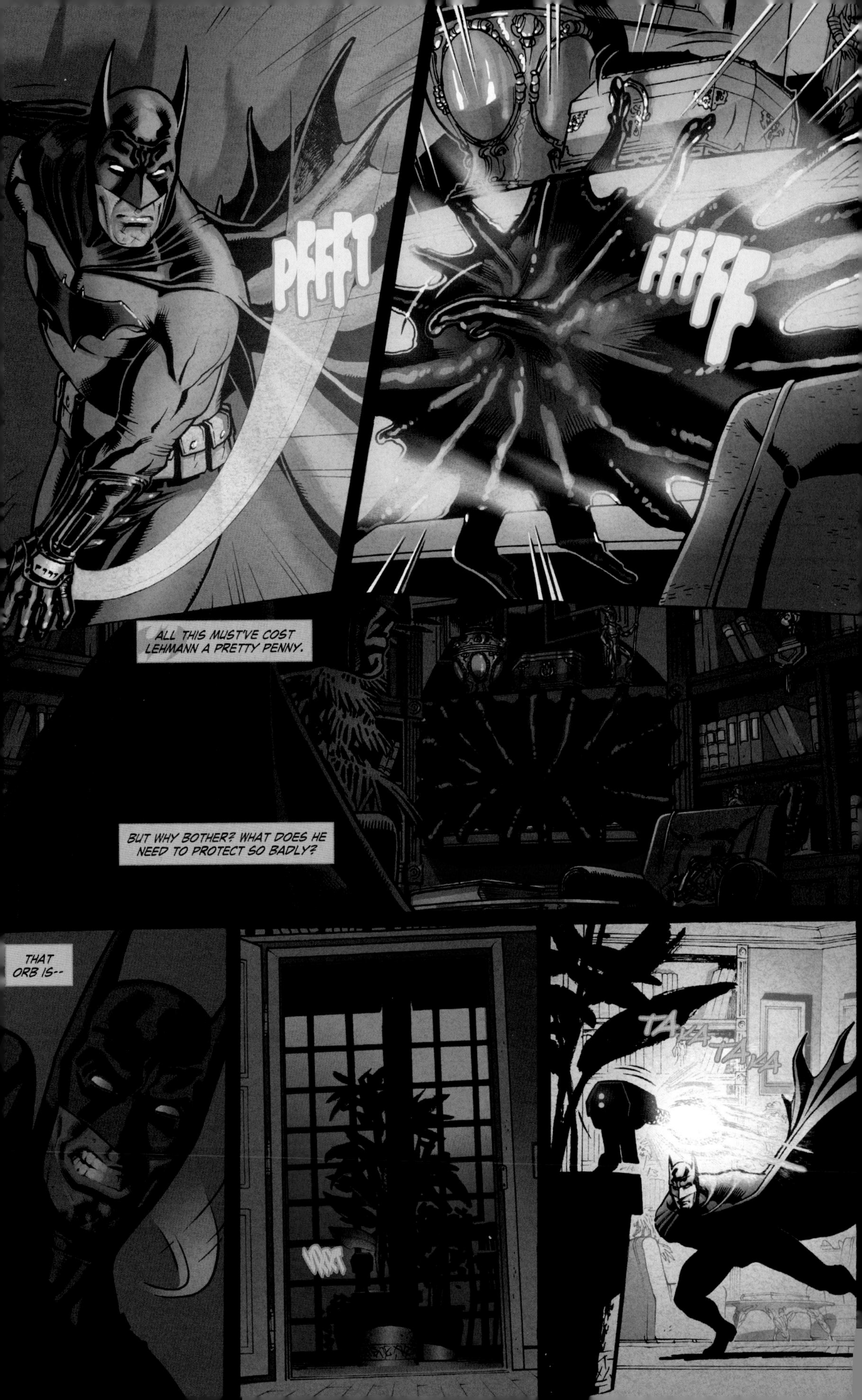
PFFFT
FFFFF
ALL THIS MUST'VE COST LEHMANN A PRETTY PENNY.
BUT WHY BOTHER? WHAT DOES HE NEED TO PROTECT SO BADLY?
THAT ORB IS--
VRRT
TAKA TAKA

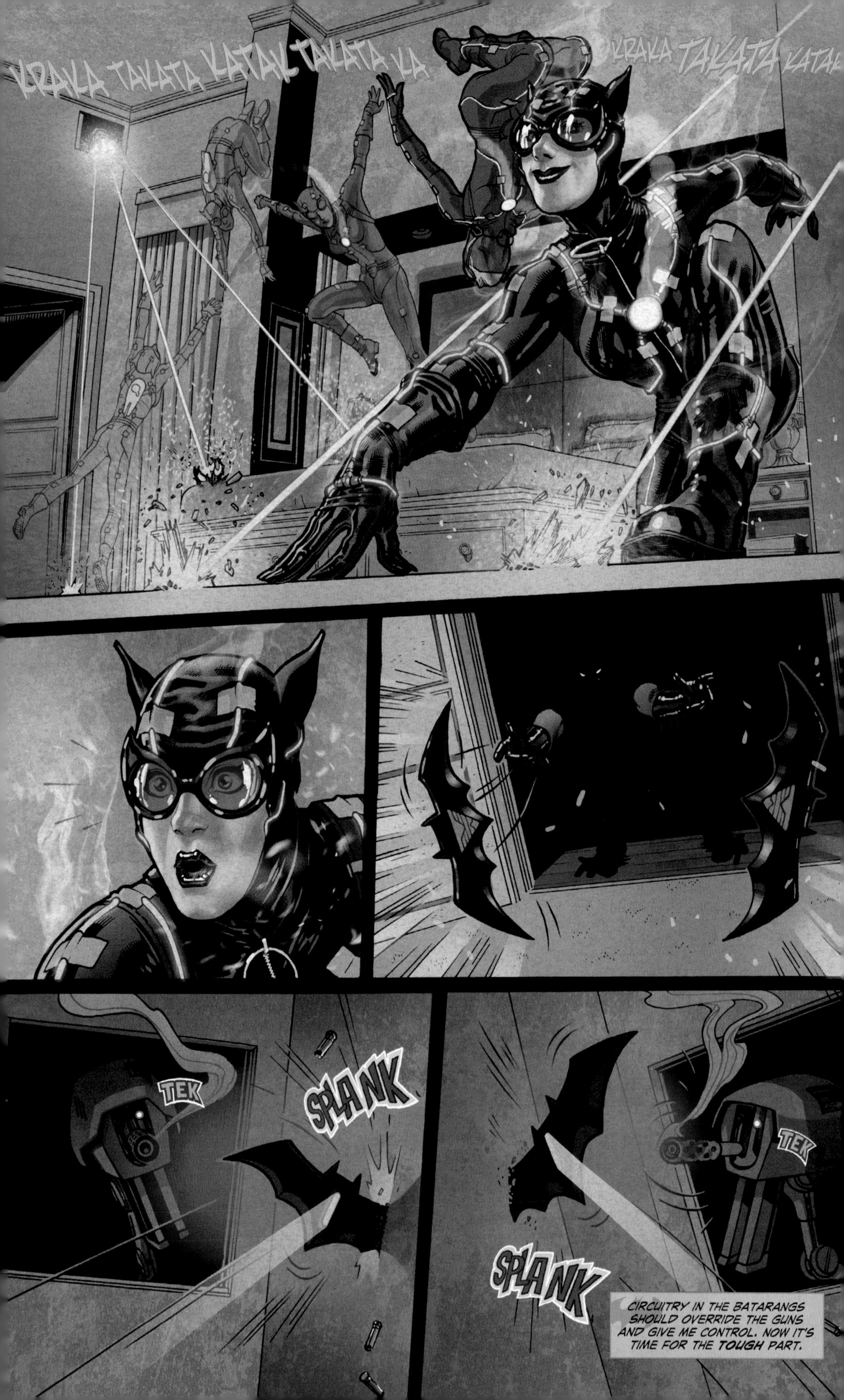
KRAKA TAKATA KATAK TAKATA KA
KRAKA TAKATA KATAK
TEK
SPLANK
TEK
SPLANK
CIRCUITRY IN THE BATARANGS SHOULD OVERRIDE THE GUNS AND GIVE ME CONTROL. NOW IT'S TIME FOR THE TOUGH PART.

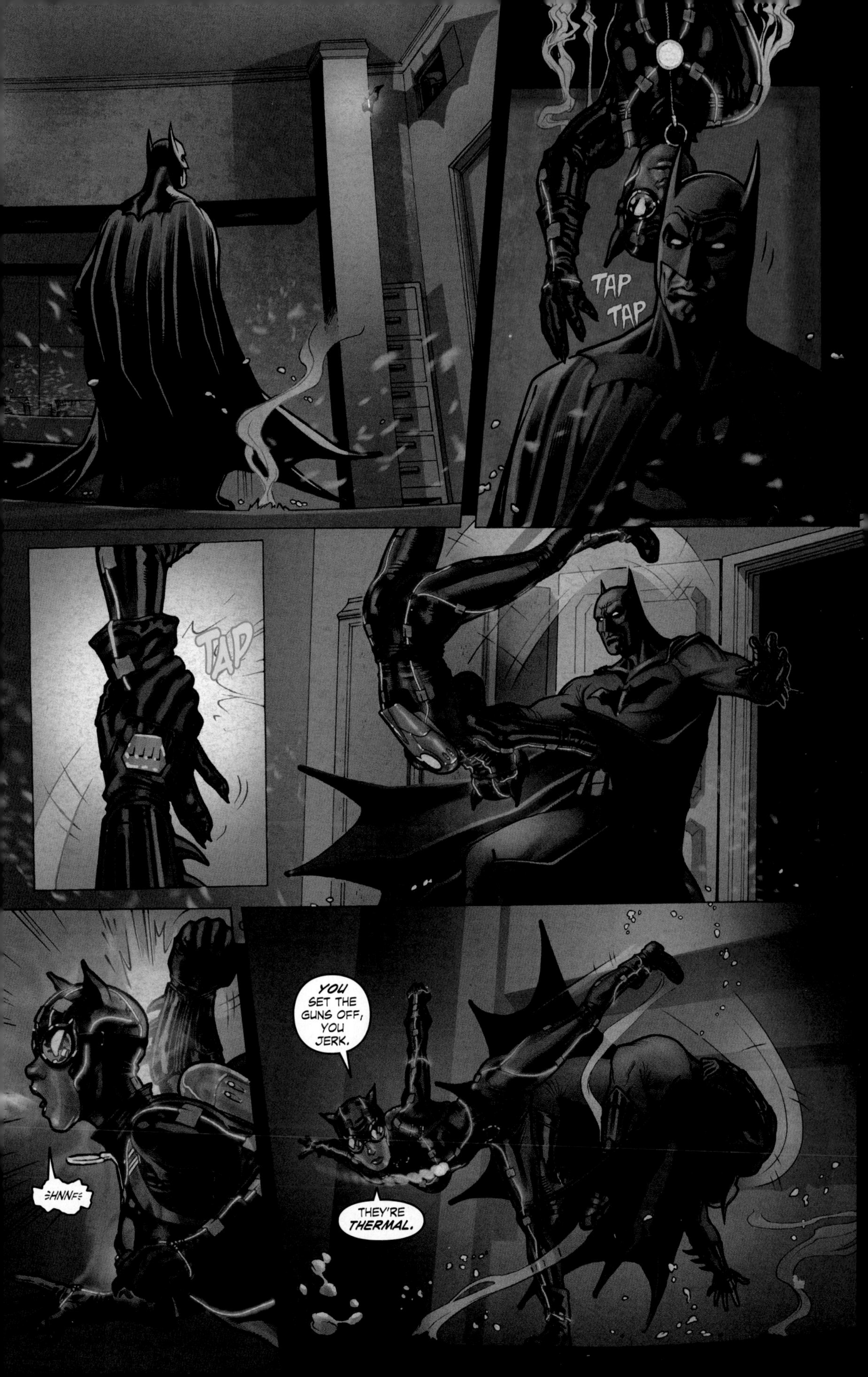
TAP
TAP
TAP
YOU SET THE GUNS OFF, YOU JERK.
HNNF
THEY'RE THERMAL.

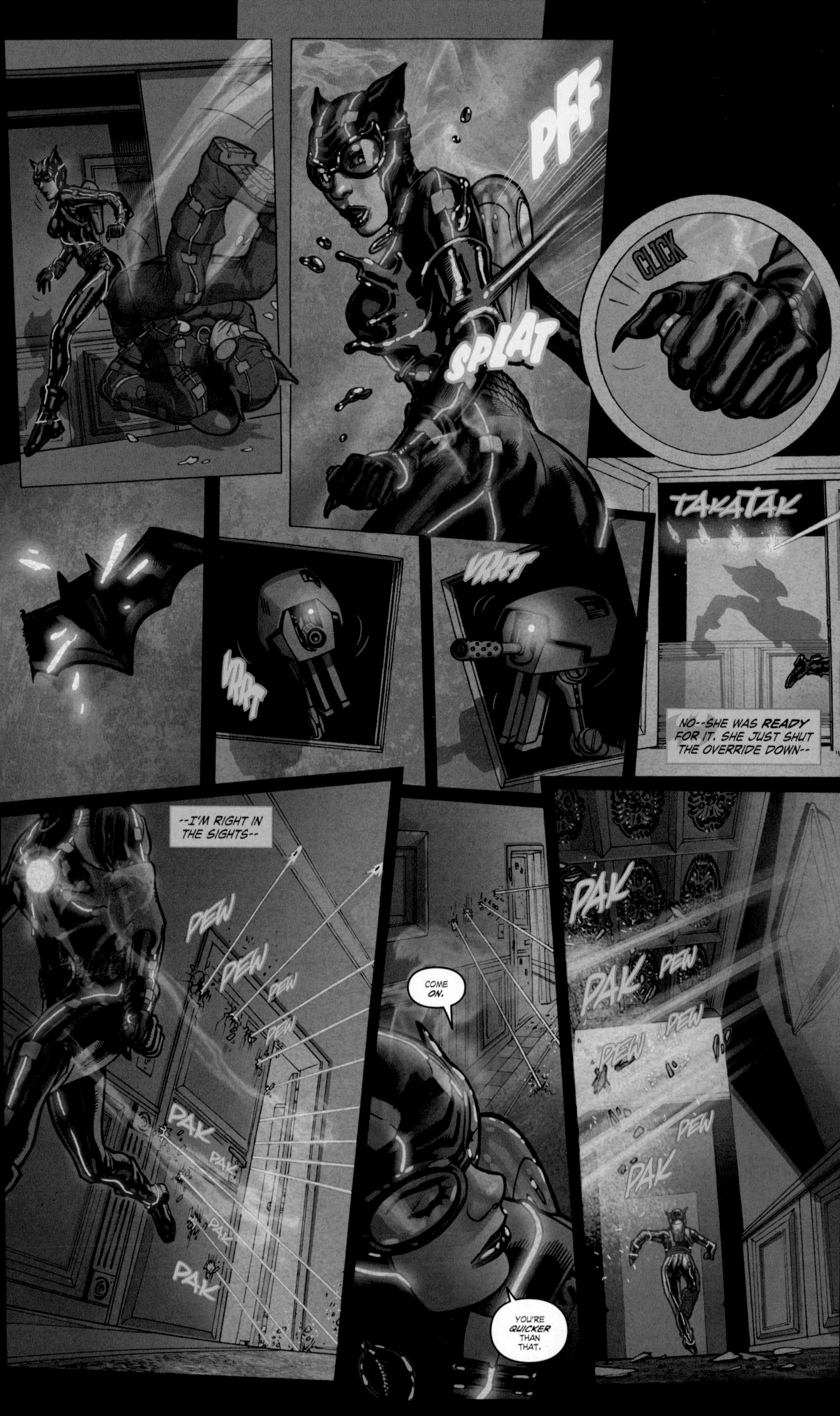
PFF
SPLAT
CLICK
TAKATAK
VRRT
VRRT
NO--SHE WAS READY FOR IT. SHE JUST SHUT THE OVERRIDE DOWN--
--I'M RIGHT IN THE SIGHTS--
PEW
PEW
PEW
PEW
PAK
PAK
PAK
PAK
COME ON.
YOU'RE QUICKER THAN THAT.
PAK
PAK
PEW
PEW
PEW
PEW
PAK

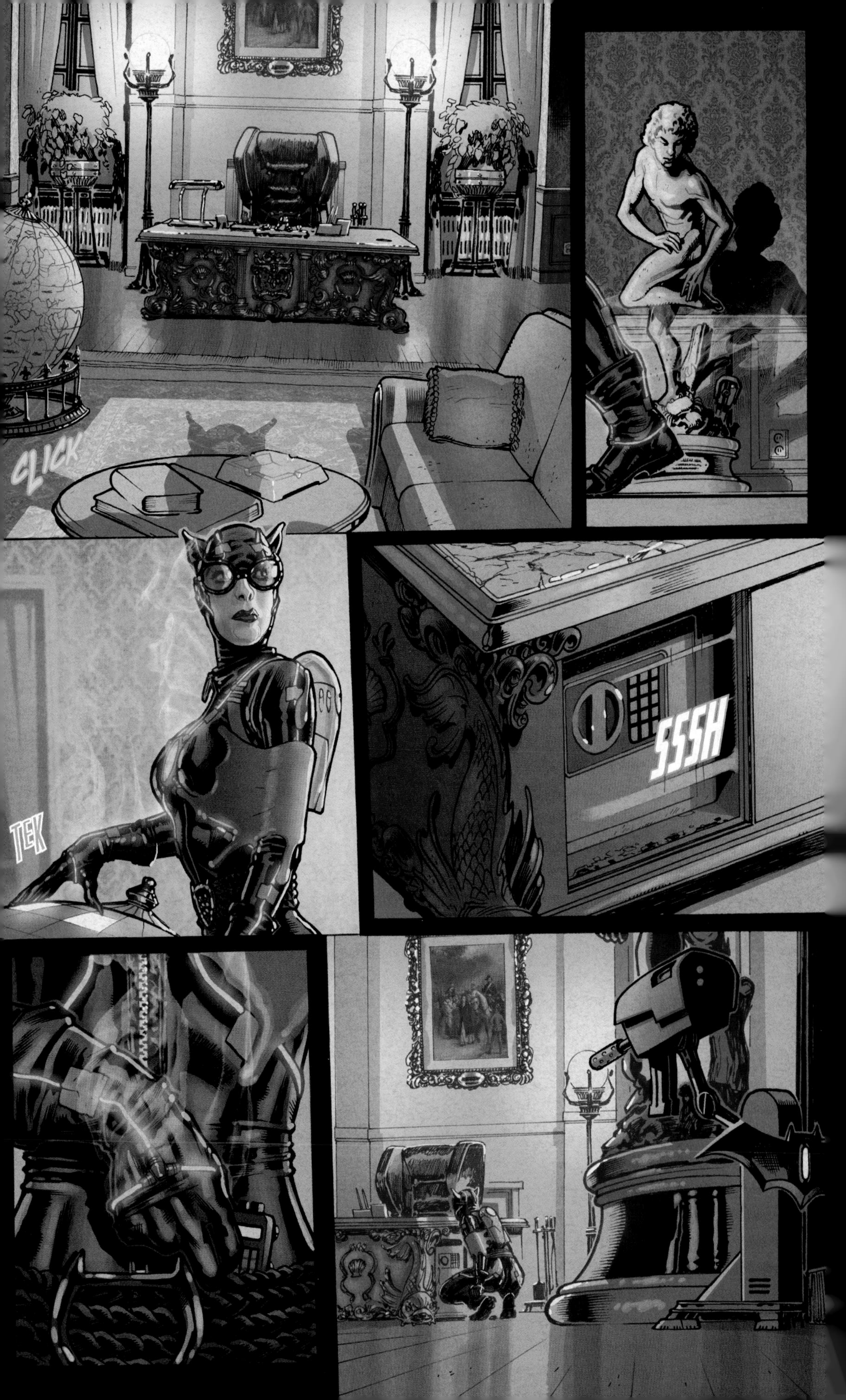
CLICK
TEK
SSSH

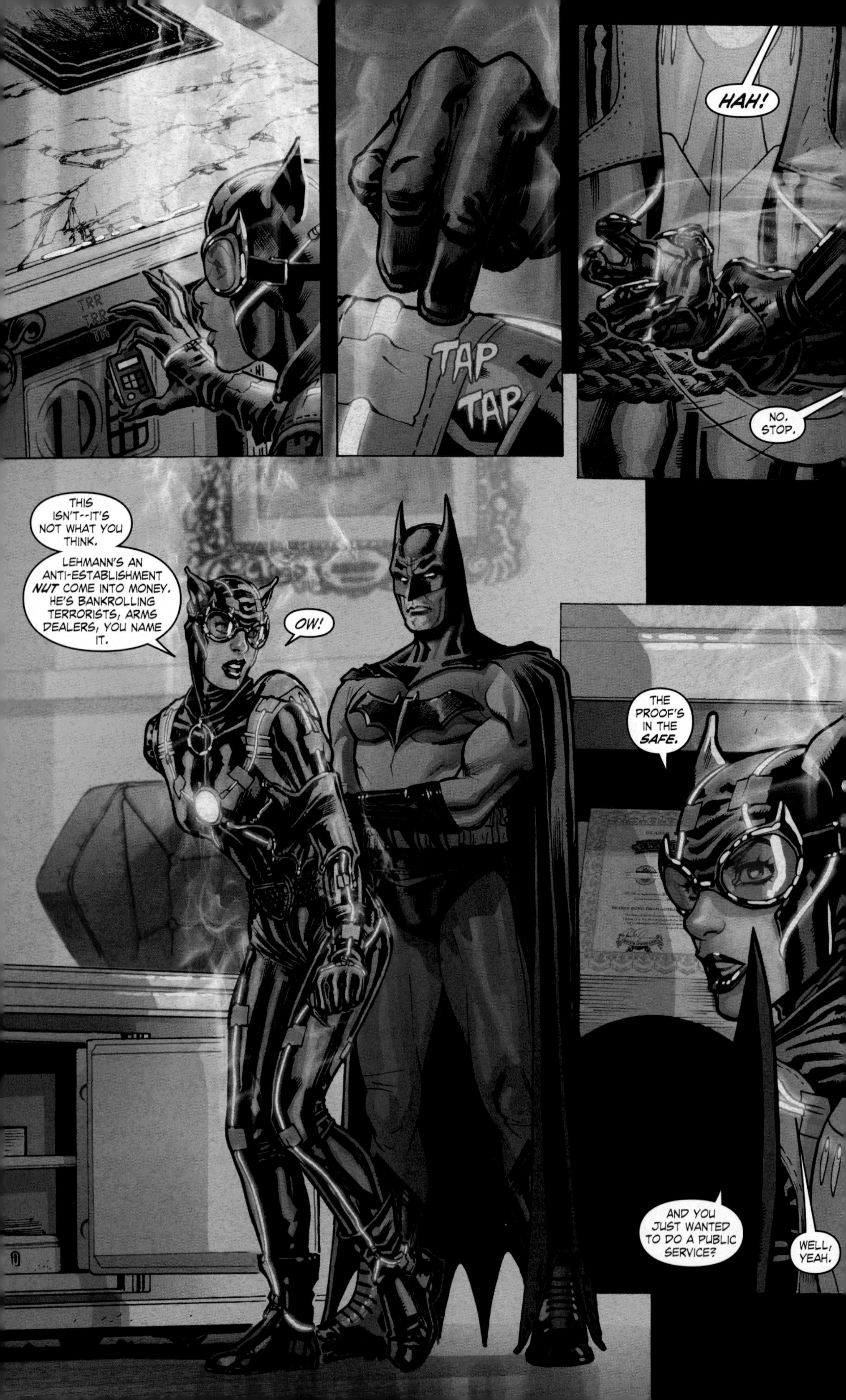
TRR
TRR
TK
TAP
TAP
HAH!
NO. STOP.
THIS ISN'T--IT'S NOT WHAT YOU THINK.
LEHMANN'S AN ANTI-ESTABLISHMENT NUT COME INTO MONEY. HE'S BANKROLLING TERRORISTS, ARMS DEALERS, YOU NAME IT.
OW!
THE PROOF'S IN THE SAFE.
AND YOU JUST WANTED TO DO A PUBLIC SERVICE?
WELL, YEAH.

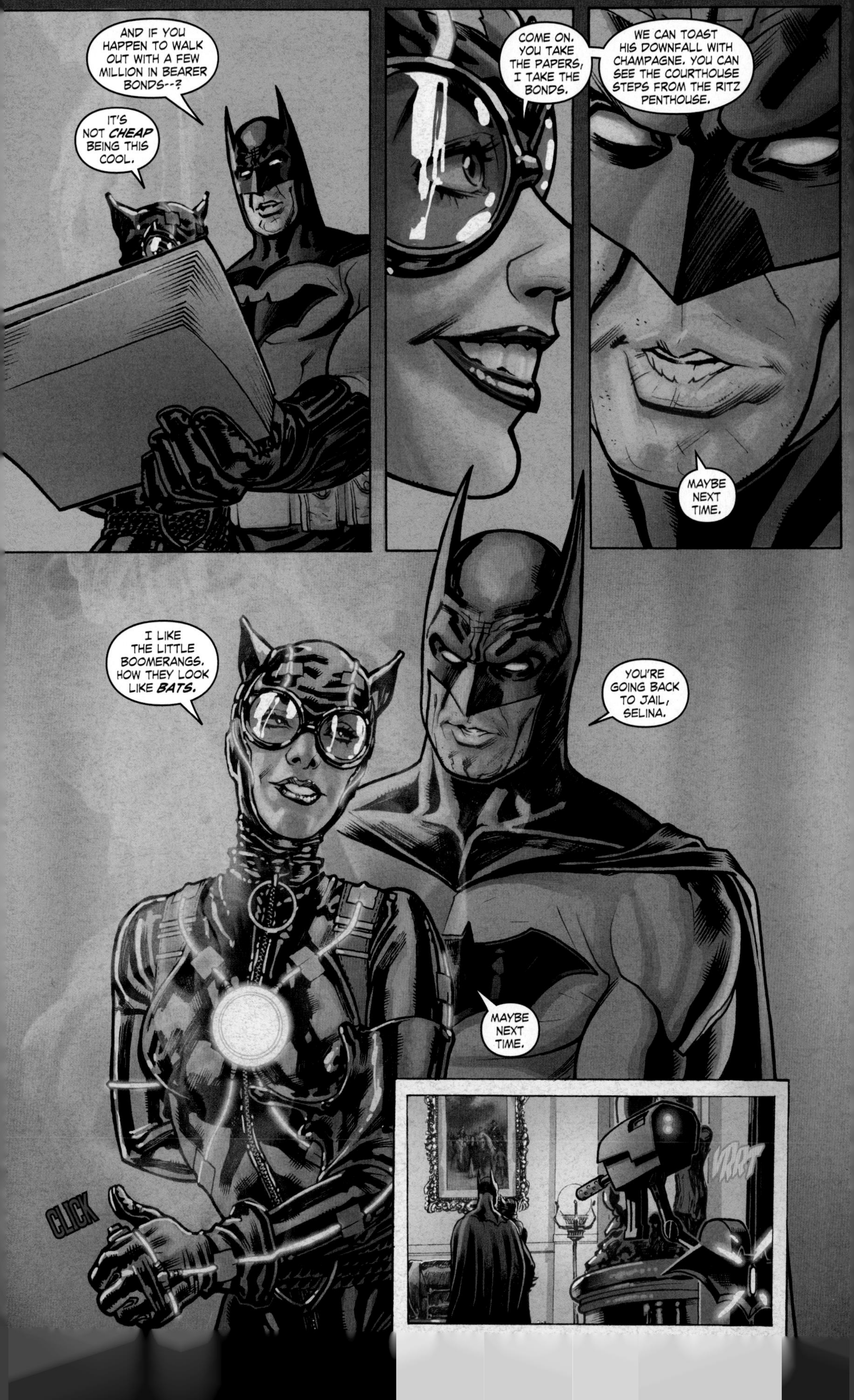

AND IF YOU HAPPEN TO WALK OUT WITH A FEW MILLION IN BEARER BONDS--?
IT'S NOT CHEAP BEING THIS COOL.
COME ON. YOU TAKE THE PAPERS, I TAKE THE BONDS.
WE CAN TOAST HIS DOWNFALL WITH CHAMPAGNE. YOU CAN SEE THE COURTHOUSE STEPS FROM THE RITZ PENTHOUSE.
MAYBE NEXT TIME.
I LIKE THE LITTLE BOOMERANGS. HOW THEY LOOK LIKE BATS.
YOU'RE GOING BACK TO JAIL, SELINA.
MAYBE NEXT TIME.
CLICK
VRRT

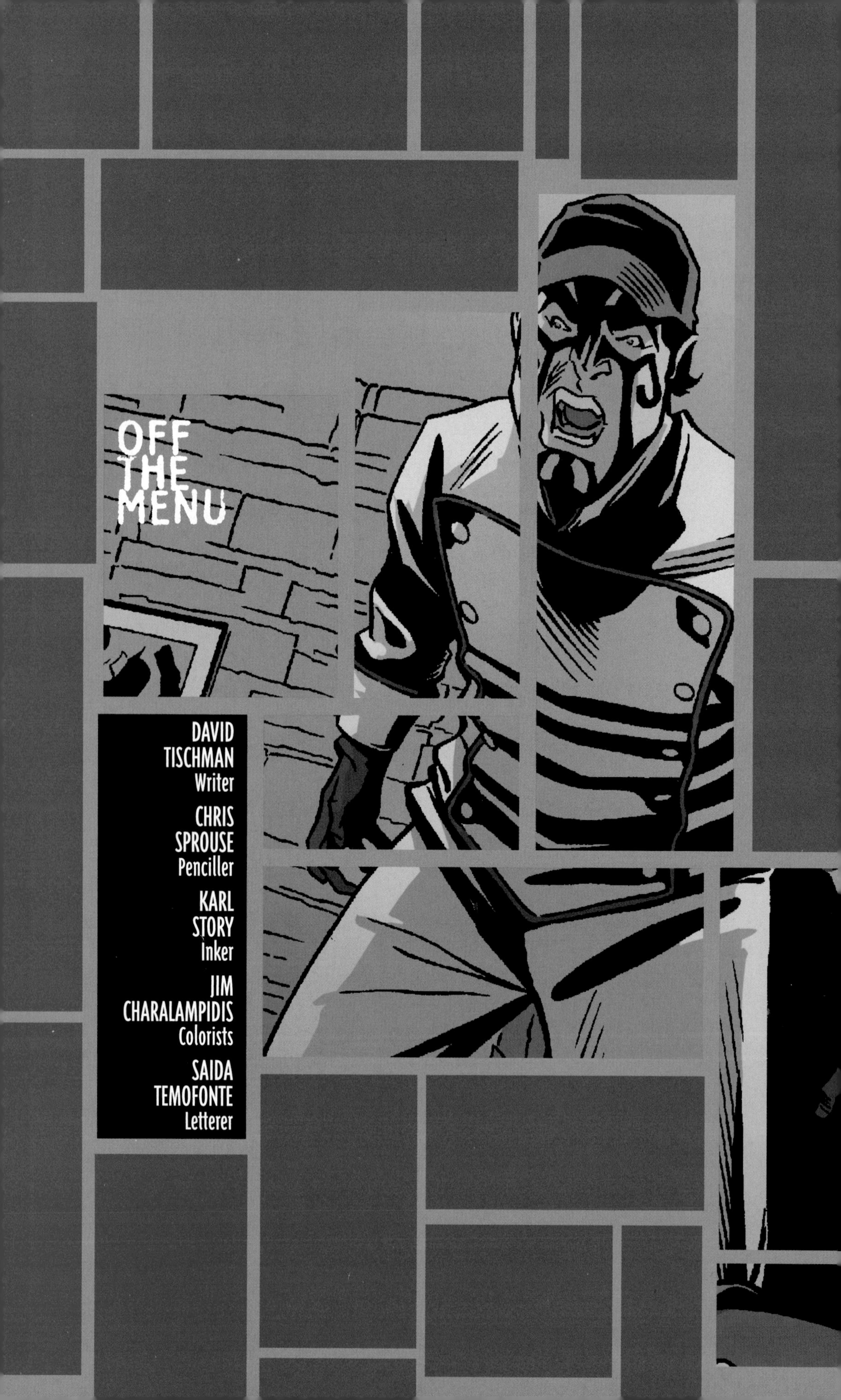
OFF THE MENU
DAVID TISCHMAN Writer
CHRIS SPROUSE Penciller
KARL STORY Inker
JIM CHARALAMPIDIS Colorists
SAIDA TEMOFONTE Letterer

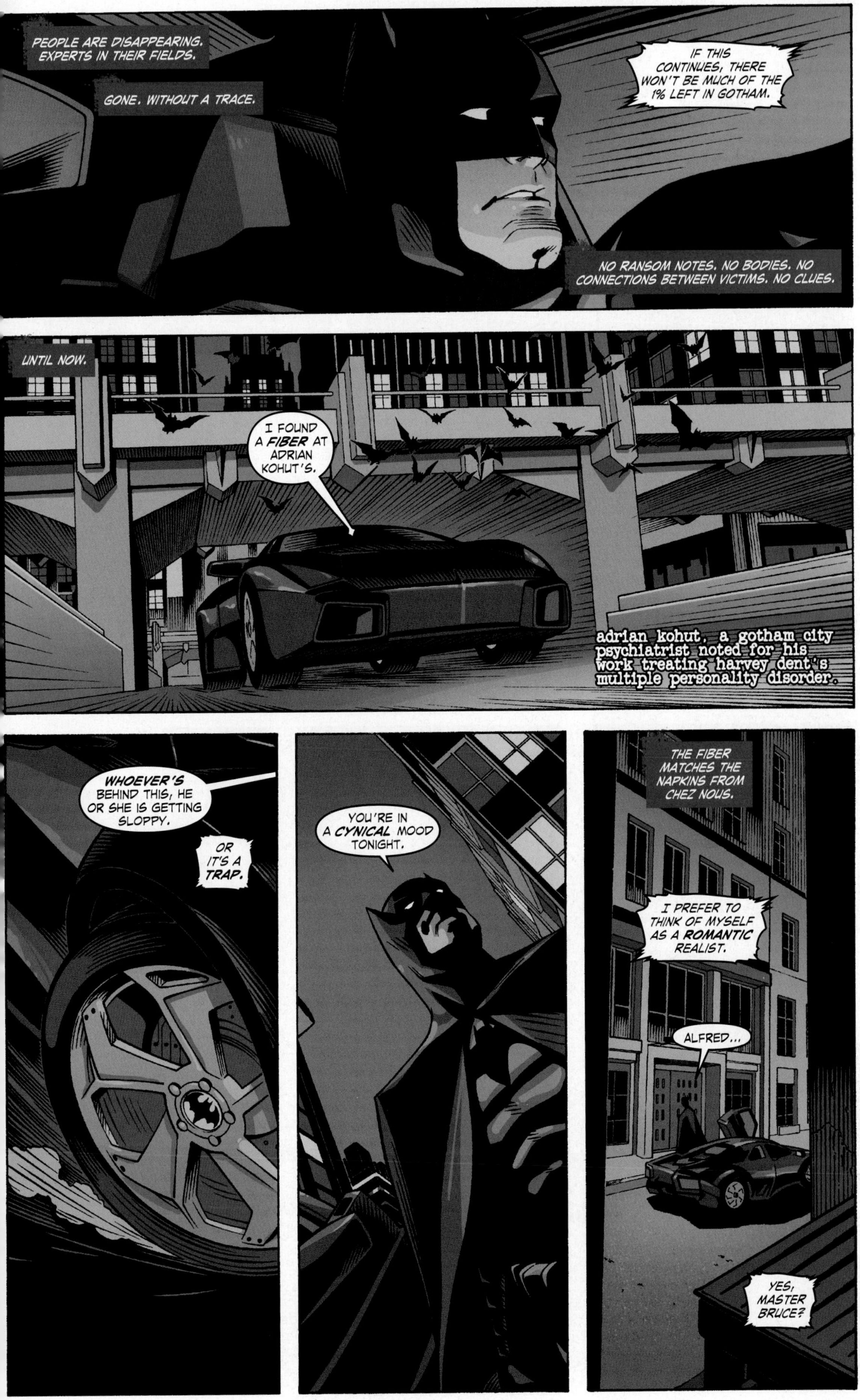
PEOPLE ARE DISAPPEARING. EXPERTS IN THEIR FIELDS.
GONE. WITHOUT A TRACE.
IF THIS CONTINUES, THERE WON'T BE MUCH OF THE 1% LEFT IN GOTHAM.
NO RANSOM NOTES. NO BODIES. NO CONNECTIONS BETWEEN VICTIMS. NO CLUES.
UNTIL NOW.
I FOUND A FIBER AT ADRIAN KOHUT'S.
adrian kohut, a gotham city psychiatrist noted for his work treating harvey dent's multiple personality disorder.
WHOEVER'S BEHIND THIS, HE OR SHE IS GETTING SLOPPY.
OR IT'S A TRAP.
YOU'RE IN A CYNICAL MOOD TONIGHT.
THE FIBER MATCHES THE NAPKINS FROM CHEZ NOUS.
I PREFER TO THINK OF MYSELF AS A ROMANTIC REALIST.
ALFRED...
YES, MASTER BRUCE?

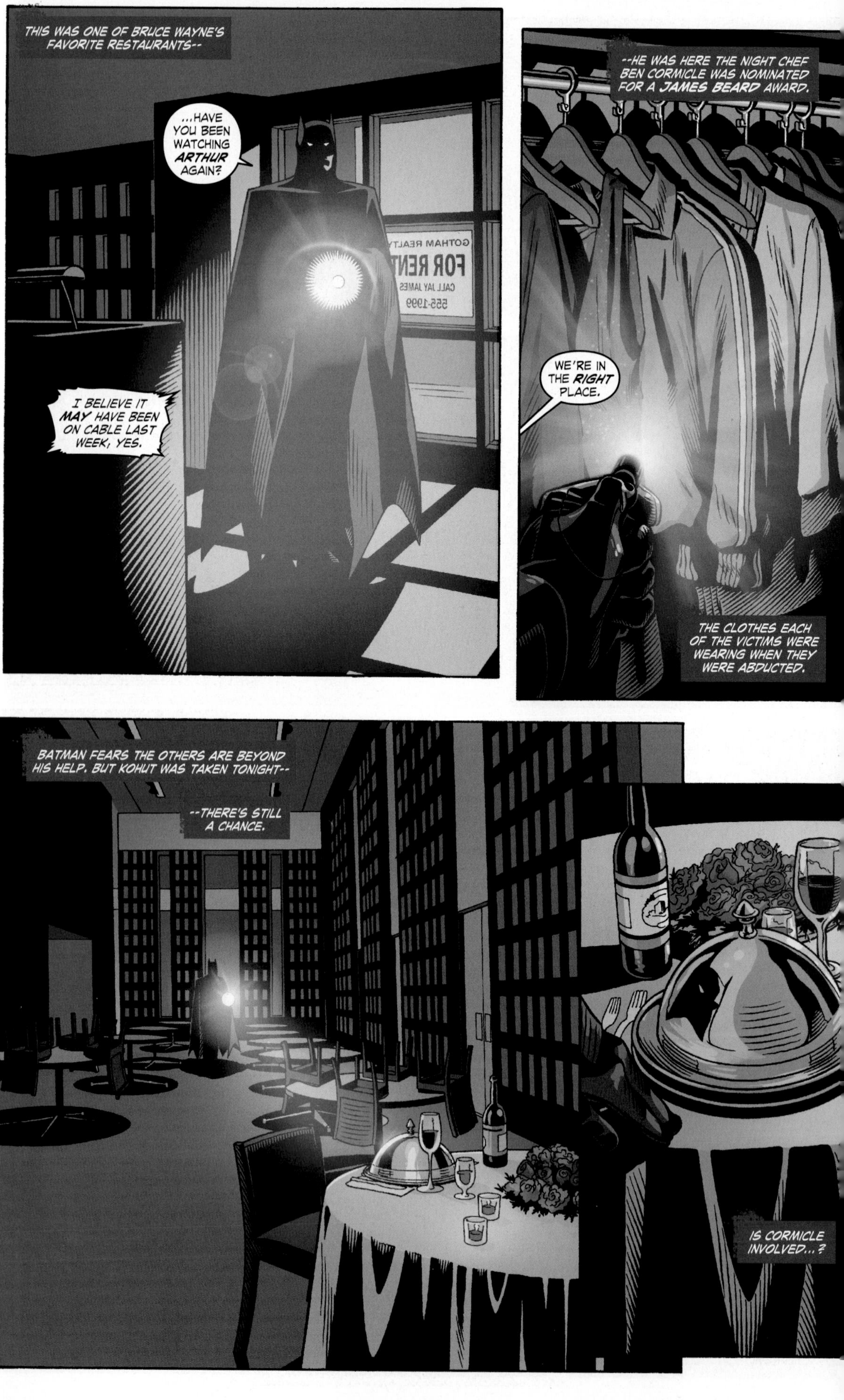
THIS WAS ONE OF BRUCE WAYNE'S FAVORITE RESTAURANTS--
...HAVE YOU BEEN WATCHING ARTHUR AGAIN?
GOTHAM REALTY
FOR RENT
CALL JAY JAMES
555-1999
I BELIEVE IT MAY HAVE BEEN ON CABLE LAST WEEK, YES.
--HE WAS HERE THE NIGHT CHEF BEN CORMICLE WAS NOMINATED FOR A JAMES BEARD AWARD.
WE'RE IN THE RIGHT PLACE.
THE CLOTHES EACH OF THE VICTIMS WERE WEARING WHEN THEY WERE ABDUCTED.
BATMAN FEARS THE OTHERS ARE BEYOND HIS HELP. BUT KOHUT WAS TAKEN TONIGHT--
--THERE'S STILL A CHANCE.
IS CORMICLE INVOLVED...?

SAUTÉED VEAL BRAINS IS HIS SIGNATURE DISH.

THE FAT IN THE DUCK EGG CUTS THE RICHNESS OF THE PERFECTLY SAUTÉED BRAINS, AND THE TOASTED CROSTINI ADDS JUST THE RIGHT AMOUNT OF TEXTURE TO EACH BITE. THE ARUGULA SALAD--

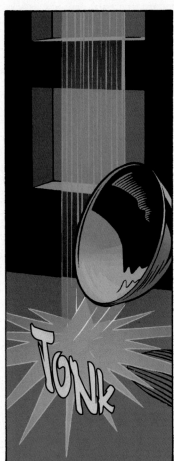

TONK

--IT SMELLS SO GOOD...

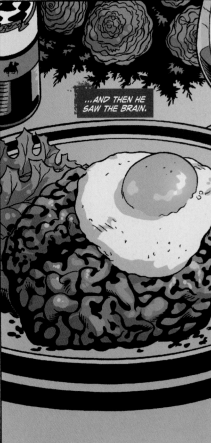

...AND THEN HE SAW THE BRAIN.

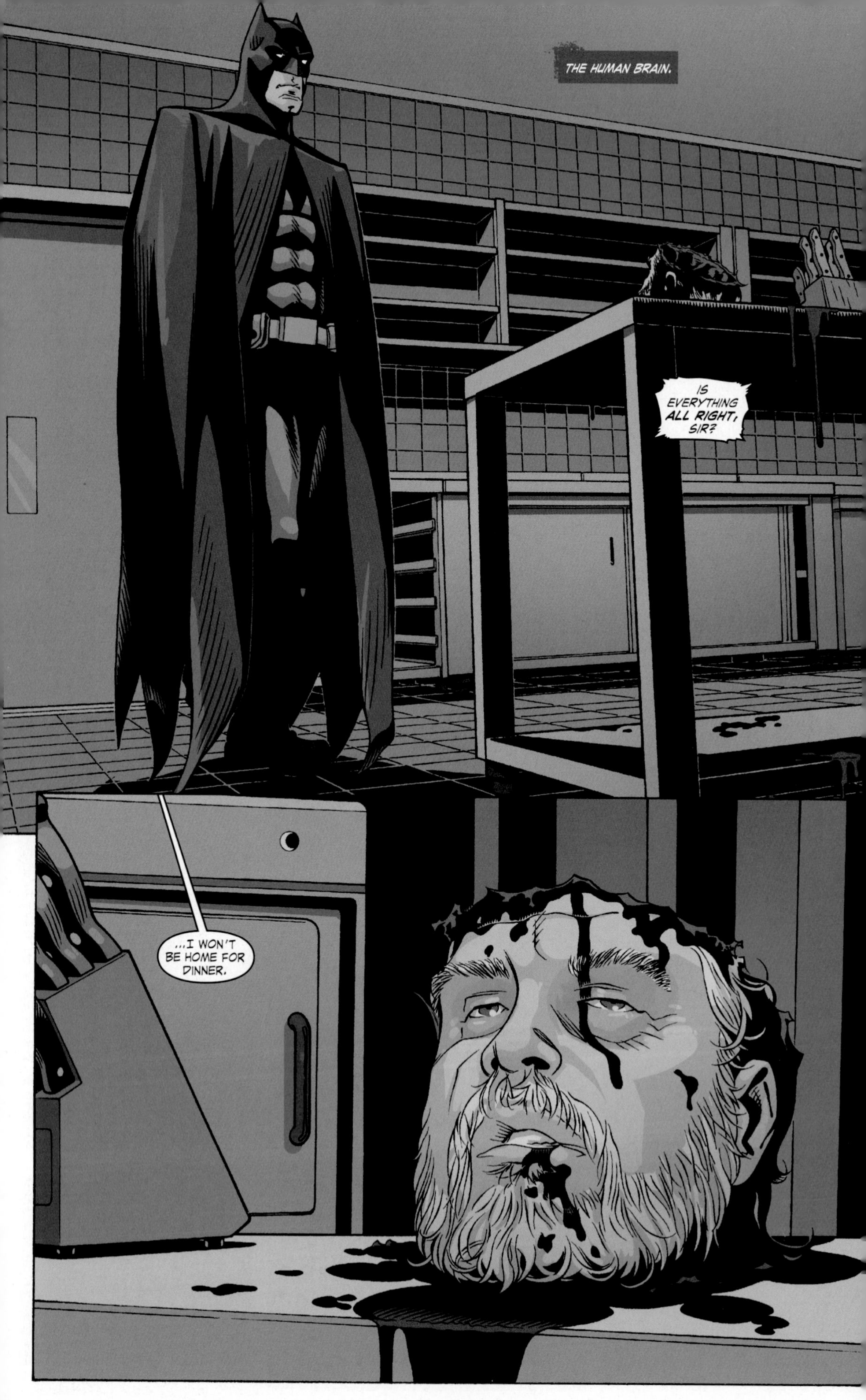
THE HUMAN BRAIN.
IS EVERYTHING ALL RIGHT, SIR?
...I WON'T BE HOME FOR DINNER.

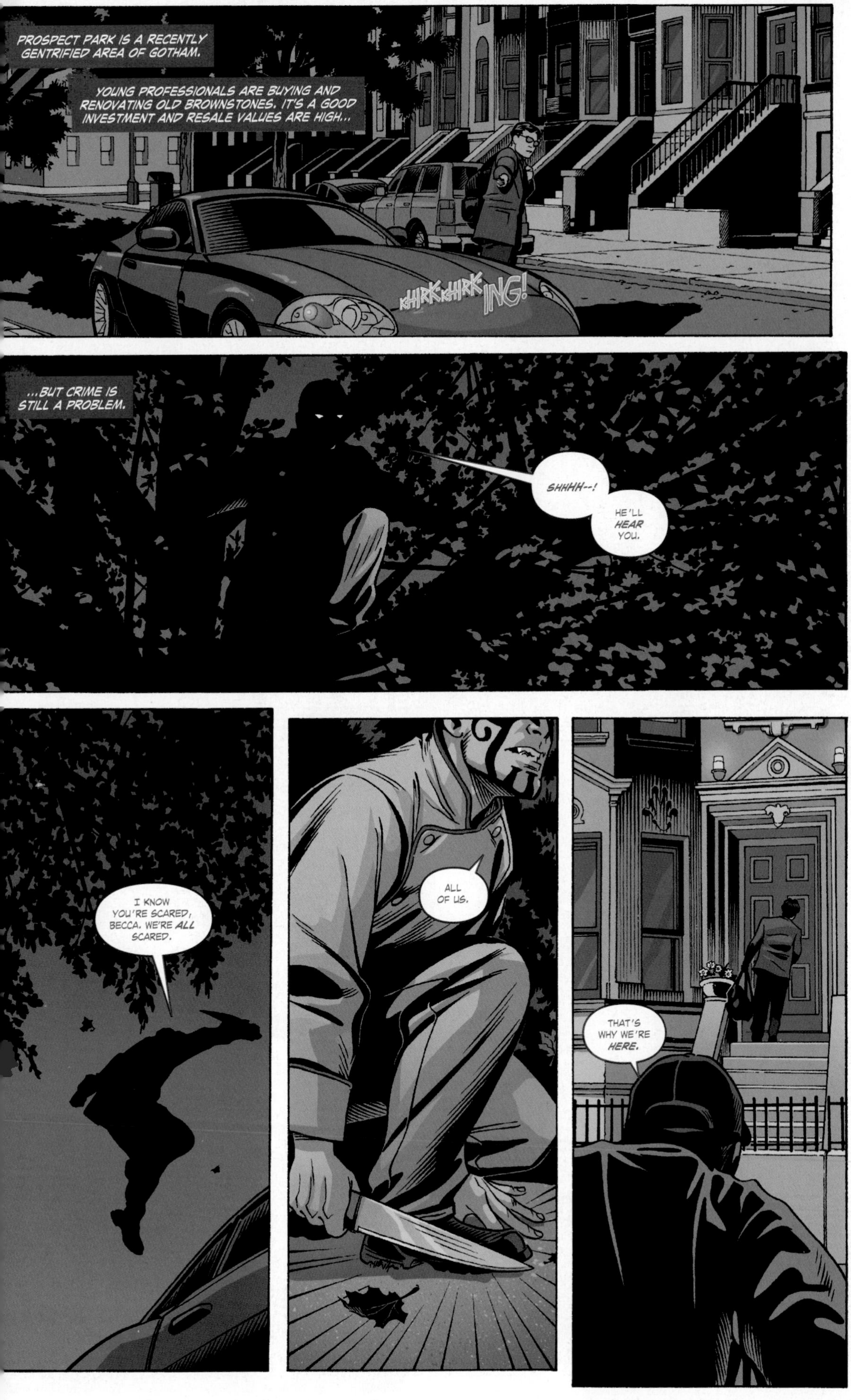
PROSPECT PARK IS A RECENTLY GENTRIFIED AREA OF GOTHAM.
YOUNG PROFESSIONALS ARE BUYING AND RENOVATING OLD BROWNSTONES. IT'S A GOOD INVESTMENT AND RESALE VALUES ARE HIGH...
KHIRK-KHIRK-ING!
...BUT CRIME IS STILL A PROBLEM.
SHHHH--!
HE'LL HEAR YOU.
I KNOW YOU'RE SCARED, BECCA. WE'RE ALL SCARED.
ALL OF US.
THAT'S WHY WE'RE HERE.

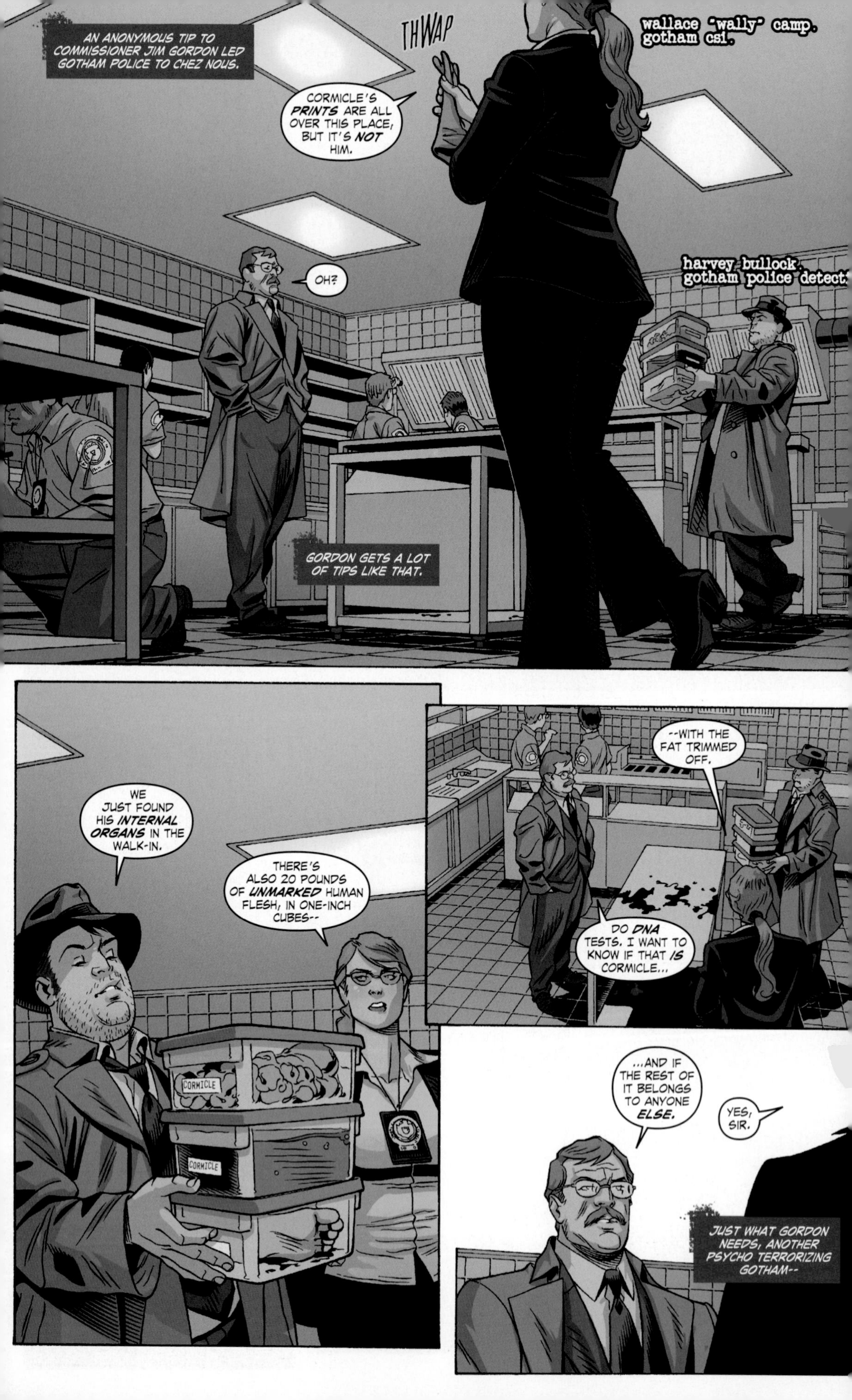
AN ANONYMOUS TIP TO COMMISSIONER JIM GORDON LED GOTHAM POLICE TO CHEZ NOUS.
THWAP
wallace "wally" camp. gotham csi.
CORMICLE'S PRINTS ARE ALL OVER THIS PLACE, BUT IT'S NOT HIM.
OH?
harvey bullock. gotham police detect
GORDON GETS A LOT OF TIPS LIKE THAT.
WE JUST FOUND HIS INTERNAL ORGANS IN THE WALK-IN.
THERE'S ALSO 20 POUNDS OF UNMARKED HUMAN FLESH, IN ONE-INCH CUBES--
CORMICLE
CORMICLE
--WITH THE FAT TRIMMED OFF.
DO DNA TESTS. I WANT TO KNOW IF THAT IS CORMICLE...
...AND IF THE REST OF IT BELONGS TO ANYONE ELSE.
YES, SIR.
JUST WHAT GORDON NEEDS, ANOTHER PSYCHO TERRORIZING GOTHAM--

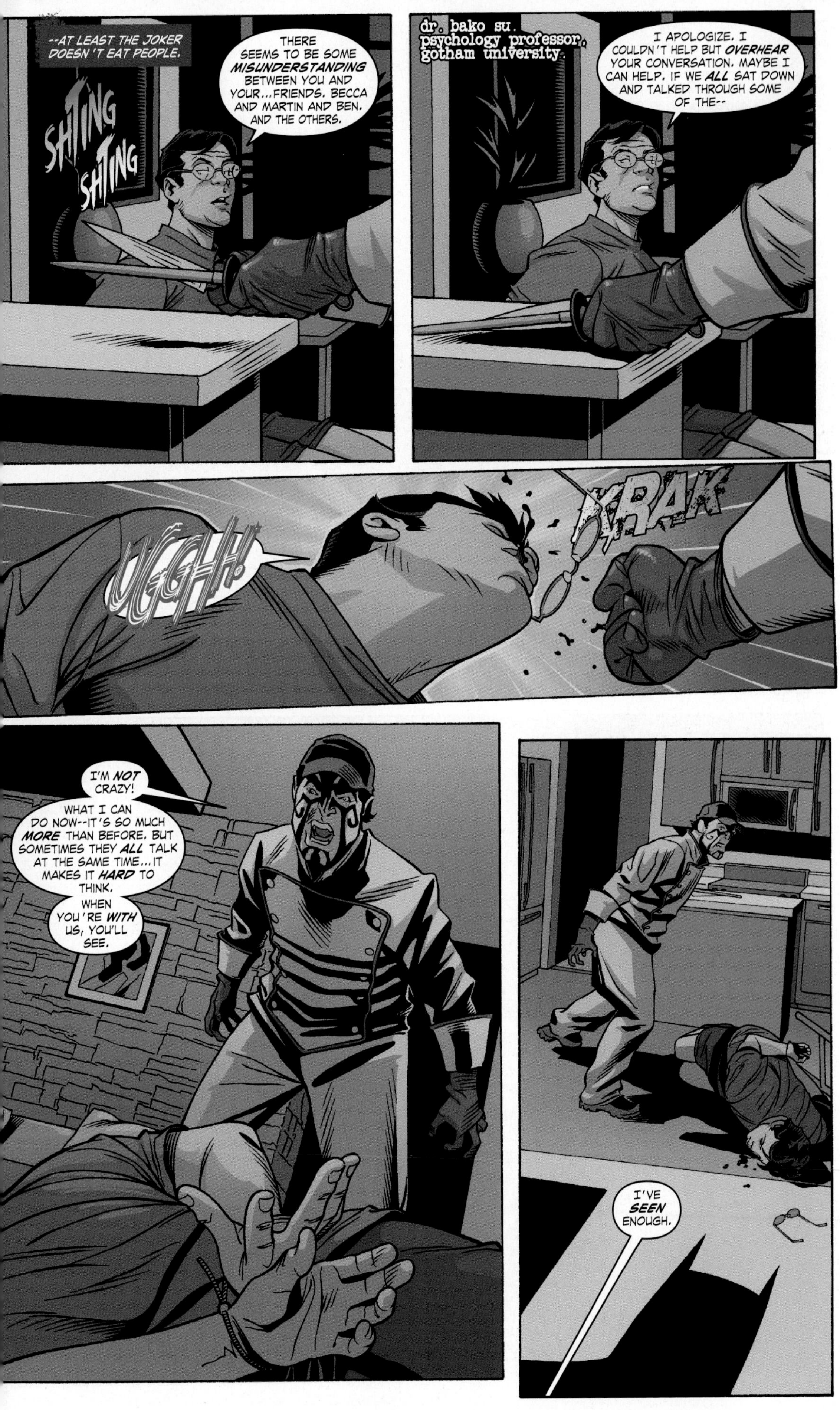
--AT LEAST THE JOKER DOESN'T EAT PEOPLE.
THERE SEEMS TO BE SOME MISUNDERSTANDING BETWEEN YOU AND YOUR...FRIENDS. BECCA AND MARTIN AND BEN. AND THE OTHERS.
SHTING SHTING
dr. bako su. psychology professor, gotham university.
I APOLOGIZE. I COULDN'T HELP BUT OVERHEAR YOUR CONVERSATION. MAYBE I CAN HELP. IF WE ALL SAT DOWN AND TALKED THROUGH SOME OF THE--
UGGH!
KRAK
I'M NOT CRAZY!
WHAT I CAN DO NOW--IT'S SO MUCH MORE THAN BEFORE. BUT SOMETIMES THEY ALL TALK AT THE SAME TIME...IT MAKES IT HARD TO THINK.
WHEN YOU'RE WITH US, YOU'LL SEE.
I'VE SEEN ENOUGH.

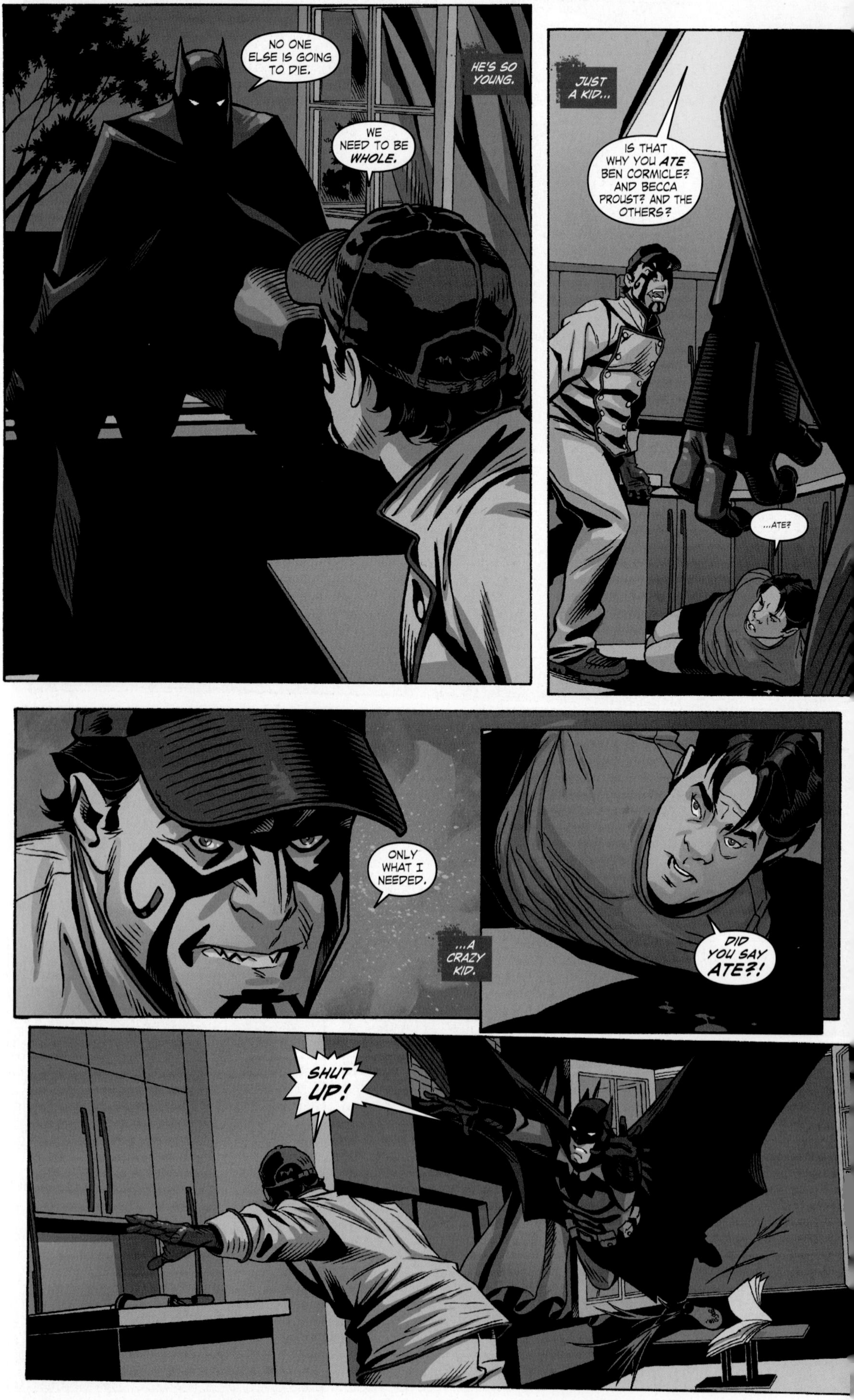
NO ONE ELSE IS GOING TO DIE.
HE'S SO YOUNG.
WE NEED TO BE WHOLE.
JUST A KID...
IS THAT WHY YOU ATE BEN CORMICLE? AND BECCA PROUST? AND THE OTHERS?
...ATE?
ONLY WHAT I NEEDED.
...A CRAZY KID.
DID YOU SAY ATE?!
SHUT UP!

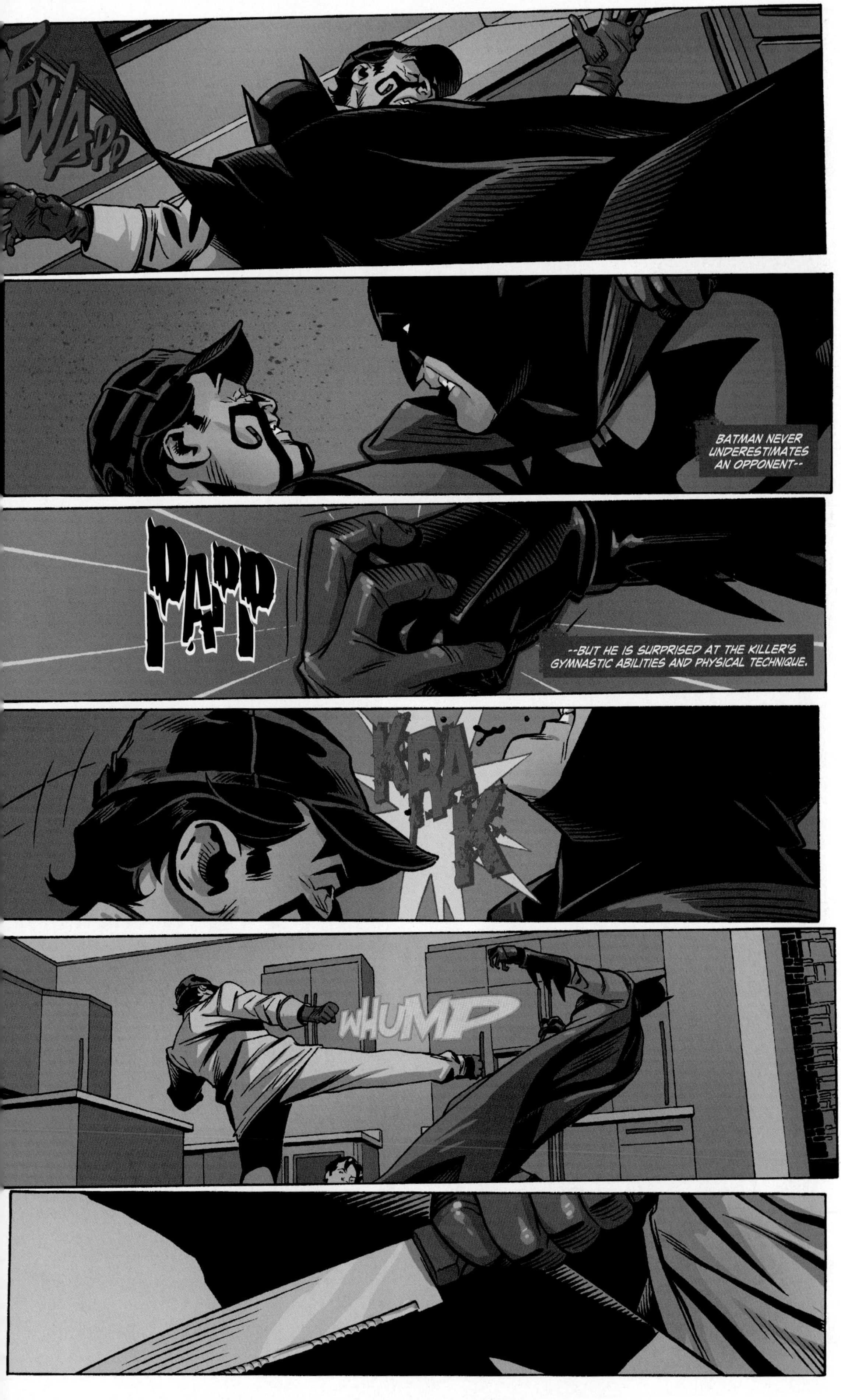
FWAPP
BATMAN NEVER UNDERESTIMATES AN OPPONENT--
PAPP
--BUT HE IS SURPRISED AT THE KILLER'S GYMNASTIC ABILITIES AND PHYSICAL TECHNIQUE.
KRAK
WHUMP

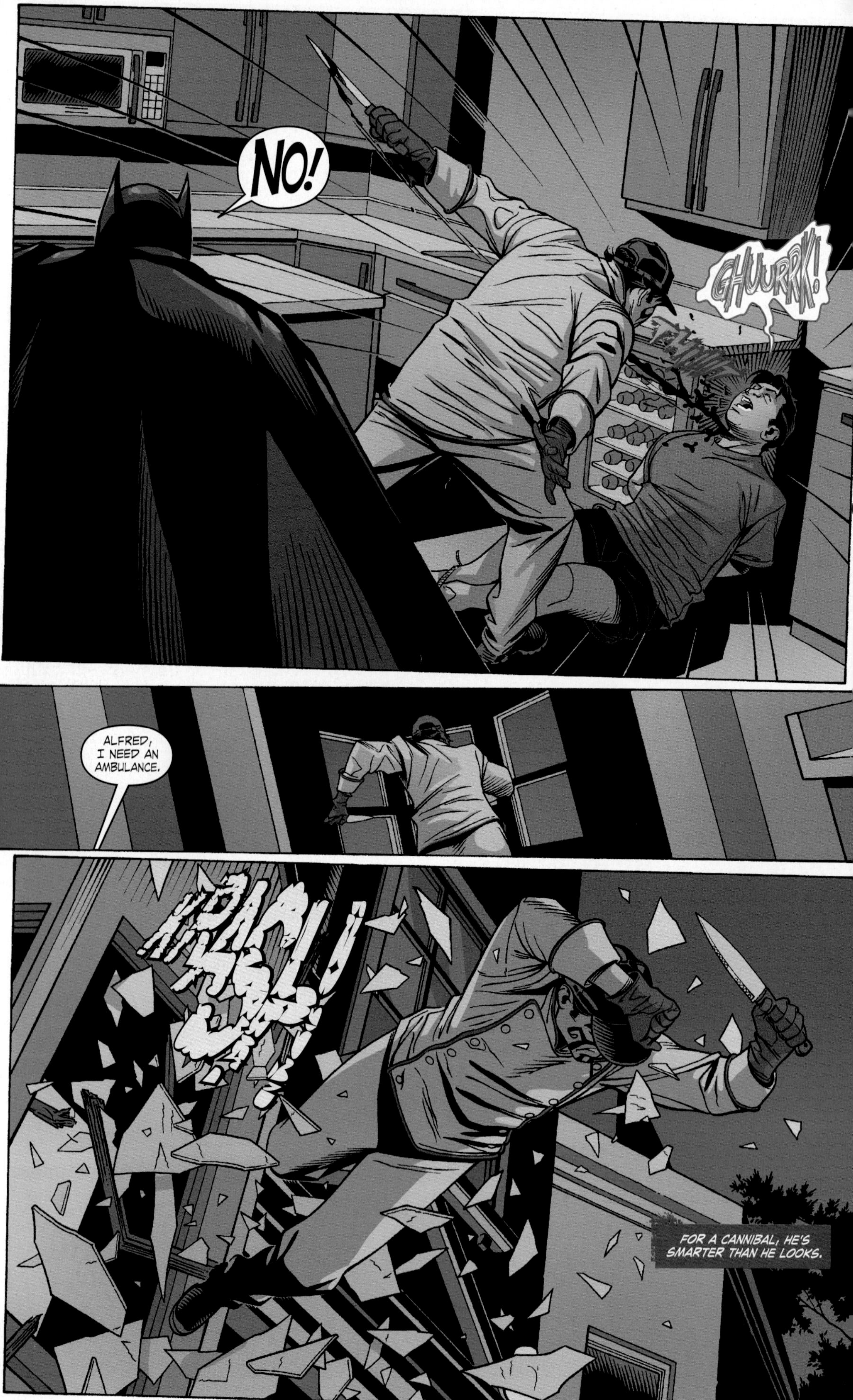
NO!
GHUURRK!
ALFRED, I NEED AN AMBULANCE.
FOR A CANNIBAL, HE'S SMARTER THAN HE LOOKS.

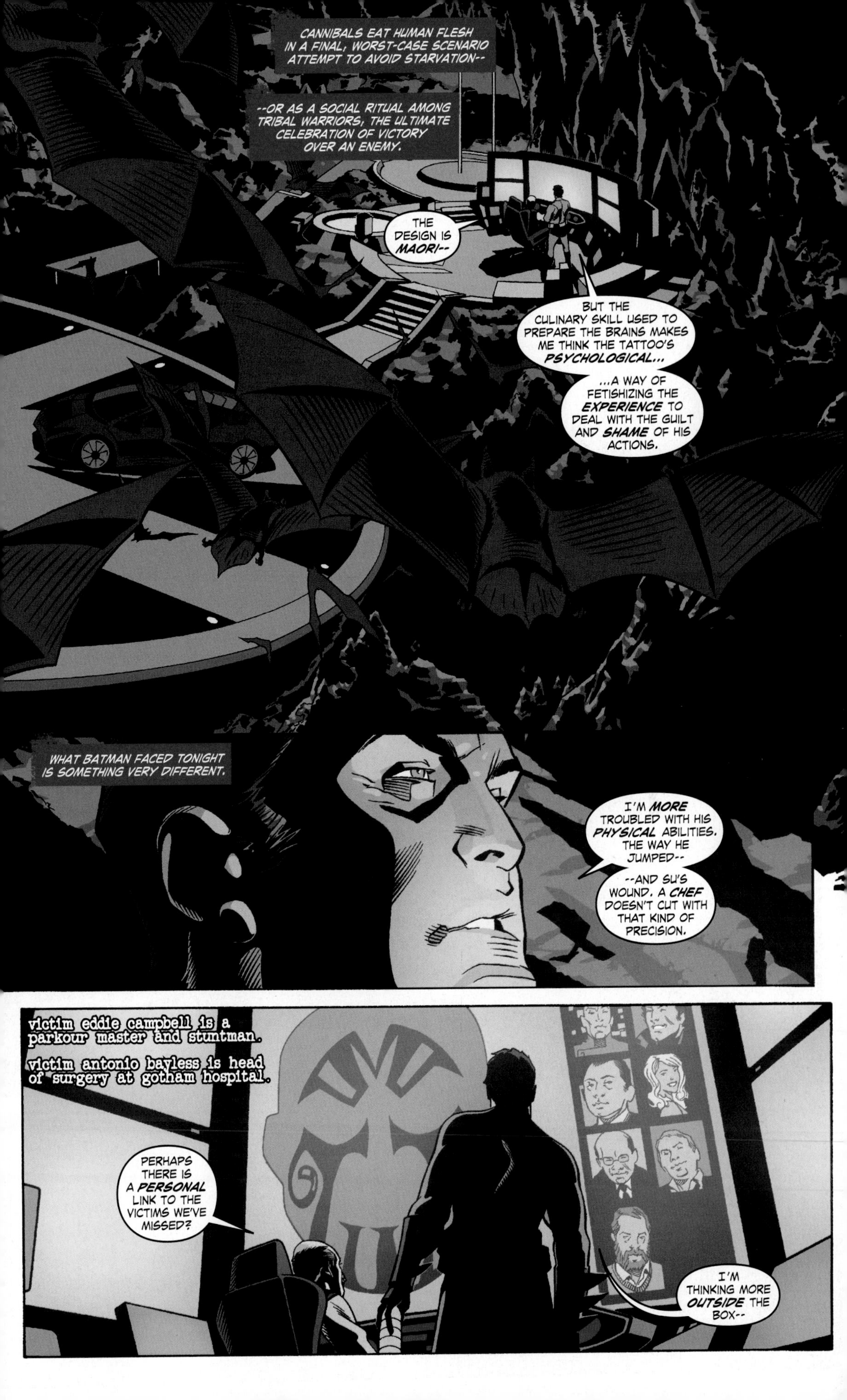
CANNIBALS EAT HUMAN FLESH IN A FINAL, WORST-CASE SCENARIO ATTEMPT TO AVOID STARVATION--
--OR AS A SOCIAL RITUAL AMONG TRIBAL WARRIORS; THE ULTIMATE CELEBRATION OF VICTORY OVER AN ENEMY.
THE DESIGN IS MAORI--
BUT THE CULINARY SKILL USED TO PREPARE THE BRAINS MAKES ME THINK THE TATTOO'S PSYCHOLOGICAL...
...A WAY OF FETISHIZING THE EXPERIENCE TO DEAL WITH THE GUILT AND SHAME OF HIS ACTIONS.
WHAT BATMAN FACED TONIGHT IS SOMETHING VERY DIFFERENT.
I'M MORE TROUBLED WITH HIS PHYSICAL ABILITIES. THE WAY HE JUMPED--
--AND SU'S WOUND. A CHEF DOESN'T CUT WITH THAT KIND OF PRECISION.
victim eddie campbell is a parkour master and stuntman.
victim antonio bayless is head of surgery at gotham hospital.
PERHAPS THERE IS A PERSONAL LINK TO THE VICTIMS WE'VE MISSED?
I'M THINKING MORE OUTSIDE THE BOX--

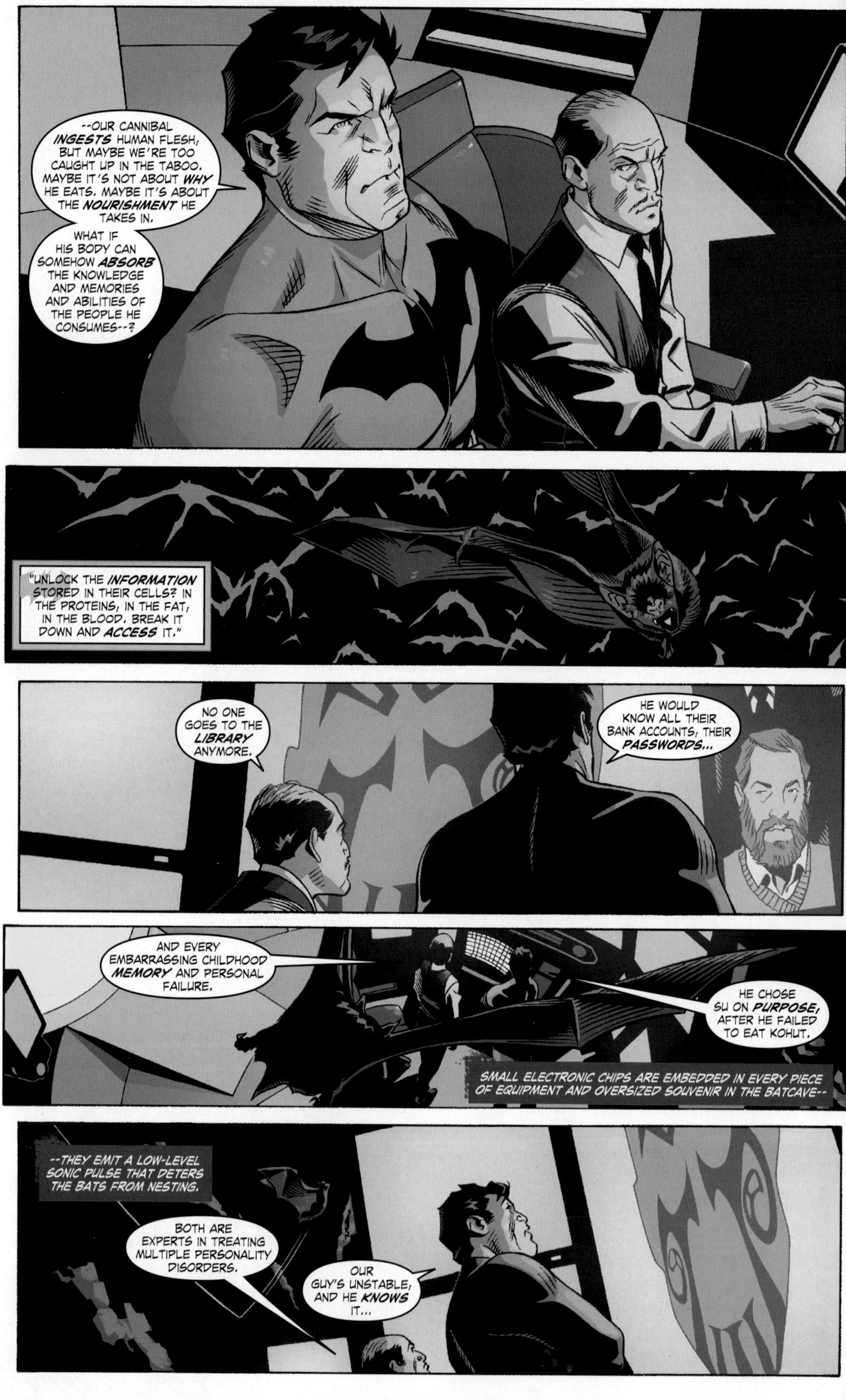
--OUR CANNIBAL INGESTS HUMAN FLESH, BUT MAYBE WE'RE TOO CAUGHT UP IN THE TABOO. MAYBE IT'S NOT ABOUT WHY HE EATS. MAYBE IT'S ABOUT THE NOURISHMENT HE TAKES IN.
WHAT IF HIS BODY CAN SOMEHOW ABSORB THE KNOWLEDGE AND MEMORIES AND ABILITIES OF THE PEOPLE HE CONSUMES--?
"UNLOCK THE INFORMATION STORED IN THEIR CELLS? IN THE PROTEINS, IN THE FAT, IN THE BLOOD. BREAK IT DOWN AND ACCESS IT."
NO ONE GOES TO THE LIBRARY ANYMORE.
HE WOULD KNOW ALL THEIR BANK ACCOUNTS, THEIR PASSWORDS...
AND EVERY EMBARRASSING CHILDHOOD MEMORY AND PERSONAL FAILURE.
HE CHOSE SU ON PURPOSE, AFTER HE FAILED TO EAT KOHUT.
SMALL ELECTRONIC CHIPS ARE EMBEDDED IN EVERY PIECE OF EQUIPMENT AND OVERSIZED SOUVENIR IN THE BATCAVE--
--THEY EMIT A LOW-LEVEL SONIC PULSE THAT DETERS THE BATS FROM NESTING.
BOTH ARE EXPERTS IN TREATING MULTIPLE PERSONALITY DISORDERS.
OUR GUY'S UNSTABLE, AND HE KNOWS IT...

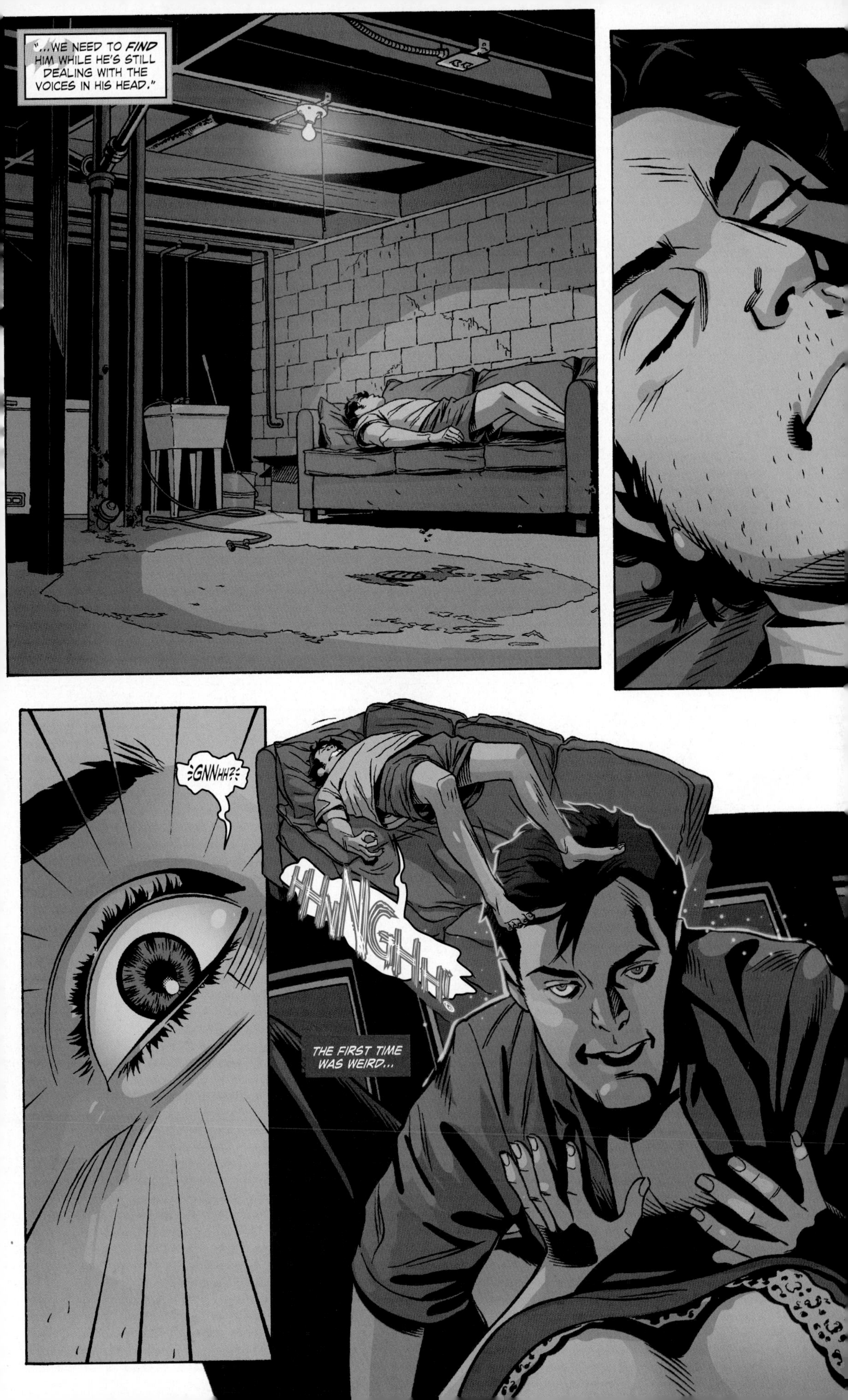
"...WE NEED TO *FIND* HIM WHILE HE'S STILL DEALING WITH THE VOICES IN HIS HEAD."
GNNHH?
HHNGHH!
THE FIRST TIME WAS WEIRD...

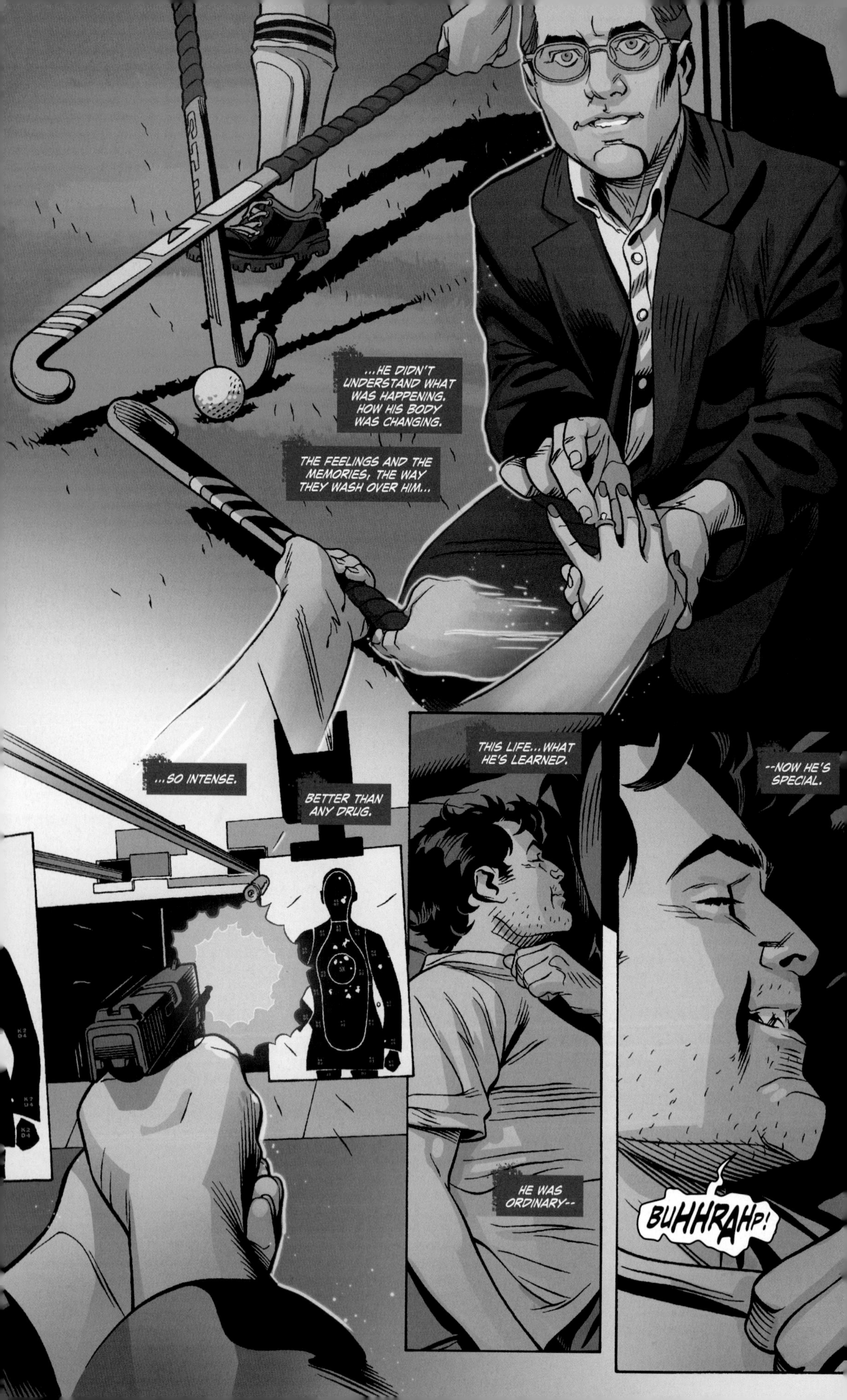
...HE DIDN'T UNDERSTAND WHAT WAS HAPPENING. HOW HIS BODY WAS CHANGING.
THE FEELINGS AND THE MEMORIES, THE WAY THEY WASH OVER HIM...
...SO INTENSE.
BETTER THAN ANY DRUG.
THIS LIFE... WHAT HE'S LEARNED.
HE WAS ORDINARY--
--NOW HE'S SPECIAL.
BUHHRAHP!

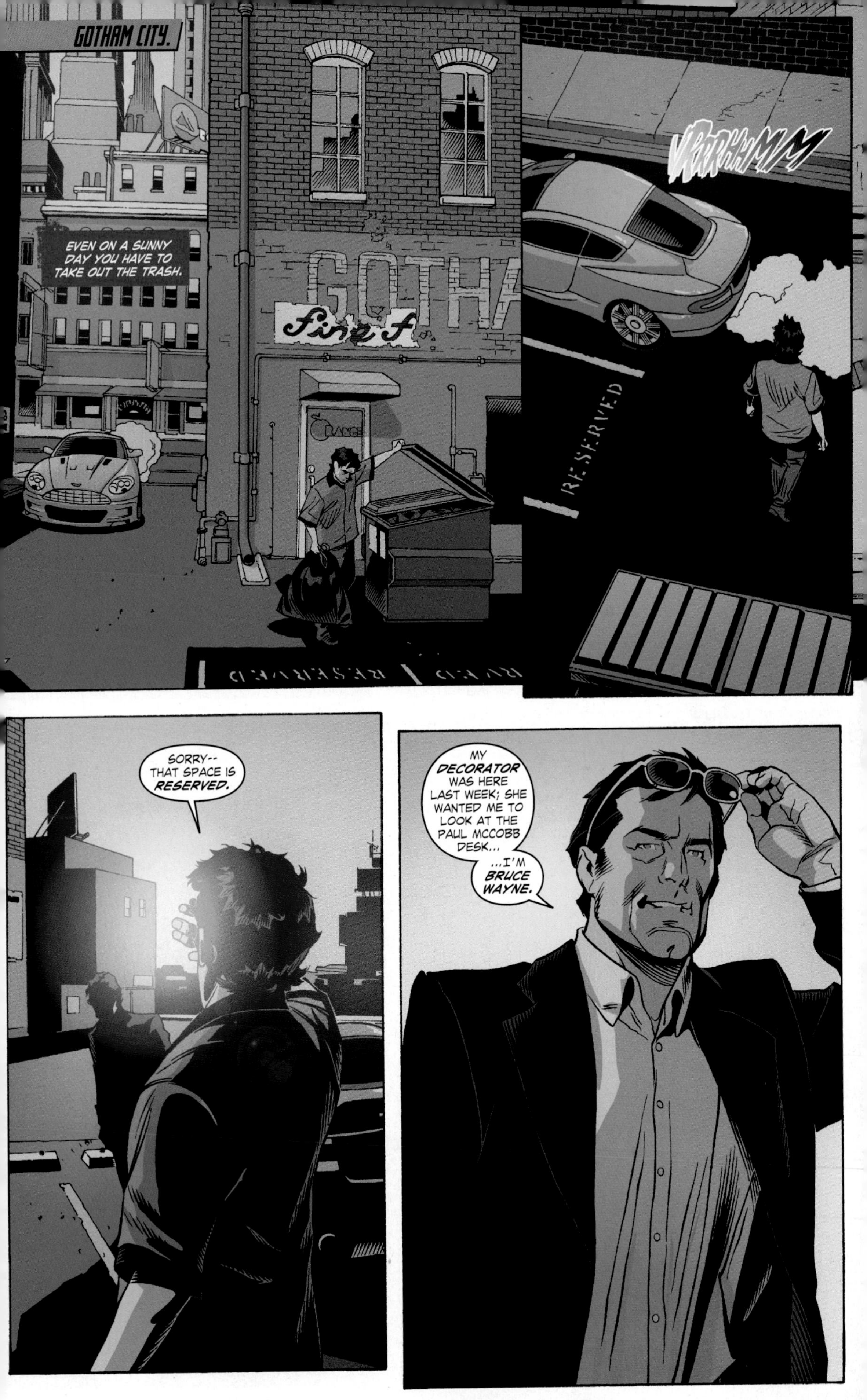
GOTHAM CITY.
EVEN ON A SUNNY DAY YOU HAVE TO TAKE OUT THE TRASH.
RESERVED
SORRY-- THAT SPACE IS RESERVED.
MY DECORATOR WAS HERE LAST WEEK; SHE WANTED ME TO LOOK AT THE PAUL MCCOBB DESK...
...I'M BRUCE WAYNE.

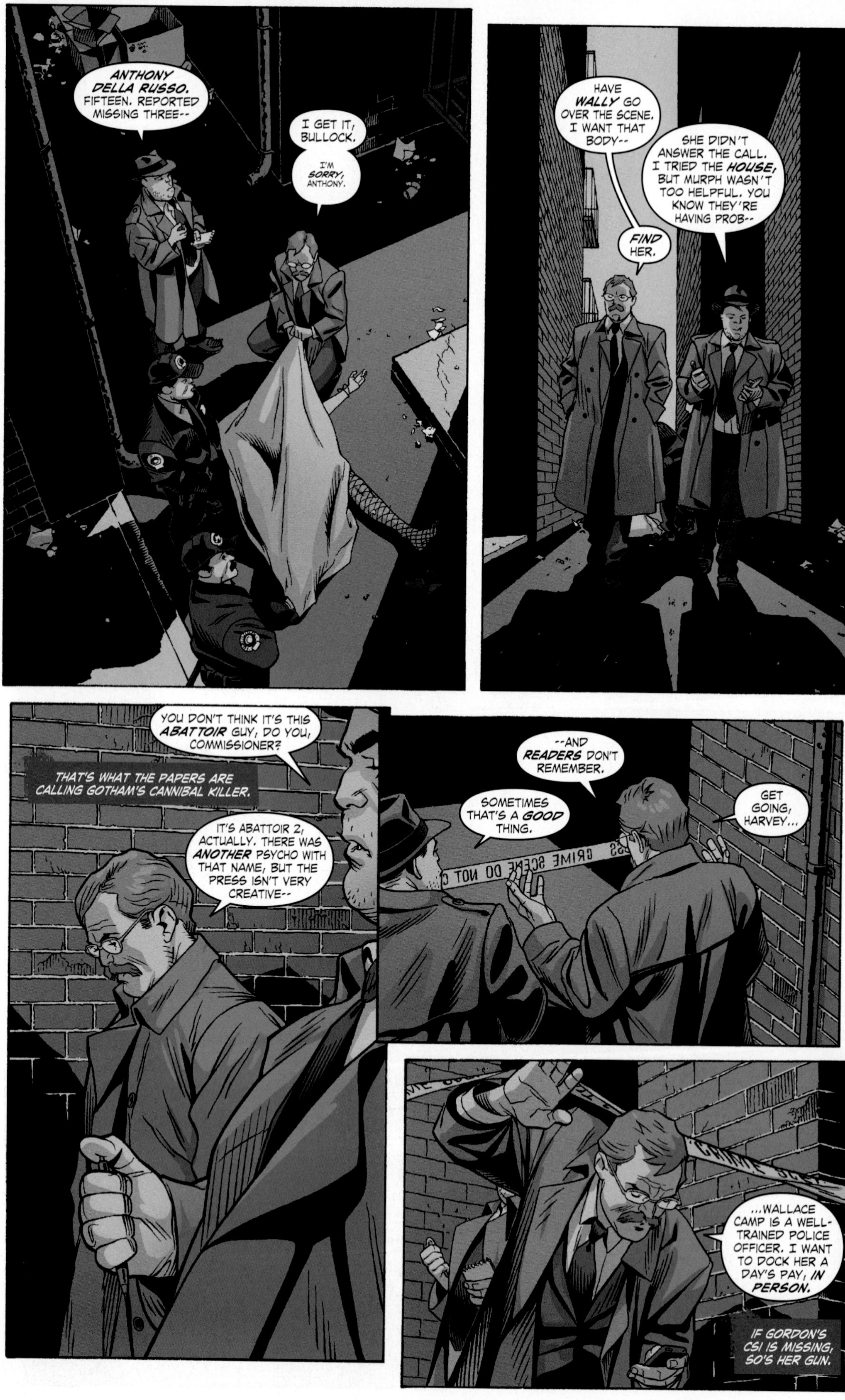
ANTHONY DELLA RUSSO. FIFTEEN. REPORTED MISSING THREE--
I GET IT, BULLOCK.
I'M SORRY, ANTHONY.
HAVE WALLY GO OVER THE SCENE. I WANT THAT BODY--
SHE DIDN'T ANSWER THE CALL. I TRIED THE HOUSE, BUT MURPH WASN'T TOO HELPFUL. YOU KNOW THEY'RE HAVING PROB--
FIND HER.
YOU DON'T THINK IT'S THIS ABATTOIR GUY, DO YOU, COMMISSIONER?
THAT'S WHAT THE PAPERS ARE CALLING GOTHAM'S CANNIBAL KILLER.
IT'S ABATTOIR 2, ACTUALLY. THERE WAS ANOTHER PSYCHO WITH THAT NAME, BUT THE PRESS ISN'T VERY CREATIVE--
--AND READERS DON'T REMEMBER.
SOMETIMES THAT'S A GOOD THING.
GET GOING, HARVEY...
...WALLACE CAMP IS A WELL-TRAINED POLICE OFFICER. I WANT TO DOCK HER A DAY'S PAY, IN PERSON.
IF GORDON'S CSI IS MISSING, SO'S HER GUN.

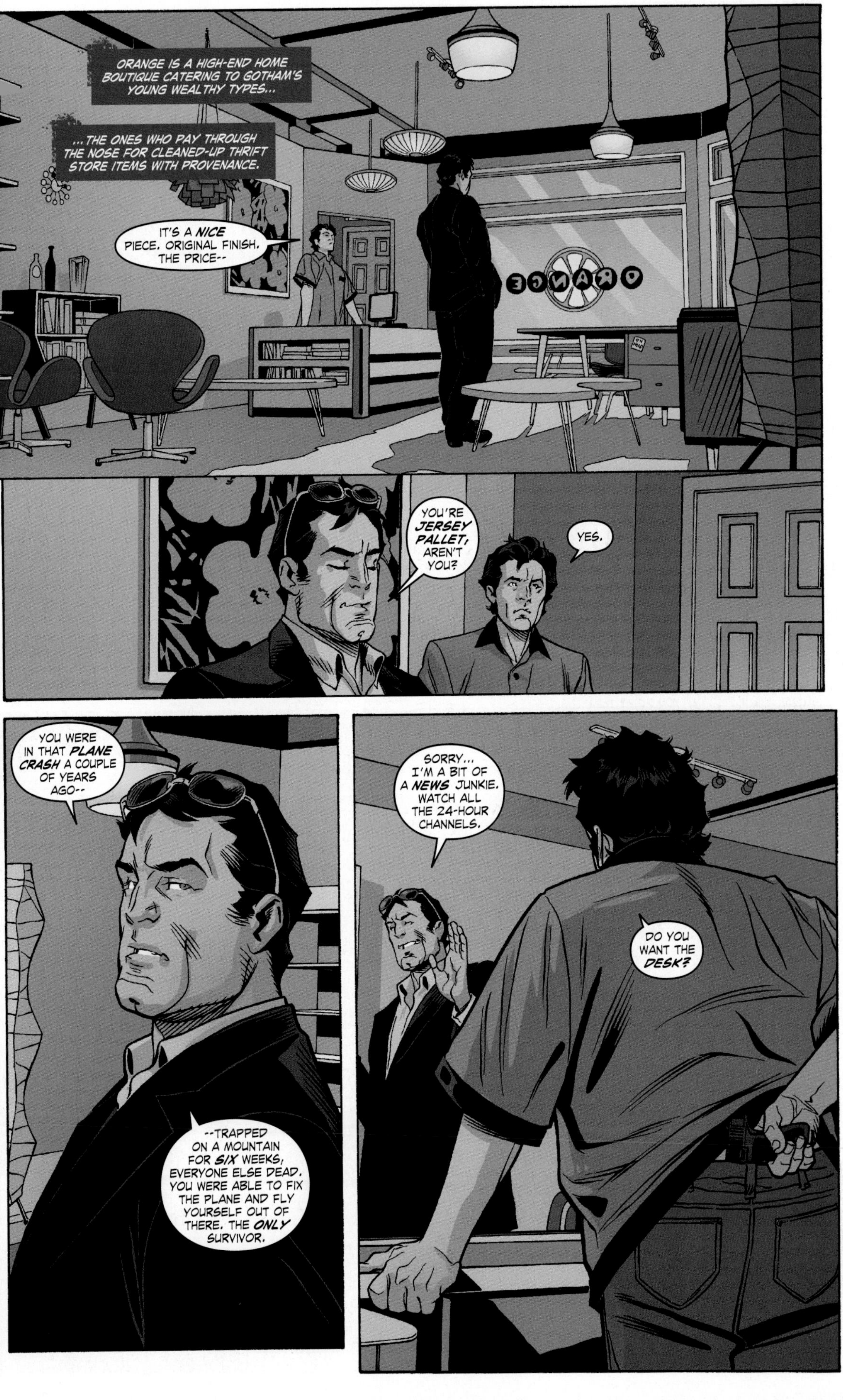
ORANGE IS A HIGH-END HOME BOUTIQUE CATERING TO GOTHAM'S YOUNG WEALTHY TYPES...
...THE ONES WHO PAY THROUGH THE NOSE FOR CLEANED-UP THRIFT STORE ITEMS WITH PROVENANCE.
IT'S A NICE PIECE. ORIGINAL FINISH. THE PRICE--
ORANGE
YOU'RE JERSEY PALLET, AREN'T YOU?
YES.
YOU WERE IN THAT PLANE CRASH A COUPLE OF YEARS AGO--
--TRAPPED ON A MOUNTAIN FOR SIX WEEKS, EVERYONE ELSE DEAD. YOU WERE ABLE TO FIX THE PLANE AND FLY YOURSELF OUT OF THERE. THE ONLY SURVIVOR.
SORRY... I'M A BIT OF A NEWS JUNKIE. WATCH ALL THE 24-HOUR CHANNELS.
DO YOU WANT THE DESK?

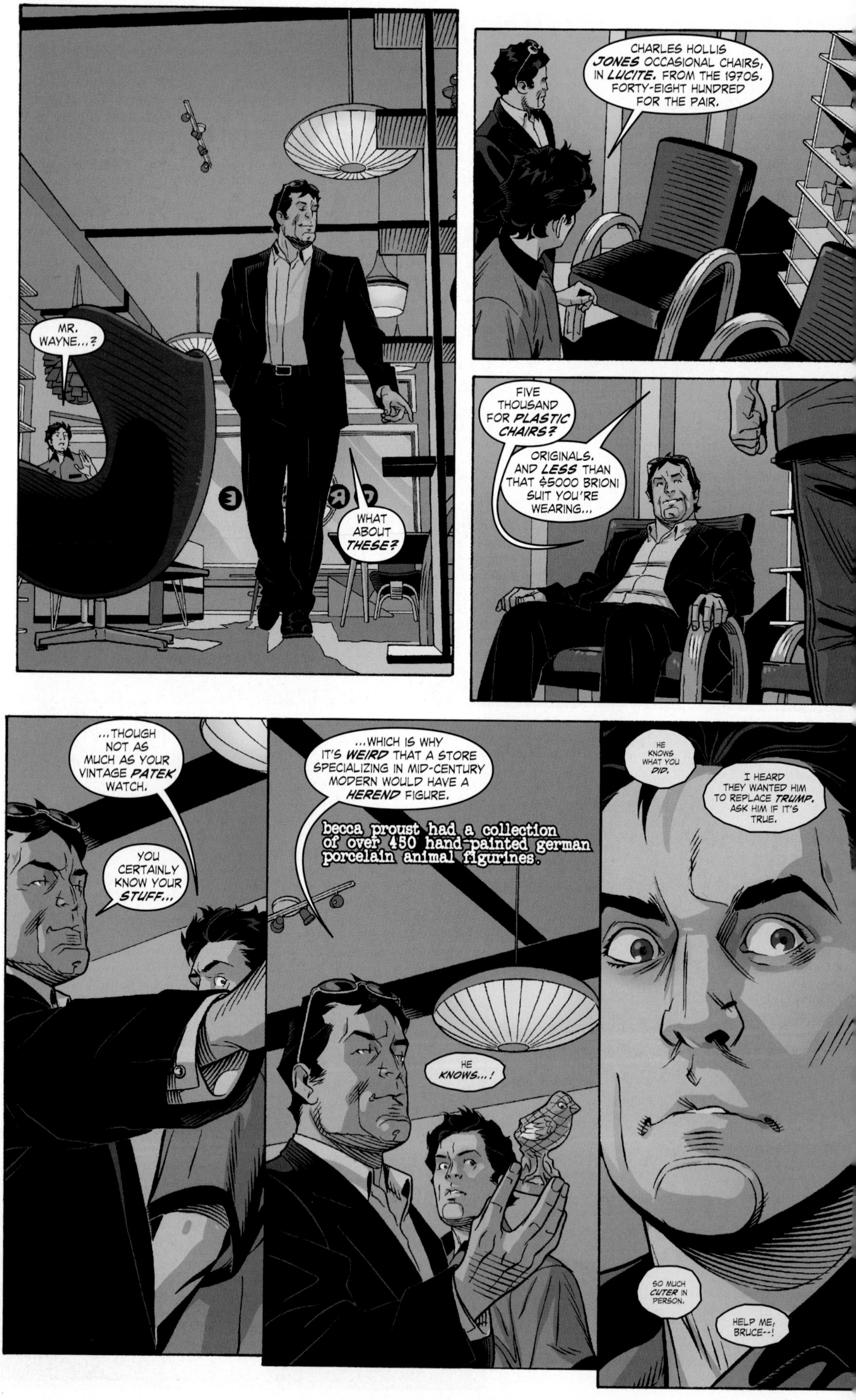
MR. WAYNE...?
WHAT ABOUT THESE?
CHARLES HOLLIS JONES OCCASIONAL CHAIRS, IN LUCITE. FROM THE 1970S. FORTY-EIGHT HUNDRED FOR THE PAIR.
FIVE THOUSAND FOR PLASTIC CHAIRS?
ORIGINALS. AND LESS THAN THAT $5000 BRIONI SUIT YOU'RE WEARING...
...THOUGH NOT AS MUCH AS YOUR VINTAGE PATEK WATCH.
YOU CERTAINLY KNOW YOUR STUFF...
...WHICH IS WHY IT'S WEIRD THAT A STORE SPECIALIZING IN MID-CENTURY MODERN WOULD HAVE A HEREND FIGURE.
becca proust had a collection of over 450 hand-painted german porcelain animal figurines.
HE KNOWS...!
HE KNOWS WHAT YOU DID.
I HEARD THEY WANTED HIM TO REPLACE TRUMP. ASK HIM IF IT'S TRUE.
SO MUCH CUTER IN PERSON.
HELP ME, BRUCE--!

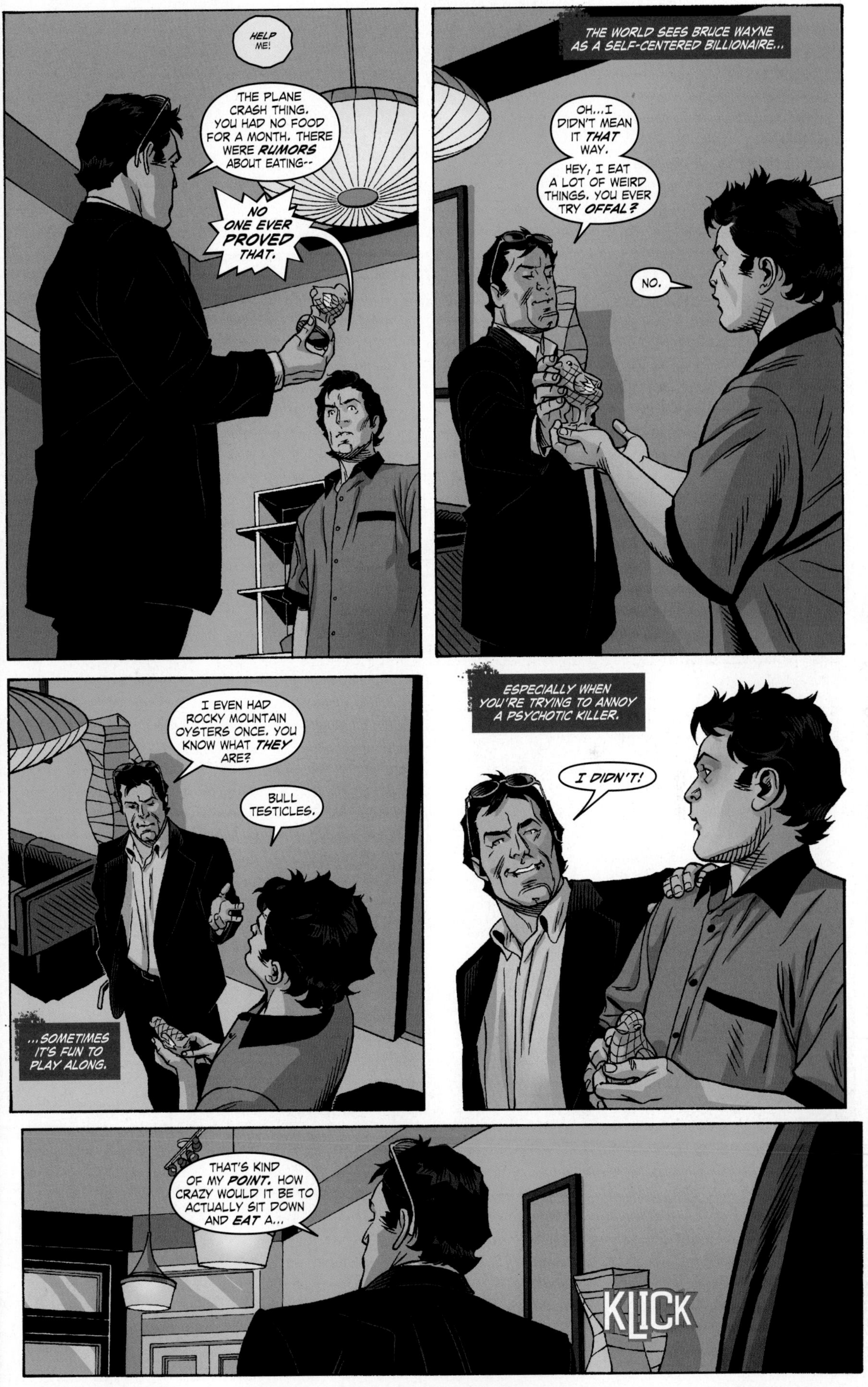
HELP ME!
THE PLANE CRASH THING. YOU HAD NO FOOD FOR A MONTH. THERE WERE RUMORS ABOUT EATING--
NO ONE EVER PROVED THAT.
THE WORLD SEES BRUCE WAYNE AS A SELF-CENTERED BILLIONAIRE...
OH...I DIDN'T MEAN IT THAT WAY.
HEY, I EAT A LOT OF WEIRD THINGS. YOU EVER TRY OFFAL?
NO.
I EVEN HAD ROCKY MOUNTAIN OYSTERS ONCE. YOU KNOW WHAT THEY ARE?
BULL TESTICLES.
...SOMETIMES IT'S FUN TO PLAY ALONG.
ESPECIALLY WHEN YOU'RE TRYING TO ANNOY A PSYCHOTIC KILLER.
I DIDN'T!
THAT'S KIND OF MY POINT. HOW CRAZY WOULD IT BE TO ACTUALLY SIT DOWN AND EAT A...
KLICK

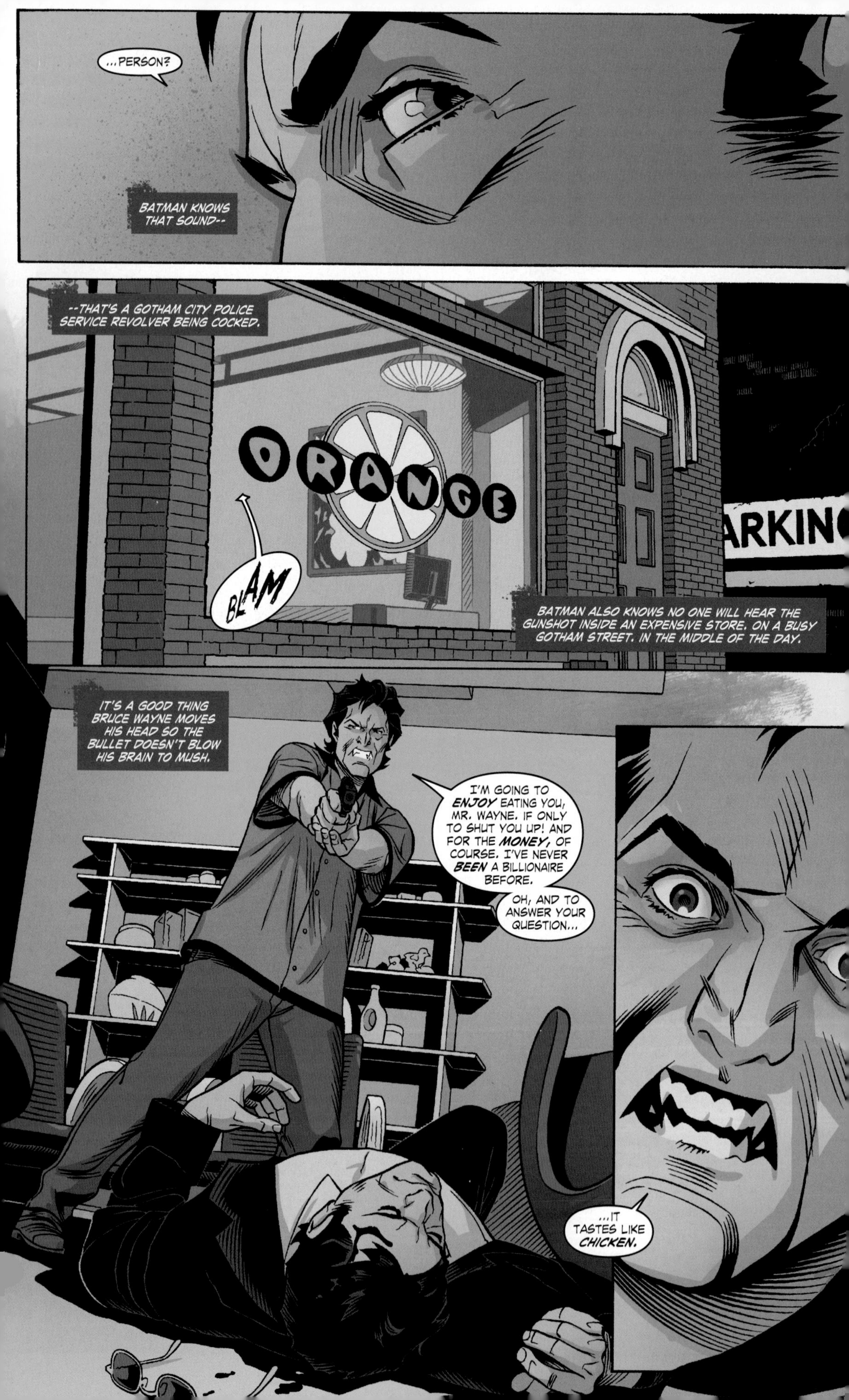
...PERSON?
BATMAN KNOWS THAT SOUND--
--THAT'S A GOTHAM CITY POLICE SERVICE REVOLVER BEING COCKED.
ORANGE
BLAM
ARKING
BATMAN ALSO KNOWS NO ONE WILL HEAR THE GUNSHOT INSIDE AN EXPENSIVE STORE. ON A BUSY GOTHAM STREET. IN THE MIDDLE OF THE DAY.
IT'S A GOOD THING BRUCE WAYNE MOVES HIS HEAD SO THE BULLET DOESN'T BLOW HIS BRAIN TO MUSH.
I'M GOING TO ENJOY EATING YOU, MR. WAYNE. IF ONLY TO SHUT YOU UP! AND FOR THE MONEY, OF COURSE. I'VE NEVER BEEN A BILLIONAIRE BEFORE.
OH, AND TO ANSWER YOUR QUESTION...
...IT TASTES LIKE CHICKEN.

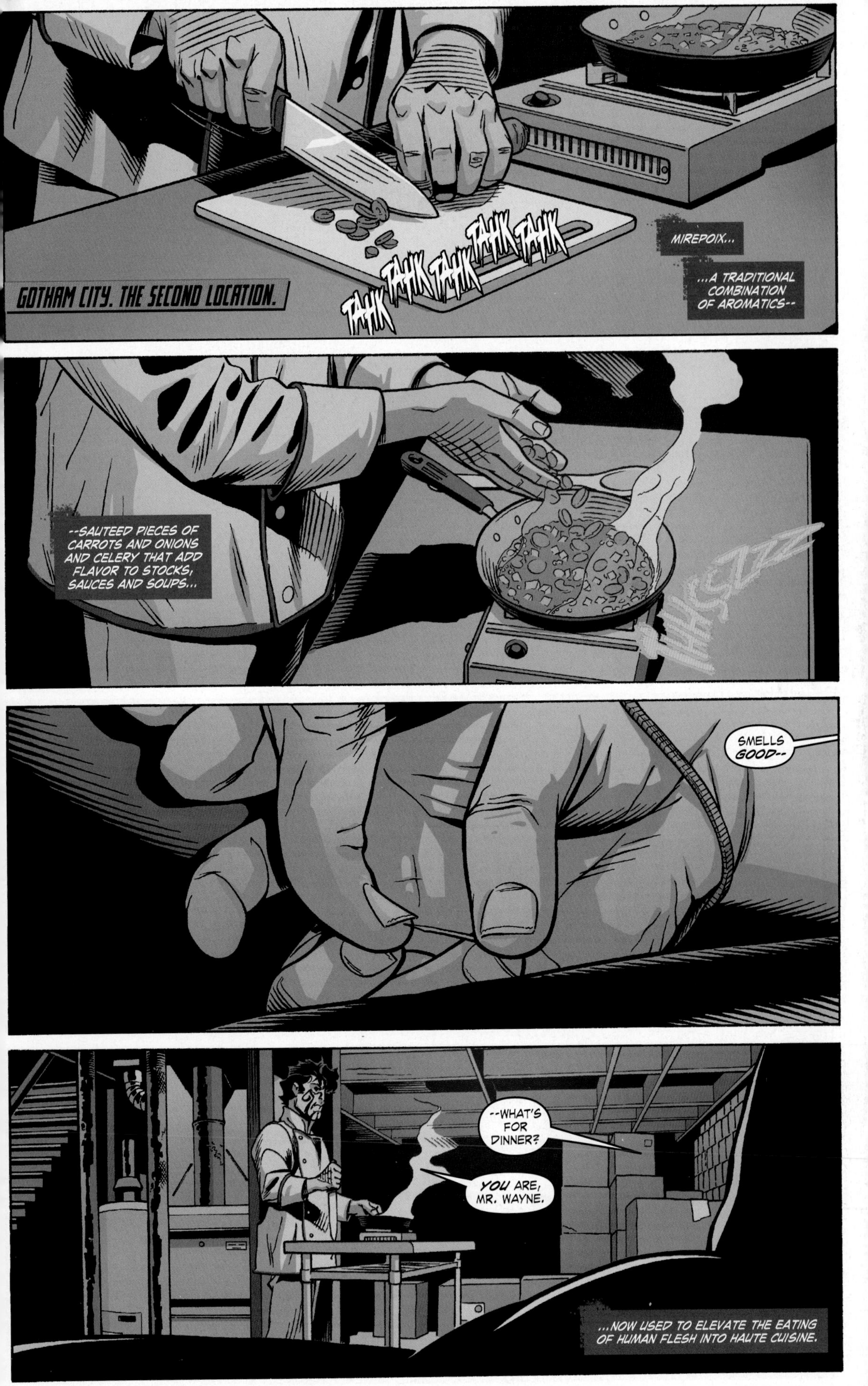

GOTHAM CITY. THE SECOND LOCATION.
TAHK TAHK TAHK TAHK TAHK
MIREPOIX...
...A TRADITIONAL COMBINATION OF AROMATICS--
--SAUTEED PIECES OF CARROTS AND ONIONS AND CELERY THAT ADD FLAVOR TO STOCKS, SAUCES AND SOUPS...
SMELLS GOOD--
--WHAT'S FOR DINNER?
YOU ARE, MR. WAYNE.
...NOW USED TO ELEVATE THE EATING OF HUMAN FLESH INTO HAUTE CUISINE.

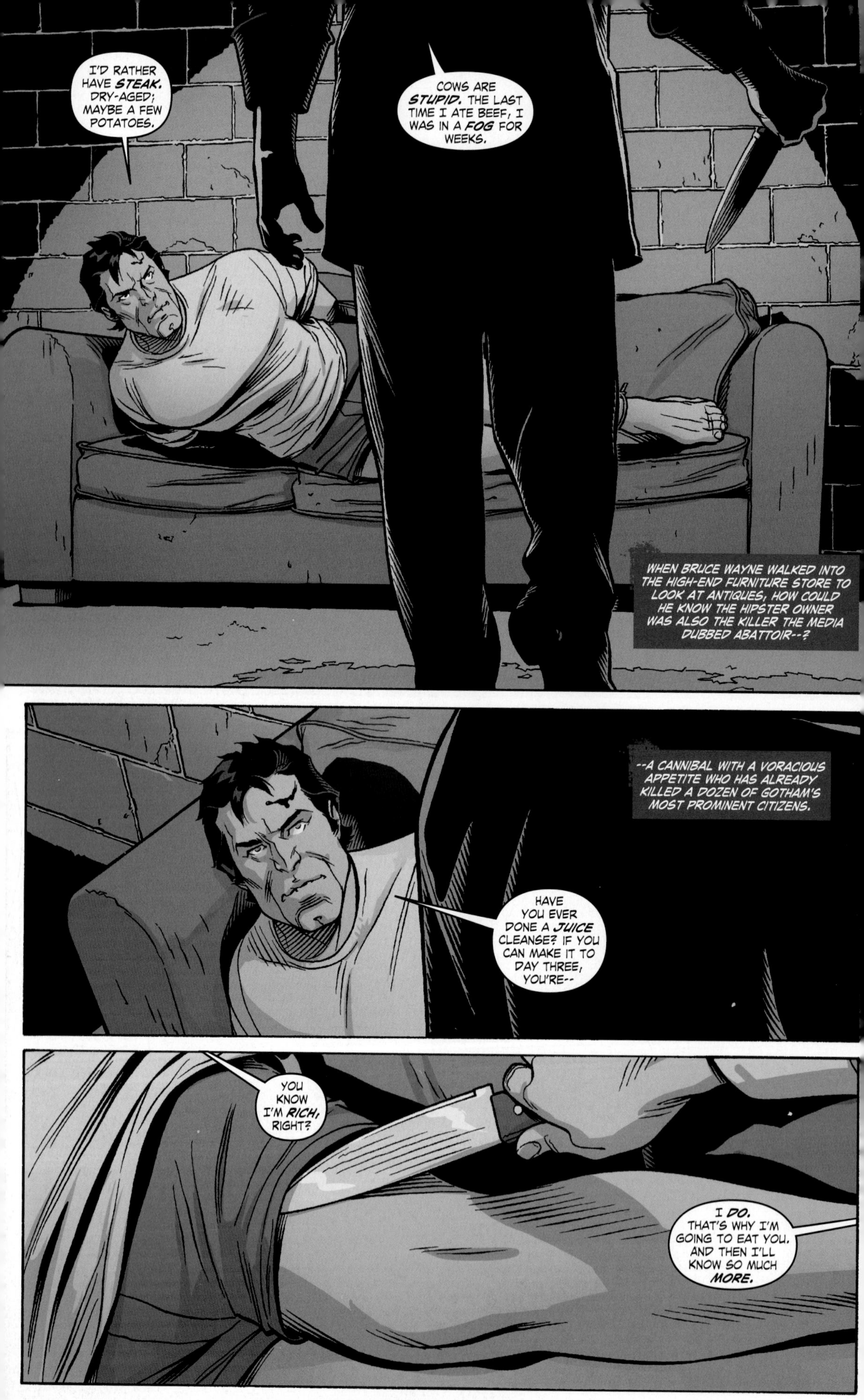
I'D RATHER HAVE STEAK. DRY-AGED; MAYBE A FEW POTATOES.
COWS ARE STUPID. THE LAST TIME I ATE BEEF, I WAS IN A FOG FOR WEEKS.
WHEN BRUCE WAYNE WALKED INTO THE HIGH-END FURNITURE STORE TO LOOK AT ANTIQUES, HOW COULD HE KNOW THE HIPSTER OWNER WAS ALSO THE KILLER THE MEDIA DUBBED ABATTOIR--?
--A CANNIBAL WITH A VORACIOUS APPETITE WHO HAS ALREADY KILLED A DOZEN OF GOTHAM'S MOST PROMINENT CITIZENS.
HAVE YOU EVER DONE A JUICE CLEANSE? IF YOU CAN MAKE IT TO DAY THREE, YOU'RE--
YOU KNOW I'M RICH, RIGHT?
I DO. THAT'S WHY I'M GOING TO EAT YOU. AND THEN I'LL KNOW SO MUCH MORE.

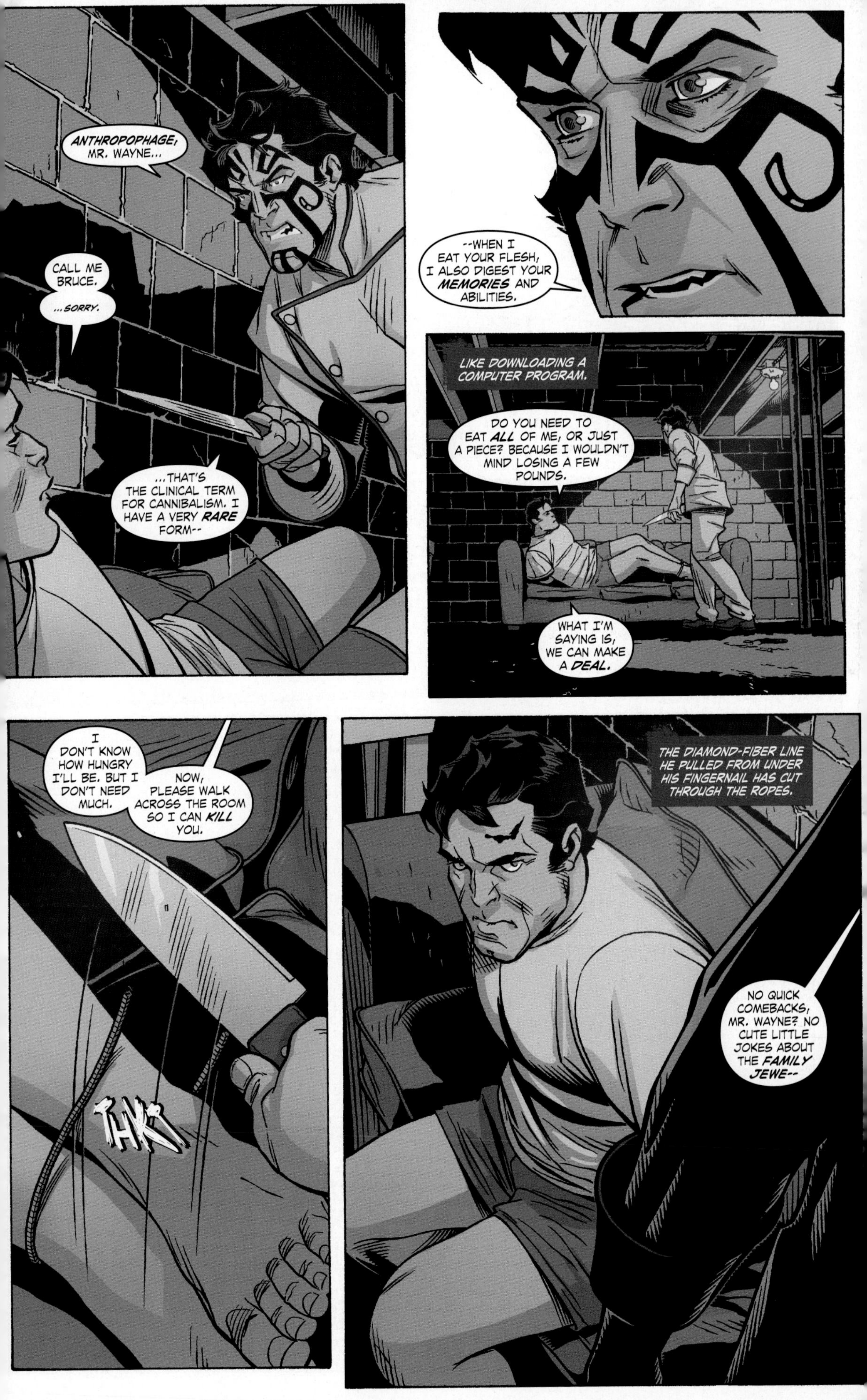
ANTHROPOPHAGE, MR. WAYNE...
CALL ME BRUCE.
...SORRY.
...THAT'S THE CLINICAL TERM FOR CANNIBALISM. I HAVE A VERY RARE FORM--
--WHEN I EAT YOUR FLESH, I ALSO DIGEST YOUR MEMORIES AND ABILITIES.
LIKE DOWNLOADING A COMPUTER PROGRAM.
DO YOU NEED TO EAT ALL OF ME, OR JUST A PIECE? BECAUSE I WOULDN'T MIND LOSING A FEW POUNDS.
WHAT I'M SAYING IS, WE CAN MAKE A DEAL.
I DON'T KNOW HOW HUNGRY I'LL BE. BUT I DON'T NEED MUCH.
NOW, PLEASE WALK ACROSS THE ROOM SO I CAN KILL YOU.
THK!
THE DIAMOND-FIBER LINE HE PULLED FROM UNDER HIS FINGERNAIL HAS CUT THROUGH THE ROPES.
NO QUICK COMEBACKS, MR. WAYNE? NO CUTE LITTLE JOKES ABOUT THE FAMILY JEWE--

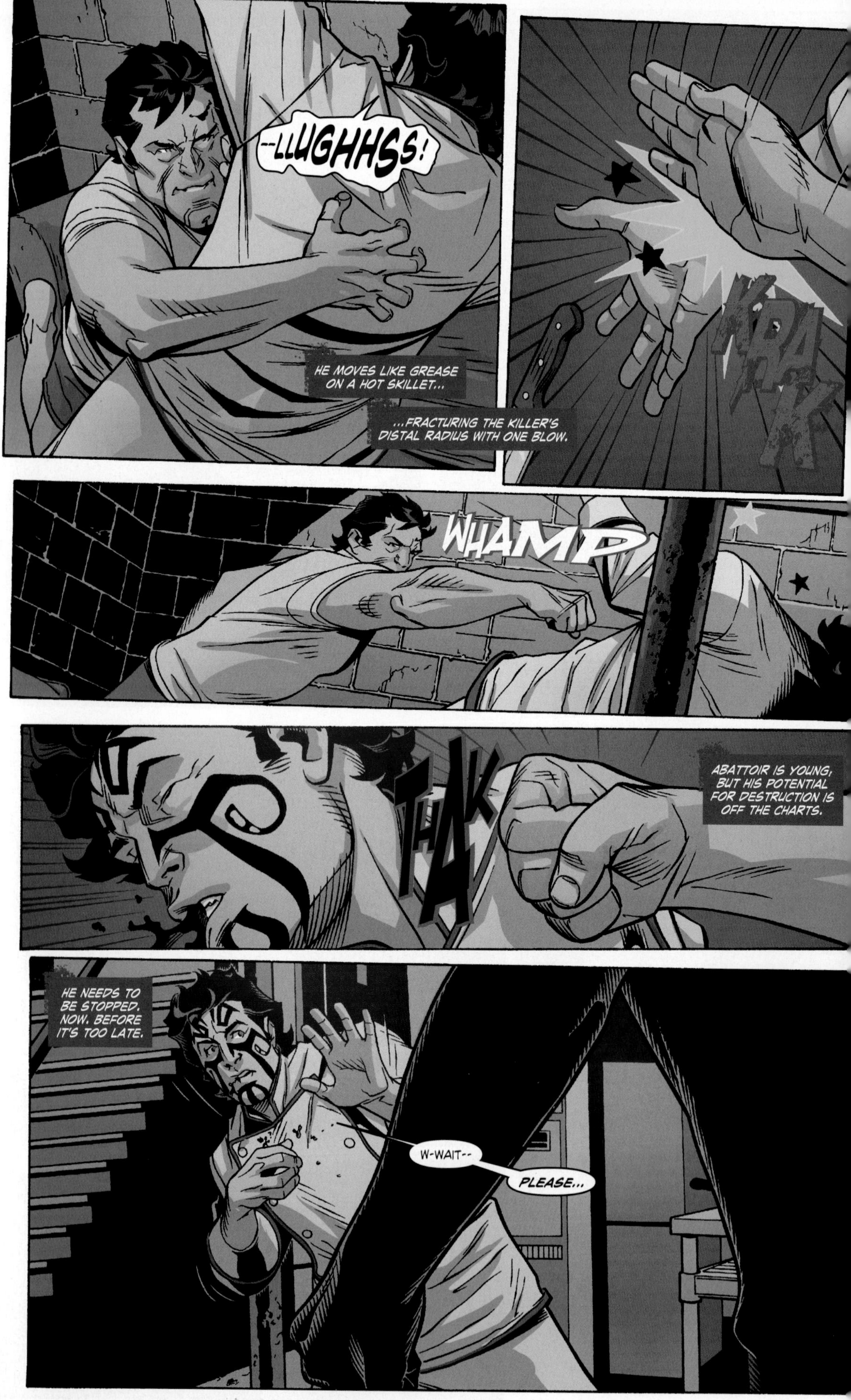
--LLUGHHSS!
HE MOVES LIKE GREASE ON A HOT SKILLET...
KRAK
...FRACTURING THE KILLER'S DISTAL RADIUS WITH ONE BLOW.
WHAMP
THAK
ABATTOIR IS YOUNG, BUT HIS POTENTIAL FOR DESTRUCTION IS OFF THE CHARTS.
HE NEEDS TO BE STOPPED. NOW. BEFORE IT'S TOO LATE.
W-WAIT--
PLEASE...

...I'M NOT HIM. I MEAN...I'M ME.

HIS BODY LANGUAGE *CHANGED*, AS WE FOUGHT. AND HIS VOICE, HIGHER *NOW* BY A FULL OCTAVE. ALMOST AS IF--

MY NAME IS *WALLACE CAMP*, MR. WAYNE. I'M A CSI WITH THE GOTHAM PD.

THE TRANSFORMATION IS ASTOUNDING...

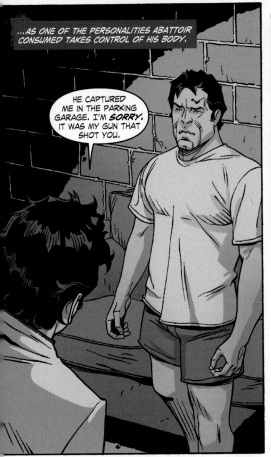

...AS ONE OF THE PERSONALITIES ABATTOIR CONSUMED TAKES CONTROL OF HIS BODY.

HE CAPTURED ME IN THE PARKING GARAGE. I'M *SORRY*. IT WAS MY GUN THAT SHOT YOU.

IT'S GOING TO BE *OKAY*, DETECTIVE CAMP. DO YOU KNOW WHERE WE ARE? IF YOU CAN GET US *OUT* OF HERE--

--I KNOW PEOPLE WHO CAN *HELP* YOU.

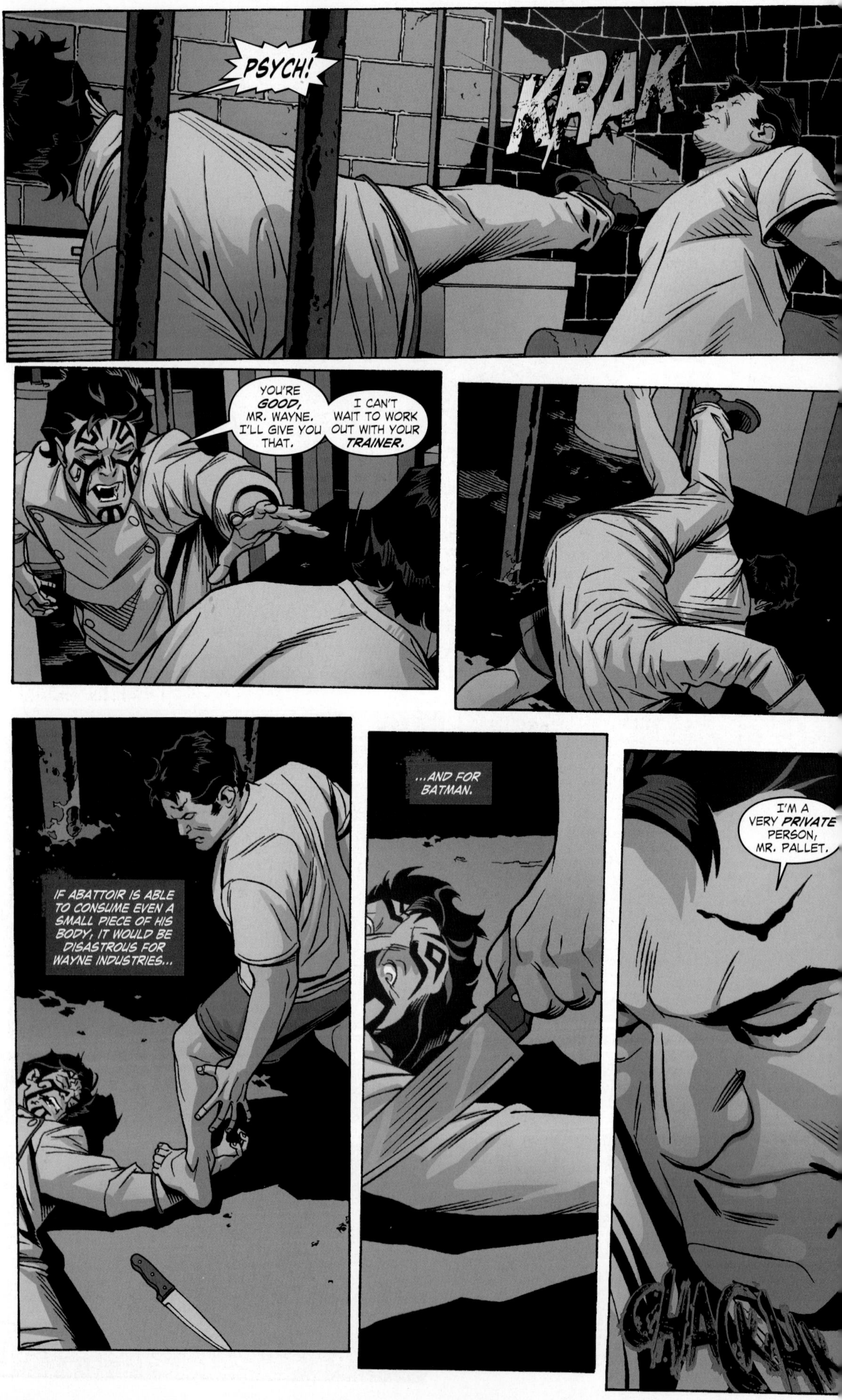
PSYCH!
KRAK
YOU'RE GOOD, MR. WAYNE. I'LL GIVE YOU THAT.
I CAN'T WAIT TO WORK OUT WITH YOUR TRAINER.
IF ABATTOIR IS ABLE TO CONSUME EVEN A SMALL PIECE OF HIS BODY, IT WOULD BE DISASTROUS FOR WAYNE INDUSTRIES...
...AND FOR BATMAN.
I'M A VERY PRIVATE PERSON, MR. PALLET.

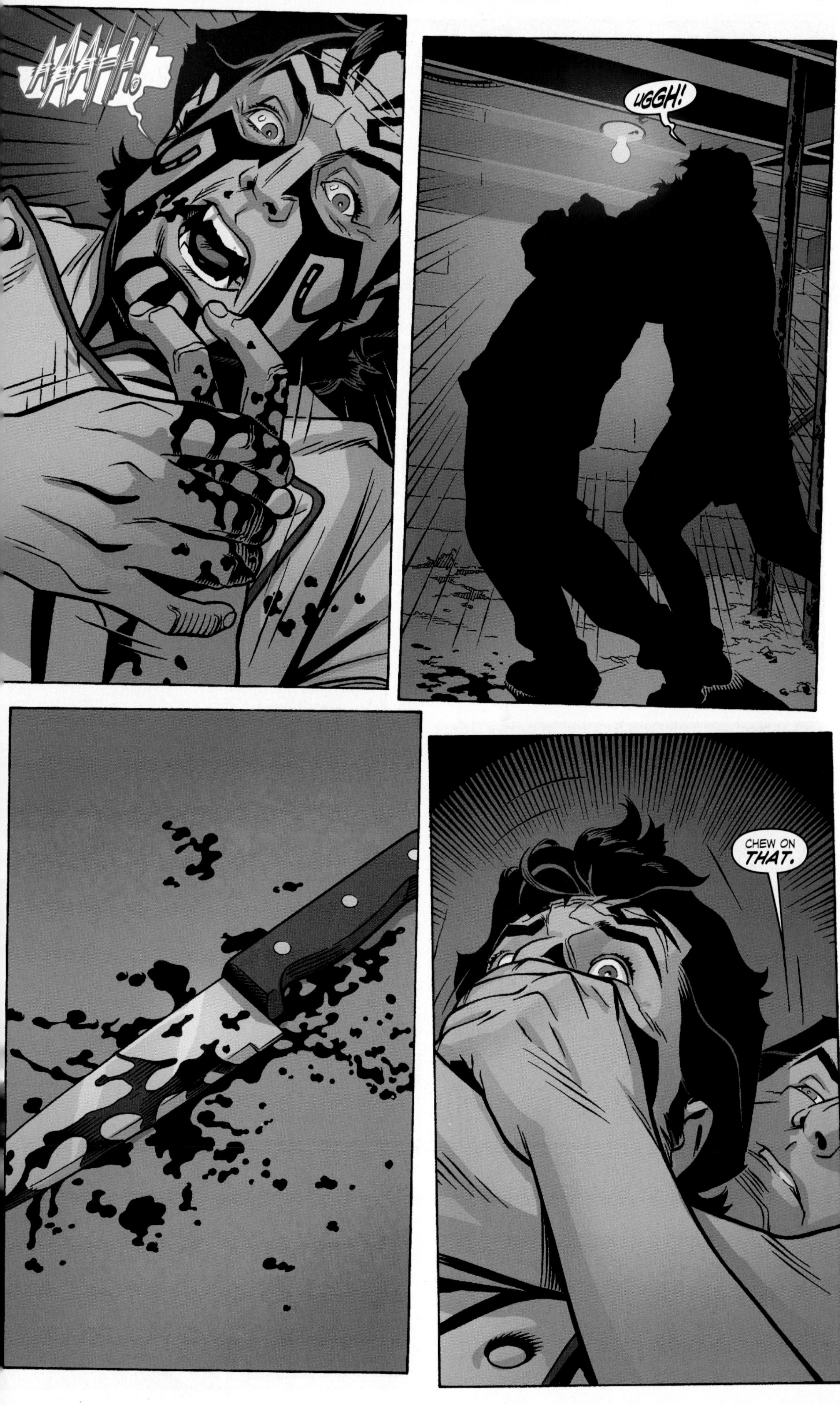
AAAHH!
UGGH!
CHEW ON THAT.

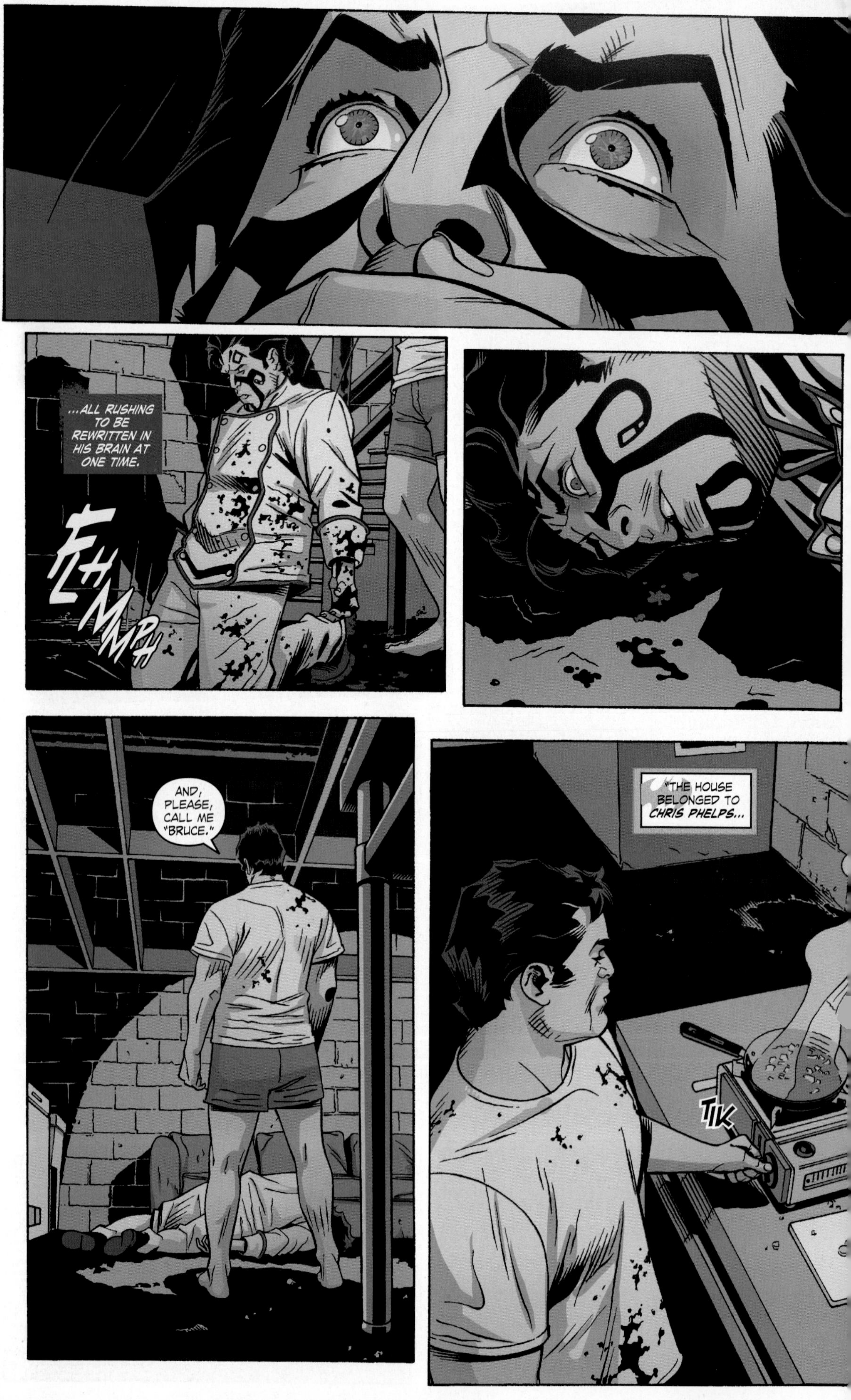
...ALL RUSHING TO BE REWRITTEN IN HIS BRAIN AT ONE TIME.
FLHMMPH
AND, PLEASE, CALL ME "BRUCE."
"THE HOUSE BELONGED TO CHRIS PHELPS...
TIK

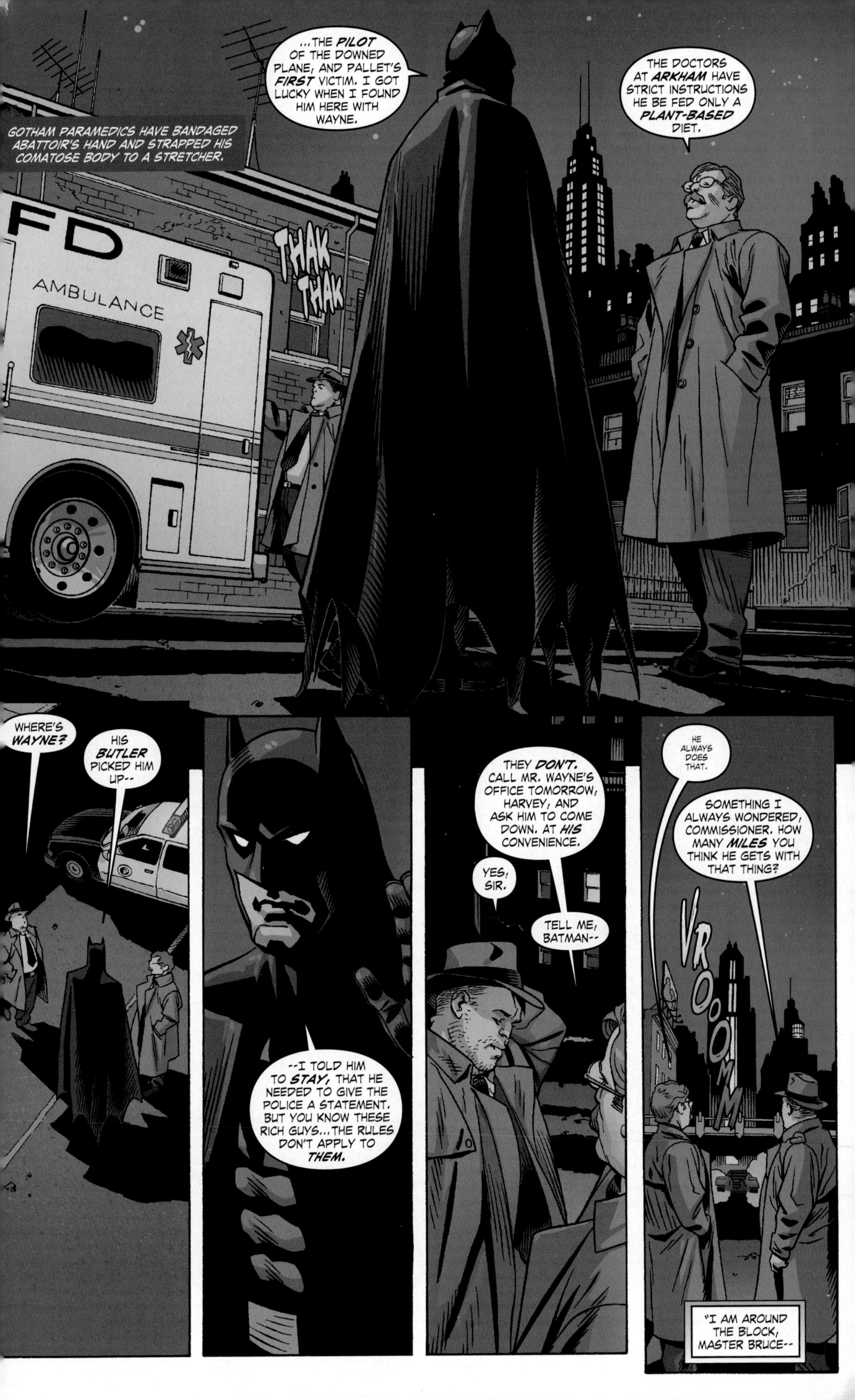
GOTHAM PARAMEDICS HAVE BANDAGED ABATTOIR'S HAND AND STRAPPED HIS COMATOSE BODY TO A STRETCHER.
...THE PILOT OF THE DOWNED PLANE, AND PALLET'S FIRST VICTIM. I GOT LUCKY WHEN I FOUND HIM HERE WITH WAYNE.
THE DOCTORS AT ARKHAM HAVE STRICT INSTRUCTIONS HE BE FED ONLY A PLANT-BASED DIET.
FD
AMBULANCE
THAK
THAK
WHERE'S WAYNE?
HIS BUTLER PICKED HIM UP--
--I TOLD HIM TO STAY, THAT HE NEEDED TO GIVE THE POLICE A STATEMENT. BUT YOU KNOW THESE RICH GUYS...THE RULES DON'T APPLY TO THEM.
THEY DON'T. CALL MR. WAYNE'S OFFICE TOMORROW, HARVEY, AND ASK HIM TO COME DOWN. AT HIS CONVENIENCE.
YES, SIR.
TELL ME, BATMAN--
SOMETHING I ALWAYS WONDERED, COMMISSIONER. HOW MANY MILES YOU THINK HE GETS WITH THAT THING?
HE ALWAYS DOES THAT.
VROOOOM
"I AM AROUND THE BLOCK, MASTER BRUCE--

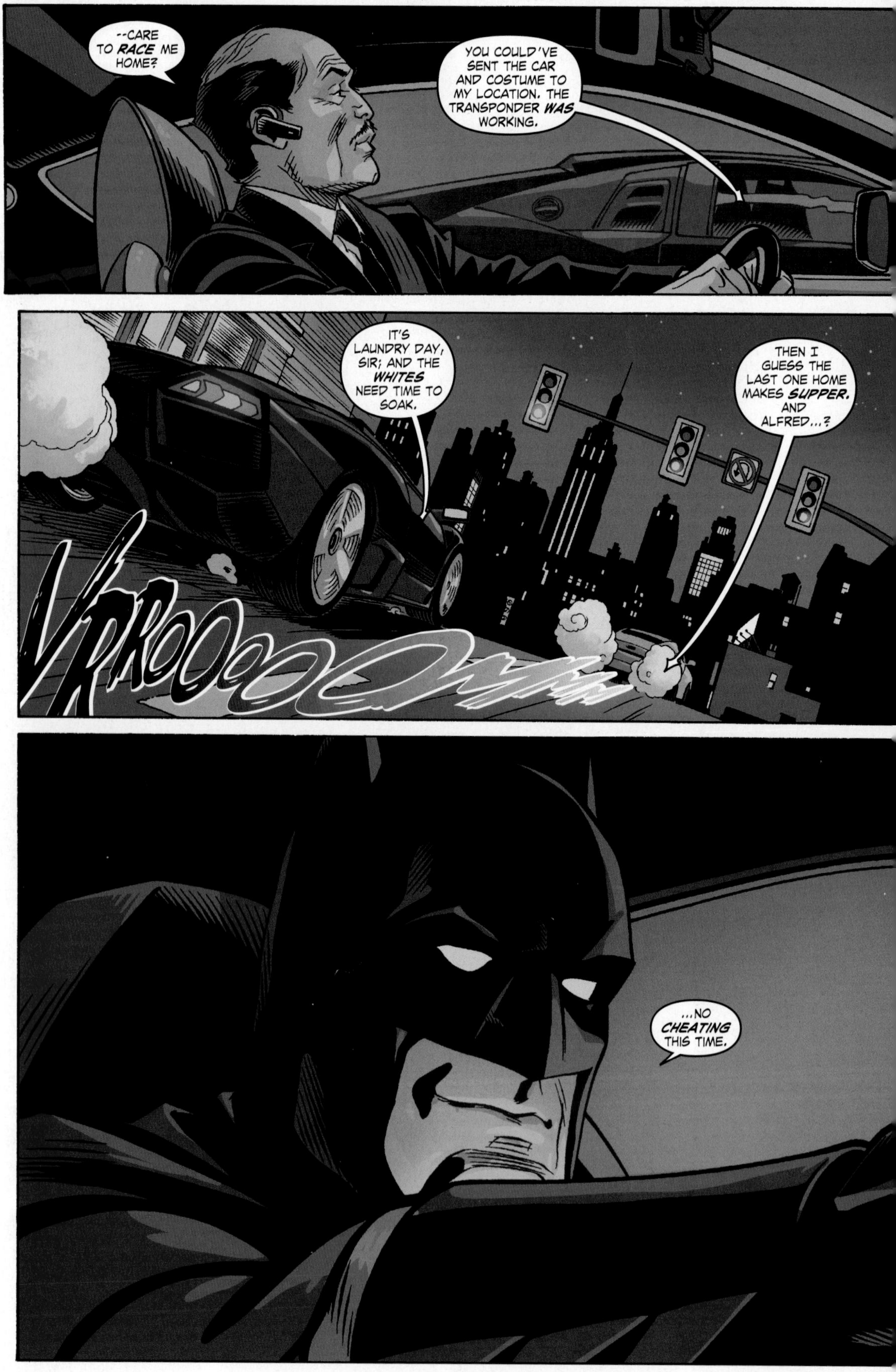

--CARE TO RACE ME HOME?
YOU COULD'VE SENT THE CAR AND COSTUME TO MY LOCATION. THE TRANSPONDER WAS WORKING.
IT'S LAUNDRY DAY, SIR; AND THE WHITES NEED TIME TO SOAK.
THEN I GUESS THE LAST ONE HOME MAKES SUPPER. AND ALFRED...?
VRROOOOOOMM
...NO CHEATING THIS TIME.

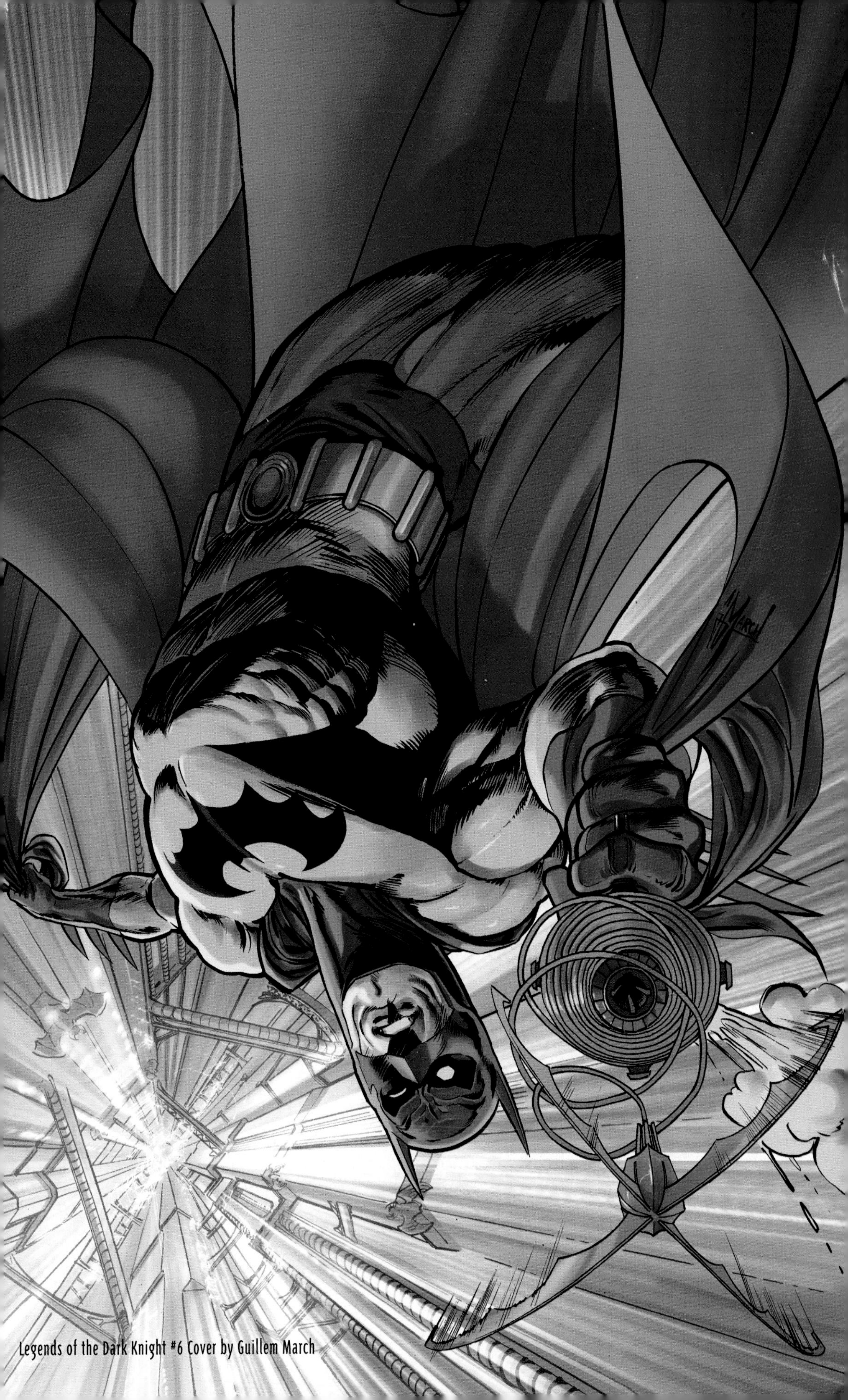

Legends of the Dark Knight #6 Cover by Guillem March

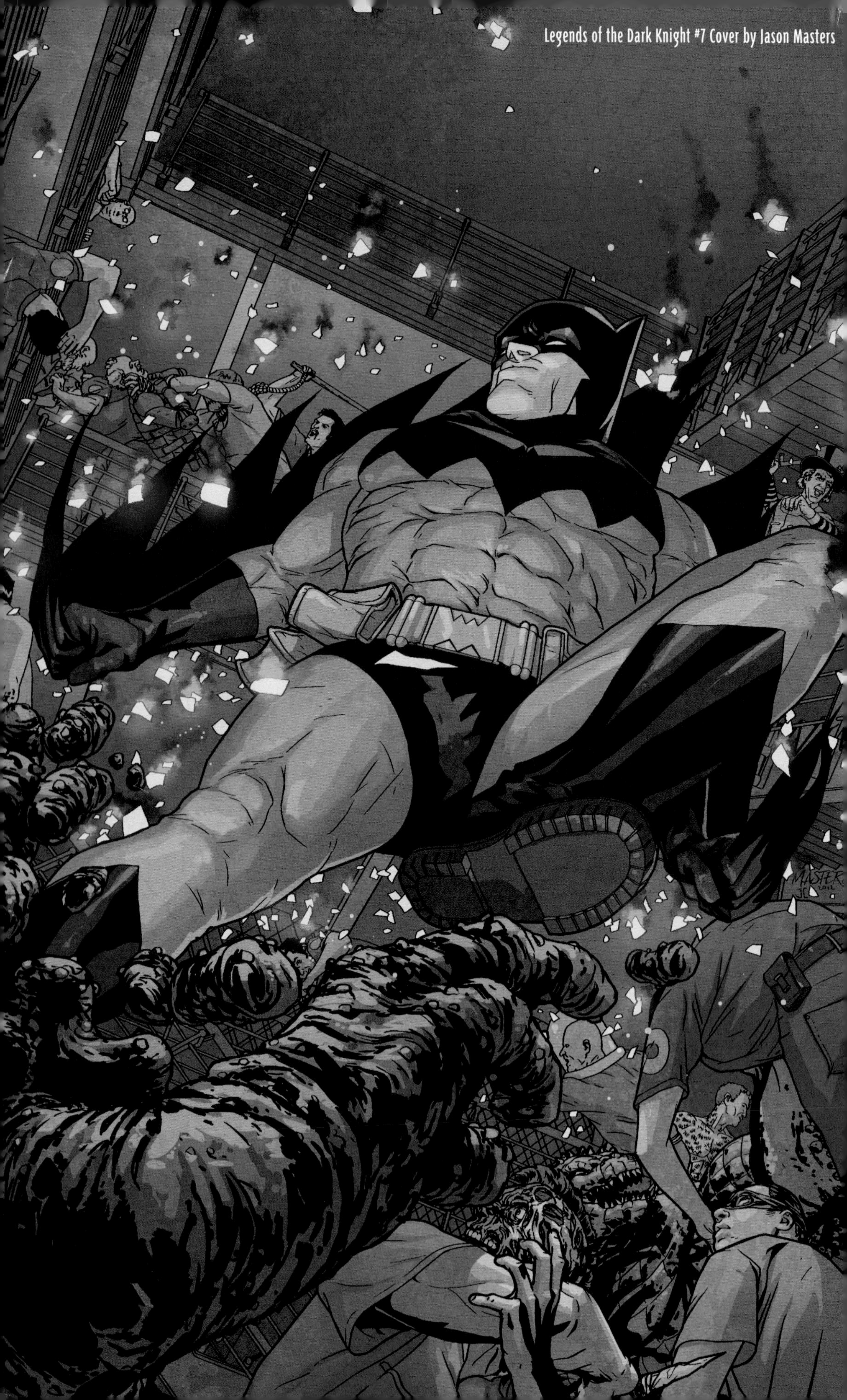

Legends of the Dark Knight #7 Cover by Jason Masters

Legends of the Dark Knight #8 Cover by Tradd Moore & Randy Mayor

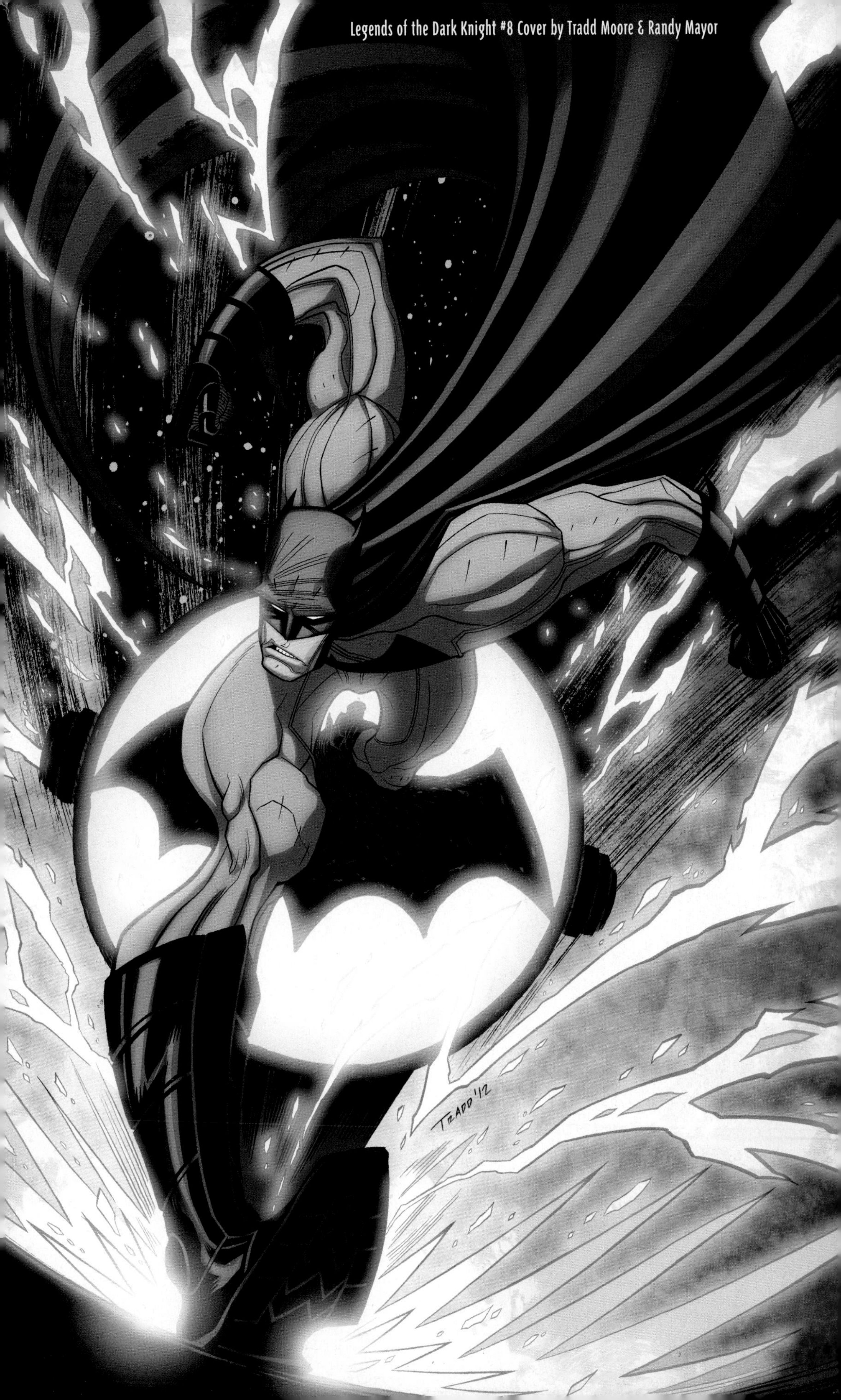
TRADD '12

Legends of the Dark Knight #9 Cover by Jheremy Raapack & Wendy Broome

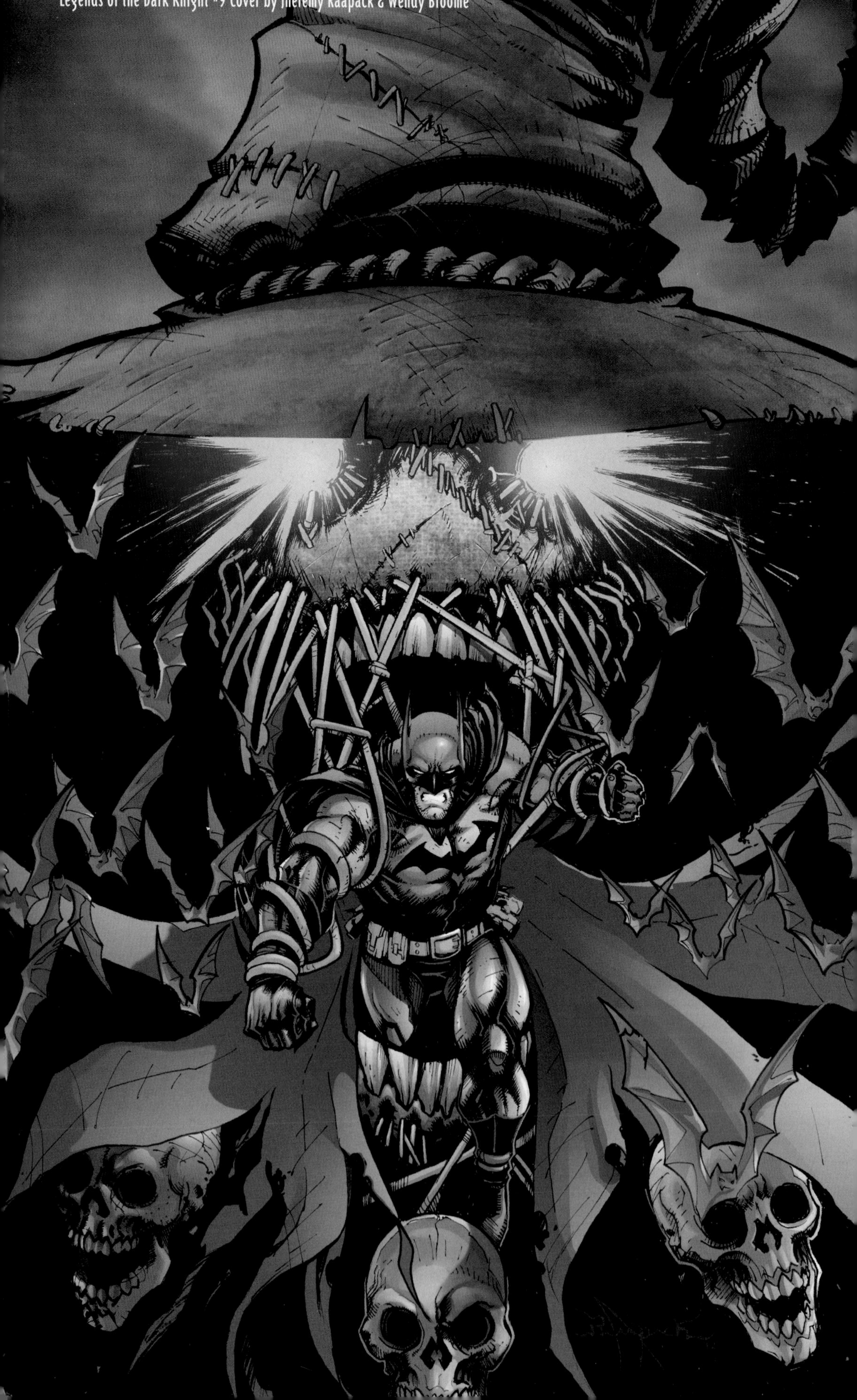

Legends of the Dark Knight #10 Cover by Chris Sprouse

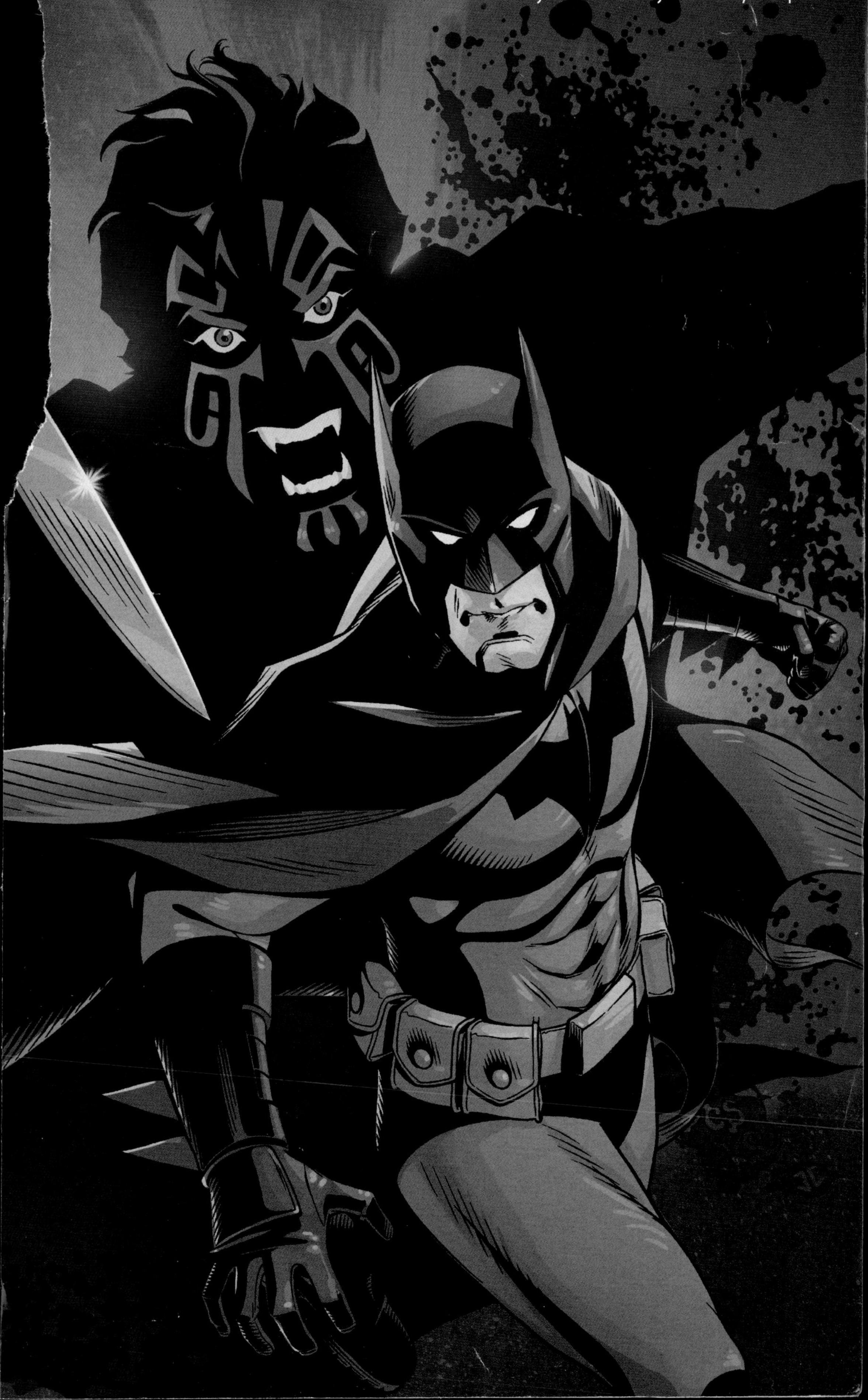

DC COMICS™

"A stunning debut. This is definitely
the top rank of the revam
—THE ONION / AV CL

"Snyder and Capullo reach new heights of collaboration he
with Capullo making inspired storytelling choices that a
additional layers to Snyder's narration and dial
—VANITY F.

START AT THE BEGINNING

BATMAN VOLUME
THE COURT OF OWL

**BATMAN & ROBIN
VOLUME 1:
BORN TO KILL**

PETER J. TOMASI PATRICK GLEASON MICK GRAY

**BATMAN: DETECTIVE
COMICS VOLUME 1:
FACES OF DEATH**

TONY S. DANIEL

**BATMAN: THE DARK
KNIGHT VOLUME 1:
KNIGHT TERRORS**

DAVID FINCH PAUL JENKINS RICHARD FRIEND

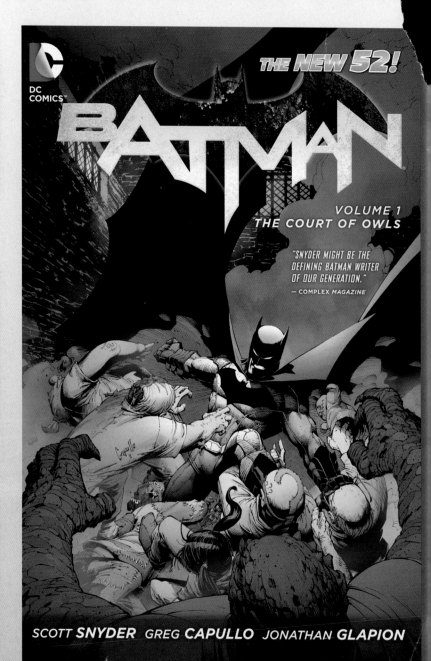